Cultural Engineering and
Nation-Building
in East Africa

Northwestern University Press
Studies in Political Culture and National Integration

edited by Ronald Cohen and John N. Paden

[Ali A. Mazrui]

Cultural Engineering and Nation-Building in East Africa

Northwestern University Press, Evanston, Illinois
1972

Permission to quote from the following works has been granted by the publishers: Okot p'Bitek, *Song of Lawino* (Nairobi: East African Publishing House, 1966); Okello Oculi, *Orphan* (Nairobi: East African Publishing House, 1968); Leopold Senghor, "The Spirit of Civilisation, or the Laws of African Negro Culture," The First International Conference of Negro Writers and Artists, *Présence Africaine*, nos. 8, 9, 10 (June–November, 1956), permission granted by Georges Borchardt; Jonathan Kariara, "Vietnam," *Zuka*, no. 2 (May, 1968), permission granted by Oxford University Press, Eastern Africa Branch; Charles Owuor, "Vietnam," *Zuka*, no. 2 (May, 1968), permission granted by Oxford University Press, Eastern Africa Branch; Rudyard Kipling, "Mandalay," in *The Best of Kipling* (New York: Doubleday, 1968), permission granted by Doubleday, and also in *Barrack Room Ballads and Other Verses* (London: Methuen, 1965), permission granted by Methuen and Mrs. George Bambridge.

Ali A. Mazrui is Professor and Head of the Department of Political Science and Public Administration at Makerere University.

To the memory of my mother

Contents

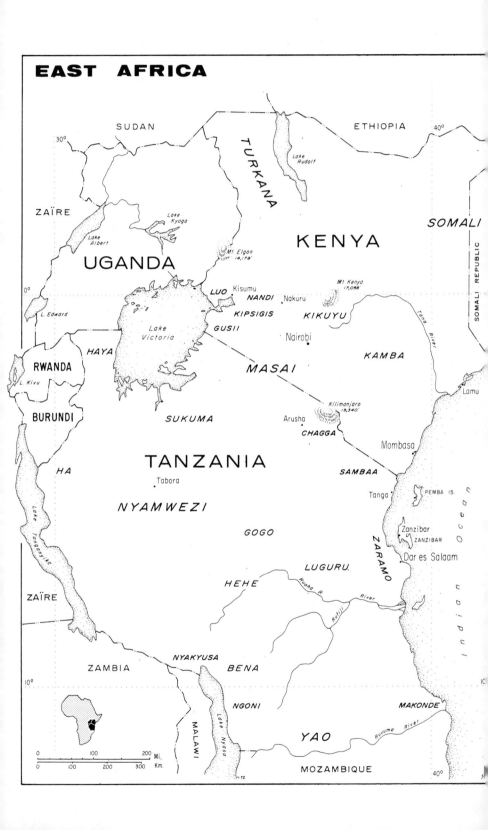

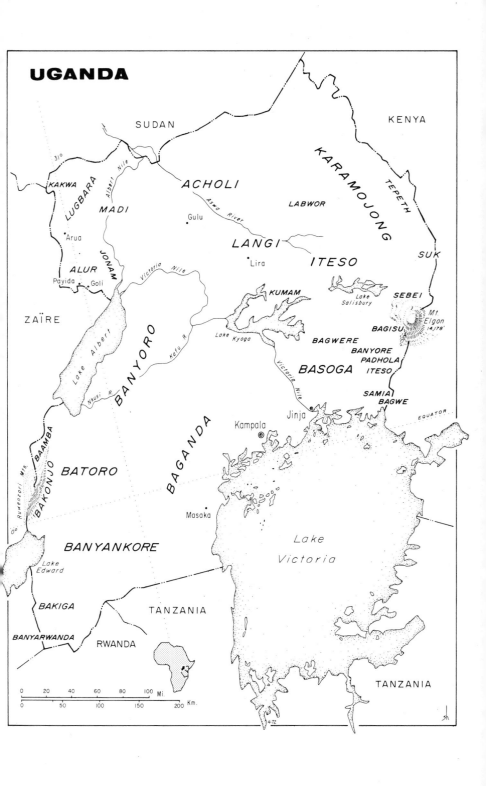

UGANDA

SUDAN

KENYA

31°

KAKWA

LUGBARA

Albert Nile

MADI

Arua

ACHOLI

Gulu

Aswa River

KARAMOJONG

TEPETH

LABWOR

LANGI

Lira

ITESO

SUK

JONAM

ALUR

Payida   Goli

Victoria Nile

KUMAM

Lake
Salisbury

SEBEI

ZAÏRE

BANYORO

Kafu R.

Lake Kyoga

Mt.
Elgon
14,178'

BAGISU

BAGWERE

BANYORE
PADHOLA
ITESO

BASOGA

Nkusi R.

Victoria Nile

SAMIA
BAGWE

RUWENZORI MTS.

BAAMBA

BATORO

BAKONJO

BAGANDA

Kampala

Jinja

EQUATOR

0°

Lake Albert

Lake
Edward

BANYANKORE

Masaka

Lake
Victoria

BAKIGA

TANZANIA

BANYARWANDA

RWANDA

TANZANIA

0   20   40   60   80   100 Mi.

0   50   100   150   200 Km.

4-72

sh

Preface

This book grew out of intellectual interaction at two universities — the federal University of East Africa and Northwestern University. The former consisted of campuses which have since become the separate national universities of Nairobi, Dar es Salaam, and Makerere. It was at the three East African campuses that I first tried out some tentative conclusions concerning the nature of East African societies. I presented these ideas to audiences well informed about that region of the continent and benefited from the questions, challenges, and debates which my provisional conclusions provoked. The challenges that made me insecure encouraged me to turn for further verification to the social evidence surrounding me, in the area where I lived and worked.

In 1969 I was invited to Northwestern University as a scholar in residence. There I interacted with scholars who did not always know as much about East Africa as I did, but who often knew far more about other parts of the continent. I gave a series of lectures at Northwestern on "Ideology and Cultural Engineering in East Africa." Some of the perspectives presented in those lectures were acquired at Northwestern as a result of comparing my East African experience with the insights of others. The lectures formed the nucleus of the book which won the prepublication prize of $1,000 from the National Unity Research Project, jointly sponsored by the Program of African Studies at Northwestern and by the Northwestern University Press.

After returning to East Africa, I delved further into the twin phenomena of cultural engineering and nation-building and elaborated on some of the issues which I had originally posed at Northwestern. I also tried to take full account of the changing political scene in East Africa, structurally and ideologically.

Academically, special gratitude is due to colleagues at the three university campuses of East Africa and at Northwestern University. Financially, I am indebted especially to the Rockefeller Foundation, which has made the most substantial contribution to political science research at Makerere. Some of the chapters in the book also benefited from research made possible by the World Order Models Project at Makerere, which in turn was funded by the World Law Fund and the Carnegie Endowment for International Peace.

An earlier version of Chapter 2, "Creative Literature and Political Commitment," was presented at a regional seminar at Makerere University in August, 1968, under the title "The Patriotic Mind and the Literary Imagination in East Africa." An earlier version of Chapter 6, "Language Policy and Political Participation," was presented at a regional seminar at Makerere University in April, 1967, and was later published in both *East Africa Journal* and *Africa Report* in June, 1967. The Conclusion, "Toward a Theory of Nation-Building," formed the basis of "Social Cleavage and Nation-Building in East Africa," a paper commissioned by UNESCO and presented in Munich at the Seventh World Congress of the International Political Science Association in September, 1970.

I would like to pay special tribute to Dr. John D. Chick and Dr. Yash Tandon, colleagues of mine who went beyond the call of duty in helping me to administer the Department of Political Science at Makerere during this period. By relieving me of some of my administrative burdens as head of the department, they made it possible for me to remain a scholar and a writer. It is not an exaggeration to say this book could not have been written without their assistance.

I am indebted to Victor Uchendu for his comments on an earlier draft of the Conclusion. To Mrs. Sue Chick and Mrs. Anna Gourlay I am grateful for many long hours of patient and sophisticated typing, with a sense of real commitment to the enterprise. To Karen Primack in Kampala and Linda Norris in Evanston I am indebted for that ruthless editorial scrutiny which is the essence of literary surgery. To my wife, Molly, and her sense of style, I owe my ambition to become a better writer. She has often rescued me from some of my literary excesses but has been indulgent when I have been too possessive about a phrase. We have spent many hours in active collaboration.

ALI A. MAZRUI

Makerere University
Kampala, Uganda

[Introduction]

The Idea of
Cultural Engineering

The rhetoric of East African development abounds with notions of reconstruction and nation-building. Indeed, the latter term is probably the most central one in the whole vocabulary of postindependence politics in East Africa. The advantage of the metaphor of *nation-building* is derived from the simple fact that so much of the work of turning newly invented, fragile states into more secure, integrated nations is analogous to construction. Institutions are to be built for the management of tensions between groups; bridges are to be constructed between tradition and modernity; calculation is necessary for the creation of new shapes and patterns of relationships; foundations are to be laid for a new national heritage. The ideas of social and cultural engineering emerge in the conceptual framework of these different aspects of nation-building.

Paul S. Kress has argued that political science and creative literature are, on some levels, comparable — "at least in that they are two symbol systems, each possessing a coherent arrangement of internal characteristics and, consequently, certain possibilities and limitations."[1] Kress also draws our attention to Murray Edelman's work. Edelman has argued: "We may be able to learn something about expressive political symbols from aesthetic theory, for an art form consists of condensation symbols. Its function, like that of the abstract political symbols . . . , is to serve as a vehicle for expression."[2] The crucial idea here is that of "condensation symbols," symbols which try to capture and condense the world of implications and associations. Like creative literature, political analysis has to resort at times to the use of analogy and metaphor. The strength of metaphor lies in its transphenomenal comparative utility. It brings forth the associations of one category of life to illuminate a different area of observation. In that lies the validation of the concepts of nation-building and cultural engineering.[3]

1. Paul S. Kress, "Self, System and Significance: Reflections on Professor Easton's Political Science," *Ethics*, LXXVII, no. 1 (October, 1966), 3.
2. Murray Edelman, *The Symbolic Uses of Politics* (Urbana: University of Illinois Press, 1964), p. 11. See also Ernst Cassirer, *The Philosophy of Symbolic Forms*, 3 vols. (New Haven: Yale University Press, 1953–57).
3. The use of analogy in political science is common. David Easton's political thought,

Cultural engineering can be related to technology in the literal sense. The idea of taming technology to serve social needs and to help in inducing social reform provides a distinctive example of cultural engineering. This is the area of what we have called *socialized technology*. But, in addition, the concept of cultural engineering echoes and overlaps two further concepts. One is the idea of *cultural management*, which was introduced by Lloyd Fallers; the other is the idea of *social engineering*, which is an older notion.

Lloyd Fallers, addressing himself to the organizational problems which were raised by the issue of relating patterns of value and belief to new national entities, said:

> The new nations, in order to achieve a degree of unity of purpose, need cultures which, first, will provide a measure of consensus among their diverse peoples and, second, will be capable of the constant innovation which existence in the modern world requires. It is perhaps not an abuse of words to speak of this as a problem in "cultural management" and to use the term "ideology" to refer to that part of culture which is actively and explicitly concerned with the establishment and defense of patterns of value and belief. Ideology is thus the apologetic part of culture.[4]

Fallers suggests that those whose task it is to "create cultures" for the new African nations — the "ideologists of nationalism" — have two main sources to draw upon: they have on the one hand the traditional heritage of the African peoples and on the other the cultures of Europe, America, and Asia.

The notion of social engineering was derived from the belief of some sociologists that the social sciences could be applied sciences as well as academic disciplines. It followed, therefore, that a social technology, designed to improve human institutions, could be developed. Value judgments might be invoked to define desirable goals, and sociological knowledge could then be called upon to yield advice on means toward these goals. Society could be reorganized in predetermined directions, and social development could be systematically induced.

The American sociologist Lester Frank Ward, like Auguste Comte and Herbert Spencer, distinguished between social statistics and social dynamics. But he went further and distinguished also between pure sociology and applied sociology. The latter he called *social telesis*, or "purposive action by man designed to influence his culture." Ward grasped the importance of state action for planned

---

for example, relies heavily on metaphorical terms like *input, output, parapolitical, feedback*, and so on; and modernization theorists in political science have creatively used neological terms like *political culture, political socialization, political goods*, and *political decay*. See Ali A. Mazrui, "Political Hygiene and Cultural Transition in Africa," *Journal of African and Asian Studies*, V, nos. 1–2 (January, 1970), 113–25.

4. Lloyd A. Fallers, "Ideology and Culture in Uganda Nationalism," *African Anthropologist*, LXIII (1961), 677–78.

social engineering. It was partly his anti-individualistic outlook which denied him acclaim in his own country; yet the state action he envisaged was supposed to be based on the will of a sociologically informed electorate. He thought of social engineering as something induced by a triangular alliance between the state, the social scientist, and the sociologically sophisticated electorate. The national welfare might be promoted by utilizing the energies and expertise of sociologists and other social analysts in the service of the administrative agencies of government, especially those concerned with planning. Social engineering was, in fact, applied social science.[5]

We use the term *cultural engineering* in this book to denote a special approach to the problems of social engineering. We are focusing on the impingement of cultural factors on issues of social reform and national development. Cultural engineering becomes the deliberate manipulation of cultural factors for purposes of deflecting human habit in the direction of new and perhaps constructive endeavors. Sometimes the effort consists in changing cultural patterns enough to make it possible for certain institutions to survive. At other times the purpose of cultural reform is basically attitudinal change. Ultimately, there is the paramount issue of identity — of how people view themselves and how far self-conceptions can be modified in the direction of enlarged empathy.

In this book an attempt is made to discern the major elements of purposeful cultural manipulation in relation to social policy in East Africa. Although East Africa, the area covered by Tanzania, Kenya, and Uganda, is the primary source of illustrative data, the book aspires to formulate propositions of wider comparative validity. The dynamics of social reform and nation-building as illustrated by East Africa's experience may yield insights relevant to the understanding of such phenomena elsewhere. Even in discussing East Africa, comparative material from other parts of the continent is often used. For purposes of analysis, aspects of cultural engineering which are directed at problems of identity are sometimes artificially distinguished from those which are directed at problems of development. In the quest for patriotic symbols for East Africa, the ambition is to move from the race-conscious nationalism which carried the countries to independence to a new state-conscious patriotism as a basis of sovereign identity. This ambition and the struggle to realize it are at the heart of the process of nation-building.

The anthems and the flags are only the more obvious symbols of identity. The role of history as a process of socialization is in some respects a more basic formula of identity-formation, and it is to this that the opening chapter addresses itself. We shall explore in Part 1 those principles of cultural engineering which are particularly relevant to identity-formation in a new African

---

5. See Lester Frank Ward, *Dynamic Sociology*, 2 vols., American Studies Series (1883; reprint ed., New York: Johnson Reprint Corp., 1969); *idem, Pure Sociology* (1909; reprint ed., Clifton, N.J.: Kelley, 1969).

state — indigenizing what is foreign, idealizing what is indigenous, nationalizing what is sectional, and emphasizing what is African. Linked to this issue are the role of the written word and the place of oral tradition in the study of history.

Identity on a societal scale is not simply a matter of self-recognition; it is also a matter of self-expression and of communication between conationals. This is where both language and literature assume a critical significance. The politics of language in East Africa is touched upon in Part 1 and Part 2. This subject inevitably includes the relative merits of the imported metropolitan language, English, as against indigenous rivals.

Language is an instrument not merely of day-to-day social function in the market place or at the political rally. It is also a medium of political philosophy, cultural creativity, and aesthetic self-expression. In this area of East African life, cultural engineering is pre-eminently concerned with bridging the aesthetic dualism which still separates the new modes of cultural expression from the older artistic experiences of traditionalism. Taking the modern culture to the people and bringing the traditional culture to the university are methods of artistic manipulation designed to help bridge aesthetic dualism in East Africa.

In Part 2 and Part 3 the term *culture* assumes a wider meaning. The cultural factors which are being observed or manipulated are ''cultural'' in the comprehensive sense of the sociologist rather than the specialized aesthetic sense of the artist and art-lover.

A major factor which is noted in the analysis is the fluidity of social structure. This has implications for electoral systems and for the process of political recruitment. Conditions which are *structurally* hospitable to a multiparty system are compared with conditions which are *culturally* hospitable to such a system. An attempt is made to discover what kind of electoral system is likely to make competitive elections viable in situations of tense ethnic pluralism.

Special attention is paid to the phenomenon of classes in transition, giving rise to the emergence of the transclass man. It is simply not correct to assume that each person must belong to only one social class at a time. In Africa as a whole in the last few decades several factors have helped to create transclass ambivalence. The intellectual dualism which came with the Western school system, the rural-urban continuum and migration of labor, the phenomenal social mobility on the eve of independence, the social nearness of the newly successful to the village communities from which they sprang, the money economy and its ramifications in a preliterate society — all of these factors combined to create a degree of transitionality which made it possible for individuals to belong simultaneously to more than one social class.

In Kenya and, to some extent, in Uganda, social policy seems designed to encourage this ambivalence and create cross-cutting social groups. In Tanzania, on the other hand, there is a great fear of conflict of interest and functional versatility, especially in relation to political leadership. The Leadership Resolutions of the Arusha Declaration have therefore sought to prevent party and government officials from owning extensive property or business shares and from holding commercial directorships.

The Leadership Resolutions and the austerity demanded by them differentiate Tanzania from Kenya and Uganda in other ways as well. In the latter two countries the quest for political legitimacy has included the manipulation of ostentatious symbols. On balance, there is less social distance between the elite and the masses in Africa than many people assume. Kinship obligations and resilient links between town and country, as well as transclass ambivalence, contribute to the interpenetration of the elite and the masses. Precisely because the elite is socially near and has not accumulated a mystique of rightful privilege, its entitlement to elite status is under constant challenge. Manipulative engineering in this case therefore takes the form of deliberately creating the *appearance* of social distance between the elite and the masses. Ostentatious consumption — from palaces to showy cars — is part of this quest for a contrived appearance of distance. While Tanzania is out to discourage acquisition and consumption by the elite, Kenya and Uganda tend to promote both. Neither side has a monopoly of rationality in the social policy it has embarked upon.

Connected with the policy of promoting the acquisitive instinct is the commitment of Kenya and Uganda to try to create an effective African entrepreneurial class. Much of the commercial sector of the economy in East Africa has been in the hands of Asian and European immigrants. Both states have embarked on programs of Africanizing commerce as rapidly as possible, but there has been a major cultural clash between the traditional prestige motive and the required entrepreneurial profit motive. Traditional economic behavior in East Africa has not isolated economic motivation from other pressures on the individual. The philosophy that "business is business" and ought not to be confused with doing favors for one's kinsmen or attending funerals during peak business hours is a philosophy which is alien to most traditional mores in this area. Yet it is perhaps precisely such a philosophy which needs to be given roots if Kenya and Uganda are to evolve an effective indigenous entrepreneurial vigor. Cultural engineering in this field therefore seems designed to foster a "business sense" through training, apprenticeship, and economic participation. What is at stake is a process of economic resocialization, as well as one of social restratification.

Tanzania is suspicious of such policies. Some opinion-leaders there are too ready to assume that a country can develop fast without forming new classes. But such an assumption is basically unscientific and certainly un-Marxist. Development inevitably entails modifications in the class structure. We cannot transform everything else in society and hold the class component constant. This question will be argued out more fully later in the book and will be related to different concepts of revolution in East Africa.

We shall also examine structural fluidity in relation to party systems and electoral systems. We shall also seek to understand the precise relationship between political control and military power. Central to this aspect will be a theoretical framework for understanding the causes of military coups in Africa. Is there a form of social engineering which can reduce the incidence of such coups?

In short, what East Africa is experiencing is the drama of interpenetration of old stimuli and new responses, old visions and new insights, old sources of animation and new modes of life. The terms *social policy* and *cultural engineering* might indeed exaggerate the degree of certainty of direction and firmness of purpose among East Africa's reformers and pacesetters. There is in this region a sense of groping, as well as a sense of resolute social direction. The twilight spell has its dangers, different both from the dangers of the blazing sun and from those of utter darkness. It is like the Mercedes Benz at dusk speeding along the Entebbe Road in Uganda. It is no longer light enough to see properly and not yet dark enough to enable the lights of the car to be fully effective. In those few minutes which separate the African day from the African night lie the peculiar dangers of visual indistinctness. The driver is in a sense an engineer, as well as a pilot. The risks of inadequate vision are there. But there is a journey to be undertaken, after all.

[Part 1]

Cultural Engineering and the Printed Word

[1]

Written History and National Consciousness

The debate about the place of history in the new countries of East Africa has been conducted on three levels: the first level concerns the methodology of history; the second is about the content of history; the third addresses itself to the application of history. While all three levels do have a bearing on cultural engineering and nation-building, the level of application is the most directly relevant. We shall discuss each of these and relate them in turn to the place of the written word in this area of cultural engineering.

At the heart of the debate on methodology is the written word itself as an exhibit in the courtroom of historiography. The older generation of modern historians in Kenya includes Prof. B. A. Ogot, of the University of Nairobi. In 1958, when Ogot, then a doctoral candidate at the University of London, decided to study the precolonial history of East Africa, he was ridiculed by some of his friends and mentors. Would he not be engaged in the pursuit of one historical mirage after another? Could there be history without the written word as the great preserver of the past?

This debate has continued for nearly two decades, and this may itself be reason to re-evaluate the place of the written word in history. In all great movements of counterinterpretation there is a tendency to sweep too far in the new direction. The old idea of the sanctity of the written word in the interpretation of history needed to be challenged, but the question which now arises is whether the challenge has been excessive. Is it excessive to regard oral evidence as the equivalent of documentary evidence in every way? Has there been too hasty an assertion of parity of esteem for what was orally transmitted and what was preserved in writing?

The debate was important for nationalism in Africa from the start, partly because to be denied history is, in some sense, to be denied full dignity as a people. In his opening address to the First International Congress of Africanists in Accra in December, 1962, Kwame Nkrumah captured the essence of this issue in the following lament:

> The central myth in the mythology surrounding Africa is that of the denial that we are a historical people. It is said that whereas other continents have shaped

history and determined its course, Africa has stood still, held down by inertia. Africa, it is said, entered history only as a result of European contact. Its history, therefore, is widely felt to be an extension of European history. Hegel's authority was lent to this historical hypothesis concerning Africa. And apologists of colonialism and imperialism lost little time in seizing upon it and writing wildly about it to their hearts' content.[1]

Nkrumah quoted one eminent Western philosopher of history, Hegel. A more recent historian and philosopher of history of the West, R. G. Collingwood, also defined history in such a way that much of Africa could be left out of it. Collingwood's approach was also one that regarded documentary evidence as a defining characteristic of history.

> History proceeds by the interpretation of the evidence: where evidence is a collective name for things which singly are called documents, and a document is a thing existing here and now, of such a kind that the historian, by thinking about it, can get answers to the questions he asks about past events.[2]

Oral Testimony versus Written Evidence

In the face of such a conception of history, three lines of defensive action are open to Africans. One is to accept the paramountcy of documents and then proceed to demonstrate that Africa does have documentary evidence for much of its precolonial history. The second is to try to establish the validity of oral evidence for historical work. The third line of defensive action is to try to cast doubt on the validity of documentary evidence in an attempt to demonstrate that countries having massive documentation for their history are no nearer certainty about their past than those lacking such evidence.

The first line of action, that of trying to demonstrate that Africa is well endowed with documentary evidence of its own about its precolonial past, has been more important for West Africans and North Africans than for Africans to the east and the south. At the First International Congress of Africanists, K. Onwuka Dike, the vice-chancellor of the University of Ibadan and one of the most distinguished of African historians, had the following to say in this regard:

> On the side of written documentary material alone we are only just beginning

---

1. Kwame Nkrumah, "Address Delivered to Mark the Opening of the First International Congress of Africanists," in *The Proceedings of the First International Congress of Africanists*, ed. Lalage Bown and Michael Crowder (London: Longmans; Evanston, Ill.: Northwestern University Press, 1964), p. 8.
2. R. G. Collingwood, *The Idea of History* (1946; reprint paperback ed., London: Oxford University Press, 1961), pp. 9–10.

to appreciate the size of the problem. Only now is it being realized, for example, that colonial government, missionary and commercial records in European languages are not the only written sources for the history of the continent outside the North African coastlands. We have hardly yet begun to take into account the fact that many of the peoples of Subsaharan Africa have for several centuries been using Arabic as an official and literary language for many different types of written intercourse. We have really only just learnt also that the Swahili and Hausa languages (to name only two) have been written down extensively in the Arabic script and may therefore, for all we know at present, have produced a further unsuspected source of written material. Again how many of us also realise how far private African citizens such as the Efik Chief, Antera Duke, were using European languages for writing in their private intercourse as far back as the eighteenth century? The private papers of African families are a potential source of historical material which to date has hardly been investigated at all. . . .

We are recovering material dating from the seventeenth century onwards in Northern Nigeria; but it is noteworthy that we are also recovering important private material in areas not usually associated with Arabic documentation such as southern Yorubaland. . . . I strongly suspect that, all over West Africa, it will be found that Arabic material exists in private hands on a scale hitherto quite unknown.[3]

Dike also referred to the remarkable dispersal of material all over the world concerning African history. He cited the work of a committee at the Institute of Historical Research of the University of London which was entrusted in 1954 with producing a series of guides to materials pertaining to the history of West Africa to be found in European archives. This material includes important works by Africans taken out of the continent over the generations by European researchers, colonial rulers, and visitors. Dike also mentioned private material in Europe, either written or acquired by visitors and retained in private hands. As the vice-chancellor of Ibadan University, he had set aside a grant to enable a beginning to be made toward copying the records which were thus dispersed.

The second line of defensive action concerns the validity of oral tradition. There is in all parts of sub-Saharan Africa an increasing awareness of the validity of oral tradition as historical evidence. The movement received an important scholarly boost with the publication of Jan Vansina's *Oral Tradition: A Study in Historical Methodology*.[4] Vansina analyzes both the strengths and the weaknesses of using oral tradition in historical research. He also distinguishes different types of oral evidence and attempts an evaluation. The work has been profoundly influential in determining the methodology of historical research in Africa and in forging new links between history and social anthropology. Universities in different parts of the continent have initiated work on collecting oral evidence and attempting to comprehend local history through this medium.

3. K. Onwuka Dike, "The Study of African History," in *Proceedings of the First International Congress of Africanists*, pp. 58–60.
4. Jan Vansina, *Oral Tradition: A Study in Historical Methodology* (1961), trans. H. M. Wright (London: Routledge & Kegan Paul; Chicago: Aldine, 1965).

[5]

Vansina discusses other potential sources for the historian — the disciplines of archaeology, linguistics, and physical anthropology, as well as written documents, where these exist. In the ultimate analysis, however, the main thrust of the book is the legitimation of oral transmission as a functional equivalent of documentation. In Vansina's words:

What the historian can do is to arrive at some approximation to the ultimate historical truth. He does this by using calculations of probability, by interpreting the facts and by evaluating them in an attempt to recreate for himself the circumstances which existed at certain given moments of the past. And here the historian using oral traditions finds himself on exactly the same level as historians using any other kind of historical source material. No doubt he will arrive at a lower degree of probability than would otherwise be attained, but that does not rule out the fact that what he is doing is valid, and that it is history.[5]

The third line of African historical defense goes beyond demonstrating Africa's possession of documentation and demonstrating the validity of oral tradition. This line casts doubt on the mystique of documentation in a bid to demonstrate that written material is no more reliable than unwritten material. In fact, according to this strategy, the danger with the written word lies in the mystique it has enjoyed among historians for such a long time; the investigator may have his guard down in the excitement of discovering an ancient and discolored page of written material. Trying to show that written evidence is itself unreliable is perhaps the other side of the coin of legitimating oral tradition, but the emphasis is certainly different. This approach seems oriented toward demonstrating that those whose history is derived from written sources are no more a "historical people" than those whose past has to be discerned from other evidence. "We are all historically naked" is the depressing message of this line of thought.

B. A. Ogot belongs more to the school which seeks to assert the validity of oral tradition than to that which seeks to discredit written material, but in the enthusiasm of debate he does at times move in the latter direction, casting serious doubt on written European accounts of Africa. The understanding of Africa and its past has been greatly bedeviled by reports written by Europeans passing through the continent. It is not at all certain that the oral tradition of living inhabitants is not a far better indication of the reality of Africa's past than the vivid and romantic accounts of European explorers. Ogot refers to the Spekes and Burtons of African historiography, with all their colorful descriptions of the "avarice," "savagery," "selfishness," and "proficiency for telling lies" that they claimed to have "discovered" among Africans. Ogot draws the inference:

It should be clear from the passages I have cited that written evidence *per se*

5. *Ibid*., p. 186; see also *ibid*., pp. 141–82.

is no more reliable than oral evidence, especially when it emanates from such biased observers. . . . The problem of conflicting accounts of the same historical events is thus not a special feature of oral evidence, as some historians and anthropologists have contended. It applies to all historical evidence.[6]

History as a Literate Skill

Has this African attack on the traditional Western conception of historiography gone too far? Is there, in fact, a residual superiority of written evidence over oral which Africa must recognize for the sake of its future? It is to this evaluative question that we must now turn.

Would the validation of oral tradition be enough to make Africa a continent with a substantial history? It is possible to argue that oral tradition is not itself history; that it is, at the most, only material for history. Even if we do succeed in proving that a legend about an event in Masailand in 1865 is the equivalent of a contemporary newspaper report about the assassination of Abraham Lincoln in the same year, we have not proved that either is the equivalent of a systematic collection of different types of evidence and analysis by a trained historian, weighing and comparing fragments of testimony and analyzing them all in a mood of cautious verification.

A notorious statement about the question of whether or not African history exists was made in 1963, by Hugh Trevor-Roper, the Regius Professor of Modern History at Oxford. He was opening a series of television lectures commissioned by the University of Sussex on "The Rise of Christian Europe." He began by dismissing the history of Africa as meaningless.

> Perhaps, in the future, there will be some African history. . . . But at present there is none; there is only the history of the Europeans in Africa. The rest is darkness, . . . and darkness is not a subject of history.

Trevor-Roper conceded that even in dark countries and dark centuries men existed and that they had political lives and cultures of interest to sociologists and anthropologists. But he declared:

> History, I believe, is essentially a form of movement, and purposive movement too. It is not a mere phantasmagoria of changing shapes and costumes, or battles and conquests, dynasties and usurpations, social reforms and social disintegration.

The world as it is today, according to Trevor-Roper, is dominated by European techniques, examples, and ideas. It is these which have "shaken the non-European

---

6. Bethwell A. Ogot, *History of the Southern Luo* (Nairobi: East African Publishing House, 1967), Vol. I, *Migration and Settlement*, p. 16.

world out of its past — out of barbarism in Africa. . . . The history of the world, for the last five centuries, in so far as it has significance, has been European history.'' He went on to urge that the study of history must therefore be Eurocentric. We cannot afford to "amuse ourselves with the unrewarding gyrations of barbarous tribes in picturesque but irrelevant corners of the globe.''[7]

Trevor-Roper was denying Africa a history by referring to the things which, he thought, went on in Africa. In other words, he was using the *content* of Africa's past as the criterion by which it could be determined whether or not Africa had a history. That kind of approach, which is one of pure cultural arrogance, shall be examined more fully below, when we come to the issue of the content of history.

A far less arrogant and more defensible proposition would be to assert that much of Africa until recent times had no history for the simple reason that it had no *historians*. A comparable situation would be the existence of many contemporary newspaper reports about Lincoln's assassination, for example, but no trained analyst to go through the material and seek answers to the critical questions about the event. R. G. Collingwood, with no special interest in conducting a debate about Africa or any colonial part of the world, enumerates four factors which together constitute history. First, history has to be a systematic answering of questions; second, it has to concern itself with human actions in the past; third, it has to be pursued by interpretation of (mainly documentary) evidence; and, fourth, it has to be undertaken for the sake of enhancing human self-knowledge.

Collingwood concedes that this is not the way in which people have always thought of history. He cites a recent account of how the Sumerians in the third millennium B.C. viewed the question of resolving historical disputes:

> Historiography is represented by official inscriptions commemorating the building of palaces and of temples. The theocratic style of the scribes attributes everything to the action of the divinity, as can be seen from the following passage, one of many examples. "A dispute arises between the kings of Lagash and of Umma about the boundaries of their respective territories. The dispute is submitted to the arbitration of Mesilim, king of Kish, and is settled by the gods, of whom the kings of Kish, Lagash, and Umma are merely the agents or ministers.''[8]

Collingwood is driven to say that the historical consciousness of the ancient Sumerians is what scientists call "an occult entity, something which the rules of scientific method forbid us to assert.'' He continues:

---

7. Hugh Trevor-Roper, "The Rise of Christian Europe,'' *Listener* (London), November 28, 1963, p. 871. For a response to these remarks, see J. D. Fage, *On the Nature of African History* (Birmingham: Birmingham University Press, 1965).

8. Collingwood, *Idea of History*, p. 11; Collingwood quotes Charles F. Jean, "End of the Egyptian Middle Empire,'' in *European Civilization*, ed. Edward Eyre (London: Oxford University Press, 1935), I, 259.

Four thousand years ago, then, our forerunners in civilisation did not possess what we call the idea of history. This, so far as we can see, was not because they had the thing itself but had not reflected upon it. It was because they did not possess the thing itself. History did not exist. There existed, instead, something which in certain ways resembled what we call history, but this differed from what we call history in respect of every one of the four characteristics which we have identified in history as it exists today.[9]

What Collingwood is suggesting is that there is a breed of analysis, conducted by professional historians with certain rules in mind, without which there can be no history in this quasi-scientific sense. Oral tradition in Africa is a form of reporting. If history were merely reporting, oral tradition might be history. But if, as Collingwood suggests, history includes a spirit of cautious verification and a technique of analyzing data, then oral tradition is not history. It is historical evidence. Its availability proves that all over Africa there is historical evidence, but it does not prove that Africa has a substantial history.

The conclusion to be drawn from this is that, although the written word is not important in deciding what is or is not valid historical evidence, it is nevertheless indispensable in determining what is or is not history. This is simply because the careful exercise of formulating propositions, comparing data, and analyzing the patterns of events in the direction of quasi-scientific plausibility is still an exercise which depends on the reduction of thought to writing. Technology has gone far enough to afford the average historian at least the theoretical possibility of using a Dictaphone to work out his ideas initially through oral transmission into a machine. But the study of history is, for the time being, tied to the notion of transcribing what is on tape into writing and then studying what is produced with greater care and thoroughness than might be possible through a purely oral exercise.

In view of the possibilities of technology, it is conceivable that in the future we will have history without the written word. But in the past and for the present all we can claim is that although historical evidence does not depend on the written word, history as analysis and cautious verification of data continues to rely overwhelmingly on the literate historian.

The Presence of the Past

Raymond Aron once said: "Man has in fact no past unless he is conscious of having one, for only such consciousness makes dialogue and choice possible."[10] Here Aron is concerned with awareness of what went on before. But there is another dimension of awareness — the dimension of whether the past is indeed

---

9. Collingwood, *Idea of History*, pp. 12–13.
10. *Chambers Encyclopedia*, 1967 ed., s.v. "History, Philosophy of."

past. This introduces an additional difficulty in the oral traditions of African communities. The distinction between the past and the present may be less sharp in some African belief-systems than might be desirable for the sake of dispassionate history. The concept of what John S. Mbiti, professor of religious studies at Makerere University, calls "the living-dead" seems to deny the need for a Western categorization of time into past, present, and future. The past is not completely past; the dead are not entirely dead. The identity of the community is tied up with the immediacy of the past. Here the debate on the *content* of history comes into play, as scholars endeavor to determine where history ends and the present begins.

In the case of written history, distance in time lends depth to the analysis. There are historians who accept the "fifty-year rule," now revised, as safeguarding not simply the personalities mentioned in documents preserved by governments but also the technique of historical study itself. In other words, the more recent the evidence, the less reliable the analysis. The passage of time enhances dependability. In the case of oral transmission, on the other hand, the passage of time reduces or dilutes reliability. The oral exercise depends on the memories of generation after generation. As more generations are called upon to remember, what is remembered becomes less reliable.

Because the past in African belief-systems is still very much the present, there is the additional hazard of projecting the present backward in time. The notions of changing values within a tribe, of social transformation, are inadequately comprehended. What is alive today as an institution or custom may be pushed back in time to a period before it actually came into being. The past and the present intertwine. While the written word as historical evidence over a span of time often has the coldness of antiquity, oral transmission has the warmth of personal interaction between the storyteller and his audience, from generation to generation. Christopher Dawson once said:

> Happy is the people that is without a history, and thrice happy is the people without a sociology, for as long as we possess a living culture we are unconscious of it, and it is only when we are in danger of losing it or when it is already dead that we begin to realise and to study it scientifically.[11]

There is an echo here of the Hegelian concept of the owl of Minerva, spreading its wings at dusk. We begin to understand our societies only when the characteristics we have comprehended are about to come to an end. Both Hegel and Dawson exaggerate the issue, but there may be some truth in the idea that a living culture is not a subject of history. That is why some historians prefer to wait for thirty or fifty years before they study a culture, making sure that what they are studying is no longer alive. The trouble in Africa until recent

---

11. Quoted in Herbert J. Muller, *The Uses of the Past* (New York: Oxford University Press, 1957), p. 27.

times was that too many of the cultures remained living cultures for too long, reluctant to let go of the past, absorbing the past in the present, fusing descendants with ancestors, and defying the tripartite division of time.

African historians like Dike and Ogot, and historians of a new generation, constitute Africa's owl of Minerva, emerging from the dusk of Africa's past. "Perhaps in the future, there will be some African history. . . . But at present there is none; there is only the history of the Europeans in Africa." Taken out of context, even this statement by Trevor-Roper is more of an exaggeration than a falsehood, if by history we mean not the content of the past but the analytical reporting of it on the basis of quasi-scientific criteria of verification. In the future there will be a substantial body of precolonial African history — going back many centuries before the white man conquered the continent. Contrary to Trevor-Roper's suggestion, Africa does have a past worth recording and analyzing; but that past has not been adequately subjected to analysis by African historians. Just as there can be no poetry without poets, no science without scientists, so can there be no history without historians. When the history of Africa's history is written, the hero has to be, in some important sense, the African historian.

The issue of methodology in history merges with the issue of the content of African history. On the question of content, the case of the African reformers of historiography is, in some respects, stronger than their arguments about parity of oral and written evidence.

Exploration and Ethnocentrism

In August, 1963, a revealing letter written by an African parent calling himself "Dume" appeared in the *East African Standard*. The parent said that in a discussion of last term's examination papers with his nine-year-old son, the child suddenly asked him, "Baba, why is it that we were taught: Speke *discovered* Lake Victoria; does it mean that there were no people living in this country at that time?" The African parent was for a while somewhat perplexed, since he had not looked at the issue in quite those terms before. But then he answered, "Captain J. H. Speke was merely the first *European* to see the Nyanza, which is Lake Victoria now. This does not necessarily mean discovery in the sense of the word as we Africans would have it understood. But to pass your examinations you have to call it discovery." [12]

This African parent was touching on an issue which has come to be linked to nationalistic sensitivities in present-day Africa. To some extent the problem is reminiscent of the comment Tom Mboya heard a European woman make in colonial days. The woman came into an office where Mboya was working

---

12. *East African Standard* (Nairobi), August 6, 1963.

as an employee. She looked around and then said more to herself than to anyone else, "Is there anybody here?" The event impressed Mboya deeply. Implicit in the woman's attitude seemed to be an assumption that Mboya was not anybody. She wanted to talk to "somebody" — but somehow this African boy was not quite what she had in mind.[13]

By the same token, Lake Nyanza had been the subject of admiration and awe and certainly had been seen by generations of Africans well before Speke cast his eyes on it. To describe Speke as having discovered the lake implied to some extent that those who had seen it before counted for little more than did Mboya to that woman. She had not deigned to notice that Mboya was there. Admirers of Speke had not deigned to notice that the lake had been seen by others before him. Who were the people who had been living around the Nyanza for generations?

Dume's letter in the *East African Standard* provoked heated discussion on the significance of the explorers for Africa. An expatriate correspondent invoked *Punch*'s answer to a similar statement apparently made by a spokesman of the Tanganyika government. The statement from Tanganyika had been to the effect that Livingstone did not discover anything, that these places had been known to African people from the beginning of time. On such remarks the satirical British magazine had the following ridicule to pour:

> It was there all the time. He just stubbed his toe on it. Why give him credit for that? "Columbus," you might as well say, "discovered America." Phooey. Discovered my eye. It was there all the time. It just happened to be in his way. And as for Pasteur and those germs — what did he ever do but notice the way they behaved? It comes to no more. By anthropoid standards he made a discovery, true — but millions of worthy bacteria knew it before.[14]

What was being claimed was that denying credit to European explorers is comparable to denying credit to those who have made discoveries in medical science, for example. The whole thing allegedly verged on being an exercise in scientific deprivation — it was like denying the right to a patent or the privilege of copyright. As another correspondent put it, "Credit must go where it is due and we should be proud of what the few have done."

Here it is worth distinguishing between discovering Lake Victoria and discovering the source of the Nile. This, too, came up in the newspaper in the course of the controversy, though the full implications of the distinction were perhaps not drawn. In a long letter, Mr. I. P. Shanks argued that Speke's intention had not been merely to see the water; what he was after was the source of the Nile.

---

13. See Tom Mboya, *Freedom and After* (London: André Deutsch, 1963), p. 29.

14. These lines, apparently written by Richard Mallett, were reproduced in the *East African Standard*, August 25, 1963, "by kind permission of *Punch*."

The point is that before he could accurately say, "This is where the great river has its source," very many separate records of observation had to be fitted in together; and it is just the accuracy and careful energy, even intuition, with which Speke carried out his task that justified, for example, the honour which the French Government did him by awarding him its gold medal for the discovery of Victoria Nyanza.[15]

This is indeed an important consideration. To discover the lake was to see something which generations of Africans before had seen and touched and utilized. But to discover the source of the Nile was something different. It did imply a larger picture of interconnections between this and other pieces of knowledge. It did signify a move forward in the evolution of human knowledge. To discover the lake was an exercise in the dissemination of knowledge, for it meant that one more person had seen it and, with his knowledge, would inform the rest of Europe. Spreading knowledge is a worthy exercise in its own right, but it is fundamentally different from augmenting the total sum of human knowledge. Europeans seeing the lake for the first time were, at best, instruments of dissemination for a body of knowledge which had already been acquired by others before them. The knowledge in this case was of the existence of this big inland sea. But establishing the connection between this inland sea and the eternal river that went down to the land of the pharaohs and the cradle of a major civilization — this was different. The discovery of this link between the lake in Uganda and the narrow pastures of the home of Cleopatra was a definite augmentation of the total sum of human awareness; it was certainly more than dissemination of something already known and understood by others.

The credit that goes to a discovery such as Speke's in relation to the source of the Nile must be distinguished from the credit that goes to someone like J. L. Krapf or G. Rebmann, who discovered snow-capped mountains in eastern Africa. The mountains had always been there. These two Germans shared a vision with black people of the region and then spread that information to their contemporaries in Europe. This was an exercise in disseminating knowledge about Africa rather than in fully augmenting the total sum of human knowledge. There was little deduction involved in discovering Mount Kilimanjaro, but there had to be deduction in discovering the source of the Nile. To discover Mount Kilimanjaro or Mount Kenya was an important event in the education of Europe, but to discover the source of the Nile was an important event in the education of mankind as a whole. The evaluation of discoveries must therefore take this dimension into account. There is less Eurocentrism in glorifying Speke than in glorifying Krapf and Rebmann.

The importance which Europe accorded the explorers was partly connected with the old vision of Africa as a "dark continent" on which the explorers

---

15. *East African Standard*, August 25, 1963.

helped to shed some light. Such assumptions have yet to disappear from the ranks of Western historians. One can almost say that there is a direct link between the assumptions underlying the European explorations of one or two centuries ago and the assumptions underlying the remarks that Trevor-Roper made in 1963. Trevor-Roper's barren picture of what African history was all about was not, of course, entirely due to the kind of information the first explorers brought back to Europe. There is no doubt that Trevor-Roper's conception of African history had much to do with the pervasive myth about the continent — the myth of an eternal savagery that seemed to stretch backward in time beyond the mists of antiquity. This, again, is a matter of the content of history. To such a mythology about the condition of Africa, European explorers made a decisive contribution at a formative period in the growth of Europe's awareness of other peoples. First reports about a distant area tend to have an impact out of proportion to their significance, let alone their accuracy. It is like the first news that is headlined — it has an impact which a later retraction can only partially negate.

The Quest for Balance

Because of past misreportings, the course of African historiography must now be more selective than perhaps one might wish. Indigenous African historians especially are faced with a dilemma as to their ultimate duty. Perhaps scholarship at large faces a crisis of divided purpose. It can commit itself either to the cause of maximizing human knowledge or to that of correcting human error. It is not often remembered that these two goals need not be pulling in the same direction. The cause of maximizing human knowledge is to some extent the more straightforward of the two. An attempt is made to accumulate as diverse a sum of knowledge as possible. Whether this form of knowledge perpetuates a myth about certain things or helps to eliminate it is not considered. The first commitment is to quantity, even if it is quantity presented with aesthetic taste and intellectual imagination.

The cause of correcting a pre-existent human error is a different form of exercise. In this case it is not enough to add to the sum total of human knowledge, lest the correction of the error be delayed. It is important that the information provided should counteract a pre-existent distortion. It is true that much in Africa's past can be intelligently described as savagery. If all that mattered for historiography was to maximize knowledge, research could add to the information about the nature of African "savagery" and, at the same time, provide information about more elevated aspects of the African past. However, if historiography was completely unselective, the addition of knowledge on the "savage" side of the African past would conceivably continue to overbalance the inflow of information from the more elevated side. After all, the information on African "savagery" is more extensively documented in available written sources in the Western world. Only counterselection can correct a pre-existent distortive selection. A whole generation of African historians — perhaps even more — is needed to concentrate on aspects of African history which do not lend themselves to being used as sustenance for disparaging mythologies.

An approach that African historians have already begun to use is to concentrate more on complex African societies and their "elevated" structures than on comparatively backward African communities. This is certainly one answer to the distortions that came with the explorers. In the case of Uganda the Afrophile historians have often paid more attention to the Baganda than to the less elevated Karamojong. However, this is an inadequate approach to the selectivity which is needed if a pre-existent distortion is to be corrected. What is required is not simply giving preference to African kingdoms rather than to less sophisticated African communities. What is at least as important is to study less sophisticated African communities with a sympathetic eye and with a willingness to discover the more favorable aspects of their organization and mores. A scholar therefore turns to the Karamojong, not in order to discuss afresh the degree to which they go naked or the extent to which they raid for cattle, but in order to find the mysteries of human justification for things that at first might look bizarre and yet, when studied in depth, might reveal rationality. The scholar is then selective in studying the Karamojong, but selective with a purpose. Even Hugh Trevor-Roper admits that "history, or rather the study of history, has a purpose. We study it . . . in order to discover how we have come to be where we are." To try to understand how a people came to be where they are is to seek the meaning of things. Where the meaning of things has been distorted, we can understand how a people arrived at the point at which they are only by selecting the kind of counterinformation which would restore the balance of historical explanation.

It is important to draw a distinction between providing information and increasing knowledge. Knowledge is a more rounded thing than information needs to be. While we can easily talk about incorrect information, to talk about incorrect knowledge is a contradiction. We often refer to someone as being misinformed or ill informed, but we would never speak of someone as being misknowledgeable or ill knowledgeable. There is something in the idea of "knowing" that implies greater certainty than is signified by the concept of "information."

To correct pre-existent human error, the scholar provides selective information that will balance the one-sided information previously available. A new half of the picture is added to the old half. Together, the two bits of information add up to a picture of knowledge about Africa. Therefore, even when a scholar is trying to compensate for prior distortion, he is still serving the cause of maximizing knowledge, although the data he provides are sufficiently partial to be more accurately described as selective information. In the ultimate analysis, the two scholarly duties — correcting error and maximizing knowledge — are equally defensible on academic and intellectual grounds. To correct a pre-existent error, even by the utilization of counterselection, is at least as defensible as a reckless, uncoordinated provision of additional knowledge regardless of its effect on existing myths. It is possible that the discipline and purposefulness of trying to correct error compensates for any apparent departures from the cult of detachment.

This is perhaps the ultimate issue in that part of cultural engineering which is concerned with the reinterpretation of African history. In Dar es Salaam the leadership in this enterprise of counterselection was assumed by Terrence Ranger, a British radical with special interest in primary resistance by Africans to the beginnings of foreign intrusion. In Nairobi, B. A. Ogot, the Kenyan historian, is committed not only to the nationalization of ethnohistory but also to the task of cutting down the size of European explorers and their place in Africa's recent past. In Uganda, M. S. K. Kiwanuka is also committed to ethnohistory in relation to national history; and Prof. Burton Webster, the Canadian head of Makerere's History Department, an apparently passionate believer in the rapid indigenization of the general syllabus, initiated relevant research toward the rapid diversification of Uganda's sectionalized history.

The place of the foreigner in the cultural engineering of East Africa still seems to be significant. Even among the leaders of the movement to Africanize historiography, one finds Ranger, a Briton, and Webster, a Canadian. Perhaps that is as it should be. A national identity based purely on mythology can afford to insist on exclusively indigenous sources. But a national identity based partly on the fruit of scholarship cannot afford to turn its back on worthy contributions from elsewhere. The African is learning that complete self-recognition is impossible without the aid of external devices.

From methodology in history we moved on to the content of history. From the content of history we must now move on to its application. It is in the application of history that cultural engineering becomes particularly explicit, though issues of national consciousness and cultural validation are inevitably involved in the methodological and interpretive debates of African historians.

The Uses of History

Four guiding principles help to determine the planning behind social engineering when the ideology is nationalistic. The principles can be formulated in terms of four imperatives: first, indigenizing what is foreign; second, idealizing what is indigenous; third, nationalizing what is sectional; and, fourth, emphasizing what is African. The four principles are interrelated and often reinforce each other. The indigenization of what is foreign — Marxism, for example — occurs when there is a readiness to adapt what is foreign to suit African conditions.

Socialism has at times been indigenized by defining its links with the tribal collectivism of traditional African societies. The indigenization of what is foreign presupposes, of course, the desirability of what is being indigenized. When parliamentary institutions were regarded as desirable, there was a constant attempt to portray such institutions as a natural outgrowth of the consensual ethos of traditional Africa — "They talked and talked under a tree until they agreed." When a one-party state became the object of political desire, the consensual ethos of traditional Africa could still be emphasized — but without stressing the freedom to "talk and talk." The consensus became more important than the preliminaries of discussion.

Included very often in this process of indigenizing what is foreign is the second process, idealizing what is indigenous. The hospitality of the village acquires romantic luster as the African genius for collective life is eulogized; and the literary movement of negritude is a romanticization of black civilized values.

One of the volumes of Nkrumah's *Encyclopaedia Africana* project, which was announced in 1962, was to be devoted to brief biographies of people of historical interest to Africa, no more than a third of whom could be foreigners who played important roles in Africa's history. Several countries were invited by the project to compile biographical data, and some had already begun when the project was adopted by the cultural wing of the Organization of African Unity. The project survived Nkrumah's fall from power, but financial difficulties have made it unlikely that the work will ever be completed.

When Uganda was invited by the *Encyclopaedia Africana* secretariat to begin to compile biographies of important Ugandans, one of the problems which arose was ethnic balance. For better or for worse, the most nationally significant Ugandans in the last 150 years had come from one or two centrally situated tribes, and the best records available concerning leading Ugandans in history concentrated on a few tribes. At that time these tribes were no longer enjoying the pre-eminence they had once had. A national biography which gave them a preponderance of entries was therefore bound to arouse the suspicion and envy of others. An ethnic balance was called for. Nkrumah's fall from power and the financial uncertainties of *Encyclopaedia Africana* postponed the problem for Ugandan historians.

The third guiding principle of cultural engineering as directed by nationalistic ideology is that of nationalizing what is sectional. J.F.A. Ajayi, an African historian, has captured the difficulty of this imperative:

> The nationalist leader attempting to rally the masses and re-establish their self-confidence by appealing to their cultural heritage soon realises that the more each cultural group takes pride in its own heritage, the more difficult it is to achieve the common loyalty to a large political unit which is necessary for development and is the fundamental goal of African nationalism. With increasing self-government the old fear of "localism" reappears under the name of "tribalism. . . ." In

East and Central Africa, with the exception of Jomo Kenyatta, it is not the nationalists but the traditional rulers opposing national integration who appeal to history and culture. In South Africa, it is the white minority government believing not in national integration but in apartheid who appeal constantly to history and culture. In West Africa where the nationalists and the traditional rulers have come closest together, and the nationalist movement is most conscious of the African's cultural heritage, the danger of "tribalism" remains — the danger that . . . the self-consciousness of the different cultural groups might tear the nation asunder.[16]

Ajayi's characterization of degrees and modes of cultural appeal in the different regions of Africa, although written in 1960, has assumed even greater relevance since then. Much of the pre-European history of Africa is in fact "ethnohistory." The unit of historical identity was the ethnic group or the tribe rather than the territorial state that we now see. The heroes were therefore ethnic heroes rather than national ones. One task of cultural engineering after independence is thus to nationalize these heroes. Kikuyu heroes must somehow be nationalized into Kenyan heroes; and heroes of other tribes should be re-evaluated and given a national stature. The Department of History at the University of Nairobi is attaching importance to the task of building a national biographical history. The department has invited scholars to study men of historical interest from different parts of Kenya — an undertaking designed to produce the first volume in a series of national biographies.

The Department of History at Makerere University in Kampala has been feeling the tensions of the dilemma also. The need to indigenize the history syllabus as far as possible is now widely agreed upon. The department of history of an African university ought to put special emphasis on African history. In addition, the department of history of a university in Uganda ought to allow special room for Uganda's history. But a simple indigenization of the history syllabus at Makerere, purely on the basis of available academic material, might once again emphasize the pre-eminence of Buganda in Uganda's history, with all the ethnic sensitivities involved in this.

It is beginning to be felt that indigenizing the syllabus is not enough; an attempt to nationalize what is sectional must also be undertaken. One method of nationalizing sectional or ethnic history is to emphasize its national implications. But, in the political climate of Uganda, it would defeat the object of the exercise if historians simply portrayed Baganda heroes as basically national heroes. Equating Buganda with Uganda is precisely what many other Ugandans objected to. The answer, therefore, in Uganda's conditions might be to create ethnic balance. Historical sectionalism is nationalized by pluralizing it, adding section to section. The heroes of the different tribes become national heroes

16. J. F. A. Ajayi, "The Place of African History and Culture in the Process of Nation-Building in Africa South of the Sahara," *Journal of Negro Education*, XXX, no. 3 (1960), reprinted in *Social Change: The Colonial Situation*, ed. Immanuel Wallerstein (New York: Wiley, 1966), p. 613.

by a process of conferring parity of esteem on the subgroups from which they emerged. The Department of History at Makerere seems to have embarked on precisely this quest for balance and for a national frame of reference in Uganda's historiography.

The fourth guiding principle of this kind of cultural engineering is that of emphasizing what is African. Obviously, this overlaps the process of indigenization, but the principles are not the same. The indigenization of what is foreign presupposes the existence of something which is foreign. In addition, it often implies that what started as foreign continues to exist but is finding local roots. On the other hand, to emphasize what is African does not imply that what is being emphasized was not always African. It simply implies that it was not emphasized before. We can talk about indigenizing, or Africanizing, Marxism; but it would not make sense to talk about indigenizing, or Africanizing, tribal loyalties or village hospitality. These latter are already indigenous; the issue is simply whether they are to be emphasized. It might make sense to talk about indigenizing or assimilating the piano into Africa's musical experience, but it would not make sense to talk about indigenizing the drum. The piano is foreign and has to become indigenously expressive; the drum is already indigenous and needs only a new emphasis in modern musical communication.

Sometimes emphasizing what is African takes the minimal form of understressing what is foreign. In 1968 and 1969, the students at Makerere were involved in a debate about renaming the buildings on the campus. The names of the halls of residence came under special re-evaluation. The six halls bear the following names: Livingstone Hall (named after David Livingstone, the missionary-explorer), Northcote Hall (named after Sir Geoffrey Northcote, chairman of Makerere Council and an expatriate British educator), Mitchell Hall (named after Sir Phillip Mitchell, a former governor of Uganda and Kenya), Mary Stuart Hall (also named after a British educator), University Hall, and New Hall. The four names that are historically inspired seek to commemorate four individuals, none of whom is African. Is this anomalous — even though the history of Makerere has owed much to the initiative of foreigners, among whom some of these four are to be counted?

After a good deal of discussion, the college gave the residents of each hall the right to suggest an alternative name if they wished. The residents of Northcote Hall had an agonizing debate as to whether the hall should be renamed Nkrumah Hall, but the debate never got beyond the issue of whether a change was needed at all, let alone whether the name Nkrumah Hall should replace the existing one. The students were bitterly divided, and the reformers lost the first round. The reformers in Livingstone Hall lost even more decisively. Most students were simply not in a mood for such exercises. The only important place name at Makerere to have fallen in this recent battle was the name of the buildings which housed the Faculty of Arts. This complex, previously called Queen's Court, was renamed Arts' Court in 1969.

Among the arguments used by the historical conservationists on Makerere Hill was the simple argument that since much of the rest of the country was still littered with "anachronistic" names, there was no reason why academics should be more impatient with residual history than politicians appeared to be. What was perhaps the most popular game reserve in the country was still called Queen Elizabeth Park. The lake which took up so many square miles of Uganda's surface was still called Lake Victoria, in honor of an imperial queen. Why should Livingstone Hall be renamed?

The issue of renaming Lake Victoria did come up before the Uganda Parliament. One difficulty in renaming it was that the lake was shared by several countries, and the problems in reaching agreement on an alternative name could be insolvable. Another difficulty was that the lake was famous, and renaming it might provoke an international controversy. The most decisive factor continues to be the simple fact that the reformers have yet to mobilize enough nationalistic militancy to endanger the lake's present name. The reformers in such matters are, for the time being, relatively isolated.

Toward the Nationalization of Memory

If economic development with its planning and projections is a future-oriented preoccupation, political development must sometimes include an obsession with the past. This accounts for the ambivalence of African nations which take pride in their newness as states and at the same time seek to emphasize or forge an antiquity.

At the 1960–61 session of the United Nations, it was interesting to listen to Nigeria's foreign minister, Jaja Wachuku, as he reveled in the innocence of the new nation. But involved in that very concept of birth was a paradoxical desire — the desire to be gray-haired and wrinkled as a nation, the desire to have an antiquity. This is directly related to the problem of national identity in Africa. Insofar as nations are concerned, there is often a direct correlation between identity and age. The desire to be old becomes part of the quest for identity.

As a result, what we have had in the newly invented states of Africa has been the paradoxical desire to modernize and ancientize at the same time. Thus the Gold Coast, on emerging into independence, first decided to wear the ancient name Ghana — and then decided to modernize as rapidly as possible. Mali is another new state that has tried to create a sense of antiquity by adopting an old name. The names Malawi and Biafra, both of which have ancient associations, have been used in efforts to strengthen identity. When the hold of the white minority in Rhodesia is one day broken, we will almost certainly have a country called Zimbabwe.

Now, if this rechristening of countries leads to a situation in which the history of the *old* Ghana, for example, is taught possessively in the schools of the *new* Ghana, the sense of historical identity of the descendants of present-day Ghanaians will be affected — even if the new Ghana does not occupy the same spot on the map as the old Ghana.[17] More specifically, there are three processes of sociopolitical change involved in an African country: first, the erosion of tribally exclusive traditions; second, the attempt to erect nationally inclusive traditions; and, third, the construction of the modern state. Here, again, the written word in relation to history assumes a critical relevance.

While it is possible to reconstruct the sectional history of the Kikuyu, the Masai, and the Luo, each from its oral traditions, it is not possible to produce a national history of Kenya purely from oral tradition. In other words, African conditions are such that oral history tends to be, on the whole, tribal history. The great historical synthesis, the merger of ethnic histories into a national history, is impossible without resorting to interlocking documentation and literate analysis.

The written word is also vital in the process of *transmitting* history to the national population. The Kikuyu may tell Kikuyu legends to each other; the Luo may tell each other great tribal deeds of the past. But an efficient transmission of Kikuyu history to the Luo and of Luo history to the Kikuyu has to be part of an elaborate educational system in Kenya. At the present stage of technology, such an educational system has to have literacy as its foundation. The national history of Kenya has to be written — and transmitted in classrooms partly through the printed word. The study of national history is a process of socialization. It is a method of helping children to acquire the rudiments of national identification. In a country of multiple and sometimes conflicting oral traditions, the slow transmission of national identification through an educational system needs the aid of the written word and the spread of literacy in the population.

Historical names, like historical monuments, are a self-conscious bequest from the past to remind the present of its ancestry. Here, again, these matters touch on not only the role of European exploration in the early versions of African history but also the critical issue of the content of history in determining the direction of cultural engineering. In other words, the application of history to social needs is impossible without due regard being paid to the other two levels of historiography — the subject matter of history and its methodology.

Behind all of this is the ghost of the first man to reduce human thought to writing, whatever his name may have been. Although his identity has been lost in the mists of antiquity, his heritage of literate thought will animate the future course of African history. Basil Davidson once wrote:

---

17. This issue is discussed in similar terms in Ali A. Mazrui, "The Role of the University in Political Development," fourth lecture in *A Crisis in Relevance in an African University*, Keith Callard Lectures, 1969 Series (Montreal: McGill University Press, 1971).

I stand with some assurance on the belief that history, whether or not it be a branch of science, is certainly a branch of *Literature*. Not the least of our problems, after all, is that of ordering an already large but rapidly growing body of material into an acceptably *readable* framework.[18]

In his own romantic way, Davidson has played a significant role in helping to reveal Africa's past in spite of the dearth of written evidence. But, from now on, the oral murmurs from antiquity need to be trapped within the walls of literate stability if they are to serve the new purposes of national awareness.

---

18. Basil Davidson, *Can We Write African History?* University of California, African Studies Center, Occasional Paper No. 1 (Los Angeles, 1965). Emphasis added.

[2]

Creative Literature and Political Commitment

Insofar as literature is concerned, much of the political commitment in Africa to date has, in some sense or another, been patriotic commitment. The relationship between patriotism and literature in East Africa has three broad dimensions.[1] The first concerns the very act of writing. In a society where creative literature is a relative novelty, and where this activity is invested with cultural prestige in response to the Western impact, the fact that people write at all becomes an act of national rejuvenation. The second dimension concerns the themes of the literature. In this case it is not merely the writing but what is written that is an expression of nationalism. The portrayal of heroic events in East African history, either through biography or fiction, is often an attempt to define moments of glory in African nationalism. The defense of tradition against modernity, of the indigenous against the foreign, is a song of self-identity that has echoed through the centuries and traversed different cultures. This song can be heard in the biography, fiction, and poetry of East Africa. The third dimension concerns the links between African literature and the literary heritage of the outside world. Within this area lies the place of translation and of languages in general in relation to cultural nationalism. There is a transition from nationalism to transnationalism. The political themes that are treated in this kind of literature are sometimes passionate exercises of empathetic identification with others abroad.

The Pen and the Patriot

National assertion is sometimes a response to prior national humiliation. In such instances the form that nationalism takes is intimately related to the kind of humiliation to which the nation has been subjected. Among the factors which contributed to the relegation of the African to a back seat on the cultural train

---

1. For our purposes in this chapter we need not distinguish sharply between patriotism and nationalism. However, one way of distinguishing the two is to regard nationalism as a more defensive and less secure form of patriotism. Nationalism might then be classified as a special kind of patriotism.

of human history was the absence of writing in many African societies. Sir Phillip Mitchell, who served as governor of both Kenya and Uganda, expressed a typical external sentiment when he marveled once at Africa's isolation from the rest of the world before Western imperialism tore open the curtains of mystery. Sir Phillip was particularly surprised that any people, particularly "a people wide open to the sea," as East Africans were, should have reached the twentieth century without an alphabet of their own.

Statements of this kind abound in the literature of imperial assessments of the African. For an individual to be illiterate was common at the time, even in Western countries; but for a society to be without the means of written expression was supposed to be a sure sign of cultural retardation. Indians, Arabs, and others in the Orient had also been colonial subjects; but, partly because they had been capable of committing their thoughts to writing independently of Western influence, they were assigned higher places than the African in the gradation of human types.

The absence of the written word affected other ways of evaluating the place of the African in world history. Among these must be included the simple point of whether the African had a history at all. This doubt goes far back in the story of Western assessments of the African. One distinguished exponent of this skepticism in the modern period is, as we have noted, Hugh Trevor-Roper, who in 1963 stated that there was no African history, only the history of Europeans in Africa.[2] This kind of interpretation is usually founded on a conception of history that is perhaps excessively literary. It thinks of historical evidence as being basically documentary evidence. A people that is without an adequate body of written evidence and records of past lives therefore falls under the shadow of historical skepticism.

The absence of written creative literature from many African societies helped to aggravate a sense of cultural inadequacy among Africans during the colonial period. Students of African cultures have lately allowed a place of respectability to oral literature — the songs, hymns, and morality stories that have formed a part of African traditional life. Yet the educational system in the colonies invested written literature, rather than oral literature, with aesthetic prestige. Classics of English and French literature were part of high culture. Even in English-speaking Africa, relatively less flamboyant than French-speaking Africa in its utilization of cultural borrowings from the metropolitan imperial power, quotations from Shakespeare, Tennyson, and Wordsworth were used in political oratory as well as in literary works.[3]

---

2. See Hugh Trevor-Roper, "The Rise of Christian Europe," *Listener* (London), November 28, 1963. This point is also discussed in Ali A. Mazrui, *Ancient Greece in African Political Thought* (Nairobi: East African Publishing House, 1967), pp. 22–25.

3. The role of English literature in political rhetoric in Africa is discussed more fully in Ali A. Mazrui, "Some Socio-political Functions of English Literature in Africa" (Paper delivered at the Conference on Language Problems in Developing Nations, Center for Applied Linguistics, Washington, D.C., November, 1966).

If the absence of the written word was intimately a part of Africa's sense of humiliation during the colonial period, the outburst of written creativity among Africans since those early days became an intimate part of Africa's vindication of itself. That Africans could write novels, plays, and even operas was in the initial stages acclaimed by Africans themselves as a phenomenon of cultural vindication. African writers have sometimes assumed heroic dimensions, not simply because of their literary skills, but because of their part in firmly placing the African on the map of global literary civilization.

In East Africa the first book-length literary achievement of political significance was not a work of the imagination as such. It was Jomo Kenyatta's *Facing Mount Kenya*, a personalized anthropological study first published in 1938. There is no doubt that Kenyatta's stature in East Africa in those early days was significantly enhanced by the simple fact that he had succeeded in becoming an author. A sophisticated book in the English language to his credit constituted part of his credentials for political leadership. Much later a fellow Kikuyu, James Ngugi, burst into prominence by becoming the first indigenous East African novelist. This was not simply a case of eulogizing an author for his success strictly as an author. It was also a case of eulogizing a cultural pioneer who was opening up new areas of national vindication for his people. He was demonstrating the ability of an East African to join the flow of creative fiction. More recently, there has been Solomon Mbabi-Katana's short operatic exercise *The Marriage of Nyakato*. Again, the significance of the work lies almost exclusively in its pioneering status. It is too brief and simple to be regarded as a major achievement, but it is a venture into a new cultural area for East Africa.

The uncritical acclamation of literary pioneering poses its own problems. Just as Africans have sometimes acclaimed each other's writing as an expression of national vindication, so have foreign critics sometimes acclaimed African writing as an assertion of their own liberalism. Dubious literary exercises by Africans have sometimes met with Western enthusiasm mainly because the exercises were from Africa. In this kind of situation, some Africans have reacted against the acclaim of the outside world. Amos Tutuola's *The Palm-Wine Drinkard* was widely applauded abroad as a great achievement in creative fantasy and unusual diction. Yet many African critics regarded the external applause as an attempt to patronize naïve attempts by an undereducated African. Therefore, the same nationalism which is capable of acclaiming mediocre African works simply because they are African finds itself deeply offended if the works are acclaimed by Westerners for the same reason. There is a conviction that indulgence by the foreigner is a form of indignity for the native. What is not good enough by the canons of European writers when judging each other ought not to be permitted to be good enough when judging the performance of an African writer.

East Africa Journal, among other publications in East Africa, has published vigorous self-evaluations by East Africans on the "barrenness" of the area in literary work. There have also been seminars, conferences, and discussions on the same theme. On the other hand, particularly since 1967, the defenders of the East African literary scene have come to the fore with the assertion that the region is abounding with innovation and literary fertility. All that it lacks are adequate avenues for expression. The new journal *Zuka,* issued by Oxford University Press and devoted entirely to creative literature and criticism, bases its right to exist on the argument that much of the creativity in East Africa has yet to find adequate outlets. Each of the universities in East Africa has one literary magazine — *Busara* at Nairobi, *Darlite* at Dar es Salaam, and *Penpoint* at Makerere. It is not clear how many of these ventures will manage to sustain themselves over a period of time. What is clear is that there is in East Africa an outburst of literary activity of very mixed quality, aided and abetted both by publishers and by academic departments of literature within the region. At least one of those academic departments has worked hard to interest publishers in getting undergraduates to write about cultural aspects of their own region and has sought to encourage graduate students to collect and record as much of the oral literature of East Africa as possible. Some publishers have been daring and courageous in the commercial risks they have been willing to take with untried students on unusual projects. Nevertheless, their critics would still insist that this is all part of a ruthless commercialism to purvey African goods on the literary market, even if many of them are defective.

Yet, as we shall indicate in Chapter 3, the argument concerning the desirability of encouraging foreign publishers to take greater, even if less discriminate, interest in the work of African students is not only in favor of one side. Although much unpublishable material may find its way into print, there may still be a gain in this quantitative approach to cultural engineering.

Biography and Culture

East Africans have sought to realize a cultural heritage not only in the act of writing but also in choosing certain themes on which to write. Lionel Trilling once discussed Freud's place within literary creativity and concluded that his place lay in the "simple proposition that literature is dedicated to the conception of the self." [4] Freud's preoccupation with the self at both conscious and subconscious levels provides a meeting point between psychology and the literary imagination in its attempt to portray selfhood. This point establishes a connection between, for example, a lyric and an autobiography. Both modes are attempts either at self-expression or at portraying an aspect of selfhood.

In discussing literature in East Africa, some attention therefore has to be paid to the struggling or nascent art of autobiography. So far, much of the autobiographical writing in East Africa in the English language comes from

---

4. See Lionel Trilling, *Beyond Culture: Essays on Literature and Learning* (London: Penguin, 1967), p. 90.

Kenya, and much of that is connected with the Mau Mau insurrection and the place of individual personalities within it. Although Jomo Kenyatta's *Facing Mount Kenya*, which was written well before the Mau Mau outbreak, is primarily an exercise in social anthropology, seeking to define and explain the tribal life of the Kikuyu, there persistently remains within the book a personal dimension which, in places, virtually converts it into an autobiographical exercise. B. Malinowski opens his introduction to Kenyatta's book with the slogan "Anthropology begins at home." He then refers to the two factors which give the book its deeply personal character. One of these is Kenyatta's commitment to the pride of the Kikuyu people, and the other is the extent to which he borrowed from the depths of his own experience in order to portray the lives of his fellow Kikuyu. "As a first-hand account of a representative African culture; as an invaluable document in the principles underlying culture-contact and change; last, not least, as a personal statement of the new outlook of a progressive African; this book will rank as a pioneering achievement of outstanding merit." [5] Kenyatta presents his credentials in the following way: "I can therefore speak as a representative of my people, with personal experience of many different aspects of their life." [6]

The nature of Kenyatta's portrayal of the Kikuyu people was probably responsible for his role as one of the earliest African proponents of the philosophy of negritude. He might not have known of the term *negritude* when he was writing *Facing Mount Kenya*, but the idea and subject matter of the book rested on some of the basic assumptions of that philosophy. Leopold Senghor defined negritude as

> the whole complex of civilised values — cultural, economic, social and political — which characterise the Black Peoples, or more precisely, the Negro African world. All these values are essentially informed by intuitive reason. . . . The sense of communion, the gift of myth making, the gift of rhythm, such are the essential elements of Negritude, which you will find indelibly stamped on all the works and activities of the Black Man. [7]

It is all very well to revel in the ways of traditional Africa. What is often more to the point is to specify those ways in concrete ethnological examples. Kenyatta did attempt to do precisely that in *Facing Mount Kenya*.

African nationalism has been ambivalent about the study of anthropology. Writing in a journal of anthropology in 1934, Margery Perham suggested that "the newly self-conscious African" was quick to suspect the academic mind

---

5. B. Malinowski, "Introduction," in *Facing Mount Kenya*, by Jomo Kenyatta (1938; reprint ed., London: Secker & Warburg, 1959), p. xiv.
6. Kenyatta, *Facing Mount Kenya*, p. xv.
7. Leopold Senghor, "Negritude and African Socialism," in *St. Anthony's Papers on African Affairs, No. 2*, ed. Kenneth Kirkwood (London: Chatto & Windus, 1963), p. 11.

which called a study of the African "anthropology" and of the white man "sociology." Seemingly vindicating Dame Perham's words, nearly thirty years later President Nkrumah suggested to the First International Congress of Africanists in Ghana in 1962 that African studies should "change its course from anthropology to sociology."

If there is such a conflict between anthropology and nationalism, why should Kenyatta's anthropological study be deemed a contribution to the nationalistic concept of negritude? The reason is that the concept of negritude is the meeting point between nationalism and anthropology. Negritude is often an exercise in romantic ethnology. Most African nationalists who share this vision have concentrated on the romance; Kenyatta provided the ethnology as well. He combined description and commitment, analysis and personal involvement; and, as he evaluated the imperial interference with the customary modes of behavior of the Kikuyu people, he was moved to reaffirm that to deny the Kikuyu the right to their traditions was to deny them not only their personality as Kikuyu but also their dignity as human beings. "It is the culture which he inherits that gives a man his human dignity." Perhaps the whole philosophy of negritude in Africa rests on this simple but fundamental premise.[8]

Kenyatta's book is also literary in the use it makes of African parables, sometimes connected with wild animals and their presumed ways and organization. Particularly memorable is the Kikuyu story about a pact concluded between an elephant and a man and the thunderstorm which led to the annexation of the man's tent by the bigger animals he had wished to befriend.[9]

A more explicitly autobiographical work linked to Kikuyu history is Josiah M. Kariuki's *Mau Mau Detainee*, an account of his role in the Mau Mau insurrection. In many ways Kariuki's book compares favorably with that political classic of African autobiography, Nkrumah's *Ghana — The Autobiography of Kwame Nkrumah*. Kariuki describes how news of Kenyatta, a leader who had returned from abroad to speak up for the rights of his people, affected him From simple, juvenile hero-worship, Kariuki drifted into the awesome ceremonies of taking oaths stark naked and committing himself to kill for the sake of a broader cause.

Another autobiography connected with the Mau Mau insurrection is that of Waruhiu Itote, or the General China of the movement, who was evidently a key figure in the insurrection. His book, *"Mau Mau" General*, has an important dimension of interest; but, though fascinating in parts, it falls considerably short of literary and historical adequacy. A weightier book is *Mau Mau from Within*, by Karari Njama and Donald L. Barnett. Barnett is basically an editor in chief, trying to put a stamp of social science respectability on the spontaneous

---

8. See Kenyatta, *Facing Mount Kenya*, pp. 196–97. This point is also discussed in Ali A. Mazrui, "East Africa in the Stream of African Thought," *Internationale Spectator* (1968), pp. 764–68.
9. See Kenyatta, *Facing Mount Kenya*, pp. 47–52.

narrative of one of the participants in the Mau Mau movement. The book does in part succeed in taking the reader behind the scenes; it describes the ideas that agitated the insurgents and tells of the fighters' relationships with their relatives and their friends who were uncommitted to their cause. Njama's account is in many ways intensely personal and is often enriched by that very fact. Barnett, who appears as "coauthor," is in fact a kind of explicator, interpreting the broader social implications of each personal sector of the Kikuyu author's account.

Tom Mboya's *Freedom and After* — acclaimed by the *New York Times* when it came out in 1963 as one of the books of the year — is also partly autobiographical and partly a personal testament. In the last decade of Kenya's struggle for independence, Mboya was in many ways the towering diplomatic symbol of the country's nationalism. He achieved international pre-eminence, and his sophistication and eloquence were often effective counters to the imperial propaganda on the atavism and primitive nature of the Mau Mau insurrection. Mboya was to Kenya what Ferhat Abbas had been to the Algerian cause. Abbas, a highly sophisticated Algerian, had served as a public leader of the Algerian government in exile. In his case, too, the polished sophistication of the man had lent greater diplomatic respectability to the cause of the rebels on the battlefield. Of course, there are important differences between the two situations. Mboya was never explicitly a spokesman for the Mau Mau rebels. What mattered, however, was that the Mau Mau, perhaps even more than the Algerian insurrectionists, had an image of primordial brutishness, which could easily have affected the image of Kenya's nationalism and its right to fulfillment. Did Kenya deserve to have the doors of political participation in the modern sense open? Many liberals abroad wanted reassurance that there was more to Kenya's nationalism than a withdrawal into primordial brutishness. Tom Mboya provided this evidence. His polish, bearing, and powers of articulation were unsurpassed in English-speaking Africa. In *Freedom and After* one gets a glimpse of Mboya's own self-conception and of his vision of the tasks to be done in Kenya.

Although many biographies have come from Kenya, other parts of East Africa have not been unproductive in this regard. Of particular note are an account by a revolutionary and one by a deposed king. The revolutionary is John Okello, who is credited with having spearheaded the Zanzibar Revolution. He has given his version of what happened in a fascinating book entitled *Revolution in Zanzibar*. He describes in a dramatic form one instance of the persistent intermingling of nationalism with racial sentiment on the African continent: the clash on the island of Zanzibar between the idea of a local nationalism encompassing both Africans and Arabs, and the broader issue of African racial solidarity. John Okello, after all, was not a Zanzibari but an imported revolutionary from Uganda. An Africa that strongly objects to white mercenaries in civil wars elsewhere applauded the intervention of a soldier of fortune from Uganda in the history of Zanzibar.

The king is Sir Edward Mutesa, the former kabaka of Buganda. In *The Desecration of My Kingdom* he tries to provide both a renewed historical vindication for the institutions of Buganda and a statement about those events following independence which culminated in 1966 in his flight from Uganda to the United Kingdom. He fled in the wake of the conquest of his palace by the armed forces of the central government of Uganda. Mutesa's book captures a theme recurrent in African history: where does tribalism end and nationalism begin? Were the Baganda a nationality? Were the Ibo a nationality? Should the kingdom of Buganda have enjoyed autonomy in spite of confrontations with the central government?

At first this seemed like the sort of book which the central government might have been tempted to ban from the country. What happened, however, was that it was serialized in *The People*, the party newspaper of the governing Uganda People's Congress. The Uganda government, in serializing a major book by its own archenemy, displayed remarkable astuteness. It undercut the publishers in what was potentially the most important single market for the book, and it let the glaring defects of the book expose themselves within the hospitable pages of a hostile newspaper.

Biographies in East Africa, perhaps by their very nature as autobiographies, provide an intermediate position between literature and political testament. There are times when the imagination is as effectively at play in an autobiography as it might be in a work of fiction.

The Song of Selfhood

Earlier, we mentioned Lionel Trilling's conviction of the centrality of selfhood in literature and the relationship of literature to the ideas of Freud and psychoanalysis. We have also indicated the place of biography in the literary productivity of East Africa and pointed out the conspicuous fact that much of it is connected with some aspect of Kenya's nationalism and with the Mau Mau insurrection. The same observations are true of the works of East Africa's most prominent novelist, James Ngugi. The theme of Kikuyu self-consciousness and the quest of this people for either collective fulfillment or collective reconciliation are recurrent in Ngugi's fiction.

Ngugi's novels *Weep Not, Child*, *The River Between*, and *A Grain of Wheat* are, in a sense, within a tradition that includes Kenyatta's *Facing Mount Kenya*. The same factors that exposed a theme of negritude in some of the postulates of Kenyatta's analysis of Kikuyu tribal life also expose themes of cultural nationalism and its clash with modernizing buoyancy within Ngugi's works of fiction. The simple faith in education — very often Western education — as an instrument both for self-preservation and for progress is sometimes overpowering. Female circumcision assumes in *The River Between* some of the social significance it had in a formative period of nationalism in Kenya. The battle between tradition and modernity, custom and Christianity, finds a battleground on this issue. Members of the tribe who want to combine the new with the old sometimes find it psychologically feasible to regard the new as tenable only in terms of the old.

> Muthoni said she had seen Jesus. She had done so by going back to the tribe, by marrying the rituals of the tribe with Christ. And she had seen Him through suffering. She had been circumcised and said she had become a woman. Nyambura too wanted to become a woman but she could only be so if Waiyaki talked to her, if he stood near her. Then she would see Christ. [10]

Even Waiyaki later attempts a reconciliation. At least he is converted to the notion of transition, of moving from the old to the new not by an abrupt change but by the slow, curative process of education.

> Yes, in the quietness of the hill, Waiyaki had realised many things. Circumcision of women was not important as a physical operation. It is what it did inside a person. It could not be stopped overnight. Patience, and above all, education, was needed. [11]

Muthoni's case illustrates not only the agonies of reconciliation but also the burden of martyrdom in attempts at reconciliation. Biblical imagery recurs periodically in Kikuyu nationalism. Sometimes it concerns the challenge of forgiving — the struggle to forgive those fellow Kikuyu who hounded and opposed the Mau Mau. In *Mau Mau Detainee* there is an echo of Jesus on the cross in Kariuki's attitude toward the former Home Guards.

> Othaya was not a good camp. If any one was found with snuff he was beaten mercilessly. The wardens there were largely recruited from former Home Guards and, although they hit us so badly, we did not quarrel with them when we were released. We decided that they must be forgiven, for they did not know what they were doing.[12]

In Ngugi's *A Grain of Wheat* there is a more explicit discussion of the meaning of crucifixion. Is a sacrifice, even on the cross, ever worthwhile if it does not encompass in its benefits one's own nation? On the basis of this critical question, Kihika, a character in the novel, concludes that Christ's sacrifice on the cross was a failure. It might have saved many people, but it did not save the Jews. It did not serve Jesus' own nation.

> Yes — I said he had failed because his death did not change anything, it did

10. James Ngugi, *The River Between* (London: Heinemann, 1965), pp. 117–18.
11. *Ibid.*, p. 163.
12. Josiah M. Kariuki, *Mau Mau Detainee* (London: Oxford University Press, 1963), p. 137.

not make his people find a centre in the cross. All oppressed people have a cross to bear. . . . Had Christ's death a meaning for the children of Israel? In Kenya we want a death which will change things, that is to say, we want a true sacrifice. But first we have to be ready to carry the cross. I die for you, you die for me, we become a sacrifice for one another. So I can say that you, Karanja, are Christ. I am Christ. Everybody who takes the Oath of Unity to change things in Kenya is a Christ.[13]

There are occasions, of course, when it is not the bearer of a new religion but the defender of an old one who is crucified. Indeed, the martyrs can sometimes be simply those who are left behind in a wave of conversion to modernity. The sense of inadequacy felt by the illiterate child in the company of young, enthusiastic bookworms or by the village girl in the company of urbanized female sophisticates — this sense of inadequacy can be a cross that bewildered tradition bears in the face of an overpowering innovation.

Okot p'Bitek, the Ugandan poet, captures both the bitterness and the bewilderment of this form of martyrdom in his long poem *Song of Lawino*. A simple married woman from the village finds herself increasingly inadequate for a husband who is becoming a fanatic of the cult of modernity. She is losing her hold over him; he has drifted into the arms of a powdered and lipsticked piece of female modernity. P'Bitek grossly exaggerates the arrogance of Ocol, the husband who is supposed to heap insults on his wife and on his tribal roots. Even if one allows for the fact that Lawino in her anguish sees too much contempt in the acts of her husband, the feeling nevertheless persists that the poet has erred on the side of excess in his portrayal of Ocol. Ocol's wife laments:

> Ocol tells me
> That I like dirt.
> He says
> *Shea* butter causes
> Skin diseases.
>
> He says, Acholi adornments
> Are old fashioned and unhealthy.
> He says I soil his white shirt
> If I touch him,
> My husband treats me
> As if I am suffering from
> The "Don't touch me" disease!
>
> He says that I make his bed-sheets dirty
> And his bed smelly.
> Ocol says

13. James Ngugi, *A Grain of Wheat* (London: Heinemann, 1967), p. 110.

I look extremely ugly
When I am fully adorned
For the dance![14]

With Lawino's account of her husband, p'Bitek has merely created a caricature that can in no way be regarded as representative of the type of person he wants to typify. Ocol is a hyperbolic deserter from his own culture. He lacks full credibility. If the exaggeration is a method of characterizing Lawino's mind rather than of giving an accurate picture of her husband, p'Bitek has made Lawino a little too simple. A mind that exaggerates so much and in such an obvious way is a mind that is not simply culturally distinct from the modernity which enchants Ocol but also too naïve to stand a chance of saving Ocol from that enchantment. The traditional ways of the Acholi deserve a better defender than Lawino. Nevertheless, *Song of Lawino* does rank as a major pioneering achievement in East Africa. It is a passionate soliloquy, an utterance of cultural nationalism.

Uganda seems to be taking the leadership in this medium of long versified discourses on important themes. Close behind *Song of Lawino* is *Orphan*, by Okello Oculi, also from Uganda. Although crude and rough in many parts, *Orphan* has passages that are strikingly more profound than anything in *Song of Lawino*. Oculi gives even commonplace ideas like the cruelty of nature renewed evocative power.

> The courting grasshopper chirps in a sun bath
> Oblivious to the pangs in the body
> Of a vagabond dog dragging along
> Against the weight of creeping rot in a limb.
> Trapped within the walls of a localised awareness,
> Nature's imposition to justify her
> Indifference to individual pains. . . .
>
> The message in the yell of the goat
> Frightened of the vision behind the slaughter,
> The glassy light in its eyes — unfinished
> Beams left bouncing off the rude opacity
> Of the sudden wall of void eternity;
> The melancholy chat of flesh in the cooking pot:
> Only arouse all appetites for heed.
> The disposed-of bones in the homestead,
> Scattered in a jumble, question the fate of

---

14. Okot p'Bitek, *Song of Lawino* (Nairobi: East African Publishing House, 1966), p. 58.

The flesh that once walled their unity
And sing the credo of the final isolation. . . .[15]

Orphan is not merely an exercise in cultural nationalism, though there are passages within it which are so preoccupied. It is also in many parts a comprehensive indictment of natural cruelty, social injustice, and the terror of inevitability. The conscience within the poem sometimes shrinks away in horror from the "poverty of the man without cows for a wife." [16]

Literature and Transnationalism

It is not merely with the localized dimension of identity that literature concerns itself. There are also moments when feelings of national assertion become intermingled with feelings of international empathy. This is when nationalism broadens its scope and becomes transnationalism. It displays the capacity to include links with the world beyond.

In East African literature, transnationalism sometimes takes the form of sympathizing with others in similarly oppressive predicaments. Many aspects of Pan-Africanism at its more immediate level are, in fact, cases of transnationalism. There have been poems about Angola and Sharpeville and, in a different dimension, about the Nigerian Civil War which have evoked a transnational empathy. Such literature has, on and off, been published in East African literary magazines. Sometimes the empathetic identification has traversed continents. The second issue of *Zuka*, for example, has a poem by Jonathan Kariara and another by Charles Owuor, both bearing the same title: "Vietnam." Lines from the two poems can be interspersed without disturbing too much the mood of a deep, shared depression.

Women sat reclining
Monuments of peace
Sculptured by death.
The river heaved, eased
Flowed on . . .[17]

quiet
depressing quiet
sombre quiet of a cathedral
as mutilated human bodies
sleep the sleep of death.[18]

---

15. Okello Oculi, *Orphan* (Nairobi: East African Publishing House, 1968), pp. 28–29.
16. *Ibid.*, p. 31.
17. Jonathan Kariara, "Vietnam," *Zuka*, no. 2 (May, 1968), p. 11.
18. Charles Owuor, "Vietnam," *ibid.*, pp. 14–15.

In the field the dead women
Sighed
Remembering the dull thud
Of the metal fist
Of the interrogator.   . . . .
No more, no more
Betrayal
The useless pain of snatching
Life from the fertile flood.[19]

Transnationalism consists not only in identification with other peoples but also in identification with other literatures. Obiajunwa Wali started a controversy in *Transition* some time ago as to whether literature written in the English language could claim to be African. Wali was convinced that no literature written in a European language could claim to be African any more than literature written in, say, Spanish could claim to be Italian. There were strong voices raised against him, and the discussion continues in literary polemics in East Africa.[20]

Within the pages of *Zuka* there has been discussion as to whether "abstract verse," encompassing a degree of obscurity that can never claim to have any one meaning, is part of African literary traditions. In particular, the poetry of Christopher Okigbo has been cited as being so abstract as to constitute "a departure from traditional poetry."

> The dilemma facing African poetry in English is whether or not it should bother to establish a connection with forms of poetic expression in Africa antedating the coming of the English language. . . . Great abstract verse demands a gifted command of words, though not necessarily a command of language. Where meaning is to be conveyed, the intellect needs to be employed. But where beautiful pictures are to be transmitted, the instrument is at best the imagination. Great poetry in African languages is a fusion of the intellect and the imagination. Abstract exercises with verbal pictures [are] a profound departure from this tradition.[21]

Finally, let us consider the place of translation in the relationship between African literature and the literary heritage of the outside world. In this respect it is not only Jomo Kenyatta who established contact with the stream of negritude;

19. Kariara, "Vietnam," p. 11.
20. Obiajunwa Wali, "The Dead End of African Literature?" *Transition*, IV, no. 10 (September, 1963), 13–16.
21. Ali A. Mazrui, "Abstract Verse and African Tradition," *Zuka*, no. 1 (September, 1967), pp. 47, 49. See also Michael Etherton, "Christopher Okigbo, A Reply," *Zuka*, no. 2 (May, 1968), pp. 48–52; Ian J. Inglis, "*Zuka* — A Journal of East African Creative Writing," *Sunday Nation* (Nairobi), November 26, 1967; Ali A. Mazrui, "Meaning versus Imagery in African Poetry," *Présence Africaine*, no. 66 (Spring, 1968), pp. 49–57.

it is also, in some other ways, Julius Nyerere, the president of Tanzania.[22] Nyerere was able to do this, not by writing an autobiography or a political pamphlet, but by translating Shakespeare's *Julius Caesar* into Swahili.

Zuka, although publishing literary material mainly in English, also tries to include some work in indigenous African languages. Of particular interest has been E. A. Ibrek's translation into Swahili of a medieval English play, *Johan Johan*, by John Heywood.

The tendency to regard translation as something distinct from creativity rests on a forced dichotomy. The task of translating world masterpieces into African languages is bound to enrich the creative versatility of the African languages. Nyerere's translation of *Julius Caesar* has contributed more to the potential of Swahili as a dramatic medium than almost any original work in Swahili which has so far emerged.[23] The enrichment of African languages through their extensive use in both translations and original works must be regarded as a nationalistic aspiration of wide influence.

The Literature of Social Conscience

In this chapter it has been shown that much of the new creative writing of East Africa has been inspired by patriotism. But what of the literature that deals with corruption among African politicians after independence? What of the fiction that deals with military coups? What of Chinua Achebe's *Man of the People* and David Rubadiri's *No Bride Price*? Do they represent a post-nationalistic literature? Do they express disenchantment with nationalism? Such literature is more an expression of disenchantment with the first fruits of nationalism — an entirely different form of reaction. To be disappointed with the first harvest of one's little plot of land is not necessarily the end of one's love for the land or of one's faith in its future. An indictment of political corruption in postindependence Africa can itself be a form of nationalism.

Wole Soyinka regards a social conscience as an integral part of African art in its primordial form.

> When the writer in his own society can no longer function as conscience, he must recognise that his choice lies between denying himself totally or withdrawing to the position of chronicler and post-mortem surgeon. . . . The artist has always functioned in African society as the record of the mores and experience of his society *and* as the voice of vision in his own time. It is time for him to respond to this essence of himself.[24]

22. Leopold Senghor, "Negritude and the Concept of Universal Civilisation," *Présence Africaine*, XVIII, no. 46 (Second Quarter, 1963), 310.

23. See Ali A. Mazrui, "The African Symbolism ot Julius Caesar," in *The Anglo-African Commonwealth* (Oxford: Pergamon, 1967), 121–33.

24. Wole Soyinka, "The Writer in a Modern African State," in *The Writer in Modern*

[Creative Literature and Political Commitment]

In East Africa the disillusion with the first fruits of independence is not as · yet acute. The region has not experienced all the political, moral, and military excesses which have agonized parts of West Africa since independence. Nevertheless, the literature of social conscience is beginning to emerge in East Africa as well. If this trend continues, a new meeting point between nationalism and literature will find its way into the East African experience, too. If that should happen, East African nationalism would not consist simply in defining the clouds of glory which lie along the trail to nationalism. It would also consist in raising the alarm against the dark clouds of impending storm on the horizon of nationhood. There was a time when criticizing Africa was considered to be an act of disloyalty. Perhaps never again will it be quite as easy to distinguish between a song of African patriotism and the anguished choke of African self-indictment.

Africa, ed. Per Wästberg (Uppsala: Scandinavian Institute of African Studies, 1968), p. 21. These words were written not long before Soyinka was detained under somewhat mysterious circumstances by the federal authorities of Nigeria for matters connected with the civil war.

[3]

Creative Literature and
Cultural Ambivalence

The central problem for creative literature in East Africa, as in much of formerly colonial Africa, is aesthetic dualism, a problem inherent in the cultural ambivalence of a colonial situation. Two artistic universes drawn from vastly different cultures exist side by side, having yet to coalesce or merge into a third, distinct phenomenon. In reality an African country has more than two aesthetic worlds, since each nation consists of several ethnic groups, each with its own civilization. For an African individual, however, the dualism is between the foreign and the indigenous, the modern and the traditional. The dualism which is most pertinent to the crisis of identity within the arts in Africa is the dualism between the pull of Western artistic influences and the stability of older modes of creativity.

This kind of problem, which is central to the process of transitional acculturation, pervades other areas of life in Africa; but there is something about the fine arts that puts them in a special category. In order to grasp the uniqueness of the arts in this regard, it is important to consider first acculturation as a general phenomenon.

Let us take a situation in which there is a conquering civilization and a conquered people. The conquered people is in the process of assimilating at least part of the new civilization. It has been established that a conquered people can learn new techniques more quickly than it can adopt new values; where new techniques are proving difficult to master, it is likely that they have come into conflict with values with which they are not compatible. The problem of economic development in much of Africa is one illustration of the fact that certain techniques and skills presuppose certain values. The techniques may be compatible with a great variety of mixtures of values — from the values of the Japanese to those of the Swedes — but certain mixtures are simply not congruent with the demands of the new skills. In such cases there is a lag in the process of change.

Acculturation is not reducible simply to a dialectic between techniques and values. Subdivisions can be made within those two categories. For our purposes we need only note that aesthetic values are frequently the most conservative of all in responding to foreign influence. It is often far easier to be converted to the ethics of a conquering power than to its aesthetics. An African is generally more easily converted to Western Christianity than to Western classical music. It is probable that formal monogamy will become part of African life sooner than will Western opera or ballet. Between societies which are very different, agreement on what is right and what is wrong is often easier to achieve than agreement on what is beautiful and what is ugly. Perhaps that is one reason why black people, as of 1970, had produced three winners of the Nobel Peace Prize and not a single Miss World.[1]

The issue of Miss World as an aesthetic problem was discussed in the Uganda press during 1967 and 1968, partly because of statements made by Miss Uganda concerning her experience in the contest. It was almost as if Africa had to breed special females, seeking advice from Western beauticians and physical statisticians. Some surgical attention might be given to the African nose or the Bantu lip should this be necessary for the African woman to be comparable to the Western female. The Uganda press discussion included a call for a separate beauty contest for blacks which would seek out the most striking black females from Africa, the West Indies, the United States, Brazil, and elsewhere in the black diaspora.

An African woman may win the Miss World competition before a world-wide beauty contest for blacks comes into being, but to do so she will have to be a "Western" beauty by every criterion other than color. Indeed, choices of beautiful women from Uganda for the 1967 Miss World contest were so influenced by Western criteria that both the first- and third-place winners in the Uganda contest were women of mixed parentage, not purely African. In 1968 the attempt to shine in London led to an emphasis in Kampala on intellectual virtues. Not only was the woman to approximate Western criteria of beauty, but she was, if possible, to be intellectually Westernized enough to feel comfortable in London society. The result was that both the first- and second-place winners in the Miss Uganda contest were undergraduate women from Makerere University. The second-place winner, Freda Lule, was the daughter of the principal of Makerere. The winner, Joy Lehai, was a student of English literature.

In 1966 Miss World was Reita Faria of India, who seemed to have broken the Caucasian monopoly of the contest. Just as decolonization in Africa had been preceded by decolonization in India and was in part influenced by it, so the Indian success in the beauty contest and the arrival of Miss Faria in Uganda and elsewhere in Africa created African hopes of standing a chance. Even Tanzania competed in 1967. But shortly after that attempt, Tanzania decided that the entire exercise was too painfully decadent for words, and the government prohibited such a contest in 1968. In any case, it should have been remembered that Reita Faria's features were strikingly Indo-

---

1. The black winners of the Nobel Peace Prize are Dr. Ralph Bunche (U.S.), Chief Albert Luthuli (South Africa), and Dr. Martin Luther King, Jr. (U.S.).

European — the beauty judges in Europe had not ventured too far from the comfort of their accustomed criteria.

From East Africa's point of view, the problem of the Miss World competition and the problem of creative literature in the English language do have something in common. They are both linked to the phenomenon of aesthetic dualism and its implications for the concept of beauty and its appreciation.

A Literature of Formal Education

To what should we attribute the conservativeness of artistic values as compared with other kinds of values in the process of acculturation in Africa? Where does imaginative and creative literature fit into this? One answer can be found in a small incident which befell two Kenyan students many years ago in an English literature class at a technical college in Yorkshire, England. The class was part of a preparatory course for the General Certificate of Education (Advanced Level), the prerequisite for university entry. Another Kenyan student and I were the only two people in the class who were not British. The course was going to include English poetry — Milton, Dryden, Pope, Wordsworth, T. S. Eliot — and it was precisely in regard to poetry that the teacher was particularly concerned about his two foreign students. He came to have a chat with us. He said we might as well realize that in a course of this kind we would be at a handicap. The British students had been prepared by their upbringing for that particular course in English literature. The preparation was not simply what they had studied in school but extended backward to nursery rhymes and playsongs, which were an integral part of the process of growing up. The world of images and metaphors, of overtones and undertones, of nuances of meaning — the world of literary response — had for the British students a firm domestic foundation. For us, the two foreign students in Mr. Threlfell's class, sensitivity to this universe of imagery was bound to be somewhat blunted by the foreignness of the exercise. The teacher offered to give us any extra help we might need in the course of the year.

In retrospect I can see in that simple teacher-pupil relationship a fact of great relevance to the viability of literature in Africa today. Although Mr. Threlfell did not carry his few words of comfort for two foreign students through to their ultimate conclusion, he was alluding to an important truth that we might re-examine for some insights into the problems affecting the viability of a literary culture in East Africa and elsewhere on the African continent.

The central point involved here is the simple but fundamental proposition that the acquisition of a new literary culture is not only a matter of education but also one of resocialization or reformed upbringing. Education in our sense is the exposure to formalized training and disciplined dissemination of knowledge, usually in schools. Socialization or upbringing in our sense is the acquisition of values and mental habits of one's society through a process which is much more haphazard than that of education, though it often includes education. The process of a child's socialization into a new culture of his own society would embrace both the school and the home, the playground and the family holiday. How Mummy and Dad talk to each other, how adults greet each other or express sympathy, are of course all part of the socialization process. So indeed — and this is the most pertinent issue in our discussion — are the nursery rhymes that Mr. Threlfell was talking about. To paraphrase Mr. Threlfell's wisdom, the foundation of Milton's *Paradise Lost* is, in a sense, the English nursery rhyme.

In East Africa the difficulty of African literature in the English language is that it remains for the time being a child of education, not of socialization. This simple fact helps to determine the writers of literature as well as the readers, whether the writing is addressed to an international audience or to a domestic one, and whether the writing comes from an impulse to intellectualize rather than from a fund of emotive sensibility. And, since African literature in English is not a product of socialization, it does not even approach aesthetic maturity.

In a paper entitled "The Teaching of Literature," T. R. M. Creighton said:

> Whatever else classics is or was, it provides a technique, a tool which anyone can learn to use. . . . [But] English [literature] is a subject in which no technique or tool or discipline ever becomes apparent to you, unless you possess certain unteachable and not particularly common faculties.[2]

In this case Creighton was contrasting the learning of a language with the learning of literature. He was suggesting that learning a language — even a classical language like Latin or Greek or Sanskrit — was something that could be undertaken by almost anyone who was intelligent enough, but that responding to an art form like literature was a different matter. Responding to the artistic code of Latin or Greek or Sanskrit would also be different from the discipline of acquiring the more functional codes of these languages.

Creighton, like Mr. Threlfell, did not push the implications of this statement for the future of academic and cultural life in Africa to their logical conclusion. The assertion here is that an African who at the age of twenty goes to a Western university might indeed develop into an accomplished historian, a great student of linguistics, a perceptive sociologist, an innovative political scientist, or even a profound philosopher using a Western idiom; but it is much more difficult for an African student to become a major musical composer in the Western idiom or even a great pianist interpreting Beethoven with new, innovative gusto. The average East African student comes from a family in which he represents

---

2. T. R. M. Creighton, "The Teaching of Literature," in *African Literature and the Universities*, ed. Gerald Moore (Ibadan: Ibadan University Press, 1965), pp. 117–18.

the first generation of literacy. Within such a family there could be little exposure to the universe of Western classical music. Why is it easier for an African to become a great historian or sociologist than it is for him to become a great composer in the Western tradition? The answer is similar to Mr. Threlfell's reference to the significance of nursery rhymes in the socialization process for art appreciation. Great creativity in art is more intimately tied to culture than is great creativity in thought and scholarship.

This situation is indeed paradoxical. Artistic creativity is, after all, supposed to be a profoundly individualistic act; and yet it is so circumscribed by the culture of the artist that an African student of Western music finds it more difficult to excel than if he were studying Western anthropology or even Western philosophy.

Literature as an art form, though sharing certain attributes with music, painting, and sculpture, also shares attributes with anthropology, philosophy, and other verbalized forms of creativity. Therefore, it is easier to produce a great African writer in a Western idiom than a great African composer in a Western idiom. There are in Africa important writers of both French and English expression. Nevertheless, literature in East Africa does suffer from the lag between education and general upbringing. As we indicated, the fact that African literature is a child of education has helped to determine what kinds of people become authors, what kinds of people are their readers, what kinds of themes receive literary attention.

A major point to note is that the leading African creative writers are unusually well educated. They have had more formal education than Shakespeare ever had, more than Dickens, Browning, Hardy, and Orwell. The fact that the language the modern African writers use is a foreign one has tended to delay major literary experiments until the writers have entered the gates of a university and mastered an alien tongue. As a result, African writing tends to be highly intellectualized, sometimes taking the form of sociological analysis or philosophical interpretation of traditional Africa. Although there is nothing wrong with intellectualized literature, there may be cause for concern in Africa if there is very little else. A balance must somehow be sought between a literature of social analysis and a literature of emotive confession.

A factor related to the intellectualism of African literature is the tendency toward didacticism. Martin Tucker once wrote an article against this didacticism in the London weekly magazine *West Africa*.[3] He complained of a tendency in much of African writing to propagandize at the expense of art. There were strong reactions to Tucker's article, not least from African writers themselves. The Society of Nigerian Authors — which includes in its membership Chinua Achebe, Cyprian Ekwensi, and M. Nzekwu — accused Tucker of seeking to "impose a false pattern on the West African novel."

---

3. Martin Tucker, "The Headline Novels of Africa," *West Africa* (London), July 28, 1962.

Chinua Achebe views himself as, in part, a teacher. He regards teaching as a continuation of the artist's function in traditional society. Achebe says:

> Perhaps what I write is applied art rather than pure. But who cares? Art is important, but so is education. The kind I have in mind. And I don't see how the two need be mutually exclusive.[4]

The Kenyan novelist James Ngugi, in a lecture given at Makerere in October, 1968, made a renewed plea for a literature of social conscience in East Africa, a literature prepared to prescribe and to protest. Ngugi resigned in February, 1969, from his lectureship at the University of Nairobi because of the way in which the college handled a crisis in the students' relations with the government. The students had boycotted classes to protest the government's action preventing Oginga Odinga, the leader of the opposition, from speaking to a students' club. The minister of education ordered the students to return to classes; when they failed to do so, the college was forcibly closed and the students evicted from their dormitories by police force. As the students were returning a few weeks later, five of the ringleaders were suspended pending further investigation. It was about this time that Ngugi resigned in protest.

As an artist, Ngugi was perhaps living up to the code that writers in their writings, as well as in their more general activities, should be socially committed. Okello Oculi has been called the George Orwell of Uganda because of the identification with victims of social deception which he expressed in his "village opera" *Orphan* and in his novel *Prostitute*. Yet this kind of commitment to intellectual causes, a commitment which is itself intellectualized, might be one effect of a literature born of academic education rather than general domestic socialization.

The African Public and the Arts

The readership of African literature is also affected by the fact that African literature is a child of education. Achebe has cited figures demonstrating that far more copies of his books are sold within Africa than in England and elsewhere in the outside world. Yet it is probably true that Achebe is read more widely for pleasure outside Africa than within Africa. In Africa, reading is very much tied to education, and a large number of the copies that he alludes to as having been sold within the continent are copies used by secondary schoolchildren in their studies. This illustrates the general problem of African literature at its present stage of evolution. It is too intellectualized, too self-consciously didactic, partly because it is a child of education and not of socialization. The very foreignness of the language, and the fact that it has to be acquired through

---

4. Chinua Achebe, "The Novelist as Teacher," *New Statesman* (London), January 29, 1965.

education and not through upbringing, tends to emphasize these deficiencies. The solution to this problem can be reduced to the following imperatives. First, take the new arts to the people as a way of building up a socialization base. Second, bring the traditional arts to the university and modern schools as a way of increasing the cultural involvement of these modern institutions. Third, diversify what is foreign in the educational institutions so that the foreignness is no longer easily identifiable as British but becomes more internationalized. Fourth, partly indigenize the English language as a medium of literary creativity. These imperatives, which are the central elements of East Africa's cultural engineering in relation to creative literature, will run through and cut across our discussion of the deintellectualization of African literature.

One enterprise in Uganda which has been quite successful in sending the new arts to the people is the traveling theater project. Every year a group of Makerere students travels throughout East Africa, presenting performances of short plays both in English and in East African languages to rural audiences and audiences in schools in the smaller towns. Productions range from scenes from Nyerere's Swahili translation of *Julius Caesar* to Tom Omara's *The Exodus*, based on a Luo myth.

The decision to start a traveling theater was made at Makerere in October, 1964, by David Cook (now head of the English Department) and Betty Baker (former tutor in English). The troupe, consisting of Makerere students, was to travel during the long vacation in 1965. The founders regarded it as fundamental to the project that productions be those that could be performed "everywhere and anywhere." Lighting and curtains were regarded as "luxuries" to be used if possible, but the show was to be able to go on without them. The only stage equipment that was found essential was a "black curtain to provide minimum entrances, a back stage for changing and some kind of definition to the acting area" — a curtain against which a great variety of plays could be acted, one "which would brighten up the drabbest setting and give some theatrical atmosphere and yet would not clash with a variety of different sets of costumes." [5]

The theater is now more fully controlled and organized by students than it was at first. Every year they give one or two performances at Makerere to raise money for transportation and subsistence while they are moving from place to place. Sometimes vehicles or petrol are provided by a benefactor like the Ministry of Culture, the British Council, or Esso Petroleum.

Many a member of the traveling theater would have nodded in agreement when Bob Leshoai, the South African literary figure, addressed the following to the readers of *Transition*:

> It is only by going to our audiences that we have any chance of succeeding in creating an African theatre audience. For us in Africa the importance of the mobile theatre is even greater than elsewhere. The majority of the people we are hoping

5. David Cook, "Theatre Goes to the People!" *Transition*, V, no. 25 (1966), 5.

to reach are those who cannot afford the cost of transport and high charges of established theatre houses. Besides, there is the additional embarrassment for the African having to dress, behave and converse "intelligently like the white people who go to these theatres." [6]

In Kenya the Chemchemi Culture Centre in Nairobi, which was headed for a while by the South African writer Ezekiel Mphahlele, has had some success in taking literature and the theater to the people and in bringing folk art to the modern institutions.

Another method of introducing the new arts to the people is to translate important works of foreign literature into local languages. The interplay between language and literature across cultures is one way of deepening the understanding of foreign influences.

The second imperative is to bring the traditional arts to the new educational system. Okot p'Bitek, author of the pioneer neonegritudist poem *Song of Lawino*, has been a leading spokesman for university reform which would make it possible to utilize local artists more effectively. In a hard-hitting public lecture at Makerere he once said: "You may be the greatest [traditional] oral historian but they will never allow you anywhere near *their* university." [7]

This imperative has also renewed interest in oral literature and oral tradition. The relevant departments at all three East African universities have been trying to look afresh at oral literature and to raise money to make the collection of this literature feasible. The Department of English at Makerere has also succeeded in persuading Oxford University Press to commit some of its resources to encouraging African students to write their autobiographies or to produce works concerning the way of life in their regions.

Recently, there has been talk of establishing projects for the collection of African music and the development of music libraries in several African universities. Mention has been made of a substantial Ford Foundation grant that would initiate a continent-wide project to collect, code, record, and study African music. Invitations have already been extended to several African universities to set up working committees to consider how best to approach the task of building up, within African institutions, libraries of music encompassing a representative cross-section of the oral arts of the continent.

Perspectives: Local and International

In general, there are important differences between the role of Uganda and Kenya on the one hand and that of Tanzania on the other in this whole enterprise

6. Bob Leshoai, "Theatre and the Common Man in Africa," *Transition*, IV, no. 19 (1965), 46.

7. Okot p'Bitek, "Indigenous Ills," *Transition*, VII, no. 32 (August–September, 1967), 47. P'Bitek was also bitter that Makerere could find no place in its recruitment policies for traditional musicians or sculptors.

to close the socio-aesthetic gap. Uganda and Kenya are the great producers of literary works in English, with Kenya in the lead at the present. James Ngugi and Grace Ogot, both of Kenya, are the two best known fiction-writers in the English language from East Africa. Of the half dozen literary journals in the region, *Ghala, Busara* (previously *Nexus*), and *Zuka* began in Nairobi, *Penpoint* and *Transition* in Kampala, and *Darlite* in Dar es Salaam. The East African Publishing House, based in Nairobi, is the only indigenous publishing firm to invest substantially in promoting local creative writing in the English language, including offering prizes for novels and novelettes. The Department of English at Makerere has produced a greater number of creative writers in English in East Africa than has any other university department, at home or abroad. Nairobi and Kampala are, in general, more important as centers of high culture than Dar es Salaam can claim to be. The live theater is a visible part of the cultural life of Nairobi and Kampala, and local dramatic groups — both amateur and semiprofessional — are active in these two capitals. Dar es Salaam is clearly behind in this respect. Even the fact that Kampala and Nairobi have television, while Dar es Salaam does not, contributes to the difference in artistic range between the capitals of Uganda and Kenya on the one hand and the capital of Tanzania on the other.

Tanzania's contribution to solving the problem of aesthetic dualism lies partly in its translation of European literature, partly in its attempts to modernize Swahili, and partly in its initiative in diversifying the foreign component in Tanzania's cultural universe. The first aspect of Tanzania's contribution, the translation of European works into Swahili, is encompassed by our first imperative in bridging the gap between education and upbringing — taking the new arts to the people. President Julius Nyerere himself has taken the lead in this venture. And here we find an important point of contact between Nyerere and Leopold Senghor. Senghor has said:

> It is a fact that French has made it possible for us to communicate . . . to the world the unheard of message which only we could write. It has allowed us to bring to *universal civilization* a contribution without which the twentieth century could not have been universal.[8]

By writing impressive poetry in French, Senghor is contributing a piece of Africa to universal civilization. On the other hand, by translating Shakespeare's *Julius Caesar* into Swahili, Nyerere is taking a piece of universal civilization and making it even more universal. For Senghor, the cause of black honor, or negritude, is served when African literature is effectively expressed in a foreign language. For Nyerere, one might say, negritude is equally served when a piece of foreign literature is effectively re-expressed in an African language.

---

8. Leopold Senghor, "Negritude and the Concept of Universal Civilisation," *Présence Africaine*, XVIII, no. 46 (Second Quarter, 1963), 310.

The latter achievement vindicates an African language as a literary medium.[9] Nyerere has more recently completed the translation of another Shakespearean play, *The Merchant of Venice*. Translations of other European works have been prepared for educational purposes — even Voltaire is now available in Swahili. Also, the Communist Chinese have provided Swahili translations of some of Marx's works. In Kenya and Uganda some translation work is also under way. Particularly noteworthy is the translation into Swahili of Machiavelli's *The Prince* by Fred Kamoga (a Ugandan linguist) and Ralph Tanner (a British anthropologist and scholar of Swahili). But on balance there is more work of this kind going on in Tanzania or by Tanzanians than in the other two countries.

The second aspect of Tanzania's contribution to solving the problem of aesthetic dualism, the modernization of Swahili, is related to our second imperative, bringing the traditional arts to modern institutions. Attempts to modernize Swahili include the establishment of a special commission to construct a Swahili legal vocabulary and efforts to perfect Swahili as a language for the mass media in diverse programs and newspaper features. Part of the modernization process involves emphasizing the literary qualities of the language. Among the East African languages, Swahili has the longest history of written literature. In 1968 John Allen, a distinguished scholar of Swahili, deposited in the library of the University of Dar es Salaam a major collection of pre-European Swahili writings from different parts of Swahili-speaking East Africa. M. H. Abdulaziz of the University of Nairobi, another academic in East Africa with linguo-cultural interests, has made a study of patriotic songs of the Kenya coast written in the eighteenth and nineteenth centuries. Lyndon Harries has produced an important collection of diverse Swahili poems and has discussed them in historical perspective. The fact that Swahili was already a literate language reduced the contrast between it and English as literary media, and the diverse uses to which Swahili is being put in Tanzania are further reducing this contrast.

There is a constant outpouring in Tanzania of what one might call "the poetry of political enthusiasm" — ranging from a satire of the *wabenzi* (the new affluent class whose members own Mercedes Benz cars) to a lament for Biafra's agony; from a eulogy of Nyerere to a political critique of the mini-skirt. The growing intellectualization of poetic themes in Swahili establishes new areas of contact between it and the intellectual themes which came with the English language.

The third aspect of Tanzania's contribution to the mitigation of aesthetic dualism coincides with the third imperative concerning the merging of education and upbringing — namely, internally diversifying the foreign part of the cultural dualism. This diversification is symbolized by the experience of the University of Dar es Salaam, which on the whole has perhaps been more open to non-British external influences than have the other two universities. Dar es Salaam has been quicker to import teachers from non-English-speaking areas of the world

9. See Ali A. Mazrui, "The Patriot as an Artist," *Black Orpheus*, II, no. 3 (1969), 14–23.

than have the other two universities, and Dar es Salaam has also been less worried about ideological diversity than have the other campuses. Curiously enough, this willingness to borrow from foreign sources other than traditional British ones sometimes alienates African undergraduates more acutely. The first major anti-American revolt in the University of East Africa occurred in 1969, when students demonstrated against the rapid Americanization of the teaching of law at Dar es Salaam.

Nevertheless, the diversification of the foreign part of aesthetic dualism is a way of reducing the sharpness of the cleavage, and Dar es Salaam has gone further in this than has been the case elsewhere. At Makerere University and the University of Nairobi the Department of English is at the center of language and literary studies; at Dar es Salaam there are two departments — a Department of Literature and a Department of Language and Linguistics — within which different languages and literary traditions are studied. There is no Department of English. The focus is on the phenomenon of language and the phenomenon of literature in different idioms rather than on the phenomenon of the English heritage. The University of Dar es Salaam is the only one of the three to offer a degree in indigenous (Swahili) literature.

However, the other two universities are also moving toward diversifying the foreign component of their dualism. At an intercollegiate meeting of literary and linguistic specialists of the University of East Africa held at Nairobi in January, 1969, all three colleges agreed to introduce into their syllabuses more African literature and, possibly, literary works from America, the West Indies, India, and Scandinavia. Two paradoxical processes were to be initiated — greater localization and greater internationalization of the curriculum. Both processes were contributions toward mitigating the dualistic cleavage.

There is a long history behind this quest in Africa for something that deepens local roots and at the same time widens international horizons. A "truly African university" has for a long time been regarded as the answer. Edward Blyden, the towering African intellectual of the late nineteenth century, was against modern European studies and strongly in favor of the classics. He thought in terms of establishing universities in Africa that would enable Africans to study the heritage of Greece and Rome and link it to the study of modern African civilization without passing through the study of modern Europe. The study of modern Europe was what he called a "despotic Europeanising influence which had warped and crushed the Negro mind." [10]

Casely Hayford of Ghana had ideas that were no less revolutionary. He felt that university education in Africa should be given in an African language as soon as feasible, and that provision should be made for the translation of books into African languages and for collaboration in scholarship not only with England but also with Japan, Germany, and the United States.

Partly with such reasoning in mind, intellectuals from British West Africa,

10. See Edward Blyden, *Christianity, Islam and the Negro Race* (1888; reprint ed., Edinburgh: University Press, 1967).

after a historic meeting in 1920, sent a petition to King George V asking that a University of British West Africa be established "on such lines as would preserve in the students a sense of African nationality." [11] They suggested that greater attention be paid to the study of indigenous cultures as well as to the study of foreign powers.

Art and Language

Part of the resocialization in the arts is the attempt to encourage literary creativity among school children. In an article in *Transition*, Bob Leshoai said:

> The African child, though almost always neglected, is a most important part of the common man. . . . It is important that our theatrical activities should evolve around him, for the children will become our future writers, critics, actors, technicians, producers, designers and audiences. Theatre for the child is not only entertainment; it is a vital educational experiment. It is here that the child's critical powers are challenged and his creativity aroused from slumber. [12]

This is another area in which Makerere University in Kampala and East African Publishing House in Nairobi have made important contributions. Makerere's traveling theater has visited isolated schools as well as isolated rural communities. *Ghala*, the literary edition of *East Africa Journal*, has made significant attempts — partly through offering prizes — to promote literary creativity among schoolchildren.

In enterprises of this kind, education and socialization are virtually indistinguishable. The task is to ensure that young East Africans begin to use English creatively before they have mastered the language. Sometimes the African schoolchild displays greater literary originality in his idiosyncratic use of the English language than does the university student, whose English is formally correct. The charm of Amos Tutuola to his readers in Europe and America partly springs from his inadequate command of the English language; yet many African literary figures have rejected him for reasons verging on intellectual arrogance. That African literature is still excessively tied to formal education is illustrated by Tutuola's struggle for literary respectability among the African educated class.

Even if many of the schoolboy compositions which are encouraged by East African Publishing House are superficial, this productivity helps to bridge the gap between education and upbringing in literary tastes. Lewis Nkosi spoke for many literary critics when he complained that foreign publishers were "in such indecent haste to put into print any mediocre talent from Africa." If that

---

11. E. N. Obiechina, "Cultural Nationalism in Modern African Creative Literature," *African Literature Today*, no. 1 (1968).

12. Leshoai, "Theatre and the Common Man in Africa," p. 44.

is a sin, indigenous publishing firms are also guilty. But is it a sin? It may be true that much literature of poor quality is published. Yet it is worth remembering that all national literatures have developed through the coexistence of both bad and good writing. That is perhaps how aesthetic discrimination becomes meaningful and standards of selectivity in taste attain sophistication. Promoting a wealth of literature in Africa might not be the same thing as promoting good literature. The desire to create a wealth of literature in Africa puts a premium on diversity, even at the cost of qualitative consistency. Included in this desire for diversity is a feeling of temporal humility — a feeling that what many may regard as "weak" in this age might conceivably be credited with some literary merit in the years ahead. For a region which has yet to build up an adequate literary heritage, the correct policy might be the one which Mao Tse-tung's China momentarily supported — "Let a hundred flowers bloom," and then hope for the best!

The philosophical position to take with regard to literary output is the conviction that quality grows out of diversified quantity. A few greater works of literature may be produced by educating a few people, but the promotion of a broadly literate culture is a surer guarantee of maximizing creative potential. The example of Nigeria before the civil war is pertinent. As Eldred D. Jones of Sierra Leone put it in 1963:

> Some of the best writing in Africa today comes from Nigeria. I think that there is a direct connection between Nigeria's leadership in African literature and the fact that the country also supports a large market in cheap pamphlets. I am told that in the market in Onitsha on any one day it is possible to count up to sixty different pamphlets on sale, on all topics.[13]

Related to the promotion of a literate culture in English at all levels of education is the development of a distinct version of English — our fourth imperative in uniting formal education and domestic socialization. It has been noted by a number of observers that East African English is more closely tied to the king's English than is West African English. In other words, West Africa has gone further than East Africa in adapting the English language to the local environment. The process of domesticating and indigenizing the metropolitan language contributes to the mitigation of dualism in the cultural life of the region.

James Baldwin once explained why he stopped hating Shakespeare. He had at one time turned away from this "monstrous achievement with a kind of sick envy." In his most anti-English days, he condemned Shakespeare as a chauvinist. Because Baldwin felt it so bitterly anomalous that a black man

---

13. Eldred D. Jones, "Academic Problems and Critical Techniques," in *African Literature and the Universities*, p. 91. See also Donatus I. Nwoga, "Onitsha Market Literature," *Transition*, IV, no. 19 (1965), 26–33.

should be forced to deal with the English language at all — "should speak" — he condemned Shakespeare as one of the architects of his oppression. Baldwin's first real understanding of Shakespeare came when he was living in France and thinking and speaking in French. His quarrel with the English language had until then been that the language reflected none of his experience. In France he began to see that if English was not his language it might as easily be his own fault as the fault of the language. Perhaps the language was not his because he had never attempted to use it but had only learned to imitate it. English could be made to bear his experiences if he could find the stamina to challenge it, and himself, to such a test.

> In support of this possibility, I had two mighty witnesses; my black ancestors, who evolved the sorrow songs and blues and jazz and created an entirely new idiom in an overwhelmingly hostile place; and Shakespeare, who was the last bawdy writer in the English language. . . . Shakespeare's bawdiness became very important to me since bawdiness was one of the elements of jazz and revealed a tremendous loving and realistic respect for the body, and that ineffable force which the body contains, which Americans have mostly lost, which I had experienced only among Negroes and of which I had been taught to be ashamed.[14]

This process of coming to terms with the English language might well be what the upsurge of literary activity in East Africa is all about. The profound and the superficial, the imaginative and the mediocre, the polished style and the halting expressions of semiliteracy, are all part of a new culture in the making. As the dualism becomes less sharp and education becomes more congruent with upbringing, at least one Kenyan will remember an English teacher in a Yorkshire school who said, way back in the days of the British Empire, that the foundation of Milton's *Paradise Lost* is, in a sense, the English nursery rhyme.

---

14. James Baldwin, "Why I Stopped Hating Shakespeare," *Insight* (Ibadan: British High Commission, [1964]), pp. 14–15.

[4]

The Press:
Freedom versus Unity

An assessment of the role of the press in national life must take account of national values. In most countries there is one particular value which, more than any other, is directly associated with the role of the press. The value is usually complex, implying a diversity of subvalues within a whole set of social preferences. In this instance it is worthwhile to place East Africa's experience in the wider context of comparison between the traditional conceptions of the role of the press in the West and the emerging conceptions in sub-Saharan Africa as a whole.

In the Western world the paramount ethical preference associated with the press is the value of *freedom*. The press is conceptualized as a buttress of free institutions and individual liberty. Freedom of the press in the United States, for example, is regarded as inseparable from civil liberties. In Africa on the eve of independence those elements of the press that were in African hands were also pre-eminently occupied with issues of freedom. In this case, however, what was being agitated for was national freedom, or decolonization, rather than the protection of individual liberties. The quest of the nationalistic press was a quest for national independence.

Since the attainment of independence a shift in emphasis has taken place in many African countries. The paramount ethical imperative has ceased to be the ideal of freedom and has become the ideal of *unity*. Whereas in the Western democracies the mass media are intended to promote and protect the liberties of individual citizens, in Africa there is a tendency to regard news media as instruments for national integration.

In some ways both the Western ethical conception of the role of the press and the African ethical conception of that role are lopsided. At its extreme, the Western vision of the press as a precondition of the people's freedom tends in its most simplistic form to regard the press almost as if it were the same thing as the voice of the people. The idea of public opinion, at least until Gallup polls began to affect political calculations significantly, was inclined to equate public opinion with the opinion expressed in the press. The government was to consult the press almost as if that constituted consulting the people. If the relationship between the government and the people is supposed to be a two-way relationship, a vision of the press as the voice of the people is a challenge to the government to find some other medium for its own voice. If the press is the people's voice, what represents the voice of the government? Within the Western ideal of the role of the press there is a suspicion that it would be evil to make the press a voice of the government. The government may use the press to provide the people with information, but the people should use the press to provide the government with their opinions. There is a lack of symmetry in thinking of the press as an instrument of the ruled rather than of the rulers.

Similarly, there is a kind of asymmetry in African conceptions of the press, only in this case in the other direction. There is a tendency to regard the press as a medium through which the government may reach the people rather than one through which the people may reach the government. The press in Africa may sometimes provide the government with information. It may also attempt to contribute to the general sophistication of the public. The binding imperative, however, is tied to the ideal of unity rather than that of freedom.

The relevance of national freedom in the history of the evolution of African attitudes toward the press should not be forgotten. Nkrumah's newspaper, the *Accra Evening News*, became a major instrument of agitation in the movement to increase African rights. The newspaper proclaimed heroically, in almost Miltonic terms, that self-government with danger was preferable to servitude in tranquility. Nnamdi Azikiwe in Nigeria was an even greater journalist. As Ronald Segal observes in his profile of Zik:

> It was by his journalism . . that Azikiwe gave a new impetus to Nigerian nationalism. He started a chain of newspapers, the most important of which was the *West African Pilot*, and revolutionised West African journalism by the daring and directness of his editorial and news coverage. Concentrating on racial injustices and the need for positive action to emancipate Africa, he energetically spread his message throughout the territory, nursing circulation by provincial news coverage and by efficient distribution, and establishing four provincial dailies, in Ibadan, Onitsha, Port Harcourt and Kano.[1]

In East Africa, Jomo Kenyatta's journalistic experience also goes back quite a while. As general secretary of the Kikuyu Central Association, Kenyatta started the first Kikuyu journal, *Nuigwithania*, in 1928.[2]

We can therefore say that the African press was from the start directed toward the attainment of collective goals. The theme of collectivity is what later led to a theme of unity as a goal to be promoted by the press.

The imperative of national unity is by no means absent as an ethical regulator

---

1. Ronald Segal, *African Profiles* (London: Penguin, 1962), p. 199.
2. See Jomo Kenyatta, *Facing Mount Kenya* (1938; reprint ed., London: Secker & Warburg, 1959), p. xix.

of press behavior in, say, the United States; but its most obvious manifestation has tended to come during great national crises — for example, during the two world wars and the Cuban missile crisis of 1962. The problem of political legitimacy and national cohesion in the United States goes back to the early days of independence. There was a turning to the law for the protection of the state quite early. The Alien and Sedition Law of 1798 was one attempt to give the government the power to protect itself from unwarranted criticism. The Federalists did much to discredit the law by utilizing it for partisan political purposes. The individual states in the Union gradually gave up the old English doctrine of seditious libel, and by the time of Jacksonian Democracy the law in its original conception was for all intents and purposes dead.

The quest for a clearer doctrine to reconcile national purpose in times of emergency with the right of free criticism entered a new phase during the two world wars of the twentieth century. Many felt that during such times serious national division could endanger the war effort. But by what formula could the press be regulated without seriously undermining the liberal ethos? During World War I the government of the United States did set up a system for censoring outgoing and incoming messages; but what the press said within the country was subject only to a system of voluntary censorship with which much of the news media cooperated. The system and its procedures were readopted during World War II and improved upon, but the basic dilemma persisted. The Supreme Court took the position that if there was a *reasonable tendency* for discussion to obstruct the war effort, such discussion could be declared criminal and those who participated in it could be punished. But there was general unease about the implications of this formula.

Shortly after World War II the Court changed its mind and adopted instead the formula originally proposed by Justices Brandeis and Holmes. Holmes introduced the formula in the *Schenck* case in these famous words:

> The question in every case is whether the words used are used in such circumstances and of such a nature as to create a clear and present danger that they will bring about the substantive evils that Congress has a right to prevent. It is a question of proximity and degree.[3]

This is the formula which became known as the "clear and present danger" test. It later played an important part in regulations affecting the activities of the Communist party in the United States, though the test was not used to suppress such Communist party organs as the *Daily Worker*.

The "clear and present danger" formula in the American system of regulated freedom is the closest that American attitudes come to African attitudes on the limits of freedom. African governments have taken the position that their situation is comparable to that of Western democracies in times of war, when

---

3. *Schenck* v. *United States*, 249 U.S. 47 (1919).

restrictions of freedom are legitimated. African leaders like Nyerere, the late Tom Mboya, and others have often asserted that the crisis of underdevelopment and the fragility of political institutions together constitute a moment of national emergency in no way less critical than that confronting the United States in its war effort during the 1940s. During the Cuban missile crisis, when the Kennedy administration legitimated governmental deception in its relations with the press, the argument was not unlike African conceptions of the limits of freedom. The naked truth could be an enemy to a nation's welfare in times of crisis.

The important difference is that American problems concerning press freedom in this century have focused on the nation's readiness to cope with an external enemy, whereas African fears since independence have more often concerned the nation's readiness to deal with internal conflict. The arguments of regulated criticism during the two world wars in the United States, as well as the American obsession with the Communist danger after World War II, have all reflected this quality. Of course there was a fear of the "enemy within," but very often this enemy was seen as an extension of the enemy without. The traitor was regarded basically as an instrument of the external foe. The ultimate fear was of compromising a nation in its international posture, though the "Communist danger" also had a presumed internal revolutionary risk.

Within Africa, however, the external danger is often believed to be political and economic rather than military. The dangers of neocolonialism and economic imperialism are often sensed and do affect African responses. But African awareness of this kind of danger, to the extent that such danger does not involve violent tampering with internal arrangements, is not normally advanced as a reason for regulating press freedom. The clear and present danger for African states is more often the danger of civil strife.

The Media and Violence

Perhaps the most ghastly illustration of the clear and present danger of internal civil strife was the 1966 radio broadcast which apparently ignited the second massacre of the Ibo in northern Nigeria. The broadcast, coming from a neighboring country, reported the killing of Hausa in eastern Nigeria by the Ibo. The north retaliated, and one of the most appalling cases of mass killing in present-day Africa took place.

There is a good deal of argument as to whether the broadcast was only a signal intended to release a criminal plot of massacre that had already been agreed upon; but there is no evidence of such elaborate premeditation. Even if such a plan did exist, it was probably predicated on the assumption that a broadcast of that kind would cause communal retaliation. In other words, the presumed conspirators who wanted the Ibo slaughtered in northern Nigeria must have known that a rumor about the killing of Hausa men in eastern Nigeria would, at that particular time of interethnic excitability, almost inevitably result in dangerous riots.

On Saturday, July 5, 1969, Kenya's minister for economic development and planning, Tom Mboya, was fatally shot while shopping on a busy street in Nairobi. I heard the news in Kampala at about 4 P.M., more than two hours after the shooting. I tuned in to the Voice of Kenya, but the station gave no indication whatsoever that a national disaster had taken place. It was broadcasting cheerful music and seemed to be rigidly adhering to the ordinary day's program in spite of the fact that the most politically significant act of violence in Kenya since the Mau Mau insurrection had just taken place. I desperately tuned in to programs abroad, seeking information and confirmation. A news bulletin from Radio Pakistan included an announcement of the assassination. The Voice of America duly covered the event. I tuned in to the Voice of Kenya again; "Listeners' Choice," a program of Gramophone records, was on the air.

The Kenya government was obviously taking no chances. The mistake that had resulted in those ghastly riots in northern Nigeria was not going to be repeated. There was a genuine danger that the Luo would react violently if the news of the assassination was not handled very carefully in those initial hours. A Luo domestic servant on Makerere Hill saw me at about 6 o'clock that afternoon and informed me that a Kikuyu had assassinated Mboya. He had heard about it from friends who had heard it on the radio. I assured him that I had been glued to the radio for a couple of hours, listening to broadcasts from different parts of the world, and nowhere had the identity of the assassin been mentioned. In fact, the news as of that time was that the killer was unknown. My domestic friend looked a bit perplexed by my information. I in turn was disturbed by the rapid ease with which the Luo, even in the surrounding countries, had concluded that the gun which killed Mboya had been fired by a Kikuyu. The rumor lent greater justification to the cautious policy of the Voice of Kenya; the station continued with pop music, while the nation gradually took in the news of Mboya's death.

Two weeks later, in the relative calm of reappraising those few days of terrorist excitement after the assassination, Kenya's National Assembly discussed the issue of freedom of the press; the media's treatment of the assassination was mentioned. Some members were uneasy about the cautious slowness with which the radio reacted to the assassination. The newspapers were "on the ball" and issued special editions in the streets of Nairobi; but the radio, which reached far more people and would normally have been the first of all the media to announce the news, was much more circumspect. S. Omweri, KANU member for South Mugirango, complained that in moments of national disaster people were driven to turn to overseas sources for news. He specifically mentioned the Voice of Kenya for omitting the news of Mboya's assassination. Omweri said that many people had to tune in to the BBC for information about Mboya's death.[4]

In January, 1969, Rajat Neogy, the editor of *Transition* magazine, and Abu Mayanja, a local politician and constitutional lawyer, were brought before the court in Uganda on charges of sedition. Mayanja had written a letter to *Transition* concerning the Africanization of the Uganda judiciary. He argued that the membership of the High Court bench was conspicuously expatriate. Kenya already had a Kenyan chief justice — a man who had qualified as a lawyer some ten years after Uganda's David Lubogo had been called to the bar. There were other lawyers in Uganda of many years standing. The Uganda Constitution stipulated that a lawyer must have five years of experience before being eligible for appointment to the High Court as a judge. On the basis of that, the court could be Africanized entirely; why then had it not? Mayanja continued:

> I do not believe the rumour circulating in legal circles for the past year or so that the Judicial Service Commission has made a number of recommendations in this direction, but that the appointments have for one reason or another, mostly tribal considerations, not been confirmed. But what *is* holding up the appointment of Ugandan Africans to the High Court? [5]

The government interpreted Mayanja's letter as suggesting that the Uganda government had vetoed the appointment of Ugandan Africans to the High Court simply on the grounds that the most promising candidates belonged to the Ganda community. The government took a dim view of this kind of allegation, interpreting it as a form of tribal incitement. The charges that were brought to the High Court alleged that the defendants had invited wanton disrespect of the person of the president of Uganda, but basically the underlying fear was the fear of tribal cleavage in a situation where the government was trying to keep the nation cohesive.

Rajat Neogy and Abu Mayanja were acquitted by the court in ringing terms defending freedom of discussion.[6] Nevertheless, the case raised important issues affecting the limits of free discussion. "Clear and present danger," though a phrase which has no special place in the Uganda legal system, was implicitly conceived in terms of the risk of intercommunal disaffection and the risk of undermining the legitimacy of the government by reference to tribal factors.

The charges of bringing the person of the president into disrepute also raised that old dilemma concerning the private person and the public personality in relation to legal protection from excesses of criticism. The laws of the United States try to protect the individual from defamation and libel, but inevitably

---

4. See "Yesterday in Parliament," *East African Standard* (Nairobi), July 26, 1969.
5. *Transition*, VII, no. 37 (1968), 15.
6. The two were rearrested, however, and detained under the Emergency Regulations. Neogy was released in March, 1969, but Mayanja was held until August, 1970.

the old problem arises about what happens when the reputation of a public official is brought into serious question. As an individual he should be protected; but as a public official should he not be subject to public evaluation, friendly or hostile? In American legal history the courts attempted to make some distinctions early in the nineteenth century, but in the end the United States gave up the game of differentiation. Public officials and candidates for public office in the United States find little protection in the law of defamation.

Related to the fear of a clear and present danger is the fear in African countries that an increase in violent crimes will result from certain ways of handling news. In 1967 and 1968 the number of violent robberies in Kenya rose significantly; there seemed to be a dangerous turn toward a style of criminality which until then had been more characteristic of Uganda than anywhere else in East Africa. At that time both Uganda and Kenya seriously considered the idea of enacting capital punishment for certain forms of robbery with violence. In Uganda some of the worst cases occurred in rural areas, where people were beaten and sometimes killed for petty sums of money. In Nairobi there was the phenomenon of urban gangsterism, including daylight robberies with *pangas*; there was also an increase in the use of firearms.

The government of Kenya began to be concerned not only about the need for devising forms of punishment severe enough to deter this form of criminality but also about the need for creating an atmosphere in which such attitudes to violence would not be fostered or encouraged. The government considered the idea of capital punishment for robbery with violence but then retreated for fear of increasing the incidence of robbery with murder.[7] The Kenya government felt that the mass media ought to play a part in promoting a climate that would reduce the mystique of violence as a method of personal fulfillment. Violence should not be sensationalized or romanticized. In Nairobi a systematic attempt was made to do away with television programs containing excessive violence. Programs like "Bonanza" and "The Saint," by decree of the vice-president and minister of home affairs, were no longer to be broadcast in Kenya. The fear of a clear and present danger was now extended from social and political violence and the risk of civil strife to the more sordid violence of ordinary criminality. A resort to censorship was regarded as unavoidable.

In the United States the use of firearms for criminal purposes is promoted by a greater number of factors. The tradition of violence is too deeply entrenched in the social and political culture of the country to be attributed merely to how the mass media handle certain social facts. However, in Nairobi the use of firearms, or even daylight robbery with *pangas*, was basically a dramatic, new phenomenon. It therefore made sense for the Kenya government to look for possible precipitating factors behind the wave of personal assault. It is far

---

7. Since 1971, however, robbery with violence has been punishable in Kenya by death.

from certain that the government's action has solved the problem. In contrast to the situation in the United States, too few people in East Africa are exposed to the media in a sufficiently sustained way for national attitudes to be changed dramatically by shifts in media policy. However, when problems are new, it makes sense to consider a variety of possible precipitating factors, even if each individual factor appears to be marginal in its relevance.

The Local versus the Foreign

In East Africa the issues of violence and freedom of the press have been complicated by the racial factor; and racial consciousness has a propensity to collectivize political questions. Until the time of independence, an overwhelming portion of the English-language press in East Africa was in non-African hands. On the whole, this press was not oriented toward libertarian issues, even in the national sense of political independence. Addressing the International Press Institute in Paris in 1962, Tom Mboya of Kenya talked about "the strange but simple fact that in many countries, especially in East and Central Africa, independence has been attained or brought within early reach despite . . . a general Press hostility." [8]

This was substantially true of the press in the colonies; but Mboya did not adequately distinguish between the local foreign-owned press and the overseas press. The local foreign-owned press had a vested interest in the colonial *status quo* and shifted its position only when it was clear that the nationalist movement was on the way to fulfillment. The correspondents of the overseas press, however, were by no means wedded to the colonial *status quo*. Correspondents of the American press in particular often favored openly the anti-imperialists and freedom-fighters. The anti-imperialist component of American liberalism has, of course, a long history. British liberalism, on the other hand, accommodated itself quite early to an imperial role. John Stuart Mill, the nineteenth-century prophet of British liberalism, argued in the following vein:

> To characterise any conduct towards a barbarous people as a violation of the law of nations only shows that he who speaks has never considered the matter. . . . Barbarians have no rights as a *nation*, except a right to such treatment as may, at the earliest possible period, fit them for becoming one. [9]

In 1885, twenty-five years after these words were published, the Berlin Conference ratified the partition of Africa among European powers. The United States

8. Tom Mboya, "The Press and Governments in Africa," *Transition*, II, no. 4 (June, 1962), 11–28.
9. Quoted in Robert A. Goodwin, Ralph Lerner, and Gerald Stourzh, eds., *Readings in World Politics* (New York: Oxford University Press, 1959), p. 325.

participated in some of these discussions and on the whole supported tolerance and broad-mindedness in handling the rights of more simple societies.

The American press was by no means neatly anti-imperialist. But within the limits of Western conceptions of the world at that time, with all the haughty chauvinism about the so-called civilized nations of the West, sections of the American press did show a sensibility which was in some respects ahead of their time. The articles on the Congo written by Frederick Starr in 1907 for the *Chicago Tribune* are among those which spring to mind. Starr observed rather cynically that "the practical man, the business man, the man of affairs, the philanthropist, the missionary, all agreed that civilized folk have a perfect right to interfere with any native tribe too weak to resist their encroachment." [10] Although Starr pretended to cater to the tastes and opinions of these "men of affairs," he made his own position clear from the start:

> Personally I dislike the effort to elevate, civilize, remake a people. I should prefer to leave an African as he was before white contact. It is my belief that there is no people so weak or so degraded as to be incapable of self-government. I believe that every people is happier and better with self-government, no matter how unlike our own form that government may be. I feel that no nation is good enough, or wise enough, or sufficiently advanced to undertake the elevation and civilization of a "lower" people. Still less do I approve the exploitation of a native population by outsiders for their benefit. Nor do I feel that even the development of British trade warrants interference with native life, customs, laws and lands. I know, however, that these views are unpopular and heretical. [11]

Starr's libertarian orientation was by no means typical of the general mood of the time. Nevertheless, it is an indication that the press within the United States did show a sensibility concerning libertarian issues abroad from quite an early period.

Later in this century, when literacy became more widespread in Africa, the image of the overseas press was in part compromised, especially in East Africa, by the attitude of the foreign-owned local press. Overseas newspapers were sometimes suspect because of the behavior of local journalism under foreign direction.

Sensitivity and Language

Two factors were involved in the process by which African attitudes to the press became collectivized in racial or nationalistic terms. One factor was that

---

10. Frederick Starr, "The Truth about the Congo," *Chicago Tribune*, January 20, 1907.

11. *Ibid*.

African leaders became more sensitive to criticism from non-Africans than from Africans. The other was that African leaders in Anglophone Africa became more sensitive to criticism expressed in the English language than to criticism expressed in the vernacular. There must have been complicated sociological and psychological factors which gave rise to the first reaction. It is not always the case that people are more sensitive to foreign criticism than to critics from among themselves. In general, European countries are less sensitive to Afro-Asian criticism than they are to criticism from fellow Europeans, who are less foreign than the Afro-Asians.

Within the Anglo-American relationship there is sometimes a high sensitivity displayed when either of these groups is criticized by the other. For example, in 1963 Dean Acheson, who was then the American secretary of state, publicly remarked that Britain had lost an empire and had not found a role to replace the imperial one. Britain was, in Acheson's estimation, "played out." The British have become quite hardened to the criticism of Africans, Asians, the French, and Germans. They have shown themselves to be at times quite philosophical when the president of France or the president of Uganda takes them to task on this or that issue. But to be criticized by a major public figure in the United States was, even to the philosophical British, more than could be accepted very readily.

The British press took up the Acheson statement with dramatic coverage. A British Member of Parliament wrote to the prime minister virtually asking him to do something — or at the very least to say something — about Acheson's remarks. Harold Macmillan, then the prime minister, took up the challenge. He publicly responded to Acheson, arguing that critics like Acheson were making the same mistake that Hitler had made — which was to underestimate Britain and to underrate the role of the Commonwealth in world affairs. There was little doubt that Acheson had offended many in Britain. They would have reacted a little less strongly if the remarks had come from the foreign minister of France or the president of an Asian or African country. Criticism from a leading American spokesman, precisely because Americans are so much less foreign than these others, increased rather than diminished British sensitivity.

There may of course have been other psychological factors at play. People are sometimes more sensitive to criticism from those they regard as their peers than to criticism from those they regard with less respect. It is a case of immediacy of relationship adding depth to the sensitivity within the relationship.

This hypothesis about criticism among peers helps to explain why leaders in Africa are sometimes more sensitive to criticism in the English language at home than they are to criticism in the vernacular. To some extent it is odd that the reaction should be in these terms. The mass media in Africa are of course much less comprehensive than those in more literate societies like the United States. The readership of newspapers is often restricted, although a newspaper in the vernacular can sometimes command a wider readership than a newspaper in the English language if the vernacular is widely used. Yet, even in countries where African languages have wide distribution, there does at times appear to be a greater reaction to criticism expressed in the English-language media than to criticism in vernacular newspapers. A major reason is that a leader criticized in English at home knows that the criticism will be read by those he regards as his peers, sometimes his most immediate rivals. The well-educated Africans seldom read newspapers in African languages. Criticism in those languages is therefore disseminated among those who are only moderately literate or moderately sophisticated. The factors which cause African leaders to react to criticism in the English-language media are therefore similar to those which make Americans more sensitive to British than to African criticism, or the British more sensitive to American than to Asian criticism.

Prior to the 1966 crisis, and the defeat of Buganda by the forces of the central government, it did appear that government ministers in Uganda were on the whole more sensitive to what was said about them in the *Uganda Argus* than in, say, a Luganda newspaper hostile to the Uganda People's Congress. In 1963 a party was given in Kampala, apparently by Europeans resident on Tank Hill. The party, ostensibly in celebration of Kenya's independence, apparently developed into a satire of the whole process of decolonization. It seems that it was a farce, complete with theatrical costumes, and that the intention was to cast doubt on African readiness for self-rule and to deride some of the ambitions of the new Africa. Milton Obote, then prime minister of Uganda, transmitted the news about the Tank Hill party to the Uganda National Assembly and gave a dramatic account of the nature of the ridicule, complete with exhibits of some of the items used in the farce. It was a remarkable occasion. The legislature seemed to be working itself into a state of political fury over the prime minister's report of the party. There were repercussions later, including the expulsion from the country of some of the Europeans associated with the party.

From the point of view of our analysis here, the particular way in which the youth-wingers in Uganda chose to punish the white community is noteworthy. The youth-wingers thought that a fitting punishment would be the humiliation of a white member of the editorial staff of the English-language newspaper, the *Uganda Argus*. The editor was kidnaped, made to carry bundles of *matoke*, the plantain staple of the region, and subjected to petty forms of disrespect. It seemed as if the fighting slogan of the youth-wingers was: "We are faced with white racialism! Let us take it out on the *Uganda Argus*!" A white-owned newspaper was to some extent a symbol of white opinion, and white opinion had been busy disparaging Africa's assumption of political power. Reaction to the Tank Hill farce in December, 1963, became inseparable from general irritation with the leading English-language newspaper of the country.

Toward an Afro-Western Convergence

In this chapter we have subsumed East Africa in a wider comparison. We have attempted to outline some of the varieties of function and behavior of the media in Africa as compared with those in one major Western democracy. We have noted that the ultimate moral imperative for the press in the United States is the promotion of freedom, whereas the ultimate imperative in African countries is the promotion of unity. Yet, as we have indicated, there is an area of convergence in the idea of a clear and present danger. The idea has served as a criterion for the curtailment of freedom in the United States; and, though the phrase is American, a similar idea has often affected African policies concerning freedom of discussion. But, while the ultimate fear in American political culture has been the fear of an external enemy or externally instigated subversion, the ultimate fear within the fragile political systems of Africa has been the fear of domestic strife and violent revolt.

The press affects social life as well as political life, and different moral imperatives might be at play in each. The fields of language choice and of race relations in Africa are among the meeting points of political and social issues. Urban violence and sex often interact also with the role of the media in the societies concerned. For example, there is an important difference between the American press and the African press in the utilization of sex as a style of journalistic presentation. Techniques of the "sex angle" are much more sophisticated and widespread in the United States than in Africa. On American television, the devices range from husky, sexy voices recommending a particular product to a suggestive portrayal of the shape of a new car or the shape of a man who eats a particular kind of bread. Africa has tended to be more subdued in its utilization of sex in journalism. One reason may be a greater degree of puritanism in attitudes toward some issues. Just as it is rare to see couples in African cities making love openly, so is it rare to see African newspapers exploiting suggestive photographs or scandal stories.

This distinction between the role of sex in American journalism and its role in African journalism is a relative one. There is some use of sex in African newspapers. The newspapers in the vernacular languages, to the extent that they are almost by definition more "popular" than those in English, have sometimes been a little freer in their coverage of social news. They are also less inhibited in handling some of the more sensational social episodes. A newspaper in a local language is more likely to ignore a major political speech and concentrate on a colorful wedding. In the parliamentary debate on press freedom in Nairobi in July, 1969, B. M. Karungaru, KANU member for Embakasi, attacked a daily Swahili newspaper which, he said, did not even report the proceedings of the House and was only "exploiting people by reporting divorce cases."[12]

---

12. *East African Standard*, July 26, 1969.

The exploitation of sex in African journalism is still modest when compared with the place of sexual symbolism and suggestion in American journalism. The reasons in this case might lie in cultural divergences. Although sex is an area of personal intimacy, it is profoundly affected by culture. Differences in cultural inhibitions are at the root of differences in journalistic style in this area of coverage.

The difference in roles between the press in Africa and the press in the Western world may be narrowing in some respects. A major factor behind this narrowing may be the global homogenization of culture being brought about by the revolution in communications. When the pope visits Uganda, European television-viewers can observe the proceedings in their homes. The communications satellites, the jet-set journalists, the multiplicity of external radio services, the spread of literacy, and the transistor revolution are all conspiring to homogenize our styles and our responses. The differences between continents are still great, but the respective conceptions of the roles of the media in Africa and the United States are decidedly not diverging any further. On the contrary, the slow process of convergence may well be under way.

[5]

The Emergence of
Documentary Radicalism

What is documentary radicalism? It can be defined as an attempt to capture in documents or philosophical tracts a vision of a new society to be created. It is the utilization of the written word for purposes of formulating new social directions and new political goals. The range of documentary radicalism in East Africa is from Nyerere's Arusha Declaration to Obote's Document No. 5, on new methods of elections.

Documentary radicalism is in some respects an older phenomenon in Kenya than in the other two countries of East Africa. This is partly connected with the seniority in age and in political experience of the president of Kenya as compared with his counterparts in Uganda and Tanzania. Kenyatta's utilization of the written word for active political purposes goes back to the 1920s and 1930s. At that time there was in his radicalism an element of nostalgia, which was perhaps inevitable in the colonial period. The nature of nationalistic assertion was not simply a commitment to transforming one's society but also a commitment to retaining one's identity as a cultural being. Nationalism, when activated by colonial domination, tends to include a love of tradition and a longing for a restoration of local independence..

Kenyatta's participation in founding an early Kikuyu newspaper was part of the genesis of documentary radicalism in Kenya. In that period the nostalgia was persistent. The vision was not simply of the future but also of the past. Kenyatta's *Facing Mount Kenya*, first published in 1938, was in part a groping to create a new identity for the Kikuyu following the devastating impact of the colonial intrusion. The book also included, in its very attempts to relate Kikuyu experience to Western concepts, the dream to revive the old in terms which take account of the new

In the 1950s the torch in Kenya passed to Tom Mboya. He entered into the field of using the printed word for purposes of expressing an inner African dignity and of demanding a restoration of what was due to the nation. After Mboya's period at Ruskin College, Oxford, he produced a nationalistic pamphlet, with the encouragement of Margery Perham, on what he called "The Kenya Question," putting forward the African case against policies then being pursued in colonial Kenya.

Much of the documentary radicalism of the period before independence was addressed to an audience outside the colonies. It was often directed to the metropolitan countries as an appeal to public opinion there, as an attempt to influence directions of policy in the capital of the empire.

Radicalism: Independence and After

At the time of independence Julius Nyerere had already experimented with the idea of capturing his thoughts in writing. Pamphlets like *"Ujamaa — The Basis of African Socialism"* and *"Democracy and the Party System"* were among his early enterprises. But the radicalism in them seemed to be tamed by nostalgia. The concept of *Ujamaa*, now defined as socialism but tied to the idea of kinship solidarity, was in the tradition of that school of innovation which sought to maintain links with the past. Even Nyerere's idea of democracy, comparing an electoral system to a system in which the elders sat under a tree and talked until they agreed, was an attempt to fuse a vision of the new Africa with a vision of the old.

Each of the three countries of East Africa had different reasons for gradually moving toward the use of documentary radicalism as an instrument for social and political reform. In the case of Tanzania, Nyerere's personality and his intellectuality were important reasons for this tendency. Educated intellectuals tend to have literary tendencies, and Nyerere is the most intellectual of all the English-speaking African heads of state. His popular designation, the *Mwalimu*, or mentor, indicates his leaning toward the world of learning. He was once a schoolteacher, and his style of leadership has a highly didactic component.

Nyerere started quite early to put his thoughts in writing and to establish a reputation as a philosopher-president. He liked to play with ideas and to intellectualize about the problems of his society. He liked to theorize about the direction of Africa's future and the nature of Africa's past. In addition Nyerere has, from quite an early date, shown an interest in "intellectual bridge-making" — the idea of establishing links between the cultural and ideological heritage of Africa and the cultural and ideological heritage of the rest of the world. His attempts at Africanizing socialism and liberal ideas fall within this general attempt at bridge-making, and he has also had an interest in translating creative literature. His translation of Shakespeare's *Julius Caesar* and *The Merchant of Venice* into Swahili has been an important aspect of this side of the *Mwalimu's* endeavor. All of these elements were important in contributing toward the consolidation of documentary radicalism in Tanzania.

Nyerere's early writings, however, were mainly speeches and papers prepared for special occasions. There was no attempt to make these documents an official embodiment of party ideology and a guide to policy-making. Nyerere's pamphlets

"Ujamaa" and "Democracy and the Party System" were basically intellectual exercises by a head of state, though they did bear a relevance to policy. Much of his early work consisted of explanations of ideological positions and rationalizations of trends. There was no attempt to form a blueprint for the future until the Arusha Declaration hit the East African ideological world.

In 1965 Kenya became the first East African country to put documentary radicalism on an official basis, with the publication of Sessional Paper No. 10 on "African Socialism and Its Application to Planning in Kenya." [1] Kenyatta described the document as the new political Bible of the country. Debates on whether or not it has been implemented will continue for quite a while. It is arguable that many of its proposals have in fact been fulfilled, either in part or in entirety. Tom Mboya, not long before his assassination, engaged in debate with Ahmed Mohiddin, of the Department of Political Science at Makerere, concerning socialism in Africa. Mohiddin's position was that Kenya's "African socialism" as enunciated and implemented was neither African nor socialism. Mboya retorted that it was both and went on to argue that commitment to development did involve systematic creation of wealth, even if some of the repercussions might, for the time being, be undesirable. Whether or not Kenya's Sessional Paper No. 10 has guided policy, it remains the first official proclamation of documentary radicalism in East Africa.

In 1969 and 1970 President Milton Obote pronounced five documents as constituting the new blueprint for Uganda — the Common Man's Charter; the National Service Proposals; the Communication from the Chair; the Nakivubo Pronouncements; and Document No. 5, concerning multiple constituencies for members of the National Assembly and the method of electing the president. [2] These five cumulatively, and with a great momentary impact, put Uganda into the mainstream of documentary radicalism in East Africa until the coup of January, 1971.

Obote was looking for both socialistic and intellectual respectability, and from 1968 onward these ambitions manifested themselves more sharply. It became clearer than ever that Obote aspired to a socialistic revolution for his country and at the same time a reputation of intellectual innovativeness for himself. The five documents of the Move to the Left and the whole phenomenon of documentary radicalism in Uganda illustrated this. In October, 1969, he issued the Common Man's Charter as a major intellectual and ideological foundation for the Move to the Left. The second document, the National Service Proposals, issued later in 1969, envisaged a growing commitment of different sections of the Uganda population to the task of nation-building and preparation for social transformation. Obote's Communication from the Chair, a speech opening

---

1. This document is available from the Government Printer, Nairobi.
2. The first four documents were published by the Government Printer, Entebbe. Document No. 5 was published by the Milton Obote Foundation, Kampala.

the new session of the National Assembly in April, 1970, enunciated austerity measures for the civil service and a new ethic for the bureaucracy as a whole. The Nakivubo Pronouncements of May 1, 1970, were short and effective; they amounted to full nationalization of the export and import trade and governmental takeover of at least 60 per cent of the shares of all other major economic undertakings in the country. Finally, in July, 1970, Document No. 5 proposed new ways of electing the president and members of the National Assembly and put forward the brilliantly stimulating idea of having each member of Parliament run for election in four constituencies — one in the north of the country, one in the south, one in the east, and one in the west. The purpose of the exercise was to reduce the influence of tribal loyalty on the relationship between members of Parliament and their constituents, to promote participation in elections based on the nation as a whole, and to require a politician to seek support from different corners of the country.

With the Common Man's Charter and the Nakivubo Pronouncements, Obote achieved a substantial measure of socialistic credibility. With the highly innovative Document No. 5, Obote achieved an intellectual success as well. In many ways Document No. 5 is the most original piece of constitutional theory to have emerged from independent Uganda and one of the most challenging political experiments to have been seriously considered anywhere in Africa.

Also important in the evolving intellectualized radicalism in Uganda was the role of Obote's cousin and confidant, Akena Adoko, the chief general service officer of the Uganda government and president of the Law Society at the time. He, too, had been eager to establish links between political radicalism and intellectual innovation. One of the more interesting accounts of the tense and far-reaching events of 1966 in Uganda can be found in Adoko's little book *Uganda Crisis*, written in blank verse. The neorepublican tendencies, derived in part from his own cultural background, form the basis of this account and sometimes lend dignity to the narration. In this case documentary radicalism becomes indistinguishable from literary radicalism.

> No dead man has any right
> To rule over the living
> Directly through his own ghost
> Or indirectly through heirs.

When the monarchic principle is unrestrained, it can be insensitive to human values. Beginning with this premise, Adoko's long poem relates an act allegedly committed by the late kabaka of Buganda, an act which seemed to have been based on the notion that the king could do no wrong.

> One morning in '64,
> He shot and killed eight people.

All the eight were Banyoro,
And that was their only crime.[3]

Adoko's interest in the possible links between intellectualism and radicalism also manifested itself in a debate I had with him at Makerere in February, 1969. The topic of the debate, proposed by the mayor after discussions with Adoko, was the role of the intellectuals in the African revolution. Adoko's position was that intellectuals should be socially and politically committed. My position was that commitment should not be confused with conformity. Intellectuals could be deeply committed without applauding every policy statement from the ruling party. Conforming with the documentary pronouncements of the regime in power was not necessarily the ultimate measure of commitment to the nation and to Africa.[4] Some of the issues discussed in that debate anticipated some of the later controversies surrounding Obote's five documents of the Move to the Left.

The Conservation of Radical Thought

Documents in East Africa have sometimes been treated with momentous reverence and acclaim. In Tanzania people walked dozens of miles to affirm their commitment to the Arusha Declaration. Even President Nyerere walked over a hundred miles in a similar demonstration of commitment to this document, which he had written. In Uganda, too, there was tremendous activity associated with the launching of the different documents in the last two years of Obote's regime. The Common Man's Charter was treated with great acclaim when it was issued, and some took long walks as a method of affirming commitment to it. The National Service Proposals were also subjected to a good deal of discussion. The relevant ministers traveled throughout the country, listening to opinions on the document and explaining its implications.

The Communication from the Chair and the Nakivubo Pronouncements were, in many ways, in a different category. There was some general discussion and some acclaim, but these documents covered enough sensitive areas to make the discussion more subdued.

Document No. 5 caused even more open debate than did the Common Man's Charter. There were no marches in affirmation of loyalty to Document No. 5, but there was more genuine discourse and analysis. Discussion of the document

---

3. Akena Adoko, *Uganda Crisis* (Kampala: African Publishers, 1968), p. 7.

4. The opening statements by the two speakers were published as articles in *East Africa Journal* in March and April, 1969. Since then, Akena Adoko has written another work in blank verse, this one about the Lea Affair of 1970, which concerned the appearance and disappearance of a British diplomat who claimed to have been kidnaped, but whose claim was rejected by a special commission of inquiry set up to investigate the affair.

ranged from extramural lectures in relatively isolated areas of Uganda to publicized debates between members of the cabinet and academics from Makerere. In short, the first of the documents in Uganda received considerable affirmation and acclaim but more subdued debate; the last of the five documents received modest popular acclaim, but it generated franker discussion and invited more candid dissent than the previous ones.

Why did this movement toward documentary radicalism ever take place in East Africa? Why, indeed, are documents so important in the African experience? The explanation must be sought in the very meaning of the printed word for man in society and in history.

The printed word is often regarded as a medium of conservation rather than as a method of transformation. Ideas which are articulated in countries that do not reduce their thoughts to writing can perish. Where is the wealth of Africa's wisdom over the centuries? Africa must have had great philosophers, great mystics, even great eccentrics, trying out new ideas; but much of that old intellectual activity has been lost to us. Africa does have an oral tradition. Some of Africa's wisdom has been transmitted, from generation to generation, by word of mouth. But oral tradition tends, overwhelmingly, to be transmission of consensus rather than nonconformity, of accepted ideas rather than innovative intellectual heresies. In Africa's history many of the latter kind of ideas, which might have been accepted one or two generations later had they been preserved, died because they were never recorded. Ancient radicalism did not find the conserving blessing of the written word.

In this observation lies a paradox. The written word is a medium of conserving the thoughts and traditions of a society; however, among the most conservative of all societies are those which have no tradition of writing. How can this paradox be explained?

One of the things conserved by the written word is the language itself; without a widespread tradition of writing, a language may change rapidly. Swahili has had a written tradition for two or three centuries, but this tradition has not been particularly widespread. One consequence of this is that the Swahili of the 1850s differs more from the Swahili of the 1970s than the English of the 1850s differs from the English of the 1970s. Luganda has also been written for a number of generations; but, because Kiganda culture in the nineteenth century was not a literate culture, the Luganda of the 1850s is probably also more different from the Luganda of the 1970s than the English of the 1850s is from the English of the 1970s. English has changed less rapidly partly because of the conserving influence of a literate culture on the language. Although literacy in the early part of the nineteenth century in England was far from universal, the literate section of the community had become so large, and its impact on the rest of the population so great, that much of the language of the upper classes of nineteenth-century England survives with little change in the 1970s.

Cultures which are not widely literate sometimes succeed in conserving much of their language, but the actual art of writing has much to do with the conservation. The influence of the Quran on the Arabic language is a case in point. The style of the Quran linguistically captured the imagination of the Arabs. Its vigor of expression and beauty of execution resulted in a new doctrine within Islam — the doctrine that the Quran was inimitable. Among the miracles that Muslims attributed to the Prophet Muhammad was the miracle of the Quran as a work of literature.

Despite the doctrine of Quranic inimitability, the book exerted such a pervasive influence that many writers attempted to imitate its style. The result is that the Quran, perhaps more than any other book or any other factor, has been responsible for the survival of classical Arabic. The Arabic spoken in one part of the Arab world can be very different from that spoken in another. Dialects can even be mutually unintelligible. But a printed page from a newspaper in Iraq is often easily understood by a literate Arab in Egypt or Nigeria. Furthermore, a literate Arab often can speak classical Arabic as well as the colloquial Arabic of his own country. When Arabs want to understand each other across national frontiers, the solution is to fall back on classical or neoclassical Arabic — transmitted from generation to generation through the influence of the Quran and the mystique of reciting it. Pride in the beauty of the language preserved by the Quran continues to be an aspect of Arab nationalism. The nature of that interaction between cultural nationalism and the printed word affords an insight into the general relationship between cultural identity and the art of writing.

This is where the paradox concerning the written word enters the field once again. A society that has no tradition of writing is beset by the fear of losing its identity precisely because oral tradition is so perishable. Because the transmission of the society's mores and values is by word of mouth, from generation to generation, the fear of losing social identity leads to a profound conservatism. Traditional societies without the printed word, precisely because they lack that great preservative of culture, are thrown back to a militant protection of their traditions. The voices of heresy rise and fall; many die unheard; certainly most die uncelebrated.

Widespread literacy could conquer this fear. The values of the society would be preserved in writing; and the populace with a moderate reading ability would have access to them. The fear of losing identity would give way to some toleration of innovation. Heresies might be unattended to for a while; but, having been preserved in writing, they might inspire rethinking a generation or two later.

Ideology and Political Theorizing

In East Africa the written word serves a purpose also in the quest to move from a society of traditional political culture to a society of modern ideology.

[73]

Each major ideology is a potential political culture, but it does not become one until it has succeeded in establishing roots. The new political culture in Obote's Uganda was a political culture in the making rather than an accomplished fact. An ideology seeking to replace an old culture sometimes needs to give itself the concrete form of written analysis and defined intentions. Documentary radicalism in East Africa might therefore be described as primarily a transition from an old political culture to a new one through a new ideology. The written word serves as a transmission device between two things which might otherwise be very different. Oral tradition is an exercise in transmitting what already has roots. Documentary radicalism, on the other hand, is an exercise in transmitting what aspires to have roots but which is, for the time being, confronting the resistance of older norms and habits.

Documentary radicalism is not merely a prescription of what ought to be done; it is also an interpretation of what *is*. Nyerere is not only a radical who documents his vision; he is also a political theorist, interpreting the nature of human society and the springs of human behavior. In an important sense, the most revolutionary thing about Nyerere is not his socialism but the fact that he is a Tanzanian political theorist. The very act of theorizing in his fashion is a fundamental departure from the social tradition to which he belongs.

Political theorizing can be profoundly artificial. Even in its most concrete form, it is an exercise in abstraction. It is an attempt to abstract from political experience a conceptual basis for political generalizations. One question which arises is whether this kind of approach is alien to the indigenous political traditions of East Africa. Is the attempt to "separate" theory from practice basically foreign in origin? What are the implications of this issue for the teaching of political theory today in African educational institutions?

There has, in fact, been a change of historical significance in the relationship between political ideas and political behavior in Africa. All traditional African societies had political ideas, and each society had a political culture of its own; but few indulged in political theorizing as a distinct intellectual tradition. A political culture is the total complex of values, principles, prejudices, and institutionalized expectations which characterize and animate the behavior of a political community. A political culture includes within it political ideas, defined in this case as units of thought in the political process. These ideas are not analyzed in abstraction but form part of the vocabulary and rhetoric of everyday political behavior.

Political ideas can cease to be primarily units of thought in the political process and can become primarily units of thought in an intellectual process. With such a conversion, political ideas become political theory — abstracted from the totality of political culture. Theories which are analyzed in abstraction by detached philosophers may then re-enter a political culture, converted into somewhat different units of thought in the process of concrete politics. This conversion and reconversion of political ideas makes the documentary as well as the oral dissemination of political ideas in Africa today relevant to the process of social engineering and national integration. We must now examine both the interrelationship of intellectual analysis and political behavior and the general evolution of the role of ideas in East African politics, traditional and modern.

The discussion, utilization, and teaching of political ideas in Africa pertains directly to the process of national integration. To the extent that ideas are related to thinking, thinking to perception, and perception to recognition, ideas become part of the total phenomenon of group identification and social discourse.

In the field of major political ideas in contemporary Africa one could technically draw an imaginary line between ideas which are basically indigenous and ideas which are basically foreign. In reality, however, the process of thinking is never that neat, and intellectual intercourse between the indigenous and the foreign admits of no clean boundary. Nevertheless, the process of national integration is a process of redefining the boundaries of group consciousness and determining what is national and what is external. The distinction between the indigenous and the foreign as an analytical hypothesis is therefore indispensable in trying to understand what is going on in the field of thought in Africa.

The transmission of political ideas is, in one way or another, part of the political process of modern Africa. Sometimes ideas of authority, values of obedience or conformity, loyalties to the community, are transmitted, not as part of formal classes in political education, but in a variety of more subtle ways of socializing young people into the mores of their society. But specific courses in political ideas are more distinctive. What functions do they serve? Here the distinction between indigenous and foreign ideas becomes particularly pertinent. The teaching of African political ideas through the mass media and educational institutions might be regarded as a way of consolidating national consciousness. The teaching of European political ideas through such devices might be regarded as a contribution to the refinement of the rhetoric that goes with those political institutions which Africa has inherited from Europe. The dissemination of indigenous ideas might then be regarded as a contribution to the evolution of a shared culture and national identity, while the dissemination of foreign political ideas might be regarded as a contribution to the expansion of political awareness.

This distinction is really a matter of emphasis rather than of sharp differentiation of roles. There is a good deal of intermingling of the ideas themselves as well as the functions they serve. Nevertheless, the teaching of African political ideas in African institutions can be rationalized mainly in terms of consolidating a sense of shared national or cultural identity, while formal courses in European political philosophy can be rationalized in terms of promoting greater political sophistication, particularly in relation to the modern institutions inherited from Europe.

Within the category of African political ideas, a distinction has to be made between traditional political ideas and modern political ideas. Of these two, modern political ideas are inevitably more difficult to disentangle from the external intellectual traditions with which they have been in communion.

Traditional political ideas have so far been relatively neglected by modern scholars in Africa. There is not even agreement that traditional modes of behavior admitted of differentiation between the political and, say, the mystical. If politics was not a distinct activity, how could the ideas of politics be so defined? Traditional village communities went about their daily business within a complex of social relationships, but these, it is claimed, were based on and guided by custom rather than abstract principles.

The term *abstract principles* brings to mind another type of objection which is sometimes raised concerning the proposition that traditional African political theory can be discussed intelligibly. The argument here is that since the time of the Greeks, political theory has been a game in abstraction. Traditional African approaches to life were fundamentally down to earth and are therefore to be sharply differentiated from the Greek tradition. Traditional Africa lacked not only political theory but also political ideology. If ideology is thought of as a rationalistic explanation of the universe and of human values, then it might also be regarded as an intellectual hypothesis or complex of hypotheses, sometimes capable of being used as a method of intellectual analysis of social phenomena. If there is a rationalistic purpose behind the concept of political ideology, it can be argued that the traditional African was not an ideological animal. According to this school of interpretation the traditional African, where he persists, continues to be intuitive rather than ideological in his search for answers.

Leopold Senghor of Senegal has described negritude as "the whole complex of civilised values of the Negro African wherever he may be." Senghor regards negritude as being "essentially informed by intuitive reason." He enumerates cultural patterns of traditional Africa and general African epistemology.

> The sense of communion, the gift of myth making, such are the essential elements of Negritude, which you will find indelibly stamped on all the works and activities of the black man.[5]

This interpretation of original Africa exposed Senghor to the charge of depriving the traditional African of the gift of rationality. Confronted with this charge, Senghor defends himself with his usual ingenuity, but insists on making the African basically intuitive.

> Young people have criticised me for reducing Negro African knowledge to pure emotion, for denying there is an African "reason" or African techniques. This is the heart of the problem.

---

5. Leopold Senghor, "Negritude and African Socialism," in *St. Anthony's Papers on African Affairs, No. 2*, ed. Kenneth Kirkwood (London: Chatto & Windus, 1963), p. 11.

Senghor then argues that, however paradoxical it may seem, the vital force of the Negro African is animated by reason.

> Let us understand each other clearly; it is not the reasoning *eye* of Europe, it is the *reason of the touch*, better still, the *reasoning embrace*, the sympathetic reason, more closely related to the Greek *Logos* than to the Latin *ratio*. For *Logos*, before Aristotle, meant both reason and the word. . . . . European reasoning is analytical, discursive by utilisation; Negro African reasoning is intuitive by participation.[6]

Senghor concludes his argument by saying that Africans should maintain the Negro African method of knowledge, but that they may integrate into it the methods Europe has used throughout its history — classical logic, Marxian dialectics, and methods of the twentieth century. But he then warns: "Let us merely be careful not to be led astray by . . . abstraction. Let us hold firmly *to the concrete*." [7]

This line of reasoning, then, regards the tradition of thought including classical logic and Marxian dialectics, which reduces the understanding of phenomena to rationalistic analysis, as basically alien to African cultures. The African mode of understanding social phenomena, whether they are connected with the polity and political authority or not, is radically different from that which was bequeathed to Europe by Greek intellectual civilization.

The Decline of Spontaneous Participation

Senghor's concept of participation almost sounds like an alternative to reflection. Descartes had asserted that the ultimate proof of existence is to think. In his own famous words, "I think, therefore I am." According to Senghor, African epistemology is based on a different postulate. For the African Negro the world exists through its reflection on his emotive self.

> He does not realise that he thinks;
> He feels that he feels, he feels his *existence*,
> He feels himself.

In short, Negro African epistemology starts with the premise "I *feel*, therefore I am." The process is radically different from the Cartesian mode of apprehension. Senghor describes Descartes as "the European *par excellence*." But the African approach to reality relies more on emotional involvement.[8]

---

6. Leopold Senghor, *On African Socialism*, trans. Mercer Cook (New York: Praeger, 1964), pp. 73–74.

7. *Ibid.*, p. 25.

8. Leopold Senghor, "The Spirit of Civilisation, or the Laws of African Negro Culture," The First International Conference of Negro Writers and Artists, *Présence*

Kwame Nkrumah, in his book *Consciencism*, also discussed Descartes's postulate. The fact that "Monsieur Descartes" is thinking, Nkrumah argued, is no proof that his body exists. It is certainly no proof that the totality of his person is in being. Nkrumah denied that matter owes its existence either to thought or to perception. In a sense he would disagree both with the reasoning that says, "I think, therefore I am," and with the reasoning that argues, "I feel, therefore I am." To the extent that "feeling" is a more "physical" experience than thought, it is a greater concession to the autonomy of matter. The kind of philosophical idealism which puts our bodies in our minds instead of our minds in our bodies was to Nkrumah no more than indulgence in "the ecstasy of intellectualism." [9]

The idea of emotional involvement as opposed to the worship of thought is at the heart of this African challenge to the principles of the Western intellectual tradition. Quiet, detached meditation is a respectable exercise in the Western scheme of values. Yet meditation can all too easily be, as it sometimes is in the Hindu tradition, a form of withdrawal from the real world. By withdrawing into the privacy of his own thoughts, an individual may commit the sin of social disengagement. Philosophizing about politics can also be a form of political disengagement if it leads to a retreat into armchair abstractions.

From the point of view of the imperative of social involvement, the political slogan is more important than the political concept. The place of rallies in political culture in Africa re-emphasizes the supremacy of the slogan over the concept. A slogan is, after all, an idea in social action.

Tom Mboya once described African political rallies as they might appear to outsiders. There is a huge crowd streaming toward the stadium or an open piece of ground, then sitting patiently for hours while a dozen politicians make their speeches. The speakers do not seem to make many new points, or at least for every new idea there is much that everyone has heard often before. Mboya described how the speaker frequently interrupts his speech to call on the crowd to repeat after him a series of slogans.

> *Uhuru* — Uhuru!
> *Uhuru na Umoja* — Uhuru na Umoja!
> *Uhuru na Kenyata* — Uhuru na Kenyatta!

Mboya continued:

The crowd is good natured, it is true, and seems to look on it as a festive occasion.

Africaine, nos. 8, 9, 10 (June–November, 1956), pp. 64–71. See also *idem*, "The African Apprehension of Reality," in Senghor, *Prose and Poetry*, ed. and trans. John Reed and Clive Wake (London: Oxford University Press, 1965), pp. 29–35.

9. Kwame Nkrumah, *Consciencism* (London: Heinemann, 1964), pp. 16–19. This point is analyzed in similar terms in Ali A. Mazrui, *Ancient Greece in African Political Thought* (Nairobi: East African Publishing House, 1967).

In fact, in front is a women's choir with bark cloth dresses and painted faces and a curious mixture of Western ornaments like dark glasses, and tincans around their ankles. But what is the point of it all? It may help to boost the people's morale a bit, but don't they get bored after the first once or twice? And why do so many leaders spend so much time at these rallies? [10]

The critical factor here is the factor of participation. A slogan is shouted out, and the crowd collectively responds. The stadium in which this is happening in Nairobi or Kampala is a modern one, and the microphone symbolizes technology. The politics involved here is supposed to be the politics of modern institutions committed to arrangements befitting a modern sovereign state. Yet between the slogan from the microphone and the collective echo from the crowd in the stadium might lie an eternity of African ritual. As we indicated, politics in traditional Africa was often regarded as inseparable from other social and spiritual arrangements. The political rally, according to Mboya, is in some ways like a festive occasion which people attend to enjoy themselves. The exchange of slogans has even deeper ritualistic connotations, almost resembling a primeval prayer.

The rally is also characterized by the sheer monotony that is profoundly African. The drum beat going on and on, the song with a persistent uniformity, and the dance culminating in an ecstatic trance are all familiar features of the African cultural experience. The negritude school was quick to perceive the centrality of monotony in African aesthetics, regarding it as part of Africa's responsiveness to rhythm. Senghor cites George Hardy's observation that "the most civilised African, even in a dinner jacket, still quivers at the sound of a drum." Senghor asserts that the sense of the drum has affected African poetry as well.

To blame Cesaire and others for their rhythm, their monotony, that is, for their style, is to blame them for being born Negroes, West Indian, or African, and not Frenchmen or Christians. It is to blame them for having remained themselves, irreducibly sincere. [11]

The African responsiveness to monotony and rhythm echoes the regularities of nature and the cosmos. Some of the most symbolic aspects of life and rebirth betray a rhythmic monotony — "the beating of the heart, breathing, the rhythm of . . . making love, ebb and flow, succession of days and seasons and, in general, all the rhythms of the cosmos." [12]

The repetitive chanting of slogans, with all its ritualistic monotony, might well be assessed against the background of rhythmic regularity within Africa's aesthetic experience. The slogan is more important than the concept because

---

10. Tom Mboya, *Freedom and After* (London: André Deutsch, 1963), pp. 62–63.

11. Senghor, *Prose and Poetry*, pp. 31, 94.

12. *Ibid.*, p. 31.

the slogan is a more immediate reflection of the regularities of nature and the rhythm of the African drum, as well as, quite simply, an idea in social action.

However, the new nation-state cannot as yet claim the kind of mystical hold over the citizens which would make intellectual rationalization redundant. Even the rallies that Tom Mboya discussed were most successful during a period of a collective sense of belonging to a shared nationalist movement against colonial rule. After independence a good deal of symbolic reaffirmation could still be evoked in cases where a particular political party or a particular leader continued to command a mystical hold over his followers. On the whole, however, there has been a decline in the unreflective singing of slogans in a ritualistic way, partly because there has been a decline in the shared sense of belonging to a common movement. People are no longer aroused spontaneously to participate. They have to think about it. They need to be persuaded. The art of political rationalization therefore needs to be improved. From this art there emerges in time a tradition of political theory as purposeful political analysis in relation to advocacy.

Nationalism and the Birth of Ideology

The growth of modern political thought in Africa constitutes a transition from a mental world of broad political culture to a mental world of more specific abstract political concepts. The initial themes of political philosophy at the dawn of African nationalism inevitably centered on questions of liberty, self-determination, and the nature of rational dignity. As the nationalist movement gathered momentum and seemed to be approaching its final victory in sovereign statehood, new ideas began to command fascination. Socialism and the issue of whether or not it was inherent in Africa's traditional political culture led to the creation of a school of thought concerned with the concept of "African socialism." Independence posed issues about the relevance of political parties, and philosophizing in Africa turned its attention to the ethics of choice in elections and the case for or against the one-party system. This was the birth of *ideology*, defined here as policy-oriented political theory. Documentary radicalism entered a new stage.

Meanwhile, a distinction emerged between the concept of political thought as understood in well-established countries like Britain and the United States, and that concept as applied to new states. A person who speaks of American political thought is not likely to be referring to the thinking of Presidents Nixon, Johnson, Kennedy, Eisenhower, or Truman. He is more likely to be referring to the ideas of American political *philosophers*. Yet, when a person refers to African political thought of the modern period, he is likely to have in mind the ideas of Senghor, Nkrumah, Nyerere, and other African political leaders. One reason for this is that contemporary Africa has no background of written philosophical works on the nature of politics. If we are interested in finding out the kinds of ideas which form the basis of African political evaluation in the modern period, we have to look for them in sources other than formal exercises in political theory. One source is the ideas of those who claim to speak for major political movements in Africa. Political philosophy and political ideology are virtually indistinguishable when the philosophers are towering politicians.

One must also pay special attention to those first leaders of African nationhood precisely because they *are* the first leaders. At least some of the ideas of a founding father become part of the foundation which he lays for the nation. The concept of American political thought might not normally denote the ideas of Nixon or Johnson, but it does include the ideas of Jefferson and Madison. In the Russian experience the ideas of Lenin, even when rejected or modified, are likely to remain in a class by themselves, regardless of any greater intellectual originality which some future Russian leader might have. Turkish political thought continues to give a place of eminence to the ideas of Atatürk. In India the thoughts of Ghandi and of Nehru seem destined to form part of the intellectual heritage of independent India.

Why are the thoughts of those who have been leaders during times of great changes given such eminence? Perhaps one reason is that the persons themselves are of unique historical interest because of the roles they played. Another reason, however, is the presumption that the first holders of authority in a new order played a decisive part in shaping that order, even if they were later rejected or overthrown. This presumption is not always vindicated; but the myth can persist, in spite of evidence to the contrary. And for certain purposes a myth can be more important than the evidence.[13]

In the last few years in Africa the ideas of those who are not in authority have also become significant in their own way. Particularly influential among black critics of black leadership after independence is Frantz Fanon, the revolutionary from Martinique who fought for the Algerian rebels, wrote books on the psychology of dependence and the purifying functions of violence, and died young, leaving for black peoples a militant school of political philosophy after formal independence.

The fact that philosophizing and theorizing now come both from those in authority and from those who have reservations about those in authority indicates a new intellectual dialectic in Africa's political experience. The spontaneous participation of traditional social behavior is giving way to ideological confrontation among competitive schools of modern African theories.

Meanwhile, foreign thinkers are beginning to assume a new relevance for African realities. It cannot be overemphasized that those who teach European political theory to students outside Europe might do well to play down the

---

13. These points are discussed in similar terms in Ali A. Mazrui, *Towards a Pax Africana* (London: Weidenfeld & Nicolson; Chicago: University of Chicago Press, 1967), pp. 215–16.

Europeanism of the theories concerned, not to make the theories more popular, but to see if they can be made more relevant. The process might involve tearing the European theory out of its historical context altogether and bringing the logic of all or some of its ideas to bear on a specific situation in perhaps one's own time or one's own area in Africa,

> the object of the exercise being to determine whether the ideas scattered within the theory help in the understanding of the situation, on the one hand, and on the other whether the situation can lend a new depth to the theory or perhaps expose an old shallowness within it. . . . What can be taken for granted is that ideas can express further ideas if they are systematically referred to one situation after another. To change the metaphor, if an idea is fertile, it may well conceive a different kind of child if it is mated to a different kind of situation.[14]

The first-year course in political theory at Makerere University is from Thomas Hobbes to Julius K. Nyerere. Throughout the course there is an attempt to assess the ideas of each thinker against experience outside the thinker's geographical or temporal context. More often than not the test is against African realities. What Thomas Hobbes's attitude to foreign missionaries would be, whether tribal loyalties are the equivalent of "particular wills" in Rousseau's terms, and whether the independence constitution of an African country is the equivalent of a social contract forming a new society are some of the issues that are brought up, providing occasion in Makerere classrooms for vigorous discussion of European political thinkers in relation to African problems.[15]

The process of national integration is facilitated by this transition from political culture to political theory in the African approach to political understanding. A re-examination of ancestral norms and a revalidation of selective aspects of the African heritage contribute directly to the growth of national identity. But the utilization of the total human pool of political theories and political ideas, from Plato to Fanon and Nyerere, must inevitably be an enrichment of analytical sophistication. Sophisticated politics becomes both an index of political development and a contribution to the consolidation of that development. We return once again to that chain whereby ideas determine the quality of thinking, thinking determines the level of perception, perception determines the depth of recognition, and powers of recognition and identification help to determine the total quality of social action and political behavior.

---

14. Ali A. Mazrui, "Edmund Burke and Reflections on the Revolution in the Congo," in *On Heroes and Uhuru-Worship* (London: Longmans, 1967), pp. 3–4.

15. See Ali A. Mazrui, "Political Theory and National Involvement in East Africa" (Paper delivered at a regional conference on Politics, Philosophy, and Creative Literature, Makerere University College, August, 1968). See also *idem* and G. S. Engholm, "Rousseau and Intellectualized Populism in Africa," *Review of Politics*, XXX, no. 1 (January, 1968), 19–32.

Philosophical Leadership and the Future

The Anglo-American thinker Thomas Paine once said, "Government, like dress, is a badge of lost innocence." When man could no longer conduct himself free of greed and sin, he began to need government to control his behavior. In the case of Africa, it is not government but the necessity to theorize about it which is the badge of lost innocence.

It has been observed that members of traditional African societies

> feel their unity and perceive their common interests in symbols, and it is their attachment to these symbols which more than anything else gives their society cohesion and persistence. In the form of myths, fictions, dogmas, ritual, sacred places and persons, these symbols represent the unity and exclusiveness of the groups which respect them.

These analysts of traditional African approaches to politics have gone on to observe that members of these societies need have no objective knowledge of the forces determining their social organization or actuating their social behavior. The mystical values of the society evoke acceptance of the social order that goes far beyond the obedience exacted by the secular sanction of force.

> The social system is, as it were, removed to a mystical plane, where it figures as a system of sacred values beyond criticism or revision. Hence people will overthrow a bad king, but the kingship is never questioned. . . . The African does not see beyond the symbols; it might well be that if he understood the objective meaning, they would lose the power they have over him.[16]

Though insightful, this description is also exaggerated. The post-traditional African societies of the newly emergent territorial states have lost this innocence of mystical acceptance, and an entirely new basis of social cohesion and political legitimacy has to be created. Political man in Africa must therefore now be activated less by the impulse of a political culture steeped in antiquity and more by the influence of concepts derived from analysis. With such a change, political theory in the modern sense comes into being; but it is emphatically derived or abstracted from Africa's own sociopolitical experience or directly tested against that experience. Citizens no longer spontaneously feel that they belong, as they might have felt in the more established of the old tribal communities. They now need to be persuaded that they belong. Hence, there is a groping for new rationalizations, for new explanations, for new ultimate reasons.

The written word assumes a new meaning in this context. Even before

---

16. Meyer Fortes and E. E. Evans-Pritchard, eds., "Introduction," in *African Political Systems* (1940; reprint ed., London: Oxford University Press, 1955), p. 18.

the population has become fully literate, their new identity — and with it, their new social directions as determined by their leaders — has to be reduced to writing. It is of this that documentary radicalism in the first decade of independence has been made.

A further factor to be borne in mind is that writing in contemporary Africa is sometimes an institutionalization of personality. Oral literature in traditional Africa, the folk tales and folk songs, was a literature without authors. There was a collectivism about that kind of literature: no one knows who wrote such and such a song; it has been sung for generations. Major works of documentation now tend to seek identification with personal leadership. Institutions are weak. Personalities are needed to compensate for deficiencies in institutions; but personalities need additional strength to make them more effective as substitutes for fragile structures. The personality of a leader who captures his ideas in documents becomes a kind of institution. Documents serve both this purpose and the additional one of being a concretization of thought.

From this point of view Nyerere is almost Mr. Arusha Declaration, if not Mr. Ujamaa. And both Kwame Nkrumah and Milton Obote sought to stabilize their political immortality by writing exercises in political theory. Since then, the military has taken over in some African countries. Soldiers in Arab Africa have sometimes toyed with documentary radicalism. Pre-eminent among such experimentalists was Col. Gamal Abdel Nasser, who wrote *The Philosophy of the Revolution* not long after assuming power in Egypt. Soldiers in Black Africa have not normally been attracted to radicalism, documentary or otherwise.

The golden age of official documentary radicalism — in the sense of radical tracts written by or attributed to men in power — may well be entering its sunset in Anglophone Africa. Nkrumah and Obote were thrown out of office, Tom Mboya has been assassinated, and Jomo Kenyatta has withdrawn from literary exercises. Nyerere's *Ujamaa* remains part of the radical scene, but his successors may be less oriented toward the arts of practical philosophy.

Nonetheless, the utilization of the written word for purposes of working out desirable social directions is in the new Africa to stay. What may happen is the disestablishment of political philosophy — the removal of the arts of fundamental political theorizing from state monopoly. Political leaders need not be leaders of thought. Yet, in Tanzania, Zambia, and, until recently, Uganda, the top political leader has also been regarded as the leading guide in the realm of social thought.

This equation of practical leadership and philosophical leadership in politics is perhaps unique to the first decade of independence. In the years to follow, neither the fountain of radicalism nor the springs of literate reflection on the polity need lie anywhere near the sources of practical power and political authority.

[Part 2]

Cultural Engineering and Political Recruitment

[6]

Language Policy and
Political Participation

Little more than a year after Uganda's independence, the government decided that the British had not taught enough English in Uganda schools. Measures were announced to increase the amount of time to be spent teaching English in primary schools. In explaining the reasons for this increase, Uganda's minister of education drew attention to the country's lack of an indigenous national language. He said, "Whether we like it or not this does emphasise what a great task we have of building up a nation."[1] The minister envisaged the English language as one instrument to be used in working toward that goal. In January, 1965, the Uganda Teachers' Association followed this up with a call for the establishment of a language institute to train teachers to teach more effectively in the English language, "from Primary One." [2] Uganda was suggesting that Britain had inadequately prepared for the future of the language in these parts. By planning to increase the use of English in nation-building, Uganda was declaring its intention to utilize the imperial language in the consolidation of the country's African independence.

In Tanzania, on the other hand, the imperial language seemed to be on the decline. A combination of cultural nationalism and socialistic egalitarianism was making Swahili a strong rival of English in certain sectors of national life. Swahili was the language of the people; it was the language of the common man. Identifying the language with the people aroused feelings of cultural nationalism; identifying it with the common man involved socialistic equality. By January, 1967, the policy of squeezing out English in major areas of governmental business had become more explicit. On January 5, the *Nationalist* (Dar es Salaam) reported Vice-President Kawawa's directive that Kiswahili was to be used for all governmental business and that the unnecessary use of English "or any other foreign languages" was to cease forthwith. The instructions were too optimistic, but they did signify a decisive state in Tanzania's national language policy.

Kenya's situation was more complex. It is sometimes too readily taken for

1. *Uganda Argus* (Kampala), December 16, 1963.
2. *Ibid.*, January 11, 1965.

granted that to adopt the Swahili language is to adopt the Swahili culture. Although Swahili culture does of course include the Swahili language, it is possible to adopt the language without adopting other aspects of culture. This brings us to the fundamental anomaly of Kenya's aesthetic situation. In terms of general dissemination, Swahili culture is more widespread in Tanzania than in Kenya. Kenya has a narrow area in which aesthetic achievement in Swahili is concentrated, but elsewhere in the country it is the Swahili language as a neutral medium of communication rather than the Swahili culture as a rich vessel of heritage which has spread. Nevertheless, it is Kenya, and not Zanzibar or Tanganyika, that is the home of Swahili aesthetic genius. Most of the classical masterpieces of Swahili poetry have come from the Kenya coast — from Lamu and its sister islands, from Mombasa and farther south. Tanzania's contribution to Swahili literature is of much more recent origin — attaining a new height of achievement in the 1950s with Shaaban Robert. But the home of the older poetic traditions of Swahili and the source of most of the great epics has been the Kenya coast.

This situation may, of course, be only transient. Before long Kenya may "nationalize" the aesthetic achievements of Lamu. Countries build up a shared cultural heritage precisely by nationalizing the local accomplishments of different regions. As Swahili becomes more established in the rest of Kenya, some of the coastal classics of the eighteenth and nineteenth centuries are almost certain to be accorded a national cultural status. For the time being, however, the basic aesthetic anomaly remains: the country that has produced some of Swahili culture's greatest achievements has only a simplified version of the language in most of its regions.

Language and Transtribal Leadership

A major difference between politics in African countries and politics in countries with more developed political systems is the simple fact that in Africa personalities are more important. A pre-eminence of personalities is a pre-eminence of individual leadership. Although Africa's experience in the 1960s has demonstrated how ineffectual individuals can be in the face of certain types of problems, it remains true that in Africa major changes in political arrangements or administrative machinery can be made by the simple decision of a couple of men at the top, civilian or military. That such a decision can as easily be negated not long afterward by the counterintervention of other leaders is a further indication of how easily change can be brought about by individual personalities. If small elites are therefore of such importance in African conditions, a discussion of language and leadership is pertinent.

There are times when a national language is necessary in order to make national leadership possible. If Jomo Kenyatta had spoken no language other than Kigikuyu, there is no doubt that his national stature would have suffered.

Members of other tribes would have found it difficult to accept him as their own leader. Julius Nyerere would also have had a reduced authority among the populace if his speeches had been delivered only in the language of the Wazanaki. Kwame Nkrumah would hardly have aroused widespread national enthusiasm at home for so long if he had made every state utterance in the Nzima language, intelligible to other Ghanaians only through interpretation. In short, effective national leadership in Africa demands the command of a transtribal language.[3]

Can an African language ever be tribally neutral? At first sight East Africa seems to provide convincing evidence that this is possible. Swahili is, after all, an African language. It is not associated with any particular tribe. Only a small minority of those who speak Swahili speak it as a first language, and the small native Swahili-speaking population does not constitute a "tribe" in the usual sociological sense. The group is an ethnically or culturally mixed community of the East African coast, not politically strong enough to arouse the linguistic jealousies of other groups and too diffuse to constitute a "tribe." The Swahili language does not suffer from the handicap under which Hausa and Luganda have labored — that of being the native language of a powerful and sometimes politically distrusted ethnic group. It could, it would seem, be safely classified as "tribally neutral."

Nevertheless, the "tribal neutrality" of Swahili is not absolute. One small but significant qualification must be made. Although Swahili cannot be associated with one particular tribe, it can be associated with a particular collection of tribes. Swahili is a Bantu language. Until recently, this did not seem to have much relevance; but, in the controversy over the establishment of Swahili as the national language which has been recurring in the Kenya press since the first quarter of 1967, many of the African critics of Swahili have been people with Nilotic names. It is possible that this is a coincidence. Furthermore, some of the so-called Nilotic names might be the pen names of non-Nilotes. Nevertheless, it is conceivable that in at least some Nilotic circles Swahili is suspect because it is a Bantu language.

If this is indeed the case in Kenya, it presents an impressive contrast to the situation in Uganda, where Nilotes are among the greatest friends of Swahili. The future of Swahili in Uganda is perhaps brighter than it has been for more than two decades. A major reason for this is the relative political decline of the Baganda, notwithstanding Obote's ouster; the Baganda — fellow Bantu people — were the greatest antagonists of Swahili within Uganda. Swahili was taught in Uganda schools for some time before World War II; it disappeared from the schools mainly because it was regarded as a serious rival to Luganda.

From 1966 to 1971 the Baganda were under a political eclipse. It was unlikely

---

3. This point is also discussed in Ali A. Mazrui, "The English Language and Political Consciousness in British Colonial Africa," *Journal of Modern African Studies*, IV, no. 3 (1966), 661–76.

all along that this eclipse would last for too long. This large and energetic group was bound to reclaim a little of its former influence. But it is unlikely that the influence recovered will ever approach what the group formerly enjoyed. Nor is it likely that Luganda will be permitted to attain the status of a national language in the foreseeable future. What is conceivable is a situation in which the non-Baganda demand greater recognition of an alternative ''language of the common man.'' The only serious candidate for such a title is Swahili. It has already penetrated some Uganda areas outside Buganda and is on its way toward conquering all Uganda towns and cities. Swahili has been crucial in the Uganda trade-union movement. It has also been professionally important in the Uganda sectors of the East African Common Services Organization. Kenya's export of manpower to Uganda has constituted a form of linguistic penetration.

In addition, Swahili is the official language of the army and the police in Uganda. Anywhere in present-day Africa, a language that has the support of the armed forces has an ally of some stature. Nor is the role of the soldier in the dissemination or consolidation of language unique to Africa. The vulgarization of Latin by soldiers in premedieval Europe was part of the genesis of the French language. It is conceivable that the utilization of Swahili in the armed forces in East Africa will have comparable long-term cultural repercussions. However, what is of more immediate significance for the future of Swahili in Uganda is that its strongest opponents are currently in decline, while some of its friends are in positions of renewed influence and power. The friends range from Batoro working women to Lugbara soldiers; the opponents are the native speakers of Luganda.

Within the Uganda government there has been an altogether different kind of interest in Swahili. To some extent Milton Obote was the Nnamdi Azikiwe of nationalism in East Africa. Azikiwe was involved in the growth of nationalism in both Ghana and Nigeria; Obote was a founding member of the Kenya African Union, as well as a major figure in Uganda's independence movement. Among the aftereffects of Obote's years in Kenya was his lingering special interest in Swahili. In 1962 a resolution of the Annual Conference of the Uganda People's Congress urged greater use of Swahili, and the following year Prime Minister Obote reaffirmed this advocacy.[4] A major stumbling block at the time was the attitude of the Baganda. In 1966 Obote subdued the Baganda, but he was still wary about giving official status to Swahili outside the armed forces. It was not until his installation as chancellor of Makerere University in 1970 that Obote announced his government's plan to introduce Swahili as a subject in Uganda schools. Four months later Obote's government was overthrown by a military coup. It seems unlikely that this will adversely affect the future

---

4. See Joseph S. Nye, Jr., *Pan-Africanism and East African Integration* (Cambridge, Mass.: Harvard University Press, 1966), pp. 66–69.

of Swahili in Uganda; Major General Amin and other members of the armed forces are among the most enthusiastic supporters of Swahili.

Language and Cultural Integration

On balance the evidence would seem to suggest that East Africa, in the process of dismantling its inherited economic institutions, is promoting greater cultural intercourse. Although some of the evidence is rudimentary, it is certainly not without significance. New, regionally conceived books for schools are being devised — for example, the major study *Zamani: A Survey of East African History*. Regionally shared broadcasting programs are in evidence — for instance, those promoted by organizations like the old East African Institute of Social and Cultural Affairs. Regional seminars and conferences are on the increase, such as those arranged by the East African Academy or the three universities of East Africa. The University of East Africa, while it lasted, was a major instrument of cultural and intellectual integration. The academy, in a more restricted way, has also served this purpose, as have magazines like *Transition* and *East Africa Journal*, *Mawazo* from Makerere, university literary magazines, and the independent literary medium *Zuka* of Oxford University Press. Most of these instruments of cultural integration serve only those with a high level of literacy. At the grass-roots level other media of cultural dissemination again seem to be in demand.

Once more, Swahili projects itself as the most important medium of cultural dissemination in a wide scope. Both *Mawazo* ("reflections"), and *Zuka* ("emerge") bear Swahili names; furthermore, *Zuka* aspires to be a bilingual medium, publishing creative writing and literary criticism in both English and Swahili. Such experiments give added weight to demand for the spread of Swahili as a cultural medium.

President Leopold Senghor of Senegal has often talked about the need for an African contribution to universal civilization.[5] Africa can make such a contribution without using an African language. African poets and novelists using French and English have added to the total sum of world culture. However, full African involvement in world culture requires more than an African use of French and English in producing novels and plays. It is not enough to make Chinua Achebe and Wole Soyinka available to British readers in England; it is also necessary to make Shakespeare available to the African. Full African integration into world culture must involve taking cultural Africa to the rest of the world as well as bringing the rest of the world to Africa. European languages should be used to project Africa abroad, but African languages should also be used to make foreign masterpieces accessible locally.

---

5. See, for example, Leopold Senghor, "Negritude and the Concept of Universal Civilisation," *Présence Africaine*, XVIII, no. 46 (Second Quarter, 1963), 310.

Here again the place of Swahili in East Africa is distinctive. Because it is the most widely understood language in the region, it has tended to be the first one used in any experimental translation of a world classic into an African medium. The first works of universal civilization to be rendered into African media were, perhaps inevitably, religious. The Bible was available quite early in several African languages, but the first translation of the Quran, the Ahmadiyya translation, was in Swahili. It is to be followed by a more orthodox Sunni translation, also in Swahili. The first Shakespearean play to be rendered into an East African language is, as we have indicated, Julius Nyerere's translation of *Julius Caesar* into Swahili. The first masterpiece of European political philosophy to find expression in an East African language is the Swahili translation of Machiavelli's *The Prince* by Fred Kamoga and Ralph Tanner. Other experiments have followed. An introduction in Swahili to the study of economics, Peter Temu's *Uchumi Bora*, has now been published by Oxford University Press; and a similar introduction to political science is under discussion. These are all instances in which Swahili has been used to bring a piece of world civilization into Africa through the medium of an African language. Tanzania's S. S. Mushi has carried this enterprise further with his translations of *Macbeth* and other Shakespearean plays into Swahili. President Nyerere's translation of *The Merchant of Venice* is also a landmark.

There is sometimes a tendency to regard translating as an activity distinct from creative work. This is a false dichotomy. The translation of world masterpieces into African languages is bound to enrich the creative versatility of the African languages. Swahili's use as a theatrical medium, for example, can be enriched both by writing new Swahili plays and by translating foreign classics into Swahili. Everyone agrees that the former kind of endeavor is to be vigorously encouraged; but the growth of Swahili as a literary medium would be slowed down if one constantly had to wait for an original Swahili masterpiece to appear. Nyerere's translation of *Julius Caesar* has contributed more to the potential of Swahili as a dramatic medium than any original work in Swahili which has so far emerged.

Literary creativity in East Africa is therefore not simply a matter of writing original works; it is also a matter of enriching the versatility of African languages as literary media. In this latter enterprise the work of translating foreign classics into an African medium can be a significant contribution in its own right.

Language and Ideology

It is not merely with products of the creative imagination that language has a relation of intimacy. It is also with works of the reasoning intellect. In translating Shakespeare's *The Merchant of Venice* and *Julius Caesar*, Nyerere was involved in work of the creative imagination; but, in writing his piece of political theory entitled "Democracy and the Party System," he was involved in work of the reasoning intellect. It is to the latter kind of activity and its relationship to language that we must now turn.

In the sporadic controversy on language in the Kenya press, it was suggested that African socialism would have received greater acceptance if it had been propagated in Swahili. The statement was originally attributed to Peter Temu, a Tanzanian lecturer at the University of Nairobi, but later discussions in the press raised doubts as to whether Temu had indeed made the remark. And the *East African Standard* said in an editorial that his authorship was in doubt.[6]

The question of which language should be nationally promoted cannot be regarded as irrelevant to the consolidation of socialism. The relevance lies in two broad areas: in the necessary link which exists between words and ideas, and in considerations of class-formation in African countries.

The movement to evolve a distinctively African socialism is, in fact, a quest for ideological uniqueness. In general, this is more difficult to attain through an international language than through a local one. Ideas have to be expressed in words. In the English language, for example, the word *socialism* carries so many European connotations that it is difficult to make the word appear distinctive in African conditions. But say *Ujamaa*, and a whole new world of subtle associations and connotations is suddenly revealed. Nothing could have given Nyerere's socialism a more strikingly African ring than that simple Swahili label which he gave it. Nyerere was using an old Swahili word in a new context. All the subtle associations of bonds of kinship, tribal hospitality, and welfare obligations of the extended family were compressed within that single Swahili expression. African socialism in Tanzania acquired an extra Africanness by the simple device of bearing an African name. No English word could possibly have achieved the same result. Nyerere, in his pamphlet on *Ujamaa*, added to the Africanness of his socialism by using an old Swahili adage to illustrate the ethic of hard work and of opposition to parasitism in Tanzania's ideology: "Mgeni siku mbili; siku ya tatu mpe jembe [Treat your guest as a guest for two days; on the third day, give him a hoe]." The Tanzanian leader was, in fact, using one Swahili concept to qualify the implications of another. The concept of *Ujamaa*, suggesting the obligations of kinship and the extended family, could be used to legitimize being supported by one's relatives; a person might go to his kinsman and exploit his hospitality indefinitely. So Nyerere qualified this notion of kinship with the notion of requiring a guest to help in the *shamba* on the third day after his arrival. Kinship hospitality must be qualified by an antiparasitic ethic.[7]

---

6. See "Swahili and English" (editorial), *East African Standard* (Nairobi), February 23, 1967. See also the report of a debate on the question at the University College, Nairobi, in *ibid.*, February 22, 1967.

7. See Julius Nyerere, "*Ujamaa* — The Basis of African Socialism" (1962), in *Freedom and Unity — Uhuru na Umoja* (Dar es Salaam: Oxford University Press, 1966), pp. 162–71.

If Tanzanians continue to utilize Swahili concepts in sophisticated political theorizing, it is to Tanzania, then, that one should look for Africa's most distinctive ideological formulations. The policies propagated are not necessarily the most original, but they might well be the most African in their idiom of rationalization. If African socialism is a quest for ideological nativeness, Swahili provides a better medium than does English.

Another point of contact between socialism and the choice of a national language lies in class-formation. There is no doubt that the English language has been a stratifying agent in countries formerly ruled by Britain. Benjamin Disraeli once imaginatively demonstrated how economic factors had divided England into "two nations," the rich and the poor. Many years later an Indian governmental commission suggested that the English language had the same effect in India that economic factors had had in Disraeli's England. In the words of the commission:

> Use of English as such divided the people into two nations, the few who govern and the many who are governed, the one unable to talk the language of the other and mutually uncomprehending. This is a negation of democracy.[8]

English has had much the same effect in many parts of Africa. Where the national language is English, the choice of leaders is inevitably restricted; it becomes anomalous to have a national leader who does not speak the national language. In a country like Tanzania, however, national leaders can be recruited from a wider sector of the society. The first vice-president, Abeid Karume, spoke no English; and many important TANU figures in high office are not fluent in the English language. It used to be said that every American is a potential millionaire. This was always a gross exaggeration, but it was a useful portrayal of America as a land of capitalistic opportunity. Today it can be rhetorically claimed that every Tanzanian is a potential TANU leader. This, too, is a gross exaggeration, but it helps to indicate the range of egalitarian opportunities in Tanzania. Tanzania's social structure is more egalitarian than that of its neighbors partly because the sector from which leadership is recruited is bigger; and that sector of political recruitment is large and varied partly because the national language, Swahili, is not an elite language.

The situation would, of course, have been different if Tanzania had had to rely more exclusively on English as the language of transtribal leadership. Of the European languages, British English is perhaps the one most closely associated with class distinctions. Alan S. C. Ross opened his famous essay "U and Non-U" with the following observation:

> Today, in 1956, the English class system is essentially tripartite — there exist

---

8. Quoted in Rupert Emerson, *From Empire to Nation: The Rise to Self-Assertion of Asian and African Peoples* (Cambridge, Mass.: Harvard University Press, 1960), p. 137.

an upper, a middle, and a lower class. It is solely by its language that the upper class is clearly marked off from the others.[9]

There is an element of satirical hyperbole in this, but there is no doubt that British English lends itself to class snobbery. Some of that snobbery, duly transformed, accompanied the English language to Africa.

Considerations such as these lend plausibility to the assertion that the cause of African socialism in East Africa might conceivably be served better by Swahili than by English. If Swahili were to replace English as the exclusive medium of national values, a major price would have to be paid; and socialism bought at such a price might not be worth it. All we have sought to demonstrate here is the plausibility of the assertion that Swahili might be a less ambiguous ally of socialism in East Africa than English can hope to be.

National Languages of the Future

East Africa presents a unique situation from the point of view of studying the problems attending the quest for a national language. Here are three countries which had achieved a degree of political marriage. Few regions of the world have been more closely integrated economically or have come so near to federation. Although each of the three countries has a distinct linguistic situation, there is a high potential for a continuing cultural interplay.

The old British policy of indirect rule had the greatest success in Uganda. The paramount aim of that policy was to preserve a good deal of the local African culture, including local African languages. Paradoxically, in the process of preserving local traditions, the British helped to ensure the country's dependence on the English language. Therefore, although Uganda is the most traditionalist of the three East African countries, it is the most dependent on the English language in its national activities.

As for the future of Swahili in Uganda, prospects are, as we indicated, brighter now than they have been for some time. However, one can anticipate that Swahili will become in time the second language in Uganda rather than the national language. The status of English as a national language is not seriously being challenged. What might be challenged is the status of Luganda as the second most important medium of communication.

In Tanzania there is a different paradox. One of the arguments against Swahili that has been brought up in the controversy in the Kenya press is that the language is a child of Arab imperialism. To some extent this is true; but Swahili is less a child of Arab imperialism than English is a child of British imperialism.

---

9. Alan S. C. Ross, "U and Non-U: An Essay in Sociological Linguistics," in *The Importance of Language*, ed. Max Black (Englewood Cliffs, N.J.: Prentice-Hall, 1962), p. 91.

Unlike the British, the Arabs did not impose their own language on East Africa; they merely influenced the development of a Bantu language. Further, the Arabic influence on Swahili is almost entirely on vocabulary. It is conceivable that in another three decades Swahili would have absorbed almost as many words from the English language as it has absorbed from Arabic. Nevertheless, the Arabs as a neo-imperial community had a crucial influence on the growth of Swahili. If this is reason enough to suspect Swahili, then Tanzania is a linguistic anomaly. Nowhere in East Africa is there a greater cultural attachment to Swahili than in Zanzibar. In fact, it was in revolutionary Zanzibar that Swahili was first proclaimed an official national language as opposed to English. Zanzibar anticipated mainland Tanzania in a total commitment to Swahili. Yet, Zanzibar is also the most anti-Arab part of East Africa.

On the other hand, it was in Tanganyika that British colonial rule had its smoothest and mildest conclusion. The nationalist movement in colonial Tanganyika sometimes seemed to be almost Anglophile. Kenya, on the other hand, had a violent anti-British insurrection; and Uganda had moments of rioting and boycotting against this or that aspect of British rule. Yet Anglophile Tanganyika has now become, in the area of language policy, anti-English.

Kenya's linguistic situation is of a different order. The country has not yet been fully conquered by Swahili but has felt its impact strongly enough to be forced into the agonies of cultural reappraisal. Kenya has produced some of the classics of Swahili. What remains to be seen is whether the country as a whole will convert them into a national heritage. The chances are that Swahili will become the language of Kenya, but there are areas of uncertainty yet to be eliminated. In 1969 Ronald Ngala once again raised in Parliament the question of whether Swahili should be made a parliamentary language. Kenyatta has also played with this idea in public. Officially, the Kenya government is not yet ready for such action.

This diversity of possibilities in the linguistic situations of East Africa makes the area fascinating for a student of social movements in search of a national medium of expression. The anomalies, the outbursts of creative experimentation, the agonies of having to make a choice, and the debates on desirability all combine to give this region a unique potential for the understanding of man's linguistic sensibilities.

[7]

Language Policy and
Political Penetration

The goals of language policy in relation to social engineering in East Africa are national integration and social integration. National integration is a process of merging subgroup identities into a shared sense of national consciousness. In Africa the creation of a supratribal or supraethnic loyalty to a national homeland is the goal of the integrative process in this national sense.

Social integration, on the other hand, is not the merger of tribe with tribe but the process by which the gaps between the elite and the masses, the town and the countryside, the privileged and the underprivileged, are gradually narrowed. Social integration is not necessarily a process by which the difference in income between the richest man and poorest man in the country is minimized. The absolute difference might remain the same, or even increase, without implying that there has been no integration. However, if the distance between the top and the bottom of the curve of income difference remains the same, the slope of the curve should be gradual and not steep. In a country where there are only very rich people and very poor people and none in between, there is a minimal degree of social integration. However, if there are between the pauper and the millionaire many people with intermediate rates of income in a gradual gradation, the social integrative process has made progress. We can have a well-integrated traditional society in this social sense of "integration," as well as a well-integrated modern society; but the prerequisites are different in each case. A well-integrated traditional society has to be largely egalitarian, with no major difference in income between the richest and the poorest. A well-integrated modern society need not be egalitarian, but the process of differentiation of structures and specialization of functions must be sufficiently advanced to have created a gradual slope of incomes from the top to the bottom.

Can a society move from traditional social integration to modern social integration without passing through the agonies of major gaps in income and life style between the new elite and the masses, the town and the countryside? Can it move from social equality (the basis of traditional integration) to social differentiation (the basis of modern integration) without passing through a stage of convulsive disparities? This is one of the most agonizing dilemmas of present-day Africa.

The place of the English language is critical in the problems of national integration and social integration in East Africa. A case can be made for the proposition that in relation to national integration in Uganda or Kenya the English language is functional, whereas in relation to social integration the English language is dysfunctional. We shall examine these two parts of the proposition in the course of the analysis.

Language Distribution

A survey of the use and teaching of language in East Africa was started in 1967, committed to compiling language data for Uganda, Ethiopia, Kenya, Tanzania, and Zambia. The survey was funded by a special grant from the Ford Foundation. A regional council, with academic and political representation from all the countries concerned, was entrusted with policy-making issues within the terms of the Ford Foundation grant. The Uganda survey, under the director-ship of Peter Ladefoged, and the Ethiopia survey, directed by Charles Ferguson, were completed in 1969. The Kenya survey, under the directorship of Wilfred Whiteley, and the Tanzania survey, started later in 1969 under the directorship of Edgar Polomé, are still in progress. The Zambia survey has been suspended.

A general picture of the distribution of languages in East Africa and the number of Africans who are bilingual or trilingual is emerging as a result of this survey. Uganda was the first to be surveyed, and the report has recently been published.[1] From the point of view of cultural engineering, the figures pertaining to the spread of Luganda and Swahili in the country as a whole are of particular interest. Preliminary indications are that Swahili may be more widely understood in Uganda than was previously assumed, though in that country it is predominantly a language of men. That significantly more Uganda men than women have been exposed to Swahili and have learned to use it for specialized purposes is due in part to the phenomenon of men's mobility in relation to job opportunities and the whole phenomenon of the rural-urban continuum.

However, although Swahili is more widely understood than was assumed, and although its political respectability has risen as a result of the decline in Buganda's influence, Swahili is not for the time being a serious candidate for Uganda's national language. Luyimbazi Zake, the minister of education, was speaking more like a Muganda nationalist than a social scientist when he said in Parliament during a debate on the new constitution in 1967 that Swahili was as foreign to Uganda as Gujarati. But each new constitution has had no alternative but to adopt English as the national language. This is the role English is intended to fill in the process of national integration.

---

1. See Peter Ladefoged et al., *Language in Uganda* (Nairobi: Oxford University Press, 1971).

The decision to make English the national language in no way implies that it is the most widely understood language in Uganda. Luganda and Lunyoro are spoken by the greatest number of people; but the problem of fair political representation and ethnic balance in political recruitment would be dangerously aggravated if one of these languages was adopted instead of English. As President Obote once put it:

> [If] we adopted [either Luganda or Lunyoro] as the official language for administrative purposes or legislation, some of us [would] have to go out of Government. I, for instance, would not be able to speak in Parliament in Luganda, neither could I do so in Lunyoro, and I think more than half the present National Assembly members would have to quit. The areas we now represent would not like to have just any person who speaks Luganda to represent them. They would feel unrepresented. So, there again, we find no alternative to English.[2]

Fairness in political representation and balance of recruitment sometimes dictate that a language which is uniformly lesser known throughout the country should have priority over a language which is very well known by one section of the community but not known at all by others. Hindi has suffered from the same disability as a projected national language of India. The opponents of Hindi felt that native speakers of the language would have an unfair advantage over others in important sections of recruitment. English, by being foreign to everyone, is a shared handicap. In situations of this kind, distributive justice becomes a question of distributive disability. A linguistic handicap uniformly distributed throughout the country becomes an important condition of political stability and a possible basis of closer integration. In terms of fluency in English, the Baganda probably have an advantage over other Ugandans. Certainly in absolute terms, and possibly in relative terms, too, the Baganda are better educated than most of their compatriots. Disparities of advantage would be compounded, however, if Luganda were to become the national language of Uganda.

Although English has become so very convenient for the task of national integration in Uganda, the lack of a grass-roots language for such a purpose puts Uganda at a disadvantage when compared with either Tanzania or Kenya. National integration is not simply a case of fair distribution of advantages and disadvantages among ethnic groups, although this might be a *sine qua non*. National integration also presupposes a high degree of socioeconomic intercourse between the different ethnic groups, a high degree of authoritative penetration from the center of the society to the periphery, and access of the periphery to the center. These variables of socioeconomic intercourse between groups

---

2. A. Milton Obote, "Language and National Identification" (Opening Address, seminar on Mass Media and Linguistic Communications in East Africa, organized by the East African Academy and the East African Institute of Social and Cultural Affairs, held at Makerere University College, Kampala, April, 1967), *East Africa Journal*, IV, no. 1 (April, 1967), 4.

and political intercourse between the populace and those in authority demand or actually mean greater communication. English is for the time being limited in its capacity to provide this kind of intercommunication involving the grass roots.

Socioeconomic intercourse between groups by way of trade, marketing, and cooperative and labor organization is served more effectively by Luganda and Swahili than by English. This is one area in which the success of English in national integration and its failure in social integration become indistinguishable. English as an intertribal language among the educated is clearly nationally integrative; but, for intertribal communication at the grass-roots level, English in intrinsically and hopelessly ill equipped to meet the challenge.

The Media and Political Penetration

Language is of course an important factor in determining the degree of political penetration that a government can achieve. How effectively and in what comparable terms can the news media, for example, reach different parts of the countryside? The national program on Radio Tanzania is in Swahili, ensuring a shared exposure to radio programs by audiences in different areas of the country. The national program on Radio Uganda is in English and can be heard (not always well) in different parts of the country. But do the people in these different areas listen to it? Outside the towns, a high proportion of those who listen to Radio Uganda's national program may, in fact, be employees of the government. Since the national radio program requires a certain standard of education in the English language, and since a high proportion of those who have attained such a standard go into government and related services, political penetration by national programs on the radio is, to a great extent, intragovernmental. It is broadcast by governmental employees under the Ministry of Information for the inadvertent benefit of other governmental employees under the Ministries of Education, Labor, Regional Administration, and others.

There is, of course, an element of exaggeration in this description. A national program in the English language in an African country may indeed have a mixed audience in the towns, but outside the towns most of the listeners are either foreigners (like European hotel managers and Asian *dukawallas*) or people connected with the government. In Uganda, where the European managers might prefer to listen to the BBC and Asian *dukawallas* might have a greater partiality for the All-India Radio, the rural audience might therefore basically be administrators and civic leaders educated enough to understand programs in the English language and isolated enough to feel starved of Kampala news and of sophisticated radio discussions.

The Uganda government is aware of the limited utility of the national radio program as an instrument of political penetration. The result is that the number of languages broadcast on Radio Uganda has increased since independence from five (English, Luganda, Lunyoro, Ateso, and Lwo) to eighteen. This certainly enables the government to reach different audiences quite effectively in regard to at least some matters.

There are two costs, however. One is that the period of time devoted to each program is necessarily limited to a couple of hours a day or less for a particular language. It is not practical to employ a full-time staff to keep programs on the air all day in a language that is restricted to one part of the country. There would also be complications in having over a dozen wavelengths constantly in use. Instead, Radio Uganda limits itself to two channels — the Red and the Blue — which are shared by well over a dozen languages, including English, for a period of about thirty-six hours of combined broadcasting time each day.

The second cost in having a large number of vernacular programs instead of one national one is that the programs tend to become less national in perspective. The medium may not be the message, but it certainly affects the message profoundly.[3] Nationalizing what is sectional becomes difficult in a situation of such sectionalized media. A news bulletin that is broadcast in a language understood all over the country has a different bias from one that can be understood only by a localized linguistic group, especially if the group is in a remote and less sophisticated area. Even a bulletin which is consciously intended to be on "national news" often becomes regionalized in perspective over Radio Uganda when it is given in a regional language. Radio Uganda is not committed to a policy of having news broadcasts translated into the fourteen or more languages with exactly the same order of news emphasis in each of them. The translators and announcers are often journalistic artists catering to a particular taste. Moreover, members of Parliament and ministers from a particular region have a way of inviting the interest of the Ministry of Information in their activities so that news of these activities will be broadcast to their own areas. The same parliamentary debate might receive a different emphasis in a Lugbara news bulletin from what it receives in one in Luganda. The most important speech for one region may be different from the most important for another. A speech made by the member of Parliament from a Lugbara constituency may be mentioned in the Lugbara newscast but not in the Luganda one.

In many ways the news is the radio feature that is most easily nationalized. If such difficulties are encountered in broadcasting the news, one can imagine how much more difficult it is to keep other radio programs from becoming relatively localized in interest. Special talks and cultural features often become narrowly restricted in interest to the linguistico-cultural group to whom they are addressed. Even in promoting local cultural activity, Radio Uganda as now constituted poses problems for cultural engineering as an attempt to nationalize the aesthetics of sectionalism. As President Milton Obote put it:

---

3. See Marshall McLuhan, *Understanding Media: The Extensions of Man* (New York: New American Library, 1964).

> Since the Radio began broadcasting these various languages, there has been a new spirit in Uganda, simple composition of songs, dance teams and various competitions around the countryside. Every village is eager to surpass the other in its cultural activities with a view that one day Radio Uganda recording vans will pass around the village and record the songs and the poems of a particular group. We find this useful although we are creating a problem of how to coordinate these activities in the future.[4]

Although a case can be made for the desirability of catering to local biases and local tastes, in such situations the radio is handicapped as an instrument for promoting a national perspective on the different events affecting the country. This is an important handicap in countries where there are relatively few alternative media for such a task. The written word is not as yet widely disseminated, or even capable of being widely read, in the rural areas. Newspapers in the English language are a phenomenon of the sizable city and a luxury to be enjoyed mainly by the intelligentsia and the subintelligentsia. The radio could be, and often is, the most important medium of political penetration. But its role in nationalizing what is sectional in political outlooks is circumscribed by its reliance on local vernaculars and by the resultant catering to local biases in taste and perspective.

Kenya's experience illustrates different aspects of the relationship between cultural engineering and the mass media. As we have observed, the more common broadcasting problems in Africa are those arising from the presence of many languages in the same country. However, the problem can sometimes be one of having one language but different subcultures. For example, only a minority of Kenyans, concentrated along the coast, speak Swahili as a mother tongue. About twenty years ago there already were radio programs in Kenya in the Swahili language, but hardly any of them catered to this Swahili subculture. It was perhaps taken for granted that the national programs from Nairobi that were broadcast in Swahili would meet the needs of these coastal people. However, the Nairobi programs were mainly directed to nonactive speakers of the language in the interior of the country. The language was the same, but the cultural universe — for example, the form of musical expression — was different. Kenyans of the coast often tuned in to the Voice of Zanzibar or the Voice of Dar es Salaam, whose programs were culturally more akin to their interests.

In order to remedy this situation, a number of coastal Kenyans in the early 1950s founded the "Sauti ya Mvita" radio programs, which were broadcast from Mombasa. Although the authorities encouraged them in this venture, first, by making available the basic broadcasting equipment at Cable and Wireless coastal headquarters and, later, by offering other kinds of help and facilities, the "Sauti ya Mvita" was started essentially as a volunteer project. I was one of those who volunteered to run the "Sauti ya Mvita" in those initial days. In addition to taking part in discussion programs, I also had a regular

---

4. Obote, "Language and National Identification," p. 6.

half-hour feature in which I read fictional stories I had written. The readings were accompanied by music from my record library. Indeed, "Listeners' Choice," a program of recorded music, also relied quite heavily on my own disc collection.[5] As a strictly regional enterprise, the program was a complete success; it was then adopted by the government as a regional program with its own studios and equipment on the coast.

As independence approached, the issue of centralizing the broadcasting medium was raised. Should all the broadcasting in Kenya be from Nairobi? If so, would this not bring about a return of the old situation in which Nairobi broadcast in Swahili, but only for those who spoke it as a second language, causing the native speakers to tune in to Dar es Salaam?

The Ministry of Information in independent Kenya has done much to avert this danger by a compromise between the demands of centralization and the demands of regional tastes and biases. "Sauti ya Mvita" is dead, and there are no autonomous broadcasting facilities on the coast or in any other region; but within the National Swahili Service different tastes are catered to. A broadcast may include a recording of the drums of Kwale, a political biography of Mzee Kenyatta, a Christian sermon, an Arabic tune imitating Cairo's Farid el Atrash, a Swahili pop song of the Nairobi dancing halls, and classical poetry from Lamu. The same language is used in all of this material, but the tastes that are represented are diverse. This integration is one approach toward effective political penetration on a nation-wide scale. It is also an approach toward the gradual standardization of Swahili in Kenya, which in time might lead to the homogenization of culture. This last is directly related to the broader goal of national integration. The making of a nation involves processes within processes in a multidimensional enterprises.

The centralization of broadcasting in Kenya has not merely been a matter of concentrating the planning and mechanics in Nairobi and merging the Swahili subprograms. The centralization has also involved a drastic reduction in the number of languages used in broadcasting. Tanzania has gone even further, limiting itself to Swahili and English. Uganda is the only one of the three countries which has felt the need to multiply its vernacular programs since independence. As President Obote explained:

> I am in Government and I have to take political feelings of the people into account in formulating policies. I would not say that all fourteen languages on the Radio are necessary . . . but we would find it exceedingly difficult to inform the Karamojong in Luganda or any other language except their own. . . . We want

---

5. The distinction between Swahili as a culture and Swahili as a language is also discussed in Ali A. Mazrui, "The National Language Question in East Africa," *East Africa Journal*, IV, no. 3 (June, 1967), 12–19; and in *idem*, "Islam and the English Language in East and West Africa" (Paper delivered at an international seminar on Problems of Multilingualism in Eastern Africa, organized by the International African Institute, held at University College, Dar es Salaam, December 15–18, 1968).

to inform the people of Uganda . . . so we have Karamojong broadcast on the Radio.[6]

The countries of East Africa are faced not only with the task of eliminating illiteracy but also with that of preventing those who have learned to read and write from relapsing into illiteracy. The ability to write, if it is minimal, can all too easily be lost if it is not utilized. The ability to recognize words and understand a passage can also disappear if the newly literate person has nothing on which to practice his reading.

A newspaper is one answer to this problem. UNESCO was interested in establishing newspapers in rural Uganda, partly to arrest the process of relapse in the newly literate and partly to provide the villager with news and information relevant to his needs and interests. Catering to local biases was precisely the object of the exercise, but in this case this goal was justified by the ambition to maintain a literate countryside. A UNESCO specialist came to Uganda, and the Makerere Institute of Social Research set up a consultative committee to help in assessing the feasibility of creating rural newspapers. The idea was not to provide official government handouts but to attempt to produce simple, relevant news sheets, entertaining as well as informative. What was needed was a product that would attract local interest, compelling the literate to read.

Ideally, the newspapers were to be privately owned, controlled by individuals sensitive to local interests and local needs. However, because of the limited size of readership in most of the local languages, it has become questionable whether it is economical — either financially or in terms of effort — to have a newspaper in Ateso, for example, or even Lunyoro, for any length of time. The lack in Uganda of an intertribal lingua franca capable of being used for a simple newspaper with a wide rural readership is one of the stumbling blocks encountered in experiments of this nature. Uganda has no national paper in an African language like those found in Kenya and Tanzania. The newly literate in Kenya and Tanzania, partly through Swahili newspapers like *Baraza*, *Taifa Leo*, and *Ulimwengu*, are partially safeguarded against the risk of relapsing into illiteracy. In Uganda, on the other hand, the only African languages that are journalistically viable are sectional, and sometimes politically sensitive, ones. The arrest of illiteracy through a local-language newspaper is possible for those who speak Luganda, but for most others this solution is impossible except in terms of brief experimental news sheets from time to time.

Language and Class-Formation

The problem of illiteracy takes us back to the issue of social integration and the narrowing of the gap between the elite and the masses, the town and

---

6. Obote, "Language and National Identification," p. 5.

the countryside. If the newly literate remain literate, that is itself a modest contribution toward narrowing that gap; but, if the newly literate suffer a relapse, the gap that was beginning to close opens up again.

In East Africa the ability to understand spoken English, let alone written English, presupposes a degree of exposure to formal education. The situation is not such that one can easily learn English by ear. This may be changed if the language becomes sufficiently widespread and its uses sufficiently diversified; but, for the time being, acquisition of the English language lies in the universe of the literate culture.

The government of Tanzania seems sensitive to the risks of this gap between the English-speaking elite and the rest of the populace. Its answer to the problem is to reduce the need for English in one area of national life after another. A combination of cultural nationalism and socialistic egalitarianism has been thrusting Swahili forward in Tanzania as a strong rival to English in the business of the nation: cultural nationalism embraces Swahili in romantic terms of loyalty to African culture; socialistic egalitarianism is thankful to Swahili for widening the area of elite recruitment. By relying increasingly on Swahili rather than English, Tanzania has greatly increased the number of potential civic leaders and functionaries. As mentioned earlier, the first vice-president of Tanzania, Abeid Karume of Zanzibar, spoke no English. Even before independence, Swahili in Tanganyika was being allowed by the colonial authorities to play a role which it would never have been permitted to play in colonial Kenya, even if it had been as well established there. In the 1950s Swahili was accepted as the second official language of the Legislative Council in Dar es Salaam; Africans were therefore no longer required to have a command of English in order to serve as members.

In Kenya during the same period, demands by Gikonyo Kiano for greater recognition of Swahili were received with derision. After all, settler Kenya enquired, could Kiano have taught his students at the Royal Technical College Keynes's theory of unemployment by using Swahili? It was not until the Lancaster House Conference of 1960 was held that Sir Michael Blundell, a leading European participant, sensed that the wind had roughly changed. More as a gesture than in earnest, he proposed that the constitutional conference in London, which was discussing the possibility of self-government under African majority rule in Kenya, should conduct its business in what Blundell possessively called "our language, Swahili." Iain Macleod, representing the British government, was hardly likely to be enthusiastic about the proposal. Tom Mboya had a very good command of Swahili, but not all of the other African delegates at the conference were as well endowed linguistically.[7]

Independent Kenya has been unable to give Swahili equal standing with English, though Swahili is used more often in education and broadcasting and within

---

7. For some of Sir Michael Blundell's reminiscences, see *So Rough a Wind* (London: Weidenfeld & Nicolson, 1964).

the work of KANU than it was during the colonial period. Mzee Kenyatta gives most of his major speeches outside the capital in Swahili, certainly those which are delivered at popular rallies. Kenyatta's Swahili is superb. As an instrument of oratory, it is better than his English. And he can of course chat with the ordinary people outside Kikuyuland in Swahili.

The Uganda government is more restricted in its ability to communicate with its people. In this respect a Ugandan leader is more typical of African heads of government elsewhere south of the Sahara than is either Nyerere or Kenyatta. In a moving statement Obote once said:

> When I move out of Kampala to talk to the people, I have to talk in English. . . . I lose a lot especially as far as the Party is concerned. The Party welcomes everybody, and some of the greatest and most dedicated workers are those who do not speak English; and yet the Party Leader cannot call this great dedicated worker alone and say "Thank you" in a language the man will understand. It has to be translated. There must always be a third party, and that is why it is said there are no secrets in Africa.[8]

Party functionaries of this kind can usually be used only in their home areas. Interregional mixing of certain kinds of officials is not easily accomplished; and transferring a promising unilingual functionary from his district to the center in the capital poses problems if his one language is not transtribal. The ability to speak English is inevitably a qualification for membership in Parliament. The pool of talent from which members of Parliament are chosen in Uganda must of necessity be more circumscribed than it is in Tanzania.

To remedy the gulf between the elite and the masses, Tanzania has already introduced a National Service, compulsory for university graduates and graduates of other major educational institutions, and designed in part to expose this presumptive educated elite to the rigors of manual self-reliance. The exercise is also intended to sensitize the educated to the needs of the masses and narrow the gulf of incomprehension between the city and the countryside. Tanzania seeks to achieve social integration through social equality (as in the case of integrated traditional societies) rather than through social differentiation (as in the case of modern developed states). Tanzania's approach may be based on error, but at least there is a commitment to a specific direction of national change. The availability of Swahili as a language of the masses has been fortunate from the point of view of Tanzania's egalitarian bias.

Kenya, on the other hand, seems to be seeking social integration by increasing social differentiation and functional diversification among the African populace. The government is deliberately trying to create an African entrepreneurial class. The controversy about the Africanization of commerce in Kenya and the gradual displacement of Asians in some critical economic functions is part of Kenya's commitment to the concept of diversifying the African's economic experience.

8. Obote, "Language and National Identification," p. 6.

The African has known what it is like to be a peasant and what it is like to be a teacher, what it is like to be railway porter and what it is like to be cabinet minister. But that is not enough. He must also have the experience of knowing what it is like to be an investor and shareholder, what it is like to run a successful modern shop on Kenyatta Avenue in Nairobi. The potential of the African man as an economically creative being ought to be given a chance to be fulfilled. Kenya, for the time being, is therefore not interested in trying to prevent the emergence of new economic classes. As far as the country is concerned, real modernization lies in rapid functional diversification and not in desperate preservation of a presumed pre-existent African social inequality. The promotion of Swahili in Kenya is inspired not, as it might be in Tanzania, by egalitarian imperatives but more purely by considerations of national integration. The gap that English might perpetuate between the elite and the masses is therefore compatible with a policy of promoting Swahili as a medium of political penetration and socioeconomic intercourse at the grass-roots level.

Uganda, in this as in so many other issues, occupies an intermediate position between Kenya and Tanzania. Like Kenya, Uganda is committed to a policy of creating an African entrepreneurial class and replacing Asians in some economic functions. To that extent, Uganda does appear to be seeking to achieve social integration through functional diversification rather than through a quest for an egalitarian society. On the other hand, like Tanzania, the country has considered the idea of a National Service for the newly graduated, partly to ensure that the educated are not isolated from the needs of the masses. There has also been speculation about setting up a commission to study land distribution, partly to provide greater social justice in landownership.

Uganda's position is clearly ambivalent. Traditional society in the kingdoms, for example, was not egalitarian; status was more often ascriptive than judged on criteria of personal achievement. Obote's government initiated a policy of creating a modern African business class. Though this was incompatible with egalitarianism, it was at least an effort to replace criteria of birth with criteria of achievement as a basis of social success. To some extent the Uganda government is still trying to attack the remnants of traditional "feudalism" by promoting a transtribal modern commercialism. Like Kenya, and unlike Tanzania, Uganda is not trying to prevent the emergence of new economic classes but is actually promoting it. The only difference between Kenya and Uganda in this regard is that the Uganda government is so ambivalent that it sometimes feels a little guilty about this quest for new classes. Even on the issue of promoting English, each successive Uganda government continues to be aware that the policy emphasizes a gulf between the elite and the masses. There is a sense of guilt about it all, but also a sense of inevitability. In the words of Obote:

> Our policy to teach more English could in the long run just develop more power in the hands of those who speak English, and better economic status for those

who know English. We say this because we do not see any possibility of our being able to get English known by half the population of Uganda within the next fifteen years. . . . Some of our people can use it in order to improve their economic status . . . [and] those amongst us in Uganda . . . who have obtained important positions because of the power of the English language are liable to be regarded by a section of our society as perpetrators of colonialism and imperialism; or at least as potential imperialists.[9]

Yet even radical Obote went on to say sadly: "We find no alternative to English." Perhaps that captures the great dilemma concerning the English language. It lends itself well, though not perfectly, to the task of national integration; but it also remains all too often an impediment to the process of social integration.

Language and Educational Opportunities

In a provocative article in *Transition*, Pierre van den Berghe once drew attention not only to the tendency toward elite-formation inherent in the role of English in Africa but also to the tendency toward elite-closure. He argued that the class structure in African countries was in a process of rapid consolidation. Knowledge in depth of a European language and culture conferred prestige and status, and the privileged class who possessed the knowledge passed it on to their children. Van den Berghe called the whole process "the crystallization of the Black mandarinate." He observed:

Indications are that this process of crystallization of a mandarinate will take no more than a single generation. Already members of the elite are frantically scrambling to get their progeny into African Etons. Concern for getting one's children into the "proper" schools (which often means formerly European ones) even begins at the Kindergarten level.[10]

Monopolizing the English language and monopolizing the African Etons are two distinct forms of elite-closure, and van den Berghe seems to confuse the two. Those African governments which have adopted English as the national language make no attempt whatsoever to restrict the dissemination of this linguistic skill. On the contrary, there is an energetic attempt to build schools and spread education. The school curricula are often so humanistic and British-inspired that emphasis on English continues to be an important part of the prevalent educational philosophy. In Uganda, government policy since independence has tended to increase, rather than to reduce, the proportion of a child's education devoted to learning the English language. If elite-closure implies

9. *Ibid.*, p. 4.
10. Pierre van den Berghe, "European Languages and Black Mandarins," *Transition*, VII, no. 34 (January, 1968), 20.

n attempt by those in power to monopolize the linguistic skill which helped
ɔ put them into positions of power, there is no evidence of such an attempt
y the reigning elites of East Africa. On the contrary, all the evidence runs
ɔunter to this particular suggestion.

Van den Berghe's point about elite monopoly of elite schools is much more
ɛfensible. In Uganda the most prestigious primary school is Nakasero. The
ɪmission procedures of this school are discriminatory not only in terms of
ɔcial class but also, by implication, in terms of race. The legitimating rationale
ɪr the discrimination is competence in the English language.

The following incident illustrates the racialism of this system. An East African
ɪofessor at Makerere submitted an application to Nakasero Primary School
ɪ behalf of his child. The application was submitted in February for admis-
ɪon the following January. Admission to the school is supposedly by inter-
ɪew, the purpose of the interview being mainly to test the child's competence
ɪ the English language. The East African professor's child had one British and
ɪe American playmate, both of whom were applying for admission to Nakasero
ɪat year. The parents of these playmates heard from the school within a few
ɪeeks that their child was accepted. There was no need for an interview. The
ɪst African professor waited to learn of his son's fate.

The first language of the East African professor's son was English; the
ɪvel of vocabulary and discourse that the boy heard at home put him at
ɪast on a par with both of his Anglo-Saxon friends. In addition, the boy's
ɪother was a WASP (the American abbreviation to denote the privileged "white
ɪnglo-Saxon Protestant"). However, because the nationality of the boy as given
ɪ the application was East African, an interview was necessary. The boy
ɪd to wait to be called for an interview and then had to wait for a verdict
ɪllowing that interview, all of which took place after his British and American
ɪaymates had had their admissions confirmed.[11]

The racialism of these procedures is obvious in the school's readiness to
ɪant admission to Anglo-American children before East African children are
ɪen interviewed. The system might look fairer if all applicants were interviewed
ɪfore any were admitted. Even if Anglo-Americans are automatically exempt
ɪom the interview, at least they should not be admitted until all the others
ɪve been interviewed and a selection of the candidates has been made from
ɪe two groups together.

Even if these niceties of fairness were fulfilled by Nakasero, the requirement
ɪ prior command of the English language biases the admission procedures
ɪo heavily in favor of those from English-speaking homes — be those homes
ɪnglo-Saxon or "Afro-Saxon." The elite in Uganda are not monopolizing

---

11. After the procedures were completed, the professor's son was offered admission;
t this does not affect the argument about neoracial discrimination in the selection
ɔcess. In protest, the East African professor declined the offer of a place for his
ɪ.

the English language; but they are perhaps using their command of the language to monopolize the best schools. In England one criterion of elite status is not command of the language but the accent with which one speaks it, and the elite accent is often derived from elite schools. In Uganda the accent of a person speaking English is associated not with a particular school or social class but with the native language of the speaker. If public school accents evolve in East Africa, superimposed over tribal accents, enabling a Munyoro from Nakasero and Budo to be differentiated from a Munyoro educated elsewhere, a new form of elite-closure might come into being. If there are intermediate accents between the most upper-class and the most proletarian, and if these accents are distributed on a curve which is gradual rather than steep, we might be able to say that the English language in East Africa has indeed been functional to social integration — but decidedly through a process of social diversification rather than one of social equality. The interplay between cultural engineering and language policy in East Africa would then have entered another exciting phase.

[8]

Culture, Structure, and the Party System

Kenya once again became a *de facto* one-party state in October, 1969, when the opposition party, the Kenya People's Union, was banned following violent incidents in Kisumu, the party stronghold. For the time being the situation in Kenya is one in which a particular opposition party, rather than the principle of institutionalized opposition, is outlawed. Technically, there is no reason why another group, or even some of the older members of the same Kenya People's Union, could not form a new opposition party, since the country has yet to decide on a one-party state.

Uganda became for the first time a *de facto* one-party state in December, 1969, when all opposition parties were banned following an attempt on the life of President Milton Obote. There has at last been a clear declaration of Uganda's intention to abolish a system of rival parties altogether, creating a *de jure* one-party state.

Tanzania was a *de facto* one-party state from the first day of independence, at which time there was only one member of Parliament belonging to an opposition party. Little more than a year after independence, plans were afoot to convert the country into a *de jure* one-party state, and this was accomplished in 1965. Julius Nyerere, the president of Tanganyika, as it was then called, said in Dar es Salaam on January 13, 1963, that the electorate's overwhelming support of the ruling Tanganyika African National Union virtually ruled out the possibility of interparty contests.

The Heritage of Westminster

The experiences of the three East African countries form a pattern that can be discerned in other parts of the continent as well. There was initially a good deal of idealism about the Westminster model and competitive parliamentary institutions, even among African nationalists. Much of the opposition to independence in the colonial period was based on the assumption that the colonial peoples were not yet capable of governing themselves. The British conception of self-government tended to be tied, for understandable reasons, to the idea of capacity for parliamentary self-government. As late as 1959 this sort of approach to problems of decolonization was discernible in the idiom of British colonial policy. In April, 1959, Alan Lennox-Boyd, speaking for the British government in the House of Commons, defined British intentions in one colony in the following familiar terms:

> The responsibility of Her Majesty's Government is to all the inhabitants of Kenya. . . . It would be a betrayal of that responsibility if we were to abandon our ultimate authority prematurely. . . . Thus, there must be in the territory as a whole a sufficient understanding of parliamentary institutions, and sufficient sense of responsibility in public affairs to hold out a reasonable prospect that parliamentary institutions, representative of the people, will produce a responsible government. . . . Self government, I think we would all agree, is but a mockery if it is purchased at the expense of personal freedom.[1]

In the context of such values, capacity for self-government was, in effect, capacity for effective utilization of parliamentary institutions. Nnamdi Azikiwe had echoed this same British conception of political capability a few years before self-government was granted to Nigeria:

> Thanks to the growth of political consciousness in this country our people are becoming acquainted with the practice of parliamentary democracy. This has been used as a criterion to determine the political maturity of any people under the rule of others and we can be no exception. As a matter of fact, it is a declared policy of Britain that no colony can be considered ready for self-government until it has made parliamentary democracy a political reality.[2]

Azikiwe at that time did not object to this criterion of eligibility for independence. He merely urged his countrymen to make possible "a full-fledged two party system in operation." The Anglo-Saxon basis of evaluating political maturity continued to affect Azikiwe's own line of reasoning.

In Nigeria parliamentary institutions did last for a while, culminating in a major catastrophe; but, elsewhere in the former British territories, faith in parliamentary institutions soon evaporated. The song of one-partyism began to be heard in different areas, lulling many into an acceptance of its inevitability in African conditions.

Are African conditions inhospitable to competitive parliamentary institutions? Is the trend toward their elimination irreversible? In much of the discussion of this phenomenon during the 1960s the belief grew, even among liberals both within Africa and without, that it had been wrong to assume that the Westminster plan could be transplanted to other areas of the globe successfully.

---

1. Great Britain, *Parliamentary Debates* (Commons), 5th ser., DCIV (1959), 563–64.
2. Nnamdi Azikiwe, *Zik* (Cambridge, Eng.: Cambridge University Press, 1961), p. 85.

There was also a good deal of vigorous defense of the feasibility of maintaining democratic values within a one-party system.

If the assumptions about the inevitability of the one-party system in Africa are valid, the reasons for their validity have yet to be fully understood. There has been one wave of theorizing in the social sciences, and a new wave of theorizing is due, particularly since much of the optimism of the original wave about African democratic instincts within a one-party system has not been entirely validated. There has also been the unforeseen intrusion of the soldier in African politics, and the consequences of this intrusion for the future of parliamentary institutions need to be looked at.

Another issue is that of reversibility. Kenya has provided a fascinating example of a movement to and from one-partyism with the same regime in power. In 1964 the Kenya African Democratic Union, the original opposition party, liquidated itself and merged with the ruling party, the Kenya African National Union. The country moved with one momentous decision from a two-party to a one-party system. Within the major party new tensions began to arise, and a faction to the left of the top leadership gradually began to be discernible as a source of challenge. By 1966 the leftist faction broke loose from the ruling party and formed the Kenya People's Union. Whereas the original opposition had been from the right, the new opposition was from the left.

The vigor of Kenya's politics entered a new phase that lasted until October, 1969, when the disastrous events in Kisumu led the regime to ban the Kenya People's Union and detain its top men. Kenya was back to a state of one-partyism. The country seemed to have a systemic pendulum, as the clock of political evolution introduced alternating structural phases of public life. If the one-party system is inevitable in Kenya, the trend toward it is not unilinear. If there is a principle of inevitability at work, it is a principle which has found areas of tactical accommodation with the realities of reversibility.

Another instance of systemic reversibility occurred in Ghana. As independence approached, Nkrumah was a believer in liberal competitive democracy. In June, 1955, at the height of the opposition challenge, he said at a rally of the Convention People's party:

> I have always expressed both in public and in private that we need a strong and well organised Opposition Party in the country and the Assembly. . . . We must not forget that democracy means the rule of the majority, though it should be tempered by sweet reasonableness in the interests of the minority.[3]

After independence Nkrumah was still keen on maintaining the format of a two-party system. He was embarrassed at first by the rapidity with which the CPP within Parliament grew, as more and more members of the opposition

---

3. *Evening News* (Accra), June 14, 1955.

crossed the floor to join the government party. Those crossings had initially been well-received indications of growing support and a useful tool of propaganda against the remaining opposition in the country. When the opposition seemed to be dwindling a little too fast, however, Nkrumah began to worry that the system as a whole would be compromised. At that time it was still important to him to maintain the image of competitive parliamentary institutions.

Nkrumah's views on this matter gradually changed, and the road toward a one-party system was taken. The regime's opponents were harassed. Ideologues in Ghana turned their talents to the rationalization of the one-party state. Ghana enjoyed the one-party system for half a decade. The end came in February, 1966, when Nkrumah's regime was overthrown and the CPP banned. The country fell under military rule with civilian advisers. Party politics took an enforced pause.

One of the most significant incidents in African political history occurred in 1969, when the political opposition reassumed its original vigor in Ghana. In August, 1969, Kofi Busia's party, the Progress party, polled 59 per cent of the popular vote and won 104 seats, or 75 per cent, of the National Assembly. No less than sixteen parties had originally come forward to contest the elections; but mergers took place, 'and the contest was finally among five parties. Of these, the major contest was between Busia's Progress party and K. A. Gbedemah's National Alliance of Liberals. Ghana was therefore back to a multiparty system, and the political philosophy behind it was the same one that Nkrumah had expressed in 1955. And then, in January, 1972, little more than two years after the soldiers had returned rule to the citizens, the military overthrew Busia's liberal system.

All of this indicates that there is a systemic pendulum in Africa's parliamentary experience. It seems, however, to be weighted on the side of either a one-party system or a no-party state. The no-party states are, of course, those which have explicitly dispensed with the party structure, as Ethiopia seems to have done, and those which have a party that is in reality nonoperational, existing merely in rhetoric and ineffectual committee meetings.

Primordial Values and Parliamentary Vigor

What social variables determine the degree to which parliamentary institutions are viable in a particular African country? Much more research into the social conditions of individual countries will have to be done before an adequate answer can be given to such a probing question. However, at a level of generality, countries which are *structurally* hospitable to parliamentary institutions can be distinguished from those which are *culturally* hospitable to parliamentary institutions.

Countries which are structurally hospitable to such institutions in Africa are those which are characterized by ethnic pluralism or other kinds of intergroup cleavage. A striking example in East Africa is Uganda, which until recently did show a great capacity for vigorous pluralistic politics arising out of a special kind of intergroup competitiveness.

Countries which are culturally congenial to parliamentary institutions are those which have, either in their traditional values or in the internalized part of their acquired values, a distrust of excessive authority and a belief in individual autonomy. Traditional values favorable to liberal democracy are to be found in such societies as the Kikuyu and the Ibo. The segmental nature of these societies and their respect for individualistic assertion made them culturally fertile for the growth of institutions seeking to safeguard the autonomy of subunits of society and to maximize individual initiative.

Neither the Kikuyu nor the Ibo constitute separate nations in which this particular cultural hospitality to parliamentary institutions can be allowed to flourish without the tensions of interaction with other groups. Where the Kikuyu and the Ibo have had to compete with other groups in society, their own internal hospitality to parliamentary institutions has been diluted by the tensions of competing at the national level with other groups. The Kikuyu have been known to be disinclined toward an open parliamentary system; perhaps they would have welcomed such a system if Kenya consisted only of the Kikuyu, but in the face of other groups their cultural liberalism has stiffened to some extent into a kind of defensive intolerance.

There is enough evidence in the history of Nigeria before the first coup to suggest fairly conclusively that, of the three major tribes in Nigeria at that time, the Ibo were in many ways the most natural liberal democrats. Liberal democracy in the Northern Region never got started. Liberal democracy in the Western Region started but then collapsed under the strain of excessive intra-Yoruba tensions. Liberal democracy in the Eastern Region of old Nigeria, though not always tolerant of the smaller tribes, seemed nevertheless to have greater inner resilience and potential viability than was discernible in the other regions.

There are important reasons connected with the interests of Africa as to why the collapse of Biafra might be regarded as a desirable ending to a disastrous episode. Strictly from the point of view of national integration and the continuing viability of fragile states in Africa, it may be fortunate that the continent was spared a conspicuously successful secessionist bid by the Ibo. However, from the point of view of experimental liberal institutions, Biafra might have become a great cultural laboratory. The vigorous individualism of the Ibo people, the segmental trends toward autonomy, the relatively fluid political stratification, and the apparent distrust of excessive authority might have converged to create a model experimental farm for the planting of liberal democracy.

Before 1965, Nigeria had displayed for a while some capacity for effective political competitiveness. If the values of Ibo society amounted to cultural hospitality to parliamentary institutions, the strength of interethnic tensions amounted to a kind of structural hospitality. Institutionalized ethnic pluralism in a polity like Nigeria was, to some extent, functionally in the same tradition as the doctrine of separation of powers. By creating a number of subcenters of power within the polity, institutionalized ethnic pluralism tended to avert the danger of absolute government. Within each region of Nigeria, and perhaps predominantly in the Northern Region, there was an intolerance of dissent. This intolerance characterized internal Buganda politics as well. Yet the strength of the regions continued for a while to make centralized authoritarianism in both Nigeria and Uganda less easy to accomplish than had been the case elsewhere in Africa.

The trouble with ethnic pluralism is that it is favorable not only to parliamentary institutions but also to violence among groups. Ethnic pluralism in much of Africa is among the most politically sensitive of all social issues. The risk of violence among tribes is at the center of Africa's twin crises of identity and integration. Britain's policy of indirect rule as a form of colonial administration tended to sharpen ethnic loyalty precisely in those places where the policy was most successful. To that extent it probably increased the risk of violence among tribes. At the same time, however, this indirect rule created the framework for genuinely competitive politics and for a spirit of energetic dissent that lasted for at least a few years after independence.

Nigeria provided a most dramatic example of the two related consequences of indirect rule. The country started off with an almost furious liberal ethos in its national politics, with all the wrangles of strong, rival political parties, all the excitement of dissent, and all the babble of competitive political journalism. Yet the tragedy of the civil war was another consequence of indirect rule. By institutionalizing ethnic pluralism in Nigeria, the British created the potential for a meaningful competitive democracy but also the framework for latent violence. Nigeria reaped both harvests, as did Uganda with its own tradition of Lugardism.[4]

It is necessary to point out important differences between Nigeria and Uganda in relation to cultural conditions for parliamentary institutions. In Nigeria there were important cultural factors favorable to the survival of parliamentary institutions, though they were overwhelmed by other factors in the social situation. There was an intellectual tradition in Western Nigeria, as well as in the Eastern Region, that was partial to some liberal values. This consisted in part of internalized acculturation, arising out of prolonged interaction with the British political tradition. This internalized acculturation was at the level of the elite. For cultural values favorable to parliamentary democracy at the level of the masses, one has to look at indigenous values — those aspects of Ibo culture and systems of value which seemed to favor a liberal democratic polity — rather than newly

---

4. For further discussion of some of these issues, see Ali A. Mazrui, *Violence and Thought: Essays on Social Tensions in Africa* (London: Longmans, 1969), chaps. 5, 6, 7.

acquired values. Nigeria was to some extent endowed with liberal values at both levels.

Uganda, on the other hand, although structurally favorable to parliamentary institutions, was culturally not so favorable. The belief in authority was a central part of the political culture of the dominant Ganda tribe. The Baganda as a group had much to do with the survival of vigorous constitutionalism in Uganda until the collapse of liberal democracy in 1966, but the Baganda believed in constitutional rights without necessarily believing in individual rights. The Baganda repeatedly challenged the central government on issues affecting their rights as a group and as a region. There was great faith in law and the process of litigation on political matters, and there was also tremendous verve in the political organization for the defense of Ganda autonomy. However, the desire was to safeguard the rights of a region or collectivity rather than to promote a respect for individual freedom. Much of the internal structure of Kiganda society and the pressures which operated within it were hostile in effect, if not by intention, to the principle of individual choice. The Baganda objected to political authoritarianism from the central government but practiced it substantially in their regional government. It was not a case of hypocrisy but a case of believing in collective autonomy and collective distinctiveness without subscribing to the primacy of the individual in the liberal sense.

Borrowed Values and Political Styles

The Ganda remain among the more Anglicized of East African tribes and communities. They have imbibed important aspects of British culture, yet what they have acquired from the British is not so much British liberalism as British traditionalism. They have responded with impressive sophistication to the side of British life that puts a premium on traditionality, refrains from too rapid a departure from ancestral ways, and respects institutions hallowed by time and experience. They have not quite as readily embraced that other side of British life, which tends to lean toward individual liberties and respect for personal idiosyncrasies.

In terms of cultural values, the indigenous groups of northern Uganda seem to be more hospitable to individualism and decentralization than Ganda culture has proved to be. There certainly has been more distrust of centralized authority among the Acholi and, to a certain extent, among the Langi than there has been among the Baganda. However, the record of Ganda supremacy during the colonial period apparently turned Obote against a pluralistic system of politics at the national level. Obote's belief in liberal institutions was shaken by the experience of tense intergroup relations which culminated in the military confrontation of 1966. Yet Obote's cultural background might be described as more congenial to liberal democratic political behavior than that of his old Ganda opponent, Sir Edward Mutesa, the king of the Baganda.

With regard to the acquired values of the northern elite of Uganda, British conservatism is not entirely absent. There has also evolved, partly in reaction to previous political styles and partly in competition with African movements elsewhere, a partiality for centralized institutions, for radical rhetoric, and, more recently, for measures of a socialistic nature.

Among the Kikuyu in Kenya, individualism has been so marked that the imperative of collective action in times of shared danger has sometimes needed the solemnity of oath-taking before its durability could be guaranteed. Structural pluralism at the national level has at times created conditions of shared danger for the Kikuyu. The competition of the Luo, especially in the struggle for political control of Kenya, has occasionally forced the Kikuyu back to primordial affirmations of loyalty. Individualism is all right if Kikuyu clans are dealing with Kikuyu clans and the freedom of political challenge does not risk the destiny of the group as a whole; but when the challenge comes from a group external to the Kikuyu and is big enough to constitute a real threat, internal Kikuyu cohesion becomes more necessary than ever.

With regard to imported cultural values in Kenya, there are some which could functionally be related to the ethic of competitive politics. The private-enterprise system as an economic arrangement has found a relationship of mutual accommodation with the values of some of Kenya's ethnic groups, especially the Kikuyu. Again, that old Kikuyu individualism, like Ibo individualism in Nigeria, is helping the emergence of entrepreneurial vigor among these people. Business enterprises and economic risk-taking are not typical of the indigenous inclinations of the peoples of East Africa, but certain elements of Kikuyu culture have turned out to be congenial to these economic functions. It is not, of course, at all certain that a system of private enterprise invariably yields a system of liberal democracy, although the two systems have been connected in the Western world. It might be true that in a country with a highly centralized economy an adequately liberal polity is impossible. It is possible, however, to have a decentralized economy alongside an illiberal polity.

Liberal ideas of Anglo-Saxon vintage among Kenyan intellectuals are discernible, but they are a little more fragile than similar ideas and values among Ghanaian intellectuals. Structurally, Ghana is not quite as congenial to the evolution of a competitive pluralistic system as is Uganda; but, culturally, both at the level of some indigenous values and at the level of acquired mores, Ghana is more congenial to such a system than is Uganda.

At the level of indigenous cultural mores, even the Ashanti have a less authoritarian political culture than the Baganda. At the level of acquired cultural mores of the intellectual elite, educated Ghanaians are among the most liberal of all English-speaking Africans. Liberal values of Anglo-Saxon vintage have in many cases been stabilized and internalized. In the process of political accultu-ration, the acquisition by the educated of mores external to their ancestral value systems has gone further among Ghanaians than among any other English-speaking African group, with the possible exception of immigrant Liberians and black South Africans. Among black South Africans it is not as yet clear which political values acquired from the Western impact are the most deeply internalized. What is clear is that educated English-speaking South Africans are among the most Westernized of all Africans.

Well-educated Ghanaians are not far behind their counterparts in South Africa. Their political values have had the opportunity to be tested, and liberalism as a system of preferences has emerged as relatively resilient in this particular section of Ghanaian society. Even when Nkrumah's personality cult was at its strongest, the most educated of Ghanaian intellectuals remained distant, somewhat resentful, skeptical, though often prudent. Westerners visiting the University of Ghana at Legon sometimes described Ghanaian academics as specimens of nineteenth-century liberalism. Many Western liberals found it difficult to sympathize with the political positions of Ghanaian intellectuals. They regarded them as excessively Anglicized in their political perspectives and therefore unprepared for real engagement in the developmental processes of the country.

The overthrow of Nkrumah was in part a success for the soldiers and in part an indication of growing popular disenchantment with Nkrumah's machine. What must not be overlooked is that the fall of Nkrumah and its aftermath were also triumphs for Ghanaian intellectuals. The national critique of Nkrumah's era bore the stamp of the prejudices and values of Ghanaian intellectuals. The distaste for hero-worship, the belief in individual liberties, the excitement with freedom of the press, the distrust of centralized power, the contempt for ideological formulas — all these aspects which saturated Ghanaian rhetoric following the fall of Nkrumah betrayed a renewed ascendancy of the intellectual in Ghana. The revival of a multiparty system and open dissent were also manifestations of this intellectual reassertion. Finally, the emergence of Kofi Busia as the head of government was the ultimate symbol of a return of leadership into intellectual hands. Busia, whose virtues were more scholarly than political, whose style was more suited to a quiet seminar than to a public platform, who seemed to have much more in common with academics than with the general run of politicians in his own country, who was bereft of some of the captivating qualities of Nkrumah's charismatic leadership, was the man who came to the helm in the new Ghana. The ship of state was entrusted to the captaincy of an intellectual.

After the 1969 elections it was not certain whether Busia and his government would remain as strikingly symbolic of the dominant values of Ghanaian intellectuals as they were at first. Power has an effect on individual leaders, and regimes undergo significant changes in the hustle and bustle of competitive politics. Although Busia was an intellectual and a scholar, it was possible for him to become, under the strain of power and its temptations, less representative of the values and prejudices of his own class in Ghanaian society than he seemed to be at the beginning.

An additional factor to be considered is ethnic pluralism. Although tribal divisions in Ghana were less deep and perilous than those in Uganda and Kenya, such differences and cleavages were by no means absent from Ghanaian politics. The 1969 elections reopened some of the old tribal cleavages, and voting showed a striking response to tribalistic factors. The Progress party gathered its support from Akan-speaking areas, especially Ashanti, and also from northern Ghana. The platform of the party tried to be of national appeal. The stature of Kofi Busia, a defiant and long-standing antagonist of Nkrumah who had spent years in exile rather than collaborate with him, helped to give the man the dimensions of national leadership. Nevertheless, the distribution of Busia's support included an unmistakable neotribal base, and K. A. Gbedemah's National Alliance of Liberals became more tribally conscious as the electioneering got under way. Some of the patterns of tribal alignment constituted a change from former alignments, but the tribalistic dimension was still there. As two observers put it soon after the elections:

> The August election marked the apparent (perhaps temporary) ending of the traditional antipathy between the Ashanti and other Akan-speaking peoples and the emergence of strong anti-Ewe feelings.[5]

But whatever forces were reactivated by the 1969 election were to be interrupted by the coup of January, 1972. A new cloud of uncertainty hung over the Ghanaian polity.

Ethnicity: Exclusive and Intersecting

The old question of party systems and ethnic pluralism demands renewed examination. Does the very nature of a multiparty system aggravate ethnic loyalties? Are there aspects of the Westminster model which are peculiarly congenial to tribalism?

It has been suggested that in a country like Ghana the way in which the single-member constituencies work tends to create strong tribal voting blocs. Districts in much of formerly British Africa were drawn on the basis of tribal lines. This is true of Ghana, of Kenya, and, perhaps even more strikingly, of Uganda. Sometimes changes have been made in the boundaries of these districts, either in response to demographic considerations or as a result of minority groups' rebelling against the dominant tribe in a given district. However, the coincidence of voting district and tribal territory can contribute to tribal cohesiveness in voting.

In most constituencies a single tribe is dominant. There may be other tribes

---

5. Emily Card and Barbara Callaway, "Ghanaian Politics: The Elections and After," *Africa Report*, XV, no. 3 (March, 1970), 11. See also Selwyn Douglas Ryan, "Ghana: The Transfer of Power," *Mawazo*, II, no. 2 (December, 1969), 47–54.

in the district, but one is clearly the focus of influence and sometimes of envy. The fact that the constituencies are single-member constituencies converts elections into tribal contests.[6] It could therefore be argued that what has tended to aggravate tribalism is less the party system than the single-member constituency.

However, this reasoning overlooks the fact that the single-member constituency quite often enforces tribal alliances, so that parties emerge not as representatives of single groups but as alignments of several tribal groups. This situation might be more desirable than one in which the electoral system encourages not only the initial eruption of multiple little parties but the survival of such parties in the course of the campaigning and subsequent voting. Ghana did begin its electoral experience in mid-1969 with a multiplicity of political parties. Although the old theory that the single-member constituency tends to encourage coalescence into a two-party confrontation has at times been challenged, the experience of Ghana in 1969 supported this theory. The single-member constituency seemed to have made groups otherwise distinct seek to align themselves with each other. The ultimate confrontation between the Progress party under Busia and the National Alliance of Liberals under Gbedemah confirms this polarizing effect of single-member constituencies. It might therefore be said that a system which forces different tribes to coalesce into a few political parties remains much more desirable than a system which gives tribes the possibility of having political parties of their own, burdening the national assembly with a variety of political parties based on tribal identification.[7]

Therefore, from the point of view of ethnic pluralism, a multiparty system is less desirable than a system of two main parties. The Anglo-Saxon model of the two-party system at least enforces coalitions and alignments of groups that might otherwise have had separate political organizations. The question still remains whether, from the point of view of coping with tribal cleavages, a one-party system would not be even better than a system of two parties.

The answer depends upon the relationship among tribes and parties within the two-party or the multiparty system. A multiparty system would aggravate tribal affiliations and antagonisms if tribes and parties were to coincide too neatly. This might be called the model of exclusive ethnicity. On the other hand, a multiparty system would help to mitigate and even eliminate tribalism from politics if parties and tribes were to crisscross. This might be called the model of intersecting ethnicity.

A one-party system is more healthy from the point of view of tribal cleavage than a multiparty system of exclusive ethnicity, but a one-party system is less

---

6. Card and Callaway, "Ghanaian Politics," p. 11.

7. For a brilliant re-evaluation of the polarization of single-member constituencies, see Colin Leys, "Models, Theories and the Theory of Political Parties," in *Comparative Politics: A Reader*, ed. Harry Eckstein and David E. Apter (London: Collier-Macmillan, 1963), pp. 305–14. See also the remaining four chapters in part 4 of that book.

healthy than a multiparty system of intersecting ethnicity. The intersecting model derives its positive integrative functions from the sociological effects of crosscutting loyalties. If some members of tribe A belong to party X, and some members of tribe B belong to party Y, and other members of tribes A and B tend to crisscross in their loyalties to parties X and Y, the situation is one which averts the danger of neat ethnic political confrontations between tribes A and B.

In more specific terms, let us consider the situation that existed in Uganda until 1969, when the multiparty system was abolished. Prior to 1966 there were three parties: the ruling Uganda People's Congress, the opposing Democratic party, and the smaller Kabaka Yekka, which was at one time in alliance with the UPC but was abandoned by the ruling party when the latter felt strong enough to dispense with its allies. The Kabaka Yekka was clearly a tribalist party. Its very name, "the king alone," identified the party with a particular ethnic group, and there was a neat coincidence of party affiliation and tribal identity. The Kabaka Yekka as a party suffered from the defects of exclusive ethnicity. However, it could not be said that the Democratic party or the Uganda People's Congress were tribalist parties. Although some ethnic communities identified themselves overwhelmingly with one or the other of the two parties, affiliations were not quite as neat as those which characterized the Kabaka Yekka. In some districts the crisscrossing nature of party affiliation in relation to ethnic identity was exemplary. Acholi was an interesting example in this regard. As one of the two leading northern districts, it seemed to belong to the new northern elite in Uganda's politics. Yet the situation was in fact much more complex. The Acholi were divided between those who belonged to the Democratic party and those who belonged to the Uganda People's Congress. If all the districts in Uganda had been like Acholi, the two-party system would have been clearly of the model of intersecting ethnicity. The Acholi who belonged to the Democratic party could not regard the UPC as a completely hostile institution for the simple reason that many of their tribal compatriots were within the UPC. The Acholi who belonged to the UPC had to retain a residual tolerance of the Democratic party for the same reason.

The process of national integration must ultimately consist of a progressive multiplication of crisscrossing communities. When social class, religion, tribe, political affiliation, and occupation all coincide in differentiating one group from another, the situation is one of explosive confrontation. But when these different forms of categorization overlap, and no one tribe can be associated exclusively with a particular religion, a particular political party, a particular occupation, or a particular social class, but all tribes have a mixture of these categories within them, then the nation is approaching the kind of complexity which should promote greater cohesiveness. These considerations would help to make the multiparty system of intersecting ethnicity more integrative as a social mechanism than either the multiparty system of ethnic exclusiveness or a one-party system.

Why should a one-party system be less integrative than the multiparty system of intersecting ethnicity? The main consideration is that a one-party system may succeed in eliminating tribally based parties and yet fail to eliminate tribal caucuses and regional factions within the single party. The one-party umbrella may only disguise ethnic factionalism in the political process. The nation would be deprived of the benefits of crosscutting loyalties, which the multiparty system of intersection would afford, and yet the tensions of tribal differences might persist behind the façade of single-party solidarity.

Another advantage of the multiparty model of ethnic intersection over a single-party system concerns the institutionalization of conflict-resolution. Social conflict is not only unavoidable in the process of national integration; it is indispensable. The cumulative experience of resolving conflict deepens the degree of integration in a given society. But what makes conflict-resolution feasible? It is sometimes a cumulative power of precedent, of having overcome other crises before. Experience of previous clashes sharpens the capacity to discover areas of mutual compatibility on subsequent occasions of tension. Another factor which makes conflict-resolution possible is awareness of reciprocal dependence. A vested interest in the survival of a particular social system is one formulation of such reciprocal dependence.

The most important institutions to be developed in a new nation are those that will help to routinize the resolution of conflicts among groups. A procedural component has to be structured into the political culture; ways of permitting conflict while preventing disruption have to be evolved. The advantage of a multiparty system of intersecting ethnicity is that it provides an institutionalization of a particular mode of resolving conflict in a way that would not be possible under the less structured factionalism which could flourish under a single-party umbrella.

Kenya's two-party system — in both the first phase, KANU versus KADU, which lasted until 1964, and the second phase, KANU versus KPU, which lasted from 1966 to 1969 — belonged more to the multiparty model of ethnic exclusiveness. Tribes en bloc tended to choose one party or the other. There were very few examples of the crisscrossing that took place in Acholi. KANU has remained to the end the most national party in Kenya's experience, but this is in terms of the number of tribes that KANU has won over en bloc. Of course, KANU has also constantly proclaimed the need for national unity and has attempted in a variety of ways to centralize the quest for nationhood. There have been aspects of KANU's policy, however, that have betrayed tribalistic tendencies. In any case, the main point to grasp here is that the unit of party affiliation was the tribe rather than the individual. Whole tribes attached themselves to one party or the other.

There is an element of gross exaggeration in this way of describing Kenya's party system. A number of exceptions, some of them very outstanding, can be cited against this formulation. Tom Mboya was a Luo but remained a towering figure in KANU in spite of the emergence of the Luo-backed KPU. Bildad Kaggia was a Kikuyu but for a while chose to be second in command of KPU. On the whole, however, the unit of political affiliation in Kenya's history has tended to be the tribe rather than the individual party member.

This pattern of affiliation was often an outcome of sociological conditions rather than a matter of deliberate ideological choice. In the early part of 1969, KPU was ideologically opposed to tribalism and highly critical of KANU for certain tendencies toward tribal preferences, yet KPU seemed to be more clearly a party with a single tribe for its base than was the rival KANU. In other words, KPU, forced to rely on Nyanza Province for its ultimate survival, was more tribal in structure. KANU, although less tribal in structure, was sometimes more tribal in general political behavior. The structure of KANU was less tribal in that a multiplicity of groups helped to give the party its national support, and the leaders — though disproportionately Kikuyu — included large numbers from other tribes. But the political behavior of KANU, on issues ranging from the choice of headmasters for Kenya schools to land rights extended to new settlements, very often betrayed the persistence of tribal nepotism. Tribalism was appparent, not necessarily in matters of policy choice, but in the way in which policy was implemented. Tribal factors intruded into areas which policy-makers at the top might not have intended to affect in such a way.

Because Kenya's multiparty system tended to be ethnically exclusive, it was basically a less healthy system than the one that evolved in Uganda with the Uganda People's Congress and the Democratic party. The Uganda two-party system seemed to be clearly a model of ethnic intersection and therefore was in many ways not only healthier than the Kenya system but perhaps healthier than a one-party system. The troubles in Uganda were not merely, or even mainly, concerned with the confrontation of the Democratic party and the UPC. The Buganda question was a bigger issue. After the crisis of 1966, the Baganda were basically disfranchised. They were, perhaps legitimately, deprived of their tribal party, the Kabaka Yekka. Because of the state of emergency within the region and the general atmosphere of the country, the Baganda were furthermore denied effective entry into the rest of the political process.

If this system had opened up and permitted those who had previously been in the Kabaka Yekka to realign themselves, the result might well have been a Buganda divided between support for the Democratic party and support for the Uganda People's Congress. Many Baganda hated both alternatives for a variety of historical reasons; but, since they were forbidden from organizing a tribal third party, they might have chosen between the existing two parties. A Buganda divided in this way between the Democratic party and the Uganda People's Congress would have revealed even more clearly that the multiparty system of Uganda was of the healthy intersecting kind, with all the potentialities for crosscutting loyalties and the promise of serving integrative functions. In the case of Uganda it is still not certain whether a one-party system might turn out in the long run to be less unifying than a two-party system of the intersecting variety.

The case of Kenya is less clear in regard to its *de facto* one-party system. The elections which took place in December, 1969, would seem to indicate that Kenya affords greater freedom under a one-party system than it did under a two-party system of ethnic exclusiveness. Had the Kenya People's Union not been banned in October, 1969, and had the elections been more clearly between KANU and KPU, it is feasible that the electorate of Kenya would have had less real choice. The regime would have been afraid of giving advantage to the opposition and risking its own survival, and would therefore have been tempted to pursue a more interventionist policy in the elections.

African regimes tend to be intolerant of situations which threaten their survival. However, while the electorate is denied the possibility of replacing the regime, it is allowed to change the regime partially, either in terms of personnel or in terms of policy. Kenya permitted the elections to be substantially free, and over eighty members of Parliament, more than half of the total membership, were rejected and replaced by new members. The turnover was impressive by any standards. Parliament, therefore, became a meaningful instrument of political recruitment, bringing in new personalities from the ranks to serve as legislators. From these new recruits in Parliament, new recruits in the executive were drawn. The personnel of the government has changed to some extent as a result of the elections, and the composition of Parliament has changed even more dramatically.

The Kenya Parliament is not a rubber-stamp assembly. There is vigorous debate within it, with accusations against the government, ranging from minor administrative complaints to grievances concerning tribal nepotism. In many ways the Kenya Parliament is, by a considerable margin, the most lively of the three national assemblies in East Africa. There is more genuine challenge and debate in the legislature in Nairobi than has been heard in Kampala for several years and more than is heard in Dar es Salaam.

Perhaps the liberal cultural values indigenous to the Kikuyu communities are being momentarily nationalized. The Kikuyu remain central to the political processes in Kenya. Such a sociological situation for a tribe has its temptations, and cases of capitulation to nepotism can be illustrated widely; but the spirit of decentralization in politics and certainly the spirit of private initiative in economics seem to be thriving under Kenyatta's leadership.

There is a continuing challenge of interaction among cultural variables, structural patterns, and electoral behavior in Africa's experience. Recent events in the East African countries and in Ghana reveal both new answers and new questions for those who seek to understand the nature of this tripartite interaction.

[9]

Culture, Structure, and the Electoral System

The ultimate function of elections can be reduced to one of two principles — the principle of choice and the principle of acclamation. Elections as an exercise of choice are part of the liberal tradition in politics. Government by consent postulates the option of withholding consent from one candidate and granting it to another. In the British system the choice is explicit; there is only one major opposition party, and the voters know at the time of elections that either party can form a government. Indeed, the opposition party usually has a shadow cabinet in existence simultaneously with that of the ruling party, and the atmosphere is one which allows for a complete alternative government to be available should the vote go to the side of the opposition. In situations of multiparty politics it is not quite as easy for the electors to know precisely which combination of parties will eventually emerge as the ruling coalition. It depends upon a range of negotiations which take place after the elections have been completed, when the different elected factions proceed to find areas of compromise. The precise composition of the winning government in terms of a combination of political platforms is not always foreseeable prior to the elections. Nevertheless, the principle of choice is still at the heart of competitive elections in a multiparty system. Democracy in this sense is conceived in terms of exercising political choice.

In another sense of democracy, elections are to be understood in terms of acclamation rather than choice. Where the electorate is faced with only a single candidate or a single list of candidates, the ballots allow the population to acclaim rather than choose the candidate or candidates put before them. In such a situation there can be degrees of acclamation, indicating the state of popular feeling. People at least have the choice of voting or not voting, of voting yes or voting no, and the size of the poll or the balance of affirmative votes as against negative votes determines the popularity of the candidates. But a selection between candidates is not allowed to the electorate.

Elections in Tanzania and Kenya

On attainment of independence, East Africa inherited the Westminster model of government, and within that liberal model the principle of elections was one of choice rather than of acclamation. The question that arose as the Westminster model seemed to be subjected to critical re-evaluation was whether the element of choice in elections would remain. The crisis of re-evaluation first occurred in mainland Tanzania. President Julius Nyerere was confronted with the embarrassment of massive support for the single party he led, the Tanganyika African National Union. If democracy meant competition between parties, what was Tanganyika to do in the face of a strong tendency toward a unanimous choice of TANU? Was Nyerere to create an artificial opposition simply to satisfy the liberal book of rules?

In response to these initial difficulties, Nyerere began to speculate about the possibility of having electoral competition between candidates belonging to the same party. His thinking almost inevitably led toward the establishment of a one-party system *de jure* in Tanganyika. A commission was set up to explore how far the principle of a one-party system could be reconciled with the other values of the Tanganyika national ethic. The presidential commission on the one-party state was not allowed to question the principle of one-partyism but was entrusted with the job of defining the appropriate one-party system for mainland Tanzania. The commission took evidence from a variety of different sources and reported to the president in 1965.

The first elections under this system took place the same year. Members of the same ruling party, TANU, competed with each other for office. It was a momentous experiment in modern African constitutional history. Choice was effectively exercised, and some ministers lost their seats. Among the most spectacular of the defeats was that of Paul Bomani, who had served as finance minister; he had apparently been so dedicated to his work in Dar es Salaam that he had allowed little time for the task of nursing his constituency and playing politics to maintain his popularity. Nyerere later decided to retain Bomani's services in spite of his electoral defeat, but Bomani's fall from power at the ballot box was an indication of the choice that was possible within one-party competitive elections.

The system had another test in 1970, and again it demonstrated its resilience. There was far less excitement about the 1970 elections than there had been about the 1965 elections, an indication that the system was becoming routinized and gradually accepted as part of the East African political scene.

In the case of the election of the president, however, the system operated differently. Nyerere was the only candidate, and voters could say either yes or no to his candidacy. Since Nyerere was popular both in mainland Tanzania and in Zanzibar, the number of "no" voters was, in both instances, flatteringly small.

An important political question was beginning to emerge. Tanzania seemed to be operating an electoral system that used the principle of acclamation for the election of the president and the principle of choice for the election of members of Parliament. What was the significance of this combination for the functionality of the electoral system?

It was not until 1969, when elections were held in Kenya, that the full import of this combination began to appear. The elections were to be preceded by primary elections within each party. There were two parties — the one in power, the Kenya African National Union, and the opposition party to the left, the Kenya People's Union. The electoral fever began to rise, but there were indications of contrived handicaps put in the way of the Kenya People's Union by enthusiastic officials on the side of the government.

In October, 1969, President Kenyatta visited Kisumu, in the heartland of the opposition party, in order to open a new hospital built with a grant from the Soviet Union. Hostility to Kenyatta among the population there soon became apparent. In the course of Kenyatta's speech there was some booing and heckling, aggravated by Kenyatta's own colorful language of ridicule against his critics. The situation deteriorated rapidly, and the special force which was there to defend and protect the president opened fire. A number of people were killed, and the nation hovered on the brink of acute civil strife. When Kenyatta returned to the capital, the opposition party was banned, and the leaders of the opposition party were subsequently detained.

Would the elections be postponed in view of these developments? The answer seemed to be decidedly no. The party candidates would compete with each other in what otherwise would have been primaries but which were now becoming full-fledged general elections. Large numbers of candidates did, in fact, emerge. In an attempt to cut down the competition, the government imposed a rule whereby any person employed in the public service who wanted to stand for election had to resign in advance of the election and could not ask for his job back. In spite of this hazard, many regarded it as worth their while to abandon the security of their careers and scramble for a seat in Parliament. There were no restrictions as to the maximum number of candidates.

The outcome of the elections was impressive. Many people had thought that the banning of the opposition party would reduce the electoral exercise to a political farce, but this was not the case. Out of a legislature of 158 members, the voters elected 93 new members. Five ministers and thirteen assistant ministers were among the electoral casualties. As one observer put it, "Kenyatta's political system was now triumphant."[1]

More specifically, what was triumphant was the principle of choice in the parliamentary elections, whereas the president ran unopposed and was elected implicitly by acclamation. The banning of the opposition party had the effect

---

1. Donald C. Savage, "Kenyatta and the Development of African Nationalism in Kenya," *International Journal*, XXV, no. 3 (Summer, 1970), 531.

of producing a two-tier electoral system. Had the opposition party been allowed to compete in the elections, the presidency would have been under challenge. Which person should be president of Kenya — Jomo Kenyatta or Oginga Odinga? Which party should have a majority in Parliament — KANU or KPU? Both questions would have had to be resolved by application of the principle of choice.

If the principle of choice had been applied at both levels, the reality of choice would have been reduced. Because the fate of members of Parliament seemed linked to the fate of the president, the pressures against free elections at the parliamentary level would have been considerable. Overenthusiastic local officials in Kenya were known to disqualify large numbers of opposition candidates in municipal elections on the slightest excuse of irregularity. The temptation for such officials to interfere in parliamentary elections in order to ensure that official KANU candidates were victorious would have been even greater in 1969 if the elections were also going to decide the political fate of Mzee Kenyatta himself. And because of the KPU challenge, the very idea of official KANU candidates would have been more rigidly enforced in spite of appearances of constituency choice in the primary elections.

Once the Kenya People's Union was banned, the fate of the president was no longer in question; only the composition of Parliament was at stake. Candidates identifying themselves as members of KANU — with no special credentials to verify their party affiliation — came in dozens to contest the parliamentary elections. The primaries were in effect substantive parliamentary elections. There was a turnover of over 60 per cent in the composition of the National Assembly. Such a turnover would have been unlikely if the opposition party had been competing for parliamentary seats and challenging the president.

The moral to be drawn from Kenya's experience, as well as from Tanzania's, is that real choice in parliamentary elections is possible only if the position of the president is not also being challenged. Pressures against free elections at the parliamentary level are greater in situations where the president as well as the members of Parliament are jointly fighting for political survival.

Therefore, in African conditions the liberal principle of choice in parliamentary elections stands a better chance of being realized in situations where the nonliberal principle of acclamation is used in the presidential election. Acclamation for the president and effective choice for members of Parliament seem at present to be the two tiers of a viable electoral system in East Africa. Electoral maturation as an index of political development has to wait until the principle of choice can be effectively applied at both the presidential and the parliamentary levels.

Obote's Search for a System

During Milton Obote's last year in office, Uganda faced a similar issue. On July 17, 1970, Obote proposed a new electoral scheme. There would be a single candidate in the presidential election, and the electorate would be empowered to vote either yes or no for that candidate. In the case of a tie between positive and negative votes, the candidate was to be declared elected. Should the candidate lose the election, the National Assembly was to hold a special meeting and select from its own membership an interim president to hold office until another general election could be held.

The National Council of Obote's political party, the Uganda People's Congress, sought to protect him from a national campaign of this kind and devised a formula whereby the president of the UPC was automatically the president of the country. Since Obote had recently been elected president of the party for a term of seven years by a delegates' conference, there was no need for him to face the electorate of the country — so these admirers of the president asserted. Obote fought this decision in an elequent memorandum which reasserted the need for the president to face the national electorate. He called a meeting of the Annual Delegates' Conference of the Uganda People's Congress in September, 1970, but the position taken by the National Council was maintained.

It was not until another conference met, called by the president in December, 1970, that Obote's resistance to this idea ultimately prevailed. A formula did emerge allowing for at least the theoretical possibility of a rival candidate in an election if enough constituency conferences (one-third of the national total) were to give their backing to such a candidate.

It was not merely with the method of electing the president that Obote's original Document No. 5 was concerned. The document also contained new proposals concerning methods of electing members of Parliament. The proposals were in many ways the most original political reform to be recommended in Uganda since independence and also represented some of the most innovative ideas to emerge out of Africa. When the Uganda coup of January, 1971, took place, arrangements were already being made to implement the proposals. Although the coup interrupted these, the proposals continue to be a major contribution to African constitutional thought.

Uganda politics was confronted with two factors — one indigenous and the other imported. The indigenous factor was the pull of tribal loyalties and the commitment of politicians to individual regions in the country; the imported factor was the electoral system. The interaction between these two factors could not but have profound effects on the country. Was the single-member constituency, inherited from the British system of elections, an element which aggravated some of the implications of tribal loyalties in Uganda? Was it possible that a different system of constituencies would promote a different pattern of political interaction? Was it conceivable that the single-member constituency slowed down the task of forging national consciousness?

These are some of the questions that normally arise as soon as one considers the likely repercussions of an electoral system on the quality of politics in a given country. President Obote decided that a major innovation was needed if the pull of tribal loyalties on a member of Parliament was to be loosened.

The proposals in Document No. 5 concerning methods of electing representatives of the people to Parliament were designed to meet this challenge. We have noted that the proposals addressed themselves to the major issue of how the president of the country was to be chosen. In many ways this was a critical factor in a country where the president wielded such enormous power. Yet these proposals, though they contained certain original elements, were in totality less revolutionary than the proposals for electing members of Parliament. It was the latter which were potentially more consequential for the future of tribal politics in Uganda.

The basic innovation was the substitution of the idea of four constituencies per member of Parliament for the old idea of one constituency per member. Under the new proposals each candidate was to indicate the constituency in which he wished to stand, which was then regarded as his basic constituency. In each basic constituency there were to be not less than two nor more than three candidates; Obote later amended the number to stand at two. A candidate registered his candidacy only in the basic constituency; after he had done so, the law would then require that he was, by the same instrument, nominated to stand as a candidate in three national constituencies, each in a different region of the country. Each voter would cast one vote for the basic candidate of his choice and one vote for each of the three national candidates of his choice, each from a different region. The popular votes cast in each constituency in favor of or against a candidate were to be computed on a percentage, counting as an electoral vote. The electoral votes for and against the candidate in all the four constituencies were to be added up; if the total number of electoral votes in favor of the candidate was greater than the number against the candidate, then he would be declared elected.

This scheme can be described as "electoral polygamy" in both a metaphorical and a literal sense. In the metaphorical sense, electoral polygamy is the idea of marrying each member of Parliament to four constituencies, with the concomitant implications which such an arrangement would have in terms of loyalties and obligations. In the literal sense, the implementation of such an electoral scheme in Uganda could result in, among other things, an increase in interregional marriages as a way of consolidating political support. There is an area of life in Africa where questions of marriage and kinship touch questions of politics and social organization. Just as Document No. 5, if revived and implemented, is likely to affect the political system as a whole in important ways, that same document might also affect those aspects of kinship and marriage which influence political behavior.

Political Confidence versus Political Consent

Let us first take the wider and more figurative meaning of electoral polygamy. What we are discussing under this heading is not only the nature of political trust in Africa but the phenomenon of trust in relation to traditional culture, tribal structure, and the ballot box. A good approach may be simply to treat Document No. 5 as a piece of constitutional theory rooted in sociological assumptions and ignore the fact that its author is no longer president of Uganda. We may, in fact, treat Obote in this regard as a constitutional theorist. There is always the possibility that the scheme may one day be re-examined for what practical insights it might afford in the field of electoral engineering in a country like Uganda.[2]

The case for the scheme contained in Document No. 5 hinges on the concept of political trust. By what means can members of Parliament enjoy the trust and confidence of the nation as a whole rather than that of only their immediate clan? What should be the criterion of popular trust? Should it be the number of supporters a man has in his own tribal area, or should it be more in terms of the national source of support?

The proposals have grasped an important distinction between government with the people's consent and government with the people's confidence. There are, in fact, occasions when government with the people's confidence is more important than government with the people's consent. The electorate may give its consent periodically to alternating regimes, each of which vies with the others for self-aggrandizement. The electorate may become cynical and have little faith in the integrity of its rulers; but as long as elections are held periodically, and the people have a chance to exercise their choice by voting for one group of politicians instead of another, the principle of government with the people's consent is satisfied. Nevertheless, the country may still have failed to devise a system that commands the people's confidence.

Obote's Document No. 5 suggests that if an assembly consists of members who are regarded as ambassadors of the different tribes, and if certain decisions do not favor certain tribes, part of the population may feel that it has been let down. The confidence of part of the nation in the national legislature is eroded, since the entire exercise of legislation is viewed as one of competing tribal interests, each tribe seeking fulfillment through a national mechanism but ultimately conscious primarily of itself and its own self-interests.

Paragraph 12 of Document No. 5 argues:

> If the pull of the tribal force is allowed to develop the unity of the country will be endangered. To reduce it to its crudest form, the pull of the tribal force does not accept Uganda as one country, does not accept the people of Uganda as belonging to one country, does not accept the National Assembly as a national institution but as an assembly of peace conference delegates and tribal diplomatic and legislative functionaries, and looks at the Government of Uganda as a body of umpires or referees in some curious game of "Tribal Development Monopoly."

---

2. See Selwyn Ryan, "Electoral Engineering in Uganda," *Mawazo*, II, no. 4 (December, 1970), 3–12.

The document discusses some of the absurd consequences of this tribal pull. A leader who is subject too much to the tribal perspective will see any project outside his tribal area as having been situated in that area purely for tribal reasons. The same person, however, will insist that the projects in his own area, for which the person responsible is a fellow tribesman, were located in that region independently of tribal considerations.

The document discusses the phenomena of nepotism and of counternepotism in both their real and their presumed versions. Recruitment into the public service is singled out for special analysis. It is suggested that there are occasions when people think that a public official is recruiting from among his own tribesmen or those who support him. In addition, there is the phenomenon of counternepotism — a public official who is so afraid of being mistaken for a tribalist that he does not encourage his own tribesmen to join him in his department. It could be a minister, eager to assert an image of absolute impartiality and forced by the circumstances of the day to discriminate against his own tribesmen as a way of securing his reputation. Paragraph 14 of Document No. 5 asserts:

> The Party and the Government must act on these accusations of nepotism . . . in recruitment wherever they are found to be valid and members of the Party must be alert and report any such violation of the law. On the other hand, the Party must not accept any warped thinking on this matter but stand firm and refuse to accept the irrational logic that all persons whose relatives and friends are in Government must not be recruited into the Public Service and if they are already there must not be promoted.

It is quite clear that the document expresses profound concern about the operation of tribal and clan factors, or family favoritism, in affairs of state. But the document also argues that citizens should not be discriminated against out of a mistaken assumption by a public official that to help a person who happens to belong to his own tribe, even if the help is deserved by merit, is somehow to do a disservice to the ethic of impartiality.

What Document No. 5 seeks to do is to nationalize confidence in government. Government by consent might be achieved by having free elections in single-member constituencies. Government with the people's confidence might also be partially realized in situations where each member of Parliament enjoys the confidence of his own little sector of society. Document No. 5 seeks to widen the boundaries of confidence and trust and to challenge each member of Parliament to realize concrete political support in areas other than his home area.

Does the document go too far in this attempt to nationalize confidence? The proposals in the document do make it possible for a candidate who receives a minority of votes in his basic constituency to win the election through the majorities he realizes in the three national constituencies. The member of Parliament would then be known as the member for basic constituency X, although in that constituency he had received only minority support.

Is there not a danger that the people of basic constituency X might feel somehow disfranchised? Only a minority of them had voted for their member of Parliament, perhaps only a small minority. He had been brought into power with the support of people distant from his own home and far from the area which he had chosen as his basic area of operation. Would not the people feel unrepresented in spite of the fact that there was a member of Parliament associating himself with them?

Political trust in African societies is sometimes related to empathy, and empathy is related to a sense of shared identity. It is true that this is not always the case. For example, there are African houseboys who trust *Bazungu*, or white employers, much more than they trust employers drawn from their own tribal communities. One does not want to overemphasize the element of shared identity in the whole phenomenon of trust. Nevertheless, the same houseboy trusts a *Muzungu* employer more than an employer from his own tribe is likely to trust his own tribesman at the ballot box. Africans voting for fellow Africans rather than for competitors from other races is a phenomenon that would surprise no one. But should Africans vote for fellow tribesmen rather than for competitors from other tribes?

As a piece of constitutional reform, Document No. 5 seeks to neutralize the tribalist tendency in African politics. However, if the nature of trust in African political behavior does often relate itself to tribal empathy, is there not a danger that the operation of Document No. 5 might reduce the confidence of the people in their representatives rather than increase it? In the attempt to nationalize that precious quality of the people's confidence, might not the proposals dilute that trust itself?

Another factor to be borne in mind in a system of multiple constituencies and candidates is the danger of putting a special premium on being well known. People who are already national figures are more likely to be known in all four constituencies than those who are struggling to emerge politically. Prior prominence would count for more in a system of four constituencies per member than in a system of one.

It may be retorted that familiarity sometimes breeds contempt rather than admiration. A candidate who is nationally known is not necessarily nationally liked. Prominence in some instances might be a liability; the relative newcomer who is a nonentity might benefit by having his weaknesses still obscure. This argument holds, but only up to a point. Detailed knowledge of a national figure can be either positive or negative. The man might be very well known in his own area; and, because the knowledge his constituents have of him is so detailed, it might sometimes be a liability rather than an asset. But to be well known in a vague sense is more likely to be an asset than a liability. The prominent man's name has a ring of familiarity; it has been heard on the radio or read in newspapers. The population is not quite clear as to what his fame is due; but he is obviously someone important, since his name is not entirely unfamiliar.

Let us consider a candidate who is a former minister. It might be said that fame in districts other than the former minister's own home might well be an asset in advance. He is known as a former minister, and by that categorization he goes up in the people's estimation. They do not know much else about him. In his own area, however, where interaction with him and his family is high, where many people have known him since childhood, where his every move is studied with possessiveness, the former minister might be revealed in all his stark reality. Suppose, then, that there is an election and that the minister loses in his basic constituency, which is his own tribal area, but wins massive votes of confidence in the national constituencies far from home. The votes of the national constituencies in this case would be votes based on very inadequate knowledge of the candidate — knowledge drawn partly from a short encounter with the candidate during the campaign and partly from the prior prominence of the man's name. Is the national support, which is based on superficial knowledge of the candidate, a greater indication of confidence than the minister's rejection by his own basic constituency — a rejection founded on deeper knowledge of him?

Another factor which gives a margin of advantage to those who are already prominent is the high selectivity of news media in a country which has had problems of instability. Those who hold public office in an African country, though not necessarily fully protected from the glare of critical public opinion, nevertheless enjoy substantial security. Criticism of ministers and their performance and complaints about the work of individual ministries are indeed still heard in some African countries; but such reports are more rare than accounts of ministers' speeches, of the applause they receive at public rallies, and of the achievements of their departments. The selectivity is sometimes understandable, given the nature of political difficulties in the Africa of this generation. There are occasions when the business of consolidating the people's confidence in the government entails protecting the government from premature scrutiny.

Precisely because news of ministers and their ministries is covered so selectively, it is pre-eminently in the basic constituencies of these personalities that their weaknesses are likely to be known. Their weaknesses may be forgiven, for the son of the tribe needs the tribe's indulgence and support. The former minister may receive an overwhelming vote of confidence in his home area; but, if he is forgiven for his failings, at least the forgiveness is not based on ignorance. He is known intimately; his services to the community are appreciated, even if his defects are also recognized.

What all these issues pertaining to Document No. 5 raise is the simple question of whether the trust, or the lack of trust, of national constituencies as expressed at the ballot box is adequately founded on enlightened information. Can trust be so founded, given the degree of selectivity in news coverage in African countries, as well as the degree of political awareness on a national level and in villages?

At the time Document No. 5 was being debated in Uganda, some modifications of the proposals were suggested. Obote was eager to discuss the issues and spent many hours with members of the Department of Political Science at Makerere answering their queries and discussing their criticisms. One modification suggested was to retain the four constituencies but to insist that a member of Parliament had to win a majority in his basic constituency as well as a majority in the total electoral votes obtained in the three national constituencies. An alternative approach was to have the candidate compete in four constituencies at election time but be required to win only three of them, provided one was the basic constituency. This could have reduced the burden of nursing four constituencies in between elections, even if the burden of campaigning in four remained the same. A candidate could be permitted to campaign in only three, but in that case he would be taking a risk. He had to win all three and had no margin of surprise losses in elections. A third possibility was a stipulation that a candidate should compete in three constituencies, win a majority of the electoral votes, a majority of the popular vote in his basic constituency, and a majority of the popular vote in at least one more constituency.

Some of the proposed modifications would have made the scheme more complex and more difficult to implement. Indeed, some carried too big a risk of leading to many inconclusive elections. However, in all these proposals what was being urged was that a candidate should be able to win in his basic constituency. He might be forgiven his failings, but the verdict of his basic constituency should indeed be "basic." The electors, in turn, had to be permitted to enjoy a sense of being represented by their own kin. Although this would cater to kinship, a nationalizing factor could be achieved by requiring the candidate to win the confidence of people outside as well as within his own area. The votes of the basic constituency could be weighted a little more than those of one national constituency, but the system would still make it impossible for a candidate to win without substantial support from the national constituencies. This would have married the idea of nationalized political trust to the older notion of a trust rooted in tribal empathy and family awareness. It represented a compromise between the ambition to eliminate tribalism and the reality of its existence.

Marriage and the Politics of Kinship

Let us now address ourselves to the more literal meaning of electoral polygamy — the phenomenon of multiple marriages, interregional in nature, arising out of the dictates of political alignment. In order to understand the hypothetical repercussions of Document No. 5 on marriage patterns, we have to look at the wider meaning of marriage in African society against the background of modern politics on the continent.

A. R. Radcliffe-Brown and C. Daryll Forde, after extensive experience in

the anthropological study of African systems of kinship and marriage, made
the following observations in a book devoted to the phenomenon of kinship
and marriage in Africa:

> In order to understand the African customs relating to marriage we have to bear
> in mind that a marriage is essentially a rearrangement of social structure. . . . New
> social relations are created, not only between the husband and the wife, and be-
> tween the husband and the wife's relatives on the one side and between the wife
> and the husband's relatives on the other, but also, in a great many societies, be-
> tween the relatives of the husband and those of the wife, who, on the two sides, are
> interested in the marriage and in the children that are expected to result from
> it. Marriages, like births, deaths, or initiations at puberty, are rearrangements
> of structure that are constantly recurring in any society; they are moments of
> the continuing social process regulated by custom; there are institutionalised ways
> of dealing with such events.[3]

On the stage of modern politics in Africa, is this really relevant? Let us
first look for an answer on the stage of Pan-Africanism. In 1957 an important
marriage from a Pan-African point of view took place. The marriage turned
out to have an inconclusive future, but while it lasted it was pregnant with
political symbolism. The bridegroom was one of independent Africa's greatest
sons, Kwame Nkrumah. The bride was an Egyptian girl, unknown until then
but suddenly acquiring a continental meaning. The marriage was a quiet trans-
Saharan bond.

Of all the English-speaking heads of government south of the Sahara, Nkrumah
went furthest in his attempt to challenge the great desert's division of the African
continent. Within months of Nkrumah's marriage to an Egyptian girl, Accra
was getting ready for the first conference of independent African states. Explaining the significance of the conference to his countrymen, Nkrumah said in
a national broadcast:

> For the first time, I think, in the history of this great continent, leaders of all
> the *purely African* states which can play an independent role in international affairs
> will meet to discuss the problems of our countries.[4]

It is significant that the countries which Nkrumah was recognizing as purely
African were Tunisia, Morocco, Egypt, Sudan, Libya, Ethiopia, and Liberia.
These were the countries whose representatives he welcomed on April 15, 1968.
He affirmed to them a slogan which he often tried to live up to: "If in the
past the Sahara divided us, now it unites us. And an injury to one is an injury

3. A. R. Radcliffe-Brown and C. Daryll Forde, *African Systems of Kinship and
Marriage* (1950; reprint ed., London: Oxford University Press, 1962), pp. 43–44.
4. Kwame Nkrumah, *I Speak of Freedom* (London: Heinemann; New York: Praeger,
1961), p. 125. Emphasis added.

to all of us.'' [5] At the final session of the conference Nkrumah returned to this theme. He said:

> The former imperialist powers were fond of talking about ''Arab Africa'' and ''Black Africa''; and ''Islamic Africa'' and ''Non-Islamic Africa.'' . . . These were all artificial descriptions which tended to divide us. . . . Today the *Sahara is a bridge uniting us*.[6]

That quiet wedding between Nkrumah and an Egyptian girl was in a sense the personalization of Nkrumah's political philosophy. From all accounts he hardly knew the girl. Nor was this a dynastic marriage between kingly houses. In a fundamental sense it was a profound personalization of Pan-Africanism in Nkrumah's own life.

As an approach to creating new links between groups, Nkrumah's marriage was in an important tradition, both from the African side and from the Arab side. In many African societies marriage often represents an alliance between two groups. The groups are not always two different tribes; more often they are subsections of a clan. But, where political questions are at stake, marriage is at times utilized as a way of uniting clans and creating an interpenetration in their loyalties and social organization.

On the Arab side, too, marriage has often served this function. In the history of Islam, polygamy has been an important instrument of statecraft. The Prophet Muhammad himself had wives from different Arab tribes as a way of consolidating alliances and initiating the process of political integration. The Muslim community as a political community was a new phenomenon, aspiring to universalistic bonds and afraid of divisive tendencies arising out of previous loyalties. Like most founders of new political communities, Muhammad was concerned about the stability of the new relationships among subgroups and the durability of the structures of authority which had captured their allegiance for the time being. Marriage in the life of Muhammad became, therefore, not simply a relationship between a man and a woman but a matter which could be important both for political integration within the new community and for the consolidation of political authority.

Nkrumah's marriage fell within the integrative tradition of political matrimony. The aim in this case was not to consolidate authority and assure allegiance to the new structures of rule but to symbolize a trans-Saharan solidarity. The marriage was not proclaimed in these terms; no trumpets of Pan-Africanism were blown to draw attention to the trans-Saharan significance of this match. Yet, against the background of Nkrumah's continental vision, the message was clear. The Lady Fathiya, the consort of Nkrumah as president of Ghana, became

---

5. *Ibid.*, p. 131.
6. Kwame Nkrumah, *Hands Off Africa! ! ! !* (Accra: Kwabena Owsu-Akyem, 1960), p. 23. Emphasis original.

the mother of Nkrumah's children; and the children were a further personalization of trans-Saharan integration.

Two forms of political unity are very critical in African affairs — the interstate variety, which we call Pan-African unity, and the intrastate version, which we call national unity. It is quite clear that Nkrumah symbolized, above all else, the first category of political unity. As long as he was in power, his was the golden voice of Pan-African solidarity. Milton Obote of Uganda was a fighter for that other kind of political unity in Africa — national unity. Few leaders on the continent had to fight harder in political tactics and strategic planning to try to leave behind them in their country a firm foundation of national cohesiveness. Obote fell far short of a conclusive victory, but he did play his part in the struggle for national integration.

President Obote's marriage seemed more of a personal affair and less of a political symbol than Nkrumah's. Yet African marriages are never entirely private; there are always social implications beyond those intended by the couple. The theme of national unity was therefore by no means absent in Obote's private life, regardless of his intentions. There was a touch of appropriateness when Obote and his bride decided to spend part of their honeymoon in Ghana as guests of his old friend Kwame Nkrumah. Both men had remained profoundly animated by a vision of greater unity. Obote's vision had been one of forging tribes into a nation. Nkrumah's vision was more distant and sometimes elusive. His was a vision of forging a nation out of a whole continent. The two leaders remained great admirers of each other. Their private lives were on the whole their own, but there were aspects which touched upon issues of wider society.

With Obote's Document No. 5, and the idea of multiple constituencies for each member of Parliament, the question of marriage seemed likely to become more explicit as a political dimension in Uganda than it had ever been in other African countries. Document No. 5, conceding that much of political trust in Africa had been connected with issues of kinship, lineage, and tribal links, proposed to challenge the idea of relating trust to kinship and tribe. Paragraph 15 states:

> The surest and strongest guard that the Party can mount in the case of National leaders is not to accept any person just because he can show that he has the confidence of his tribe or clan. A national leader must have a high degree, in as much as is possible, of the confidence and support of the people outside his tribal area. The aim should be that a Member of Parliament should not base his representative status on the substantial votes he might have obtained from his clan or his tribe.

Could the habit of looking to kinship relationships for political allies and support be eroded that easily? Was there not a possibility that the politics of kinship ties would be expanded if a candidate from one basic constituency were to marry someone from one of his national constituencies? If Document

No. 5 were to be implemented, it seems likely that within a decade there would be more members of Parliament married to wives from other regions than there have been so far in independent Uganda. The trend need not, of course, be toward a situation in which each member of Parliament has four wives, one in each political port of call. It would not be surprising, however, if a large number of members of Parliament were to turn out to have at least two wives, each from a different region.

Two related factors would be particularly important in linking matrimony to constituencies in this way. One factor is the member of Parliament's need for more than one home; the other is his need for more than one political base. The need for an additional home arises out of considerations for maintaining contact with a constituency. The member of Parliament who hopes to retain the support of a national constituency in the next round of elections has to "nurse" the constituency. That means attending to its needs and desires insofar as that is practicable. Periodic visits to the constituency are therefore inevitable.

The party may arrange special hostels and provide facilities for visiting M.P.'s, but some M.P.'s may feel that visiting a constituency and always staying in a hostel creates a sense of social distance. One remains a stranger in a national constituency if one invariably has to act like a passerby. There will therefore be a temptation for some M.P.'s to establish homes in their national constituencies. In a number of cases this might well mean that the M.P. will have a second wife and will equip her with a house in which he can live during his periodic visits to that part of his political world.

What would be at stake here is simply a politicization of a common experience in Africa. As a child, I commuted every week between two homes. My father was not a politician in the usual sense, but he did have two occupational interests — a job as an Islamic judge and civil servant in the city, and a little farm in a rural area. In a nonpolitical sense one might say that my father had two occupational constituencies — and, as it happened, he had two wives. My mother was in the town, consort to my father in his role as judge and civil servant; my stepmother was on the farm, looking after my father on weekends. As a young boy, I accompanied my father to his country home every Saturday and returned to my mother's home during the week, when my father returned to the city and put on his working robes as a Muslim judge. In that kind of situation, and against that background of cultural arrangements, it was almost inconceivable that there should not be a separate wife for each occupational constituency.

If Uganda's members of Parliament in the days ahead were to have four constituencies, as Obote proposed, it is doubtful that they would attempt thoroughness and have four wives. But two wives, or even three, would be a tempting proposition under the political system proposed by Document No. 5.

The other factor which would encourage this trend is the need for a second political base. A member of Parliament in a national constituency could be a complete stranger, unknown to the local people, promoted only in the depersonalized sense of party enthusiasm. If he comes from another tribe, he cannot, by definition, have immediate kinsmen in a national constituency unless a significant number of people from his own area have settled there. An alternative to the advantage of having kinsmen by blood in a constituency is the advantage of having kinsmen by marriage. The precise pattern of relationships would vary in different areas of Uganda and among different communities. There is, after all, diversity in cultural patterns. There are some groups with matrilineal and some with patrilineal relationships, and the variations would have implications for the progeny of the marriages. There are bound to be differences in how the phenomenon of electoral polygamy operates from constituency to constituency, but in many instances new links established by a political marriage would promote a nucleus of political relatives. Echoes of Radcliffe-Brown and Forde, the two distinguished social anthropologists we quoted earlier, might well be heard again, were the matrimonial consequences of Document No. 5 to unfold themselves.

What would be the implications of such marriages for nation-building? One cannot be sure about the details, but the effect as a whole should be positive. The phenomenon of creating interpenetrating linkages of this kind is by no means novel in African social structures. Even in politics, marriage has already played an important part. The 1962 elections in Uganda were not without instances of alliances between clans in support of candidates — alliances based ultimately on relations by marriage. Of course, a good deal depends on whether a clan is endogamous or exogamous. The single-member constituencies permitted matrimonial factors to influence political alignments at the transclan level. What Document No. 5 might promote is the phenomenon of transregional as well as transtribal matrimonial alignments in politics.

In this connection the ironic precedent of Gen. Idi Amin is also to be taken into account. In January, 1971, Amin captured power from Obote in a military coup. At that time Amin had three wives, each from a different tribe — a Musoga, a Lugbara, and a Langi. When he took over power, Amin used his matrimonial record as evidence that he was not a tribalist. On March 20, 1971, Amin went to Lango, Obote's tribal area, and reminded the Langi that he had taken a wife from among them on the recommendation of President Obote and of Akena Adoko, Obote's cousin and head of the Intelligence Service in Obote's regime, who was also of the Langi tribe.[7]

If Document No. 5 were to be saved from the ashes of militarized Uganda and implemented, matrimonial effects would take time to consolidate themselves. The building up of alignments from evolving kinship relations might take at least a decade, or even a generation. If Document No. 5 were not only

---

7. See *Uganda Argus* (Kampala), March 22, 1971. In March, 1972, President Amin took a fourth bride, a Muganda.

implemented but also maintained, it seems likely that some kind of matrimonial reorientation might begin to appear in between elections.

Integration through Electoral Engineering

National integration often presupposes substantial interaction among regions. This interaction can be economic, as exchange relationships are evolved and trade among different groups assumes a new importance, but it must also, if it is to result in national integration, include political dimensions. Obote's Document No. 5 sought to promote precisely such a widening of political interaction, as it proposed to force candidates to rely on areas other than their own and proposed to force voters to think of politics in terms beyond their immediate localities.

Cultural interaction is the area of nation-building that necessitates the gradual accumulation of shared norms and values and shared perspectives on the universe, in spite of variations of emphasis. That meeting point of politics and personal intimacy, of elections and kinship ties, could be one of the most important areas of the integrative process. Members of Parliament who are scattering their Maker's image through the land could be nationalizing the concept of kinship itself. Transregional and transtribal marriages might facilitate cultural intercourse and greater mutual awareness. To the extent that such marriages also emphasize the bonds of kinship solidarity in politics, instances of electoral polygamy in the literal sense might turn out to be a major factor in the inter-regionalization of at least the ruling elite. The most politically influential of all groups might in time become, through the very links they have established in different regions, the vanguard of a new race of Ugandans.

Should the political elite maintain and enhance its social prestige and become a pacesetter in the cultural as well as the political sphere, there might develop a significant demonstration effect in the field of transtribal matrimony. Such matches have already begun to be promoted by forces of urbanization and general economic migration. If politics were also to lend a hand in facilitating these mixed marriages, a new dimension would be added to the most fundamental of all levels of national integration — the level of mixing the blood of the nation. If ever implemented, Milton Obote's Document No. 5 might turn out to be not only a new breakthrough in African constitutional thought but an important experiment in social and biocultural engineering.

Polygamy is normally thought of as premodern. So is tribalism. What Document No. 5 might initiate is the mobilization of polygamy for the fight against tribalism. To mobilize polygamy for the purpose of national integration is to utilize once again a primordial custom for the task of modernization.

In parts of Nigeria following the civil war, polygamy has been thought of as a solution to some of the consequences of national disintegration. Communities in what was formerly Biafra — some devoutly Catholic, but beset by a shortage of marriageable men following the costly war — seemed in 1970 and 1971 to have been turning once again to the solution of sharing the men. The alternative was perhaps a problem of large numbers of unemployed, unmarried, and indigent women, with the concomitant social costs of widespread illegitimacy and subsequent juvenile delinquency. The Roman Catholic church was reported in mid-1970 to be understandably disturbed by this polygamous solution to the demographic imbalance between the sexes. Yet the task of restructuring kinship relations, averting widespread female indigence, and containing illegitimacy and subsequent delinquency seemed to invite the careful consideration of polygamy as one approach to national reconstruction.[8]

In the case of Obote's Uganda the trend toward mobilizing polygamy was for the process of winning political battles rather than for coping with the after-effects of a civil war. In Uganda there was potentially a clearer instance of engaging social primordialism for purposes of political modernization.

Document No. 5 would have added a new dimension to an older story in Uganda — the story of a society which has often found areas of accommodation and interplay between tradition and innovation in the process of political development. But Obote's electoral proposals have to be seen also in the wider context of the principles of choice and acclamation as functional foundations of elections. The voters in each of the four constituencies were to vote for three national candidates. The location of the constituencies covered the four points of the national compass — east, west, north, and south. The political experience of tribesmen from the four corners of the nation jointly choosing from the same set of electoral candidates would itself have been in the direction of political integration.

With regard to the election of the president of Uganda, Obote's final amended proposals were in fact, though not in name, based on the principle of acclamation rather than choice. His final proposals to the party in December, 1970, provided not only for an official candidate put forward by the party but also for the possibility of a contested election if a third of the total number of constituency conferences of Uganda as a whole nominated a rival candidate. This appeared to be a system based on the principle of choice. However, the minimum number of constituencies required for a rival nomination was thirty-two, and at that stage of Obote's rule no constituency was likely to put forward a rival candidate. Therefore, it was almost certain that the party's candidate would be unopposed.

The political realities of Uganda at the time therefore converted Obote's proposals on the election of the president to a scheme founded on the *de facto* principle of acclamation, though his proposals for the election of members of

---

8. For an example of the kind of thinking that was going on in parts of Iboland, see the report from a special correspondent, "Nigerian Town Decides in Favour of Polygamy," *The People*, August 20, 1970.

Parliament remained firmly based on the principle of choice, both in law and in practical design. Yet the success of such parliamentary elections as exercises in popular choice depended, in part, precisely on the security afforded the top man by the assurance of presidential acclamation.

The three East African countries adopted three different approaches to electoral engineering; but they retained an area of similarity of experience in the relationship between popular acclamation and popular choice in the electoral process.

[10]

Social Distance and
the Transclass Man

On the day following the coup which overthrew the regime of President Modibo Keita in Mali, a leading politician on the east coast of Africa advanced a theory to try to explain the relative ease with which military coups were accomplished. Speaking to the United Kenya Club in Nairobi, Martin Shikuku, the Kenya government's chief whip, attributed military coups in Africa mainly to the tendency of political leaders to "get out of touch with the people," accumulate as much wealth as possible, and engage in personal rivalries.[1] One possible safeguard that a political regime might have against the danger of a military coup is popular support, and popular support might be seriously undermined in situations where leaders "get out of touch with the people." However, our concern here is not with the causes of military coups but with the allegedly growing distance between leaders and followers which Shikuku found in contemporary Africa.

The social distance between leaders and followers is much narrower in Africa than it is in most developed regions. In fact, there is so much interpenetration in Africa between the world of the elite and the world of the masses that the elite has resorted to the trappings of social grandeur as a way of creating an artificial distinctiveness. This phenomenon, which I have called "the quest for aristocratic effect," has taken the form of social ostentation among the African elite. More specifically, it has meant a partiality for splendid attire, for large, expensive cars, for palatial accommodations, and for other forms of conspicuous consumption.[2]

Although this conspicuous consumption may have a tendency to erode political legitimacy by creating disaffection with leaders among the rest of the populace, this disaffection arises from social nearness rather than social distance. In situations where the leaders are identified too readily as people who have risen

---

1. *East African Standard* (Nairobi), November 21, 1968.
2. This is also discussed in Ali A. Mazrui, "The Monarchical Tendency in African Political Culture," *British Journal of Sociology*, XVIII, no. 3 (September, 1967), 231–50, reprinted in *idem*, *Violence and Thought: Essays on Social Tensions in Africa* (London: Longmans, 1969), pp. 206–30.

from the ranks, it is easy for those who remain in the ranks to become envious of the privileges enjoyed by their former peers. The "lower classes" are more likely to forgive long-established aristocrats for their luxurious living than they are to forgive newly successful members of the privileged classes. Those who have been rich for generations have established their social distance and have made it appear natural, if not deserved. The newly opulent are more easily accused of "giving themselves airs" and are more easily resented as a result. What ought to be grasped, however, is that the resentment arises not from a clearly defined social distance, but from a persistently residual social nearness of these newly opulent to their poorer relatives.

Classes in Transition

A major factor involved in all of this is the phenomenon of the transclass man. There seems to be little doubt that one of the major faults of certain schools of Marxism is the assumption that man must belong to only one class at a time. Marx allowed for social mobility, and even for the merger of classes, as the historical process approached the polarization of class conflict. What even he did not adequately allow for, however, was the phenomenon of the person who, in a situation of great structural fluidity, is compelled to belong to more than one class. In such a situation a dual- or even a polyclass personality becomes conceivable.[3]

Before one can fully understand the nature of social distance and social nearness in Africa, it is necessary to analyze the causes and implications of this experience of transclass ambivalence. In a traditional society the phenomenon of the transclass man rarely occurs. Ascriptive hierarchy has a certain rigidity about it, and people tend to be "kept in their place." The notion of a primeval contract between different levels of the social order, both living and dead, assigns a certain "functional specificity" to the members of each level. Conservative thought in the West turned back to such a contract, precisely at a time of revolutionary transition and mobility. At the time of the French Revolution, Edmund Burke's conception of such a contract was that of

> a partnership not only between those who are living, but between those who are living, those who are dead, and those who are to be born, [a partnership in which] each contract of each particular state is but a clause in a great primæval contract of eternal society, linking the lower with the higher natures, connecting the

---

3. The concept of the transclass man was first developed in Ali A. Mazrui, "Political Superannuation and the Trans-Class Man" (Paper delivered at the Seventh World Congress of the International Political Science Association, Brussels, September, 1967). The paper was subsequently published in the *International Journal of Comparative Sociology*, IX, no. 2 (June, 1968), 81–96. This chapter is based in part on that paper.

visible and invisible world, according to a fixed compact sanctioned by the inviolable oath which holds all physical and all moral natures, each in their appointed place.[4]

The idea of each having an appointed place permeates Burke's thought on social stratification. Burkean conservatism has mystical links with the ethos of traditionality in other parts of the world. This relative rigidity in stratification makes traditional society inhospitable to the idea that anyone might belong to more than one class.

The phenomenon of belonging to more than one class at a time is a feature of modernized society, but it is sometimes disguised by the very complexity of the economic and social patterns of that society. It becomes difficult in a modern situation of functional diversity to determine where occupational and income differences end and class variations begin.

Therefore, the transclass man is inconspicuous in both traditional and modern societies, though for radically different reasons. In traditional society he is inconspicuous because the ascriptive tendencies in stratification make it difficult for such a phenomenon to emerge. In modern societies the transclass man is inconspicuous because the complexities of socioeconomic patterns disguise the soft transition from occupational differences to class distinctions. A man in a modern society may be seen to have more than one job, but it may seldom be clear that the nature of those jobs could conceivably give him a footing in more than one class camp.

The figure of the transclass man becomes sharp, neither against the shadows of tradition nor against the blazing sun of modernity, but against the twilight sky of a transitional society. Daniel Lerner was right to divide the social world of today into traditional, transitional, and modern sectors.[5] Entire countries in Africa may be thought of as being in some sense basically "transitional" in their agonies of detraditionalization. Such countries are therefore all the more hospitable to the emergence of transclass specimens.

There is first the very coexistence of the old universe of ascriptive gradation and the new universe of achieved status. A dual system of stratification is fraught with possibilities of dual- or even polyclass identity. A person of lower status in the traditional gradation could be a member of the modern elite in terms of achievement. If his tribe is unsure which gradation should prevail, the man may have to retain a transclass ambivalence.

Linked to this dual system of stratification in a transitional African society is the duality of African economies. The traditional sector, with its tendency toward subsistence, has to coexist with the modern sector, with a market

---

4. Edmund Burke, *Reflections on the Revolution in France* (1790), in *Works* (London: Bohn's World Classics, 1907), IV, p. 107.

5. See Daniel Lerner, *The Passing of Traditional Society* (New York: Free Press, 1958), esp. pp. 69–75.

economy.[6] This economic bifurcation of society has implications for class and status in society. As Simon Ottenberg said of Ibo experience:

> The situation of culture contact has, of course, accentuated and expanded other possibilities of individual achievement. Trade has increased greatly since the cessation of traditional intergroup warfare. . . . New avenues of achieving prestige have opened, such as sending children through school.[7]

Earlier, Pius Okigbo, the Biafran-Nigerian economist, had taken the analysis further. He had argued that innovation and increasing monetization in West Africa had all too often led to a revaluation of "the traditional basis of obedience." Okigbo said:

> New statuses arise with the emergence of a new class, the rich who have made their fortune in trade either by selling the raw produce of the land or by retailing imported articles manufactured abroad. The growth of this new class of rich, divorced from the land that was so important a link in the chain that bound the society to the elders, has weakened the authorities of the elders, especially if they happen to be, as is often the case, impecunious.[8]

Okigbo sometimes exaggerates the extent to which old forms of social gradation have actually been replaced by new ones. He mistakes the direction of change for its actuality. West Africa in 1956 was far from attaining the following condition, though the trend of social change was certainly in that direction:

> The indigenous institutions are cracking. . . . With the disintegration of class groupings based on age, the society acquired a fluidity which made it easy for an individual to move up from the present status by acquiring some wealth or education. . . . In postwar West Africa, especially in the British territories, the artificial obstacles of vertical mobility appear non-existent; within the ambit allowed by the facilities of self-improvement, the individual seems to have boundless opportunities of moving to the top.[9]

---

6. There are a number of useful background studies about dual economies. A useful introductory work on Africa is Guy Benveniste and W. E. Moran, Jr., *Handbook of African Development* (New York: Praeger, 1963). See also United Nations, *Enlargement of the Exchange Economy in Tropical Africa* (E/2557, St/ECA/23), 1954. The thesis of the U.N. study is that the rate of economic development will depend on the rate at which the subsistence sector is absorbed by the exchange sector.

7. Simon Ottenberg, "Ibo Receptivity to Change," in *Continuity and Change in African Cultures*, ed. William R. Bascom and Melville J. Herskovits (Chicago: University of Chicago Press, Phoenix Books, 1962), p. 137.

8. Pius Okigbo, "Social Consequences of Economic Development in West Africa" (1956), in *Africa — Social Problems of Change and Conflict*, ed. Pierre van den Berghe (San Francisco: Chandler, 1965), p. 420.

9. *Ibid.*, pp. 423–24.

By any standards this is an exaggeration. It is particularly so in Nigeria, where ascription among the Yoruba and Hausa is still a major element in stratification. Yet Okigbo's analysis is useful in highlighting the general condition of transformation in West African societies. And it is in such conditions of intermediacy that the phenomenon of transclass ambivalence thrives.

The Rural-Urban Continuum

Class differences are not always vertical. They are sometimes horizontal. Marxists often appear to take it for granted that class differences necessarily mean class inequalities. However, two classes can be distinct without being unequal. A poor peasant need not be socially superior to a well-paid urban wage-earner. Indeed, the rural peasantry and the urban proletariat came to be regarded by Marxists as "natural allies," though each group belonged to a different "class" in the Marxian sense of the term.[10]

In contemporary Africa the feasibility of horizontal transclass identity is demonstrated in both the bottom and the top levels of stratifications. The most interesting form is perhaps the peasant-proletarian ambivalence. If the landholding peasant, on the one hand, and the wage-earning urban worker, on the other, are normally classified as belonging to two distinct classes, then African experience has often bridged the gulf of class identity. The peasant-proletarian identity, when merged in the same person, is connected with the phenomenon of "the rural-urban continuum" in Africa. The connection between the urban worker and his rural roots is as yet not fully broken; the bonds of the countryside affect much of the style of life in the city.

The peasant-proletarian ambivalence is even more dramatically manifested in the phenomenon of migrant labor in Africa. From the mines in South Africa and the Copperbelt of Zambia to Kilindini Harbour in Mombasa, the number of migrant workers within the labor force remains striking.[11] Walter Elkan

---

10. For an excellent discussion of class inequality in relation to class difference, see John Plamenatz, *Man and Society* (London: Longmans, 1963) II, pp. 294–98.

11. There are a number of good studies of this phenomenon. See, for example, Philip Mayer, "Migrancy and the Study of Africans in Towns," *American Anthropologist*, LXIV (1962), 576–92; J. Clyde Mitchell, "Africans in Industrial Towns in Northern Rhodesia," in *Report of the Duke of Edinburgh's Study Conference* (London: Oxford University Press, 1957), Vol. II; Walter Elkan, "Migrant Labor in Africa: An Economist's Approach," in *The Study of Africa*, ed. P. McEwan and R. Sutcliffe (London: Methuen, 1965), pp. 278–87; Philip H. Gulliver, "Incentives in Labor Migration," *Human Organization*, XIX, no. 3 (Fall, 1960), 159–63; A. W. Southall and P. C. Gutkind, *Townsmen in the Making* (Kampala: East African Institute of Social Research, 1957); E. P. Skinner, "Labour Migration and Its Relationship to Socio-cultural Change in Mossi Society," *Africa*, XXX, no. 4 (1960), 375–401; J. Van Velsen, "Labour Migration as a Positive Factor in the Continuity of Tonga Tribal Society,"

regards the persistence of migrant labor in Africa as a significant point of difference between the history of urbanization in Europe and the trend in Africa.

> Why does temporary labor migration persist [in Africa]? In Europe the growth
> of towns was associated with the growth of a new category of people: the urban
> industrial working class. In Africa, too, the towns are growing rapidly, but, although
> some of their houses may be built to last a lifetime, those who live in them
> seldom stay for long. Sooner or later they return to their original homes.[12]

A number of theories have been advanced to explain this phenomenon and
to point out possible differences between urbanization in Africa and urbanization
in Europe. Elkan refers to theories of "the target worker." Africa is regarded
as blessed with a bountiful nature in which a minimum effort can yield fairly
adequate subsistence. Partly because of this, and partly because of certain cultural
and even climatic factors, there is less inducement in Africa to work hard
and continuously than there might have been in the bleak conditions of England
during the Industrial Revolution. Men in Africa therefore work only long enough
to accumulate the cash they need to buy things that only cash can buy. These
target workers then leave their jobs and return to their subsistence farms. The
urban wage-earner assumes the role of rural peasant once again.

Another theory advanced to explain African labor migration is that in some
African societies it is simply an initiation rite. Schapera and other anthropologists
have reported that young men in certain rural communities are not regarded
as fully eligible to marry until they have worked for a while away from home.
Other theories blame bad economic conditions in the country for the migration
to the towns and then blame bad economic conditions in the towns for the
maintenance of a "security link" with the home village. Some theories connect
migrancy with the special meaning that land sometimes has in African conceptions
of tribal identity. In such cases, there is a persistent psychological reluctance
to sever completely all lingering ties with ancestral soil.

All of these theories succeed, to a degree, in explaining some of the differences
between the effects of industrialization in Europe in the nineteenth century
and the effects of urbanization in present-day Africa. By the nineteenth century
England had lost some of the elements of tribal identity and the spiritual mystique
of ancestors in relation to land. The newly urbanized English worker's link
with his village was more easily cut, and the proletariat grew more rapidly
as a distinct class. In Africa the urban worker often retains a transclass
ambivalence; he is compelled to be at once a wage-earner in some industry
and a landholding peasant "at home."

---

in *Social Change in Modern Africa*, ed. A. W. Southall (Chicago: University of Chicago
Press, 1961), pp. 230–41; I. Schapera, *Migrant Labour and Tribal Life* (London: Oxford
University Press, 1947).
  12. Elkan, "Migrant Labor in Africa," p. 281.

It is in part this interpenetration of town and country which forms the basis of the interpenetration of different classes in transitional Africa. Frantz Fanon captured an aspect of this phenomenon when he made the following simple observation:

> The country people are suspicious of the townsman. The latter dresses like a European; he speaks the European's language, works with him, sometimes even lives in the same district; so he is considered by the peasants as a turncoat who has betrayed everything that goes to make up the national heritage.[13]

The critical concept in this observation is that of "turncoat." The peasant regards the townsman as something of a traitor to his origins. For the peasant to regard the townsman as a traitor, he must first see him as one of his own kind, since a traitor is one who betrays his own people. The capacity of the peasant to empathize with the town-dweller sufficiently to recognize him as one of his own kind must itself rest on a relative nearness. The town-dweller is near enough to the country to be recognized by the peasant as kindred, yet distant enough to be suspected of betrayal.

A danger arises when these townspeople become national leaders, not because they are out of touch with the people, but because they are in this intermediate position of social ambivalence. For example, it is not social distance but social nearness which gives rise to the incidence of nepotism in Africa. The leaders are constantly under pressure from people of their own kind who look to them for special favors in the struggle for jobs and other opportunities. The capacity of the leaders to resist these pressures is reduced, precisely because the leaders are a little too near their tribal or rural origins.

Within each ethnic group the ties between the highly successful and the socially less fortunate serve many a positive function. Pre-eminent among these functions is that of distributing widely some of the dividends of social success. The poor look to the successful within their own community for a variety of favors. An African who has successfully accumulated wealth is seldom permitted to be completely free of ethnic obligations. There is recurrent pressure to help or subsidize needy relatives and aspiring kinsmen. One can therefore say that, intraethnically, nepotism is functional by being a distributive factor but that, interethnically, nepotism is dysfunctional and a disruptive factor. Within the community the act of helping one's kith and kin helps to distribute the benefits of individual achievement. When this sharing is at the expense of other tribes, the sense of fellowship within one community tends to disrupt relations with other communities.

---

13. Frantz Fanon, *The Wretched of the Earth*, trans. Constance Farrington (New York: Grove, 1963), pp. 90–91.

Tribalism versus Class-Formation

On a visit to the office of an African minister, I saw a queue of simple folk, some of them apparently from the rural areas, waiting for an opportunity to see the minister. He later indicated that this was quite common in his working week, though there were seldom as many people to see him as there were on that particular day. Evidently he was not a leader who had succeeded in creating distance between himself and the people from whom he sprang. This was an instance of the continuing interplay between the new elite and the masses. The pressures for nepotistic favors are widespread. Some ministers succeed in combining a sense of obligation to their own ethnic group with the fulfillment of their duties to their fellow citizens of other tribal origins. There is a constant battle to balance these two areas of social obligations, each of which is honorable in its own right but capable of conflicting with the other in the demand for priority.

The transclass minister's links with the "lower classes" in Africa are basically tribal in their confines. Put in an extreme way, the minister mixes on terms of equality with more humble citizens only if they are from his own tribe. On the other hand, the minister's links with his horizontal peers — fellow ministers, successful businessmen, and leading intellectuals — are often transtribal. It is perhaps these considerations which make it possible to argue that one major factor in the erosion of tribalism in Africa must be a restructuring of classes.

There is sometimes too ready an assumption, perhaps especially among some Tanzanians, that a country can develop fast without forming new classes. Such as assumption is basically unscientific and certainly un-Marxist. How society can be transformed to new levels of socioeconomic development without affecting the class struggle is not easy to see. The price of rapid economic development must inevitably be a changing social structure.

By the same token the means toward detribalization might well be a new economic reclassification. The theory of "crosscutting loyalties" as a method of achieving national cohesion becomes relevant here. When the tribes are divided too neatly, without overlapping affiliations, the danger of tribal confrontation is most acute. But when, for example, a Muganda finds a religious tie with a fellow Catholic who is a Munyoro and an economic tie with a fellow coffee-grower originally from Lango, the situation is one in which people are divided in some matters and united in others. They might be divided as members of different tribes and united as members of the same social class or the same religious denomination. The danger of a neat tribal confrontation is strongly reduced when there are alternative areas of alliance.

Former President Obote once suggested that arguments which recommend class-formation as a method of reducing the significance of tribal affiliations implied an opposition to African nationalism. This is a defensible line of reasoning. But an alternative line of reasoning is to say that purposeful class-formation might be inconsistent with African socialism but perfectly compatible with African nationalism. After all, nationalism presumably puts a premium on the erosion of tribalism. Should it prove correct that Africa can be detribalized rapidly only if it succeeds in evolving a relatively complex class and occupational structure, the means used would be quite compatible with the ultimate ambition of African nationalism. Tribalism as an enemy of nationalism would be effectively reduced in power by the emergence of socioeconomic complexity and crosscutting sociological affiliations. However, such a road to detribalization might run counter to the ambition of African socialism, which seeks to perpetuate or create a classless society. My own position would be that a classless society is beyond the bounds of possibility. All that one can aspire to is the reduction of class privilege.[14]

This brings us back to the argument that there can be class differences without class inequalities. In the words of John Plamenatz:

> In the Marxian sense of class, peasants who own their land and artisans who own their workshops belong to a different class from landless labourers and factory workers; but they need not be socially superior or inferior to them. . . . People whose incomes consist mostly of rent or interest belong, in the Marxian scheme, to a different class from people whose incomes consist mostly of wages or salaries; but they need not be, and often are not, socially superior to them. . . . There can clearly be differences of class without social inequality; that is, if we take the Marxian sense of class.[15]

In other words, diversification of the class structure in an East African society need not mean intensification of class privilege. The task of preventing gross inequalities between groups does not necessitate a struggle to suppress the emergence of more functionally specialized interest sectors in the society. The crosscutting loyalties which would emerge with this structural differentiation and functional specialization as East African societies become more complex might indeed serve to reduce the potency of tribalism as a disruptive factor in the body politic.

Yet the struggle of the new classes to become more distinctive does for a while entail manifestations of privilege. This is where the phenomenon of "the quest for aristocratic effect" emerges as a quest to create an artificial social distance. African leaders are still so much a part of the people that social ostentation becomes a mode of escape from commonality.

The Mercedes Benz assumes relevance in our analysis of the quest for social distance. African ownership of cars in Uganda is a matter of longer historical

---

14. In a speech in Parliament on October 21, 1968, Obote said, "For a Professor of Political Science to say that Uganda must create a class society is to do a disservice to African Nationalism" (*Uganda Argus* [Kampala], October 22, 1968).

15. Plamenatz, *Man and Society*, II, pp. 296–97.

standing than African ownership of cars in Kenya. The mere possession of a car in Kenya is therefore more of a status symbol than it might be in some sections of Uganda society. Yet in both countries ownership of cars is restricted to a small group and therefore constitutes an important status symbol. However, in the last ten years there has been a significant spreading out of African ownership of cars. This has been partly due to more elaborate systems of car loans to people in certain categories of employment. For special status within the elite, one now needs more than the mere possession of a vehicle. The Mercedes can afford this special status to the most affluent of the new elite.

The significance of the Mercedes Benz is not simply that it signifies affluence but also that it signifies a *modernized* form of affluence. The Mercedes has equivalents lower down in African social hierarchies. As Philip Gulliver recounts:

> In this kind of [African] situation wage-labor becomes more than merely fulfilling youthful needs for clothes, bridewealth contributions, and a little ready cash to establish a man as a husband, father and householder. Wage-labor is involved in obtaining goods and services which are not obtainable in the tribal areas and with standards which are not those of the home community — bicycles and radios, a wide variety of clothing, cash for luxuries, travel by bus and train, as well as a greater demand for the more traditional cloth, cattle, tools and utensils which are involved in tribal life.[16]

Prestige comes to be attached to some of these new standards. Young men aspire to own one day at least a few of the symbols of a "European" way of life. In the words of Mitchell and Epstein in their analysis of social status in Zambia:

> Success in achieving this "civilised" way of life is demonstrated conspicuously by the physical appurtenances of living. The most important of these is clothes, but personal jewellery (especially wrist watches), furniture and European-type food-stuffs are also important.[17]

The Mercedes Benz as a symbol both of wealth and of modernity is only a high-class equivalent of the wrist watch or the bicycle. At the lower level, the transclass ambivalence is in part a product of the rural-urban continuum. The appurtenances of "modern" living which the townsmen acquire and exhibit, particularly when they visit their villages, represent their desire to create the appearance of social distance where in reality such distance is relatively limited. In the case of the transclass man whose duality is the vertical one, combining an upper- and a lower-class status, social ostentation becomes even more dra-

---

16. Gulliver, "Incentives in Labor Migration," p. 160.
17. J. Clyde Mitchell and A. L. Epstein, "Occupational Prestige and Social Status among Urban Africans in Northern Rhodesia" (1959), in *Africa — Social Problems of Change and Conflict*, p. 211. These points are also raised in Mazrui, "Monarchical Tendency in African Political Culture," pp. 233–34.

matically a quest for appearances of social distance, although the reality of relation between the high and the low still involves a good deal of inter-penetration.

Class Limitation and the Future

We opened this chapter with the assertion by Martin Shikuku of Kenya that the critical factor behind military coups in Africa was the tendency of political leaders to get out of touch with the populace. Two months before making this observation, Shikuku had, in fact, had occasion to relate the danger of social distance more specifically to the expensive appurtenances of state leaders. He told his fellow members of Parliament on September 4, 1968, that when many of them had entered Parliament they had not even owned bicycles. Now they had two cars. Where did they get the money?

> There is a danger somewhere. Either the taxation policy is not enough, or some-where, somehow, some people are getting extra money and exploiting other peo-ple. . . . You will find when we talk of reduction in salaries everyone opposes with the exception of nine members out of 170. But still we can afford Mercedes cars while the people are going out naked.[18]

In his reply, Tom Mboya, the minister for economic planning and development at the time, found it pertinent to refer to government measures aimed at reducing the number of big cars being purchased in Kenya. He argued that it could be statistically demonstrated that the number of big cars being sold in Nairobi had "dwindled to a trickle." Correspondingly, the number of small cars being bought had increased to a point which was the highest in the history of the country since independence. The changing pattern of consumption in relation to the sizes of cars was, he said, due to the government's tax measures. The government was continuing to fulfill its pledge to the House that it would pursue a policy involving the equitable distribution of earnings and wealth, the minister asserted.[19]

In this case the control of certain forms of luxurious consumption in Kenya was, in its repercussions, also a control of certain forms of contrived social distance. Yet, on the whole, Kenya seems to have adopted a policy of encouraging functional versatility and of deliberately creating crosscutting classes. The govern-ment's campaign to spread the practice of shareholding in all sectors of society is an exercise in bourgeois-formation. It may result in creating a transclass ambivalence — in creating, for example, the phenomenon of peasants holding shares in highly modernized technical industries in the capital city.

Theories of class analysis have tended to underestimate possibilities of dual

---

18. *East African Standard*, September 5, 1968.
19. *Ibid.*

or multiple class affiliations in the same person. As we have indicated, these possibilities are by no means absent in developed societies, but they are less conspicuous. Both structural differentiation and functional specialization in a developed society tend to maximize occupational mobility. But these same socioeconomic complexities in developed societies make it more difficult than ever to distinguish between simple occupational differences on the one hand and actual class distinctions on the other.

It is true that the concept of "class" is elusive, and definitions are almost always vulnerable; but a lawyer who is also a congressman may belong to only one class, whereas a poorly educated trade-unionist who becomes a cabinet minister in a developed country is probably leading a transclass existence. An academic who is also a regular correspondent of a serious newspaper may conceivably have obtained occupational versatility (university work and journalism) without a transclass identity; but an academic who is also a business tycoon, or a very successful landlord, does become ambivalent in his class affiliation. It is certainly true that one cannot always tell where occupational and income differences end and class distinctions begin. But to the question What is a class? one can give the same evasive but fundamentally correct answer which Edmund Burke gave to the question What is a natural right? It is "in a sort of *middle*, incapable of definition, but not impossible to be discerned."[20]

The delimitation of classes, as distinct from their conceptual definition, is nevertheless more clearly revealed in a less developed society than in a developed one. The reason is, once again, that grosser categories come with socioeconomic simplicity. We have tried to show that transclass ambivalence becomes more visible in such situations and that such ambivalence may become prevalent because of the transitionality of the society. Migrant labor in Africa, for example, is a manifestation of rural-urban ambivalence, leading to the transclass duality of a person who is both an urban wage-earner and a rural landholding peasant.

Karl Marx did allow for social mobility and for merger of proximate classes, but he did not adequately allow for the transclass man. Yet the classless society might well be a society of transclass men. This might have been implicit in the belief shared by Marx and Engels that when real communism is at last reached, functional versatility will reign supreme. The same person will then be able to "hunt in the morning, fish in the afternoon, rear cattle in the evening, criticize after dinner . . . without ever becoming hunter, fisherman, shepherd or critic."[21]

---

20. Burke, *Reflections on the Revolution in France* (1790), in *Works*, III, pp. 312–13. The Marxian concept of class is tied to the idea of variant forms of property, including labor itself as a special kind of property. People belong to different classes according to which form of property they control or fail to control. For a good analysis of the Marxian concept, see Plamenatz, *Man and Society*, Vol. II, as well as *idem*, *German Marxism and Russian Communism* (London: Longmans, 1954).
21. Karl Marx and Friedrich Engels, *The German Ideology*, ed. R. Pascal (New York: International Publishers, 1963), p. 22.

Perhaps unwittingly, the founders of communism did seem to have nearly grasped the fundamental fact that creating the classless man might not be very different from creating the polyclass personality. The road to a classless society might indeed be through functional versatility and multiple crosscutting affiliations. What must not be overlooked is that the same road is in the direction of maximum transclass ambivalence.

East Africa has by no means arrived as yet at such an optimum functional diversity. All that is demonstrated by the region's state of development is the dream of interpenetration of different classes, accompanied by a psychological compulsion to sharpen the *appearance* of distinctiveness through the medium of artificial ostentation. The gap between the elite and the masses in East Africa is much narrower than it is in developed countries. The danger lies in the quality of intermediacy. The elite is not long enough removed from the masses to have acquired a mystique of political legitimacy, and yet it is often adequately removed from the masses to create envious resentment and a sense of social betrayal. Here again we will repeat that the twilight spell has its dangers, different both from the dangers of the blazing sun and from those of utter darkness. It is, once again, like the Mercedes Benz at dusk speeding along the Entebbe Road. It is no longer light enough to see properly and not yet dark enough to enable the lights of the car to be fully effective. In those few minutes which separate the African day from the African night lie the peculiar dangers of visual indistinctness.

[11]

Political Control and
Military Power

On January 25, 1971, the Uganda Army, under the leadership of Maj. Gen. Idi Amin, took over power in Uganda. President Obote was out of the country at the time, having just attended the Commonwealth Conference of Heads of Government in Singapore. The army declared Obote deposed and, in a list of eighteen points, told why it was necessary to take control of the country "before the situation got any worse." The eighteen points were an indictment of Obote's policies and ranged from charges of corruption in high places in spite of protestations of socialism to a denunciation of the practice of detaining political opponents without trial.

The date of the coup was in a sense uncanny. It was almost precisely the seventh anniversary of Idi Amin's dramatic promotion following the first case of military insubordination in independent Uganda. On January 25, 1964, 450 soldiers from the Scots Guards and Staffordshire Regiment seized the armory in Jinja at dawn and, without any casualties, disarmed disruptive elements within the armed forces.

The trouble in Uganda had followed the outbreak of a mutiny among troops of the First Battalion of the Tanganyika Rifles, who had risen against their British officers on January 20, 1964. On January 22, Uganda's minister of internal affairs, Felix Onama, gave a radio address in Uganda in which he expressed confidence in officers seconded from the British army to the Uganda Army, and outlined his plans for Africanizing the officer corps as soon as possible. The plan, at the time, was that eight companies were to be commanded by Ugandans by the end of 1964, and that all battalions were to be commanded by Ugandans by the end of 1965. Onama reported that there were already two Ugandan majors, one of whom was Idi Amin. There were also fourteen Ugandan captains, thirty-six lieutenants, and fifteen cadets in training.

The following day there was a sit-down strike in the First Battalion of the Uganda Rifles at Jinja. Onama was held hostage by two companies of the First Battalion, and some expatriate officers were also detained. Onama was held until he apparently signed an order agreeing to increase the salary for privates, enhance the ration allowance, and improve general amenities for troops and their families.

On January 24, Prime Minister Obote reported on the situation at the barracks in Jinja and explained why he was inviting British troops from Nairobi to help avert the danger of general military insubordination in the country. Obote expected that the sit-down strike which had taken place in Jinja would be followed by strikes in other barracks and that, before long, unruly elements in the society as a whole would "run amok, looting . . . and lives and property would [be] in danger." On January 25, the job of general pacification was completed by the Scots Guards and the Staffordshire Regiment. Civilian supremacy was rescued by the intervention of British troops. After the mutiny, Obote dismissed large numbers of soldiers and promoted Idi Amin, along with some other trusted men.

Exactly seven years later, civilian supremacy came to an end in Uganda, with the Idi Amin coup. Four hundred miles away in Kenya there were British troops in 1971, as there had been in 1964. Indeed, 750 British grenadiers had arrived in Kenya only a few days before the army coup in Uganda. Their presence in Kenya had been denounced by leading members of the Obote government, partly in response to reports that the troops had arrived in Kenya in anticipation of probable rioting by Africans in neighboring countries should Prime Minister Heath of England decide to go ahead with his plan to sell arms to South Africa.

Why indeed were those troops in Kenya? Could they have been there to avert the risk of an army coup in Kenya itself? If so, how defensible in nationalistic terms was such a policy? What alternative solutions were there to the risk of military challenges to military authorities? What, in short, had happened in East Africa in the seven years between the region-wide military mutinies of January, 1964, and the military coup in Uganda of January, 1971?

Kenya: Nonalignment versus Civilian Supremacy

After the mutinies of 1964, the three East African countries had to consider how to prevent similar incidents from occurring in the future. One answer was to transform the army altogether, creating a force based on a different principle of military service and motivated by different considerations. The other solution was to maintain the original principle of military service inherited from the colonial power, complete with military cooperation with the colonial power. It was, after all, such unofficial military cooperation which had made it possible for the three East African governments to borrow the troops of the former imperial power for the purposes of disarming local military mutineers.

Tanzania adopted the first solution and totally transformed the nature of military service. Kenya adopted the second solution and consolidated the inherited imperial tradition, complete with British cooperation. Uganda adopted neither strategy; it preferred to cut off the link with the British military but did not transform the army.

The mutinies of 1964 had revealed the devastating political significance of the power of the gun in the hands of an army which had not yet learned never to question the principle of civilian supremacy. If there was violent trouble among the Somalis in the northeastern province of Kenya, or among the Baganda in Uganda, the government could send the armed forces to restore law and order. The question which arose in 1964 was what solution the governments could invoke if the trouble was not among members of an ethnic group but among the armed forces themselves. Rebellious civilians could be disciplined by the security arm of the state; but who was to discipline the security arm if it, in turn, decided to be rebellious?

The immediate solution in all three countries was the solution of countervailing power. The power utilized was external to the country — British troops to cope with the armed insurgency of local ones. It was Obote who made the critical decision, in many ways a courageous one. In the climate of opinion in Africa at that time, the idea of reverting back to the colonial power for assistance to quell a local troublemaker was deemed to be a manifestation of a dependency complex.

Not long after the mutinies I had the opportunity to visit Nigeria, and in several conversations with Nigerians I, as an East African, was put in the dock and asked to answer for the humiliating decision of East African governments to seek the military assistance of an imperial power that had just departed. At that time, neither my Nigerian critics nor I could foresee the tragic irony which would befall Nigerians barely three years after East Africa's humiliation. Nigerians, too, were destined to find it necessary to invoke a residual principle of *Pax Britannica* in order to deal with their own, more serious, insurrection. British aid came in great amounts, accompanied by a British commitment to help in saving federal Nigeria. But in 1966 I had to defend East Africa.

It is said that the British high commissioner in Kampala was so impressed by Obote's decision to invite British help that he asked that the request be made in writing. After all, the return of British troops could be widely denounced as an imperial invasion, a neocolonialist reassertion of power. The return of Belgian troops to the Congo in 1960, following the mutiny of the Force Publique, was a case in point. The British high commissioner wanted to make quite sure that Uganda's invitation to British troops to return was voluntary on the part of the African government concerned and that it could be proved to be so in a documentary way.

Once Obote had set the precedent, it was easier for Nyerere and Kenyatta to follow suit. All three East African countries invoked the principle of external force to counter the armed insurgencies of their own soldiers.[1] But what was to happen after the disarming of the mutineers? How were similar incidents of military insubordination to be averted?

Kenya adopted a continuation of the principle of external countervailing force, which involved continuing military cooperation with the United Kingdom on at least some matters. When the mutinies took place in 1964, Kenya had been independent for less than two months, and there was still a British military presence in the country. It might be said that one of the precipitating factors behind the mutinies in both Tanzania and Uganda was the demand for rapid Africanization of the officer corps in the army. Kenya had not been independent long enough for disaffection with the expatriate officer corps to have developed to such an extent, but the demonstration effect of the mutinies in Tanzania and Uganda did have an impact on Kenya.

The issue which remained after the crisis was whether to maintain appropriate links with the British, and the government of Kenya rapidly decided to do precisely that. Discussions about landing rights and about joint exercises of British and Kenyan troops took place not long after the 1964 crisis, and the principle of joint exercises has been retained ever since. In addition, British advice on military reorganization and training has been a continuing feature of the armed forces of Kenya.

The most widely publicized of all these preparations for joint exercises was the arrival of 750 British grenadiers in Kenya in January, 1971, at a time when Britain was considering selling arms to South Africa. Such a decision was likely to create resentment in the East African countries. Indeed, as we have already indicated, when the Commonwealth Conference of Heads of Government was meeting in Singapore in January, 1971, and the deliberations

---

1. The actual chronology of events was of the following order: *January 12, 1964*, the sultan's government of Zanzibar was overthrown. *January 17*, Tanganyika police were sent to Zanzibar to help restore order. *January 20*, the men of the First Battalion of the Tanganyika Rifles stationed near Dar es Salaam mutinied, demanding higher pay and complete Africanization of the officer corps; President Nyerere's whereabouts was unknown to the public. *January 21*, the Second Battalion of the Tanganyika Rifles stationed at Tabora mutinied; Nyerere appeared in a broadcast to the nation; order was temporarily restored. *January 23*, Uganda's minister of interior, Felix Onama, was reportedly manhandled by two companies of the First Battalion of the Uganda Rifles over the issue of increasing the salary for privates; the Uganda government requested British military assistance; 450 British soldiers were sent from Nairobi. *January 24*, troops of Kenya's Eleventh Battalion mutinied at Lanet Camp, near Nakuru; units of the Third Royal Force Artillery were called to restore order. *January 25*, British troops broke up a sit-down strike of mutinous troops at Nakuru; British troops descended near Dar es Salaam and at Tabora and disarmed the Tanganyikan mutineers at the request of the Tanganyika government; three Africans were reportedly killed in the engagement near Dar es Salaam. For some of the implications of these activities, see Ali A. Mazrui, "The Soldier and the State in East Africa: Some Theoretical Conclusions on the Army Mutinies of 1964," in *Violence and Thought: Essays on Social Tensions in Africa* (London: Longmans, 1969), pp. 3–23.

were dominated precisely by the arms issue and the security of the Indian Ocean, the arrival of the British grenadiers in Kenya resulted in widespread speculation about British precautionary measures to deal with popular rioting in East Africa. But the government of Kenya and the British High Commission both repudiated these rumors, reaffirming that the grenadiers had arrived for the sole purpose of the usual joint exercises with their Kenyan counterparts.

The use of an external countervailing force like Britain inevitably raised the issue of consistency with the policy of nonalignment. The problem occurred to President Julius Nyerere in the course of the crisis in January, 1964. Nyerere called for a special meeting of the foreign ministers of the Organization of African Unity to discuss the crisis in East Africa and the implications of utilizing British troops. As headquarters of the liberation movements for southern Africa, Dar es Salaam was acutely aware of the nationalistic embarrassment implicit in a resort to the troops of the former imperial power. Kenya and Uganda were not enthusiastic about the special cleansing ceremony which Nyerere was trying to arrange by calling on the Organization of African Unity. But the organization did respond positively to Dar es Salaam's request for such considerations, and on February 12, 1964, Nyerere opened the conference at the Diamond Jubilee Hall in Dar es Salaam.

The president explained that Tanganyika's position as a border state adjacent to the white-dominated areas of southern Africa, as well as its status as the headquarters of liberation movements for Mozambique and southern Africa, made it necessary for the country to consult with African states about how best to deal with the situation which had arisen. He explained that from the point of view of domestic political factors, Tanganyika's humiliation arose from the necessity of using foreign troops, regardless of their nationality; but, he went on, from the point of view of the international implications of the situation, it did make a difference what the nationality of those troops was. The nationality, in this case, was British.

> The presence of troops from a country deeply involved in the world's Cold War conflicts has serious implications in the context of African nationalism, and our common policies of non-alignment.

Nyerere argued that the success of the policy of nonalignment "may depend not only on remaining outside such [cold-war] conflicts but also on being seen to remain outside them." How could the government of Tanganyika convince other African countries that it had no alliance with a big power when it was prepared to call in British troops? [2]

What was arising out of the situation was a basic tension between two principles

---

2. *East African Standard* (Nairobi), February 13, 1964. See also Julius Nyerere, *Freedom and Unity — Uhuru na Umoja* (Dar es Salaam: Oxford University Press, 1966), p. 288.

of political neutrality. One was the principle of domestic political neutrality for the armed forces as a safeguard of civilian supremacy in government. The other was the principle of international military neutrality as a cornerstone of the policy of nonalignment. The question that was arising in East Africa in 1964 was whether these two principles could, in fact, be combined. Could a newly independent state succeed both in maintaining the domestic neutrality of the armed forces and in pursuing the international neutrality of nonalignment? If the two forms of neutrality could not be reconciled, the question which inevitably followed was whether a new African country was endangering the doctrine of civilian supremacy in government by pursuing a policy of nonalignment.

In absolute terms there is no logical incompatibility between a policy of international nonalignment and the doctrine of civilian supremacy in government at home. Moreover, it is also possible to have a military regime in a new state that is basically nonaligned, just as it is possible to have a civilian regime in a state that is committed within the terms of the cold war. But, although the idea of civilian supremacy in government is not logically incompatible with nonalignment, and in practice there are empirical examples which illustrate this consistency, on balance the evidence would seem to suggest that a policy of absolute nonalignment puts a strain on the principle of domestic political neutrality of the armed forces. If, therefore, civilian supremacy in government rests on the political neutrality of the armed forces, international nonalignment does, by extension, put a strain on the maintenance of this civilian supremacy.

One reason behind this causal relationship is the simple fact that nonalignment tends to aggravate the problem of military idleness. It is true that Africa does have border disputes of varying degrees of magnitude, and it is true that social upheavals that draw in the military forces are recurrent in at least some African countries. But in very few African countries do these phenomena demand military attention frequently enough to give the armed forces a sense of national purpose.

An active involvement in the cold war, even as a small country, can afford a sense of military mission. A climate of having a world-wide enemy and world-wide allies could give meaning to military life. A military confrontation with the Communist countries might not be immediate, but the international atmosphere always includes discussions of the arms race, the security of the Indian Ocean, residual ideas of ideological containment, and a vague, but politically significant, fear of international subversion. A small country involved in the cold war could share in such a pervasive sense of military mission and occasionally engage in high-level discussions with its allies concerning strategy, containment, and antisubversion.

Therefore, alignment in the cold war by the civilian authorities of an African country could mitigate the risk of military anomie, which arises in situations of inadequate professional commitment by the soldiers, inadequate absorption of military values in relation to one's society, and an inadequate sense of purpose as an armed force. Military anomie is quick to arise in countries where the tradition of military service is very new, and it is bound to be aggravated if no sense of military purpose can be credibly created. The East African armies did have some historical background, in view of their links with the King's African Rifles. But the King's African Rifles was a local extension of the imperial forces of the metropolitan power, and the sense of mission created was inseparable from the tradition of *Pax Britannica*. On attainment of independence, the three countries of East Africa evolved separate armed forces; and these forces, in the context of newly created states, had no roots in national history, no tradition of devoted combat. By the very nature of a new state, the armed forces of such a country are acutely exposed to the danger of military anomie as a malaise of rootlessness. Problems of loyalty to the territorial entity that is now a separate nation arise, as do problems of submission to civilian authority in situations of such malaise.

In the absence of a military tradition which commanded pride in past performance, East African countries needed, in effect, to devise a new and credible sense of purpose for their soldiers. Nonalignment, while giving the politicians a sense of diplomatic mission, denied the soldiers a sense of military purpose. When Jawaharlal Nehru of India died, Milton Obote went on the radio and paid him the following tribute: "Nehru will be remembered as a founder of non-alignment. . . . The new nations of the world owe him a debt of gratitude in this respect." [3]

Nehru's nonalignment shared an ideological ancestry with Gandhi's nonviolence. Gandhi had contributed passive resistance to one school of African thought during the colonial period, a school which included Nkrumah's strategy in the late 1940s and early 1950s. Nehru had contributed nonalignment to almost all African countries as a cornerstone of their diplomatic posture on attainment of independence. In India, Gandhi's nonviolence was a method of seeking freedom, while Nehru's nonalignment came to be a method of seeking peace. Yet nonalignment was, in some ways, a translation into foreign policy of some of the moral assumptions underlying passive resistance in the domestic struggle for India's independence. Gandhi once said:

> Free India can have no enemy. . . . For India to enter into the race for armaments is to court suicide. . . . The world is looking for something new and unique from India. . . . With the loss of India to non-violence the last hope of the world will be gone.[4]

In spite of Gandhi's vision, independent India did not abstain from violence. Gandhian nonviolence was not fully translated into a foreign policy. Suspicion

---

3. *Uganda Argus* (Kampala), May 29, 1964.
4. *Harijan*, October 14, 1939. This point is discussed in a related context in Ali A. Mazrui, *Towards a Pax Africana* (London: Weidenfeld & Nicolson; Chicago: University of Chicago Press, 1967), pp. 200–201.

of Pakistan in particular was too strong to permit that. Yet, of all the countries in the world, India under Nehru came nearest to symbolizing the search for peace. For a crucial decade in the history of Africa and Asia, India was the diplomatic leader of both continents. In reality, much of the diplomatic behavior of the nonaligned countries was motivated by a desire to maximize their own flexibility and diplomatic autonomy. But there can be little doubt that much of nonalignment was inspired by the ideal of peace in the world, a distrust of military alliances, a rejection of military bases, and a substantial air of military autarky. Again, a policy of this kind, while inflating the sense of diplomatic mission on the part of the politicians in new states, aggravated the feeling of aimlessness in the barracks. The phenomenon of military anomie among the soldiers was inclined to deepen in such circumstances.

It is against this background that Kenya's qualified nonalignment has to be evaluated. The country has indeed retained the principle of nonalignment as a cornerstone of its foreign policy; nevertheless, there is not only a clearly pro-Western orientation in Kenya's nonalignment at the diplomatic level but also a residual military connection with the United Kingdom in terms of advice and joint training. Kenya has not gone as far as the Ivory Coast in relying on the former colonial power for external security. In March, 1962, almost exactly two years before Kenya had to ask for British troops to cope with its mutinies, a report in the *New York Times* described the Ivory Coast in the following terms:

> The most striking anachronism to the radical African nationalists is that M. Houphouet-Boigny has practically abdicated sovereignty in the military field. The Ivory Coast has only a small force for internal security. And even this force has French officers. The French army assures the external defense of the country. It has been asked to do so, M. Houphouet-Boigny says, because "we wish to devote our modest means to economic and social development." [5]

By relying on the French so extensively, Houphouet-Boigny not only was ensuring the availability of more resources for economic development but also was helping to ensure the principle of civilian supremacy in the government.

President Kenyatta has refrained from going to that extent in his reliance on British forces and British military expertise and has therefore taken more risks with the principle of civilian supremacy in Kenya than Houphouet-Boigny has taken in the Ivory Coast. Neither country is coup-proof; but both have invoked this idea of an external countervailing force as a method of ensuring the political neutrality of the armed forces within them, therefore safeguarding the principle of civilian supremacy in government.

Nonalignment in Kenya is not as puristic as it is in Tanzania. It can even be argued that Kenya's pro-Western orientation is derived partly from the evolution

5. Henry Tanner's dispatch, *New York Times*, March 25, 1962.

of a private-enterprise preference in its economic policies as well as from the decision in 1964 to continue military interaction with the United Kingdom. The atmosphere against Communist China in Kenya's internal history and the debates between the pro-Western foreign policy of the Kenya African National Union and the Eastern-oriented position of the Kenya People's Union under Oginga Odinga from 1966 to 1969 were connected both with the evolving private-enterprise system in Kenya and with the continuing military cooperation with Great Britain. Kenya sacrificed a little nonalignment for the sake of greater civilian authority in government.

Tanzania: Political Commitment versus Military Anomie

Of the three East African countries, it was Tanganyika which perhaps felt most deeply humiliated by the army mutinies. Two factors were particularly humiliating for a leader of Nyerere's sensibilities. One was the personal factor of having to go into hiding: in the face of an armed insurrection against the background of a bloody revolution in Zanzibar hardly a week earlier, Nyerere was prevailed upon to seek safety in concealment. It was his colleague, Oscar Kambona, who had to come out and negotiate with the soldiers in a bid to get them to return to their barracks. The other factor of humiliation was, as we indicated, the need to invite British troops to disarm the mutineers.

Nyerere never felt the need to explain why he left it to Oscar Kambona to deal with the mutinous soldiers in the early phases of confrontation. Nyerere never apologized for having gone into hiding. But he did feel deeply both this personal dimension and the political decision to invite British troops to return. In a nation-wide broadcast following the disarming of the Tanganyika Rifles by British troops, Nyerere said:

> I am told that there is already foolish talk that the British have come back to rule Tanganyika again. This is rubbish. . . . Any independent country is able to ask for the help of another independent country. Asking for help in this way is not something to be proud of. I do not want any person to think that I was happy in making this request. This whole week has been a week of the most grievous shame for our nation.[6]

The shame was brought upon Tanganyikans by "those who tried to intimidate our nation at the point of a gun." In the face of this bitter experience, Nyerere proceeded to reconsider the country's military organization, which was based on that of Britain. Since World War II, Britain had combined that old principle of the domestic neutrality of the armed forces with a policy of external military alignment. Such alignment helped to give the British armed forces

6. *Tanganyika Standard* (Dar es Salaam), January 27, 1964.

a continuing sense of mission. It is true that with the decline of the empire, a sense of military purposelessness is hitting even Britain. In January, 1971, the Royal Academy of Sandhurst was so worried about problems of recruiting into the army that it broke with tradition and advertised for recruits in *The Times*. The defense of the empire had previously been one important bulwark against the danger of military anomie in the British armed establishments. The noble vision of defending the different outposts of the empire, romanticized by Kipling's poetry in the late nineteenth and early twentieth centuries, helped to give even the deprived British private a sense of ultimate national fulfillment.

> For the wind is in the palm trees,
> and the temple-bells they say:
> "Come you back, you British soldier;
> come you back to Mandalay!"

Behind the new empire was a tradition of previous adventures on the part of British soldiers, former glories consolidating into a romantic national memory. Songs of patriotism and tributes to bravery, such as Tennyson's "Charge of the Light Brigade," had formed part of the military history of the grenadiers.

> "Forward, the Light Brigade!"
> Was there a man dismay'd?
> Not tho' the soldier knew
> Some one had blunder'd.

The French army, on the other hand, sustained periods of military anomie as a result of the sheer futility of the colonial wars in Indochina and Algeria after World War II. It is even arguable that the military insurrection which led to the return of Charles de Gaulle to power in 1958 was ultimately brought about by the inner sense of frustration of the forces in Algeria and the military's growing sense of purposelessness. It is true that the French army, unlike the armies of new states, had a tradition behind it. But even the reassurance of an honorable tradition cannot always avert a growing sense of anomie in a situation of wavering confidence, uneasy conscience, and declining military morale. De Gaulle, after finally disengaging France from the futility of colonial wars, gave the French military a new sense of purpose with his vision of a nuclearized France, seeking parity of esteem with the super powers of the world.

Nyerere in 1964 was bereft of both an honorable military tradition behind his armed forces and a high military purpose. Indeed, he had had grave doubts about building up any large military establishment or having a major military ambition for his country. He had at one time even considered having forces no bigger than those necessary for police work within Tanganyika, hoping somehow to leave the question of external defense to Pan-African arrangements, should these be feasible.

With the disarming of the Tanganyika Rifles by British troops, Nyerere took another look at the country's military principles. The cold war had given the British a functional equivalent of empire in the form of a global commitment demanding national exertion. The Conservatives, especially, saw in the cold war and the defense of distant oceans against Russian threats or Chinese influence a mission worthy of succeeding that old imperial vision of *Pax Britannica*. But Tanganyika had opted for nonalignment. Could it combine this international form of neutrality with the principle of domestic neutrality for the armed forces?

Here again were two matters to be taken into account. One was the danger of military anomie, as the soldiers became restless in the barracks in the face of functional redundancy. The other was the interconnected problem of providing a countervailing force to the military, should the soldiers be tempted to challenge civilian supremacy.

After the 1964 mutiny, Nyerere distrusted the inherited British principle that an army must be politically "neutral" within the domestic system. After all, an army that is politically neutral is an army that consists of *pure soldiers* — soldiers with little experience beyond the barracks and the battlefield. Soldiers who are trained only in the arts of warfare have their horizons too narrowly restricted. Warfare is an exercise in physical power — and pure soldiers tend to be too dangerously preoccupied with those arts of physical force. Therefore, while Nyerere remained a believer in civilian supremacy, he was also becoming a convert to the concept of a *developmental militia* — people trained not merely in the use of guns but also for participation in certain sectors of nation-building.

By June, 1964, the second vice-president of the United Republic of Tanganyika and Zanzibar, Rashidi Kawawa, was addressing new army recruits in the following terms:

> You are just as much citizens of the country as are farmers or fishermen. There is no reason therefore for refusing any citizen of the country permission to have a say in the politics of the country.[7]

Political discussions between officers and soldiers were to be encouraged, and the army was to be represented on the National Executive of the Tanganyika African National Union.

Police and soldiers responded to TANU's invitation to join the party. Officers were entrusted with the responsibility of being liaisons between the party and the armed forces, and the responsibilities of soldiers in national development were to be systematically explained. On November 6, 1964, a political commissar of the Tanzania Defence Forces was appointed. Representation for the armed forces within the party was being institutionalized.

These developments signified a rejection of the idea of political neutrality

---

7. *Nationalist* (Dar es Salaam), June 27, 1964.

for the armed forces. Nyerere was insisting that the soldiers should, in fact, become politically committed — but, of course, on the side of the ruling party, accepting the principles of party discipline and civilian supremacy.

Political commitment is thus one answer to the problem of military anomie. It provides a kind of national purpose for the soldiers — a purpose which is not purely military but which might be enough to mitigate the sense of functional redundancy within the armed forces.

But what about the second question, of providing a countervailing force to the military? As we have indicated, Kenya decided to opt for an external countervailing force, even if this meant the dilution of Kenya's nonalignment. But Tanzania, far from deciding to dilute its nonalignment, proceeded very soon after 1964 to give its nonalignment greater military purity. Nonalignment is sometimes defined in terms of having no links with either East or West; an alternative form is to have links with both East and West, diversifying one's military contacts and the sources of one's military advice. Not very long after the mutiny, Nyerere decided to accept the help of Communist China in certain aspects of military training. The Chinese training team arrived, to the consternation of Western opinion. President Nyerere, in an angry press conference, made it clear that Western links with Tanzania were still very strong, and that what he was trying to do was to introduce certain diversifications as a way of deepening the meaning of Tanzania's nonalignment. The worst the Chinese could do would be to make the soldiers inclined to rebel against authority; and Tanzania had experienced such a rebellion, although the training until that time had been provided by the British.

Nonalignment as diversification in military advice and cooperation became a cornerstone of Tanzania's foreign policy. The Chinese participated, and so did the Canadians, the Israelis, the West Germans, and, indirectly, the East Germans. Some of these sources of military advice and training were later changed or abandoned, according to negotiations and the exigencies of international politics. The point to be grasped is that Nyerere, after the 1964 insurrection, proceeded to diversify his military links as a way of emphasizing his international neutrality. His relationship with the Chinese seemed so intimate at times that when the Commonwealth Conference of Heads of Government was meeting in Singapore in January, 1971, to discuss the issue of Britain's proposed arms deal with South Africa, rumors started afresh about an impending military alliance between Tanzania and Communist China. Nyerere once again firmly rebutted such insinuations, emphasizing the continuing commitment of Tanzania to positive neutralism in the cold war and in international diplomacy.

Because of Tanzania's international neutrality, the countervailing force to the military had to be domestic rather than external. The domestic countervailing force that Nyerere adopted was the National Service, which helped to disseminate the skills of weaponry to civilians as well as to soldiers.[8] One of the consequences

---

8. The details of the National Service in relation to issues of economic conscription are discussed in Chapter 14 below.

of this scheme, first formulated in its ideological version in 1964 following the mutinies and elaborated in 1966 to bring in graduates of higher institutions of learning, was to break the soldiers' monopoly of military skills in Tanzania. Although only a modest level of military training was given within the National Service scheme, even that modest amount constituted a breach in the soldiers' monopoly of physical force. Indeed, some of the villagers on the Mozambique border were at times called upon to arm themselves in the face of incursions by the Portuguese. The National Service created an atmosphere in which soldiers realized that it would be more difficult for them to hold the nation to ransom with their guns in the future than it might have been when they mutinied in 1964.

There is evidence to suggest that part of the distrust which the Uganda Army had of the National Service of Uganda emanated from the belief that it was going to be similar to that of Tanzania. However, unlike the Tanzanian scheme, the one in Uganda did not envisage military training. On the contrary, it explicitly excluded it. As the proposals had not as yet been finalized, and as the Uganda Army was beginning to feel insecure in the face of apparent moves by Obote to seek countervailing power, a suspicion arose that the National Service was, in part, designed to provide balancing power and break the monopoly in military skills which the professional security forces seemed to have. The Ministry of National Service was the first casualty in the governmental reorganization in Uganda following the military coup of January 25, 1971.

But while Obote had not, in fact, intended to disseminate military skills through the National Service, Nyerere's vision of the new Tanzania sought to cope with the risk of military ambition by providing a domestic countervailing force.

Uganda: Ethnic Arithmetic and Separation of Powers

Following the mutinies of 1964, Kenya adopted the strategy of external countervailing force by maintaining military cooperation with Britain, and Tanzania adopted a strategy of internal countervailing force by breaking the professional soldiers' monopoly of military skills. What solution did Uganda invoke to avert future dangers?

The twin problems of military anomie and military ambition were present in Uganda. The problem of military anomie as a problem of functional redundancy was partially met by an implicit doctrine of northern leadership in nation-building and consolidation of national unity. It was a doctrine which could never be officially formulated or proclaimed without defeating its aim of reassuring the different ethnic groups and leading them toward national integration. Nevertheless, a factor which was plain in Uganda politics from 1964 was a kind of Manifest Destiny of the Nilotes to lead the country toward modernity and unity.

Before the British came, the Baganda were among the more warlike of the tribes of East Africa, converting the principle of military service for the kabaka into a point of high honor. During the nineteenth century there did develop a special Royal Guard Corps, which was the nearest thing to a regular army that Uganda had had until then; but the bulk of the army continued to consist of peasant militia. Military glory was greatly emphasized. Military weakness by individuals was a matter of public concern. There were occasions when cowards were burned alive or forced to go about dressed in women's clothing.[9]

Under the British the Baganda were increasingly demilitarized, although they enjoyed special privileges in the country on the basis of the 1900 agreement, which extended British "protection" to Buganda. Before colonization, Buganda had enjoyed autonomy on the basis of power; during the colonial period, Buganda enjoyed semiautonomy and a privileged position on the basis of a legal contract. This transition from an autonomy based on power to an autonomy based on contract had long-term consequences for the region and the tribe. By the time Uganda attained independence, in 1962, the Baganda were still the most privileged single group in the country, but they had lost their former tradition of military engagement.

What had happened during the colonial period was the evolution of a system of separation of powers based on ethnic specialization. The Bantu peoples of the south, led by the Baganda, had captured administrative and political influence under British hegemony. The Nilotic peoples of the north, on the other hand, had come to dominate the military profession. In the enjoyment of their privileged status, the Baganda had gradually boycotted the profession of arms as undignified for them, while significant numbers of northerners had embarked on military careers in the face of limited opportunities in other areas of endeavor.

The military profession in colonial Africa was, in an important sense, a profession of the underprivileged. Its impact on the political system after independence can be thought of in terms of equalizing power. The ascendancy of educated Africans came to be challenged by semiliterate soldiers.

During part of the colonial period it almost seemed as if Uganda was endorsing Plato's system of stratification. The Baganda provided the ruling elite, holding administrative positions not only in Buganda but in other districts of the country, and imposing their notions of administration and political organization on societies very different from their own. The British played the game of fostering a Ganda elite in the administrative system of the country. The Acholi provided the nucleus of a Nilotic class of auxiliaries, entrusted in part with the security of the nation, while the Baganda shared with the British the control of administration. What was missing from the Platonic stratification was a well-defined class of economic producers. This area of endeavor, initially dominated by outsiders, was beginning to be significantly shared by Ganda traders and growers; but it was still an area wide open to both the Nilotes and the Bantu.

---

9. See L. A. Fallers, assisted by F. K. Kamoga and S. B. K. Musoke, "Social Stratification in Traditional Buganda," in *The King's Men: Leadership and Status in Buganda on the Eve of Independence*, ed. L. A. Fallers (London: Oxford University Press, 1964), pp. 111–30.

This ethnic separation of powers began to be threatened by the process of democratization in colonial Uganda. The emergence of political organization and the growth of agitation for popular elections made it increasingly difficult for the Baganda to retain their political pre-eminence in the country. True to their regional interest, the Baganda resisted the democratization of Uganda and even boycotted the 1961 elections as part of the strategy to defend Buganda's autonomy against indiscriminate franchise.

The country entered into independence, however, with an alliance between northerner Obote's Uganda People's Congress and the Buganda-based Kabaka Yekka party. What this meant was that the Nilotes were retaining control of the military but at the same time were seeking to share the political domain with those who had previously been politically privileged.

For the first fifteen months of independence, the Uganda Army could derive no sense of national purpose from a political arrangement which appeared to be a makeshift alliance between Milton Obote and Sir Edward Mutesa. Indeed, when the governor general departed, Mutesa took the headship of state, while Obote had the headship of government. We might therefore say that when the soldiers mutinied at Jinja, there had not as yet emerged in Uganda any special function which could capture their imagination.

For a while the Baganda were not aware that although northerners were sharing administration and government with them, they were not significantly sharing the military profession with the northerners. But, by January, 1964, matters were beginning to be strikingly evident to Mutesa. Obote's invitation to the British to send in troops was apparently extended without official consultation with President Mutesa, the commander in chief of the Uganda Army. Following the disarming of the mutineers, Obote proceeded to make suitable changes in the armed forces to strengthen his position. He reportedly dismissed five hundred men and promoted those he thought he could rely upon. Pre-eminent among those who were immediately promoted was Maj. Idi Amin. Mutesa was later to confess:

> I was sadly and vividly aware that he [Obote] had from that moment on complete control of the Army, which was filled with northerners of his own stock. . . . The Buganda Police Force could be controlled by Obote if he wished. We knew from this time on that if it came to force, we could not hope to win.[10]

Although Mutesa remained commander in chief, he learned that Obote had specifically forbidden Amin to approach Mutesa without first obtaining permission from Obote. As Mutesa later put it:

> Amin was a comparatively simple, tough character. He had been to the Palace, and I watched him box, which he did efficiently. Later Obote told him never

10. Mutesa II, *The Desecration of My Kingdom* (London: Constable, 1967), p. 179.

to approach me — which might seem a natural thing to do, as I was his Commander-in-Chief — without first obtaining permission from the Prime Minister himself.[11]

Within little more than six months after the army mutinies, the political alliance between the Uganda People's Congress and the Kabaka Yekka came to an end at Obote's initiative. The official link between Obote and Buganda as shareholders in the government of Uganda was thus institutionally ended.

Mutesa remained head of state for a year and a half longer. In 1966, a motion was brought before Parliament by Daudi Ocheng, a northerner but a close friend of Mutesa, charging Obote, Amin, and others with corrupt practices involving gold and ivory from Congo. This motion precipitated a crisis, culminating in Obote's suspension of the constitution, his deposition of Mutesa as president, and his assumption of power as the president of Uganda. He had previously ended the Kabaka Yekka's share in the government of the country; now he was ending Sir Edward Mutesa's honorific share as well. The Baganda came to interpret this in ethnic terms and proceeded to ask Obote to remove his government from "Buganda soil."

In the first half of 1966, before Obote had suspended the constitution, Mutesa had discussed with the British high commissioner and with the ambassadors of some African states the possibility of a loan of troops to handle the problem of constitutional upheaval in Uganda. The movement of troops without adequate consultation with either Brigadier Opolot, the head of the army, or President Mutesa, the commander in chief, had already caused serious speculation. Mutesa's account was as follows:

> It was at this stage that I sounded out the British Commissioner and some African ambassadors as to whether it would be possible to fly in troops if the situation got out of hand. I did not invite a foreign force to invade Uganda. I had in mind something similar to the successful intervention by the British which Obote had authorised two years before. It seemed to me likely that a coup was imminent.[12]

As it turned out, the coup was an internal one, within the system, in the sense that the prime minister was the one to overthrow the president, suspend the constitution, and assume executive powers as a self-appointed head of state.

Obote's assumption of supreme authority tilted the balance more sharply to the side of northern dominance in Uganda. The old principle of the ethnic separation of powers, which British colonial policy had tended to foster, came to an end. The idea of a Bantu pre-eminence in politics and administration with a Nilotic preponderance in the military could not have been sustained during the independence period in any case, but the brief alliance between Obote and Mutesa and the reign of Mutesa as the first president of Uganda

---

11. *Ibid.*, p. 195.
12. *Ibid.*, p. 186.

had together helped to give the Baganda a continuing central role in Uganda affairs. But this uneasy solution came to an end in 1966. Far from an ethnic separation of powers, there now seemed to be developing an ethnic concentration of powers.

In fairness to Obote, it ought to be emphasized that he did want to become a unifier of Uganda, a historical figure who managed to forge the different ethnic communities into a coherent nation. To that extent he never wanted to reserve the top positions in the country for his own people. On the contrary, the Baganda retained a disproportionate share of the civil service as a whole. Obote was quite often very sensitive about allegations that he was discriminating against any group. His furious reaction to Abu Mayanja's letter in *Transition*, which suggested that the judiciary in Uganda was kept wholly expatriate simply because the best-qualified local lawyers were Baganda, can be understood in terms of Obote's determination to be a reconciler rather than a discriminator. Abu Mayanja and the magazine were charged with sedition on the basis of these insinuations of ethnic discrimination. The court acquitted the accused, to Obote's indignation, but Obote took no action to interfere with the judicial process.[13] In spite of Obote's determination to pursue a policy of reconciliation, and in spite of his desire to go down in Uganda history as the nation-builder, the theme of Nilotic leadership in this endeavor was persistent. To some extent Obote was a victim of a particular period in African history, a period in which ethnic pulls and ethnic visions were omnipresent in politics.

When Obote assumed the top position in Uganda, the armed forces had, at last, a meaningful national purpose. This was the Nilotic Manifest Destiny — to back a northern man in cutting the Baganda down to size and to determine the course of the country's history from the north. There is little doubt that if Grace Ibingira and Mutesa and the other critics of Obote had succeeded in ousting him from the leadership of the UPC in 1966, the army coup in Uganda would have come sooner. Indeed, there might have been an army coup that year, soon after Obote's ouster. Obote's retention of military support was substantially due to ethnic bonds of solidarity, just as Mutesa's inability to capture military support was substantially due to a historic ethnic cleavage between the northerners and the Baganda. It may well be that from a civilian point of view, one of Obote's enduring achievements was his success in delaying a military coup in Uganda for another five years. It took a great deal of manipulative skill. But it also took the simple device of giving the army a sense of national purpose.

Why was it that every six months Parliament went through the motions of extending the state of emergency in Buganda? In order to give the armed forces a sense of mission in unifying the country, and in order to cut the Baganda

---

13. For a discussion of Obote's style as a reconciliation leader, see Ali A. Mazrui, "Leadership in Africa: Obote of Uganda," *International Journal*, XXV, no. 3 (Summer, 1970), 538–64.

down to size, the sense of urgency in the political situation had to be maintained. An atmosphere of continuing national emergency was sustained simply by putting the most populous and historically the most uncooperative tribe under emergency regulations. That was Obote's answer to the problem of military anomie. He gave the armed forces a sense of national purpose partly by maintaining tension in the country.

In December, 1969, an attempt was made on Obote's life, and the cabinet decided to extend the state of emergency beyond Buganda to the country as a whole. To that extent the attempted assassination gave the army an additional reason for national involvement. The soldiers were needed to avert a violent Ganda attempt at a political comeback.

In 1970 the idea of holding elections gathered momentum. Obote issued Document No. 5, outlining a new method of electing members of Parliament and the president of the country. Elections were expected sometime before April, 1971. Some preliminary steps involving party elections in constituencies had been taken. Constituency boundaries had been determined. Would there be a full return to civilian politics? Would there be an end to the state of emergency not only in other parts of the country but also in Buganda? Would there be a reduction in the army's role in national affairs? Some sectors of the army, perhaps partly influenced by the special privileges arising out of a state of emergency, might have had mixed feelings about Obote's unilateral decision to move toward full restoration of civilian authority.

Institutionally, the move toward such a restoration began at the top. From 1966 to 1968 the Defence Council of Uganda had had a major role in the decision-making process. But in 1969 Obote's growing commitment to the concept of a socialist Uganda was leading him toward ideas of civilian supremacy. He began to bypass the Defence Council, and more and more decisions were made either by Obote or by the cabinet. When the coup came in January, 1971, one of the main grievances expressed by the soldiers was that Obote had transferred too much of the military business to the cabinet. The Defence Council had not met since 1969. Moreover, Obote had — in Amin's absence — promoted a number of officers for purely political considerations. This gradual bypassing of the military machinery helped to reduce the sense of national involvement among important sections of the army.

But the Nilotic leadership in nation-building continued. A change which Obote reportedly contemplated was in the direction of discrimination within the northern sector. Those who staged the army coup of January, 1971, claimed that Obote was veering toward basing his military support more on the Langi, possibly in alliance with the Acholi, and less with the Nilotic groups of West Nile. It may have been that Obote was experimenting with a new equation of ethnic calculation, designed to maintain his civilian supremacy and thus to retain a Nilotic leadership in national integration.

Whatever the case, Obote's approach toward mitigating military anomie turned out to be not as effective as the strategies pursued by Tanzania and Kenya. Obote's and Akena Adoko's secret distribution of arms to loyal civilian supporters — which was discovered after the coup — was, by its secrecy, ineffective in *deterring* a coup. In spite of these secret arms, Obote's strategy can still be said to have involved giving the military a sense of purpose without devising a countervailing force. The sense of purpose coped with the problem of military anomie but it did not cope with the problem of potential military ambition for power.

On January 25, 1971, Major General Amin took over. Amin's strategy did seem to continue to emphasize northern leadership, but the shift was away from Lango to West Nile. Moreover, Amin committed himself fairly early to a new basis of ethnic balance in the army. The Baganda had been demilitarized when they moved from a concept of autonomy based on power to a concept of autonomy based on contract during the colonial period. After the coup, Amin committed himself to a system that would increasingly involve other tribes in the armed forces. He stressed, at his first press conference, his intention to step up recruitment in the army, partly with a view to making the armed forces more ethnically representative of the groups within the country. An armed force that was thus representative had to include a sizable Ganda component. The *remilitarization* of the Baganda could end, once and for all, the ethnic separation of powers which British imperial policy had bequeathed to the political fortunes of Uganda.

Three Approaches to Civilian-Military Relations

We have discussed in this chapter the dynamics of civilian-military relations in East Africa in the light of the first military coup in this region of the continent. The countries of East Africa, as chance would have it, were among the few that were forewarned by actual experience about the power of the military without actually experiencing a military takeover. In almost all other African countries an actual coup was the first instance of violent military insubordination. By that time it was too late for the civilian authorities to restructure the army.

Kenya, Tanganyika, and Uganda did have the exceptional experience of first coping with modest military mutinies before having to confront the threat or reality of an actual takeover. The 1964 events were mutinies oriented toward terms of service for soldiers and opportunities for promotions rather than toward the acquisition of political power. Tanganyika experienced the worst case of mutiny, and in its case the distinction between a pay-packet mutiny and a threat to the survival of the political system was at one stage very narrow. On balance, however, it remains true that Kenya, Tanganyika, and Uganda enjoyed the distinction of having a realistic forewarning about the potential power of their armed forces. That forewarning provided on opportunity to reconsider in entirety the issue of civilian-military relations and the precise organization of the armed forces in these societies.

It ought to be remembered that, at that time, military coups in Africa were not as yet a fact of life. In fact, the only explicit and successful coup which had taken place had occurred in Togo, where President Sylvanus Olympio had been assassinated and a military regime had taken over. The situation in Congo-Leopoldville was a more complicated one, since it involved general chaos and undisciplined soldiers, as well as the first exercise in alliance between Colonel Mobutu and President Kasavubu. In other words, the situation was one of general social and military disintegration rather than one of the military taking over control of government from the civilians.

An attempted coup in Gabon took place at about the same time as the East African mutinies. In the case of Gabon, the French flew in to restore the overthrown civilian authority. In East Africa, the governments had not been asked by the soldiers to step down. British troops came to make civilian authority more effective rather than to restore to power governments which had been overthrown. Indeed, the mutinies in both Kenya and Uganda were very modest exercises, little more than what Obote called "a sit-down strike."

Taking the region as a whole, we see that Kenya's solution of *limited* military cooperation with Britain is more effective in providing a countervailing force than in mitigating military anomie. Uganda's solution of northern leadership in disciplining Buganda and uniting the nation was, by contrast, more effective in mitigating anomie than in providing a countervailing force. Tanzania's experiment, which has included making the soldiers ideologically committed and establishing a domestic countervailing force, has been a more imaginative endeavor to cope with both problems.

Meanwhile, the first military government in Uganda, under Idi Amin, abolished the principle of ethnic separation of powers as well as that of ethnic concentration of powers in Uganda's sociopolitical arrangements, and espoused instead the principle of ethnic representativeness in the composition of the armed forces. It may well be that this strategy, if fully implemented, will be Uganda's equivalent of an internal countervailing force. A system of checks and balances would be produced within the armed forces itself, rather than between the armed forces under Nilotic dominance and civilian administration with Bantu preponderance.

But will ethnic representativeness in the composition of the armed forces be adequate not only for purposes of providing a countervailing force but also for purposes of averting or mitigating the danger of renewed military anomie? Will the Uganda Army succeed in finding national purpose short of continually challenging civilian supremacy in the government? The intentions following the coup in January, 1971, were excellent; but keeping military ambition in check is, in itself, a major moral ambition. It remains to be seen whether Uganda will succeed in containing the risks both of anomie and of excessive ambition among its forces and provide what is conceivably an even more durable answer to these tendencies than has been devised elsewhere in East Africa.

[Part 3]

Cultural Engineering and Socioeconomic Change

[12]

Political Culture and
Concepts of Revolution

Political culture can be defined as the values, mores, and assumptions which animate or underlie the political behavior of a given society or of a given collection of social groups. There is an important school of thought in East Africa, sometimes powerful and influential, which believes that "revolutionary policies" constitute the only adequate approach toward meeting the needs of the countries concerned as determined by their political cultures. The term *revolution* has itself become persistent in the rhetoric of social reformers in Uganda, Kenya, and Tanzania. What does this quest for revolutionary transformation mean? Are there important differences in the three countries? If there are, what factors can explain these variations? But the first challenge lies in the concept of "revolution." What kinds of phenomena does the word describe?

Types of Revolutions

There are a number of ways to classify revolutions, but two sets of twin classifications might be particularly significant in East Africa. In this regard, revolutions are either structural or systemic; they are also either instigated or spontaneous.

A structural revolution is one that brings about major transformations *within* a given social system without fundamentally changing either the main outlines of the system or the power relations on which the system rests. A structural revolution can entail rapid urbanization in society, important new trends in belief systems, a fast rate of industrialization and the growth of new social groups and classes, and a rapid rise in the standard of living and swift changes in the style of living, while the main outlines of the sociopolitical system remain relatively constant. The rapid industrialization of Japan after the Meiji Restoration is a case in point. It is true that in this period Japanese political and social institutions were changing in spite of apparent continuities. But what is being suggested here is that the Japanese social system remained substantially neofeudalistic, while the internal structural content of the system was changing rapidly with industrialization and modernization. Japanese Confucianism, which had been substantially affected by Shintoism, Buddhism, and a feudalistic military society, put a social premium on each man's recognition of his own place in the social universe. The phenomenon of *deference* as an organizational resource and a basis for discipline became one of the factors behind the industrial miracle of Japan. The highly structured class system of the Japanese was transferred to the work relations of the factory. In some ways feudalism in Japan was modernized without being abandoned during the Meiji period. Feudalistic relations moved into the structure of the workshop, conditioning relations of production in a modern economy almost as deeply as they had affected relations of production in pre-Restoration Japan. These considerations make the Japanese ascent to industrial and military pre-eminence from the 1860s to the Second World War a matter of structural revolutionary change, combined with systemic continuity.

No less revealing an example is the case of the Industrial Revolution in Britain in the eighteenth and nineteenth centuries. The main outlines of British society did adjust to meet the kinds of changes that were affecting the structure of society. But the changes in the inner content of British life, in the structure of British arrangements, were more revolutionary than the changes in the British political system and power relations. The rapidity of change brought about by the Industrial Revolution in England could easily have resulted in a political revolution committed to a transformation of the system itself. Although there was much social unrest and many demands for reform as a result of the structural dislocations of industrialization, the British system of government was not overthrown; it was modified. The great Reform Bill of 1832 and the legislation that followed later in the century extended the frontiers of political participation. A major reason why greater difficulties were averted was perhaps connected with the primary reason why Britain has continued to have more years under Tory rule than under Labour government. This is the factor of deference in the class structure of British society. The acquiescence of the workers in the leadership of the upper classes has contributed much to the stability of the British system, in spite of major structural changes within that system. The dislocations coming with industrialization and urbanization did not result in a systematic upheaval.

Of the three countries of East Africa, Kenya comes nearest to affording an example of a structural revolution unaccompanied by a systemic one. Structurally, the economy of Kenya is changing faster than that of Uganda or Tanzania. The movement of people from the countryside to the cities, the growth of the cities themselves, the increase in social mobility and resultant changes in the class structure, the emergence of indigenous entrepreneurs, and the more rapid growth of an educated cadre are all aspects of a transformation in Kenya which is in some respects more fundamental than anything as yet experienced in either Uganda or Tanzania. However, Kenya's revolution is, like the Industrial Revolution in England in the eighteenth and nineteenth centuries, a revolution without *revolutionaries* at the helm. Major structural modifications in the society and the economy are taking place largely in the sheer momentum of unguided social change.

Systemic revolutions are those which entail a renunciation of old institutions and a transformation of values. Examples include the Russian, Chinese, Egyptian, and Cuban revolutions.

This brings us to the other set of twin classifications concerning revolutions — those that are instigated and those that are spontaneous. An instigated revolution is one that has revolutionaries in positions of influence and effective activation. It is also quite often a guided revolution. The instigation is primarily what happens before the actual initiation of major change; the guidance is what is provided to ensure that the change follows a purposeful direction. A revolution which has been instigated and guided by revolutionaries tends to have behind it a set of idealized objectives and sometimes even a coherent ideology. East African examples of instigated or guided revolutions now include Uganda in the last year of Obote's rule, as well as Tanzania. Both Uganda under Obote and Tanzania under Nyerere committed themselves to socialism. The idealized objective seemed to be primarily a systemic change, leading, it was hoped, to structural transformations as well.

A spontaneous revolution is one that erupts without sustained preparation or organization, a mass uprising rather than a planned insurrection. Examples include the revolutionary eruptions in different parts of Europe in 1848.

Nationalization of certain industries causes a change in the system but, in itself, does not imply any structural revolution. Even a coup is merely a takeover of the state; it need not result in a revolution. Likewise, nationalization of the means of production is a takeover by the state. This change of ownership is, in itself, not a structural revolution, though it may constitute an important systemic change. Sometimes nationalization in East Africa has seemed at best to be aimed at transforming the legal basis of ownership. The ownership passes from one group of impersonal owners (often foreign investors) to another (the state) without fundamentally changing the work relations within the particular industry or the nature of the industry's interaction with the world of consumers.

In contrast, a policy that seeks to promote an indigenous entrepreneurial culture and to create successful African businessmen where none existed before might well be a policy that seeks to transform the economic man in East Africa. We have discussed the distinction between the prestige motive, which animates much of the economic behavior of traditional communities in East Africa, and the profit motive, which is more individualistically oriented as a spur to economic action. The Trade Licensing Acts passed in Kenya and Uganda in 1969 and the whole complex of inducements and protection for African businessmen as potential successors to Asian entrepreneurs are measures that can result in a drastic revolution in the economic behavior of indigenous Kenyans and Ugandans.

That revolution, as it learns the tricks of commerce and trade and the philosophy of "business is business," might result in precisely the kind of fundamental psychological and sociological changes which form the foundation of structural transformation. In other words, creating successful African entrepreneurs in Kenya and Uganda can be structurally a more revolutionary process than the mere nationalization of a particular industry — in spite of the fact that, ideologically, it may sound less revolutionary than the legal exercise of changing the ownership of an industry.

History and Change

What factors have determined whether a country is to undergo a structural rather than a systemic transformation? What has produced a spontaneous structural revolution in one East African country and an instigated systemic transformation in another? Such questions cannot be adequately dealt with at this stage in the history of the countries concerned. There is a good deal that is still inconclusive. But, as so often happens in an evaluation of postcolonial Africa, we find that some of the differences between one country and another can conceivably be explained in terms of the immediate colonial past. Some differences can be explained, for example, by the kinds of colonial policies that operated in particular countries and the distinctive features of the local response. How pertinent toward understanding the different levels of revolutionary commitment in Uganda, Tanzania, and Kenya is the imperial factor and its variations in the three countries?

The experience of East Africa as a whole would seem to suggest that the more an African country suffered in the struggle for independence, the less "revolutionary" in a leftist ideological sense it was inclined to be after independence. Kenya suffered most in the great battle for sovereignty, paying for that independence with blood, death, and humiliation. Yet Kenya today is the least "revolutionary" in the leftist sense of socialistic instigation.

Tanganyika suffered least in its struggle for independence. There were no detention camps in colonial Tanganyika with hundreds of miserable freedom-fighters. Tanganyikans did not have to endure dark and wet nights in the depths of jungles, hiding from colonial security forces. During the latter half of the British period in Tanganyika there were no instances of collective physical brutalization, no bodily mutilations ordered by sadistic colonial officers, and no record of castrations inspired by a sense of political revenge against an indigenous community. The sacrifices that were made by Tanganyikans for *uhuru* were modest when compared with what was exacted on the other side of Kilimanjaro. There can be no doubt about it — Tanganyika had a smooth approach to independence. The country was under the brilliant leadership of Nyerere, a man widely considered at the time as the moderate African par excellence. Yet this country, regarded once as a paragon of moderation, is carrying the torch of socialistic revolution in East Africa.

Uganda suffered more than Tanganyika but less than Kenya. Some of its agonies were concerned with internal divisions; others, however, were more specifically rooted in imperial relations. Over the generations Uganda did know the death of nationalists, the imprisonment of freedom-fighters, the exile of kings. Yet in the actual nationalistic movement the casualty rate in Uganda was drastically smaller than that in Kenya, though higher than that in Tanganyika.

Is it a consequence of these differences in experience that Uganda has been less revolutionary in its commitment than Tanzania but, perhaps even yet, more so than Kenya? The question that is being raised here is whether we can at this point infer that the experience of agonizing suffering for independence is not the best preparation for socialistic fervor once independence has been won. Is there a degree of suffering in the fight for independence which is *deradicalizing* in its consequences? The evidence on the African scene as a whole is by no means conclusive; but the experience of East Africa is suggestive enough for us to pose this question, even if the answer remains yet to be adequately confirmed.

Malawi, which is less radical than Zambia, is another good example in East Africa from this point of view. The real leadership in the struggle for the breakup of the Central African Federation was taken by Malawi (then Nyasaland) rather than Zambia (then Northern Rhodesia). In the struggle for independence many Malawians were imprisoned or detained. For example, David Rubadiri, who later represented Malawi at the United Nations, was once a nationalistic detainee in colonial Nyasaland. Hastings Banda was also detained. There is no doubt that Banda suffered more under colonialism than either Kenneth Kaunda of Zambia or Julius Nyerere of Tanzania. Again it appears that those who really suffered for their country's independence are not prepared to force their people to make further sacrifices, after independence, in the name of socialism.

It may be too early to determine whether the agony of fighting for freedom simply *delays* a taste for socialism or whether it kills that taste altogether. In addition, one must always bear in mind that there are other factors operating, factors that may mitigate, or even neutralize, the effect of one historical dimension on postindependence orientations. It is quite conceivable that great suffering for independence results in *delayed* radicalization after independence. Yet this effect could be reduced, or even neutralized, if other factors in the social and national situations were to accelerate the trend toward radicalization. This is the old problem of determining the causes of social phenomena.

It is possible that Malawi will one day go the way of Zambia, in a leftward direction. It is also possible that Kenya will one day move to the left. But, for the time being, this seems quite clear — of the three East African countries, Kenya sacrificed the most for independence. There may well be important sectors of the population within Kenya who feel that those who sacrificed much for independence should reflect before pursuing further horizons of sacrifice.

In the early 1960s Tanzania achieved historical distinction by attempting to bring about an East African federation. Mzee Kenyatta supported Mwalimu Nyerere in his vision, and Obote joined them in issuing a declaration in June, 1963, asserting their readiness to form a federation and urging the British government to grant independence to Kenya so that this federal ambition could be brought to fruition before the end of the year. Two years before that formal declaration I was having a conversation with a young Kikuyu in New York. Nyerere had publicly declared himself in favor of an East African federation. My Kikuyu friend had the following observations to make:

> It is easy enough for Nyerere to take the larger view and offer to give up Tanganyika's sovereignty before he has even won it. Only someone who had not suffered for his little plot of land can be so cosmopolitan. How can Tanganyika be expected to know what it is like to suffocate under humiliation? Tanganyika never suffered the way Kenya did.

At the time, "Kenya" was the broadest concept to which my young Kikuyu friend was honestly capable of feeling loyal. I disagreed with him then; I still feel he was wrong. But I was struck by the argument that those who had suffered so much should not be asked to enter into further agonies of self-denial and visionary ambition.[1] His argument is perhaps a fragmentary explanation as to why independent Kenya, with a Kikuyu pre-eminence in government, is for the time being devoid of self-conscious revolutionaries at the helm and yet is undergoing structural change at a dramatic pace.

Culture and Change: The Kikuyu

It is not merely the imperial experience which helps to shape postcolonial orientations. It is also the texture of the values and customs inherited from the traditional life of the dominant tribes in the African countries concerned. The Kikuyu in Kenya provide a striking example of this kind of phenomenon. The evidence since independence would seem to suggest that, on balance, the Kikuyu are politically conservative but economically innovative. The conservatism of the Kikuyu has, in part, lain in their rural nationalism. During the colonial period Kikuyu rural nationalism, combined with economic dynamism, helped to give the Mau Mau movement the image of a revolution. The Kikuyu uprising in the Mau Mau insurrection seemed inspired by radical fervor as well as by a rebellion against racial humiliation and foreign control.

At that stage it almost appeared as if the Kikuyu were expressing the same kind of peasant radicalism that animated the Chinese under Mao's leadership

---

1. See Ali A. Mazrui, "On Heroes and Uhuru-Worship," *Transition*, Vol. III, no. 11 (November, 1963), reprinted in *idem, On Heroes and Uhuru-Worship: Essays on Independent Africa* (London: Longmans, 1967), pp. 19–34.

just a few years earlier. The Mau Mau insurrection, like the Chinese Communist Revolution, has been interpreted in historical perspective as basically a peasant revolt. The argument has been to the effect that land hunger in Kenya created a situation of peasant grievance, and that this initiated a transformative self-assertion.

Sometimes the term *peasant* is used to denote a person who owns a modest piece of land. But much of the agitation behind the Mau Mau insurrection was by people who were landless, living as squatters on estates owned by Europeans. They could see large tracts of land — sometimes uncultivated and unused, sometimes richly cultivated and foreign-owned — all beyond their capacity to acquire. As Donald L. Barnett put it in his introduction to Karari Njama's *Mau Mau from Within:*

> It is not only the brute fact of landlessness, land hunger, and insecurity of tenure which conditioned Kikuyu involvement in the nationalist movement and peasant revolt; it is also the fact that for a people who attach such sacred meaning to the land the areas alienated remain within their field of experience, unattainable yet in considerable measure unused by its new [white] owners.[2]

The final outcome was the revolt of the rural dispossessed — and the long years of the state of emergency in the 1950s. The rural assertion in Kenya had the garb of a traditionalism which was at times almost primeval. The nature of Mau Mau oaths administered as a way of commanding loyalty indicated a profound traditionality in Kikuyu nationalism, which was, in turn, to remain the basis of Kikuyu political conservatism after independence. But, as long as the battle was directed against the elimination of colonial rule and the British settler presence, the Kikuyu uprising had the reputation of being a radical, even a revolutionary, movement.

At the time of the uprising many could not quite reconcile Kikuyu radical assertiveness with the strange ritualism which consolidated it. Western observers could understand killings and torture, having tried that sort of thing themselves on many occasions, including the occasion of fighting Mau Mau. Even Elspeth Huxley — hardly a friend of African nationalism, let alone of Mau Mau — concedes that atrocities during the emergency were perpetrated by both sides. Anyone who expected different standards from government forces had, according to Mrs. Huxley, "read no history." Rebellions could not be put down "without brutalising."[3] What Western commentators and observers could not understand was the bad taste of the Mau Mau rituals. The rituals ranged from drinking

---

2. Donald L. Barnett and Karari Njama, *Mau Mau from Within: An Analysis of Kenya's Peasant Revolt* (New York and London: Monthly Review Press, 1967), p. 34.
3. Elspeth Huxley, review of Josiah M. Kariuki's *Mau Mau Detainee*, in *Sunday Times* (London), August 4, 1963.

menstrual blood to taking the Mau Mau Batuni oath standing naked, with one's male organ inserted through a hole in the thorax of a goat. There did not seem to be enough precedents for these oaths in history books to enlighten those who, like Mrs. Huxley, had "read their history."

Whereas the Chinese peasant assertion had culminated in a Marxist revolution, the Kikuyu peasant assertion came to assume a more conservative orientation on Kenya's attainment of independence. The nature of those oaths during the insurrection might have been an indication of the innate ruralism of Kikuyu political behavior.

The tendency to invoke oath-taking and sacred ritualism manifested itself again after independence. In 1969 the Kikuyu began to feel insecure once again, partly in the face of a growing challenge from the Luo, the second of Kenya's major ethnic groups. Oath-taking erupted once again. There was a tendency to seek reassurance in the solidarity of shared rituals and a determination not to permit the Kikuyu to be in the political wilderness ever again. The Luo challenge had replaced settler intransigence as an igniting factor behind traditionalist assertiveness among the Kikuyu.

The traditional aspect of Kikuyu political behavior has led to other problems associated with such an orientation. In recruitment to the civil service and the parastatal bodies, in the awarding of licenses for trading, in the allocation of land rights in areas other than those reserved for individual communities — in all such instances of the distribution of benefits and privileges, Kikuyu traditionalism has, at times, come into conflict with modern criteria of merit and rational eligibility. Ethnic nepotism in Kenya has sometimes been more frank and less disguised than elsewhere in Africa, partly because the universe of values of the dominant tribe still puts a premium on solidarity rather than rationality as a principle of distribution. There has been widespread concern in Kenya that powerful positions and fruitful opportunities are disproportionately, though not exclusively, allocated to Kikuyu.

There is, then, in much of Kikuyu political behavior a kind of traditionalism which distrusts both excessive rationalism and excessive egalitarianism in political arrangements. The relative antirationalism as well as the relative antiegalitarianism of Kikuyu traditionalist behavior in a modern context have been important conditioning factors behind the Kikuyu attitude to communism.

In contrast to Kikuyu political conservatism is their economic innovativeness. There seems to be little doubt that the Kikuyu are among the most economically dynamic of all tribal communities in East Africa. They are rapidly responding to the policy of Africanizing commercial activity in Kenya and are thrusting themselves out into different parts of the country in a bid to establish themselves economically. In many ways the Kikuyu are reminiscent of the Ibo in Nigeria. The readiness to seek economic opportunities in other parts of the world, the acceptance of the need for risk-taking, and the mystique of self-improvement as a traditional imperative have all contributed to an economic resurgence among the Kikuyu.

Perhaps this economic innovativeness can be traced back to the colonial days and the extent to which the Kikuyu responded more positively than some of their neighbors to the impact of modernity and Western educational challenges. They built their own schools during the colonial period in a bid to acquire the necessary skills for modern success. Even land, in some ways a profoundly sacred entity among the Kikuyu, was more a commodity to them than to other African tribes. The idea of parting with land as an exercise in exchange was by no means an alien doctrine among the Kikuyu.[4] In the midst of the Mau Mau emergency, entrepreneurship was seeking new outlets among those not directly involved in the war. In 1955 L. S. B. Leakey observed:

> The Kikuyu have over the past ten years developed an absolute craze for "company" formation. There are hundreds, possibly thousands, of unregistered "Companies," as they call them, comprising anything from three to ten shareholders, who invest their money with the hope, often a forlorn one, that it will multiply much more quickly than it would in the Post Office Savings Bank or in any other organised concern.[5]

The range of companies and types of enterprise attempted was quite wide. The mere fact that the Kikuyu preferred to invest in such companies rather than to put away their money in a Post Office Savings Bank augured well for the spirit of risk-taking which seemed to characterize Kikuyu economic behavior after independence. The small companies that were organized in the colonial period ranged from commercial transport firms to small grocery shops in the villages. There was no doubt that something in Kikuyu culture which responded to economic innovation would make the tribe commercial masters of the country, should the political climate one day become more congenial to their full economic maturation.

And then independence came. The principle of personal success as a measure of social achievement began to find legitimacy in a Kenya under African rule. In the first two years of Kenya's independence the term "African socialism" was still part of the official vocabulary of politics. But, meanwhile, changes were taking place in the direction of greater African involvement in the economic organization of the country. The policies of giving Africans a greater share in the former White Highlands of Kenya, of encouraging more efficient forms of land settlement among Africans, of bringing under cultivation land which was before underutilized, and of pushing harder than ever the idea of creating an African commercial class to replace, at least in part, the cadre of businessmen

---

4. See Greet Sluiter, *Kikuyu Concepts of Land and Land Kin* (M. A. thesis, University of Chicago, 1960); John Middleton and Kershaw Greet, *The Kikuyu and Kamba of Kenya* (London: International African Institute, 1956), pp. 52–56; Jomo Kenyatta, *Facing Mount Kenya* (1938; reprint ed., London: Secker & Warburg, 1959), pp. 20–40.
5. L. S. B. Leakey, "The Economics of Kikuyu Life," *East African Economic Review*, III (1956), 177–79.

which had previously consisted of Asians and Europeans — all of these were aspects of a vigorous move to Africanize more substantially the central parts of Kenya's economy. A question which remained was whether the Africanization of the economy had to be in the direction of creating African capitalism. Again Kikuyu traditional predispositions, activated in part by Jomo Kenyatta's style of leadership, helped to provide an affirmative answer to that question. Kenya took the highroad toward an African private-enterprise system, partly because within Kikuyu traditional predispositions there was an ethic which accepted personal success as a measure of social achievement.

President Kenyatta once tried to "disgrace" a prominent Kenyan leftist at a public meeting by pointing out that the leftist did not own a big house or a private business. The leftist, Bildad Kaggia, was present at the meeting. President Kenyatta compared Kaggia with other old colleagues of his who had since become prosperous. Addressing Kaggia directly, Mzee Kenyatta said:

> We were together with Paul Ngei in jail. If you go to Ngei's home, he has planted a lot of coffee and other crops. What have you done for yourself? If you go to [Fred] Kubai's home, he has a big house and has a nice shamba. Kaggia, what have you done for yourself? We were together with Kungu Karumba in jail, now he is running his own buses. What have you done for yourself?[6]

What is significant here is the conviction that failure to prosper is an argument against a leader. As a socialist radical, Kaggia was, at the time, urging distribution of land in Kenya to the poor. Kenyatta was suggesting that a person who had failed to prosper through his own exertions should not be "advocating free things." [7]

From this kind of reasoning it was an easy transition to the feeling that enforced economic equality was an insult to the dignity of labor. The principle that wealth should be distributed "to every man according to his work" made sense; it did not make sense to strive for a principle of distribution "to each according to his needs." The official distrust of communism in Kenya's ideological orientation is therefore to be traced not so much to Western influence as to the influence of the traditional mores of one of the dominant ethnic groups in Kenya politics. The Kikuyu distrust of economic egalitarianism was sometimes shared by other groups, or by individuals from other groups converted to a similar orientation. From all of this emerged the official conviction in Kenya, crystallized in Minister Ronald Ngala's assertion that "communism teaches people laziness." [8]

---

6. *East African Standard* (Nairobi), April 12, 1965.
7. *Ibid.* This point is discussed more fully in Ali A. Mazrui, "The Monarchical Tendency in African Political Culture," *British Journal of Sociology*, XVIII, no. 3 (September, 1967), 231–50, reprinted in *idem, Violence and Thought: Essays on Social Tensions in Africa* (London: Longmans, 1969), pp. 206–30.
8. See BBC Monitoring Service Records of African Broadcasts, Nairobi (in English), ME/1892/B/2, June 22, 1965. In Lenin's terms, the principle of "from each according

Marginality, Centrality, and Innovation

Both the Kikuyu and the Baganda are heartland tribes; that is, they are communities important enough and central enough to have been at the heart of major events in the history of their countries. The Kikuyu were an underprivileged heartland tribe during the colonial period. Their nearness to the white settlers of Kenya made them vulnerable to some of the more brutal aspects of settler colonialism. The Baganda, on the other hand, were a relatively privileged community under British rule; they enjoyed a degree of autonomy and attentiveness from the imperial authorities which was the envy of others.

One question which arises concerns the very quality of being a heartland tribe, central and important regardless of whether privileged or underprivileged. Does this quality promote the kind of self-confidence which psychologically facilitates a capacity for economic risk-taking? Such a hypothesis may help to explain the positive economic responsiveness on the part of both the Kikuyu and the Baganda.

We have suggested above that, since independence, the Kikuyu have been politically conservative but economically innovative. To some extent the same can be said of the Baganda, both before and after independence, but with some important variations. The Baganda have a record of minimal response to political reform but one of effective response to economic modernization.

During the colonial period the privileged position of the Baganda facilitated economic risk-taking but, at the same time, created a vested interest in maintaining the political *status quo*. After independence the Baganda began to decline, especially following their confrontation in 1966 with the central government of Uganda under Milton Obote. The coup of January, 1971, cannot be expected to restore their former pre-eminence. The Ganda decline in power has inevitably undermined their interest in the *status quo*. Does this mean that the Baganda are now ready to mobilize into a movement for political reform? In their case the issue could go either in the direction of nostalgia for the *status quo ante* or in the direction of impatient elimination of the present arrangements and substitution of a new political system. The evidence so far is that the Baganda's response has been nostalgic rather than revolutionary, to restore the past rather than to create a new future. Ganda political conservatism has therefore persisted in spite of the new situation of relative decline.

But what has happened to their innovative capacity in the economic sphere? Although the evidence is incomplete, there are signs that Ganda economic innovativeness may be enhanced as a result of their political decline. Before 1966 many of the best minds, skills, and entrepreneurial qualities of the Baganda

---

to his abilities to each according to his work'' is a transitional principle characteristic of the lower phase of communism. But the ultimate aim of justice in communist terms is, according to Lenin, "from each according to his abilities to each according to his needs.'' See Lenin, *State and Revolution* (1917; reprint ed., New York: International Publishers, 1932).

were involved in competing for office within the kabaka's system of government rather than in engaging in economic investment and trade. During the 1940s and 1950s, attempts on the part of the Baganda to promote vigorous commercial activity were seldom spectacularly successful, though often more successful than those undertaken by some of their neighbors. Commerce and trade enjoyed limited prestige as compared with the prestige of landownership or of entering the Mengo establishment.

The Kikuyu, now in power in Kenya, have consolidated the self-confidence which makes economic risk-taking feasible. If the Kikuyu economic upsurge is partly due to their centrality in the power structure, this would be a case of economic vigor deriving its sustenance from political ascendancy. On the other hand, if, as the evidence so far seems to suggest, Ganda entrepreneurship has increased since 1966, this would be a case of a community becoming economically more vigorous because of political decline, rather than political ascendancy, and the closure of some of the alternative opportunities. The Kikuyu are still in a position to *diversify* their hegemony; but the Ganda have been forced to *specialize* if they are to retain some pre-eminence in Uganda society as a whole.

The economic success of the Baganda falls within that category which is sometimes attributed to sociological marginality. Marginal communities are those on the borderline between belonging and not belonging, those which have to specialize in a particular area of endeavor in order to make an impact on society. The case of the Jews in Europe and America is one example of this type of community. The case of the Asians in East Africa, though in some ways less clear, is also a viable illustration.

Yet there is a difference between such cases of marginality and the case of the Baganda. Unlike the Baganda, the Jews in Europe and America were never privileged and then cut down to size. Economic assertiveness arising out of the phenomenon of losing status must therefore be regarded as somewhat different from the pattern of motivation characteristic of continuously marginal communities.

The case of the Baganda is more like the case of some categories of the samurai in the history of the modernization of Japan.

> In Japan, the feudal group known as Tokugawa, who gained national power in 1600, imposed a peace which deprived the Samurai of some of their traditional functions; imposed rigid distinctions among social classes which had the effect of relegating the so-called wealthy peasants, descendants of the lesser elite, to the rank of the peasant; and to some extent demeaned other feudal groups, so-called outer clans. It was the lesser Samurai and wealthy peasants, apparently of the outer clans, who were the innovators of the industrial revolution.[9]

---

9. Everett E. Hagen, "How Economic Growth Begins: A Theory of Social Change," *Journal of Social Issues*, XIX (January, 1963), 31.

The Baganda afford a similar case of demotion — a withdrawal of political status resulting in renewed readiness to experiment in alternative areas of endeavor.[10]

Radicalism and the Uganda Nilotes

If traditional culture helps to determine responsiveness to an entrepreneurial ethos in a particular African community, does it also help to arouse socialistic radicalism in others? Much of the debate in Africa about African socialism has been tinged by a socialistic idealization of traditional society. Nyerere's concept of *Ujamaa* is itself an assertion that traditional collectivism and the solidarity of kinship systems can provide a foundation for socialistic endeavors in the modern world. But not all African communities in East Africa have, by any means, displayed a responsiveness to socialism as a matter of course. The word *socialism* does enjoy wide respectability, even among those who only pay lip service to it. But in the empirical situation of East Africa, we remain inadequately informed about the precise relationship between the cultural background of an individual and his potential response to socialistic values. What the short history of independent East Africa has so far illustrated is the simple fact that in Uganda and Kenya much of the left-wing radicalism has been initiated or led by sections of the Nilotic peoples. In the case of Uganda, Nilotic radicalism, where it has existed, has been partly structural and partly cultural. It has been structural because, until recently, northerners have occupied a relatively underprivileged position in relation to Buganda and other Bantu kingdoms. The Nilotic readiness to engage in the politics of radicalism might in part be a rebellion against a tradition of being underprivileged. But the Nilotic response to radicalism has at times also been cultural because of the egalitarian and republican elements in their traditional system of values.

In many ways the Nilotes have not been especially more egalitarian than the Kikuyu, but they certainly have been more egalitarian than the Baganda and some of their other Bantu neighbors. There were times when certain northern groups in Uganda, in an effort to assert their parity with Buganda, created the equivalent of a paramount chief comparable to the kabaka. The Kikuyu in colonial Kenya had similarly been tempted at times to seek dignity in monarchical devices. Their own cultural heritage did not include a hierarchical system of rule or institutions of monarchical power. But Buganda's demonstration effect on its neighbors, the degree of respect and autonomy it had received from

---

10. For discussion of the wider issues concerning motivation and economic performance, see David C. McClelland, *The Achievement Motive* (Princeton, N.J.: Van Nostrand, 1961); Bert F. Hoselitz and Wilbur E. Moore, eds., *Industrialization and Society* (The Hague: UNESCO and Mouton, 1963). See also Chalmers Johnson, *Revolutionary Change* (London: University of London Press, 1966).

the British, helped to arouse in some of those neighbors the desire for a similar system of centralization as a means of acquiring greater dignity and respect from the colonial authorities.[11]

After independence the Kikuyu in Kenya found themselves at the heart of power, and their own traditional modes of organization were enough to give them political effectiveness. Their individualistic orientations were therefore released to become part of the emerging entrepreneurial culture of Kenya.

In the case of Uganda, Milton Obote first accommodated himself to the historical realities of the country and even formed an alliance with Kabaka Yekka ("the king alone"), the party in defense of the monarchical principle in Buganda and of the autonomy of the region. But by the time of independence it had become less fashionable to seek parity of esteem with Buganda by creating hierarchical structures similar to those of the Baganda. Obote was coming to the view that one day it might be possible to establish parity among the different communal groups by abolishing all the kings in the Bantu areas rather than by creating new kings in the Nilotic areas. Ideologically, as well as by virtue of cultural background, Obote had reservations about centralized monarchies. The idea of having chieftains was, of course, very much part of the Langi heritage. Obote himself came from a family of chiefs. But these dignitarian and influential institutions were not the same thing as centralized ones. In general the dominant structures in the northern communities were segmentary and neorepublican. The fact that such societies suffered in comparison with the respect accorded to the kings increased their self-conscious republicanism soon after independence.

Nevertheless, Obote was prepared to let the Bantu retain their kings as long as national cohesion was not threatened. But with the crisis between him and the kabaka of Buganda in 1966, he became more convinced than ever that regional kings could be dysfunctional to the cause of national integration. In general, what probably forced Obote to impose republicanism was not a quest for equality but a quest for unity. Most fanatical opponents of the institutions of kingship develop reservations about such institutions for reasons of egalitarian commitment. The very notion of royalty and its power and splendor connotes a relationship of privilege. Opposition to monarchical institutions has therefore very often been inspired by an impulse which seeks to end privilege. Although the egalitarian element was certainly present in Obote's republicanism, the integrative element was stronger. As a national leader, Obote was opposed to kings less because monarchical tendencies were incompatible with egalitarianism than because monarchical institutions in Uganda seemed to him to be incompatible with his vision of a united country.

In what way was Obote's radicalizing mission facilitated by the cultural factors in Nilotic experience? Were the values dominant in his northern political base congenial to the political reforms he had in mind? In the words of Aidan W.

11. For Kikuyu examples of this phenomenon, see John Nottingham and Carl G. Rosberg, *The Myth of "Mau Mau" : Nationalism in Kenya* (New York: Praeger, 1966).

Southall: "The popular view of the Nilotic peoples as a whole has certainly been one of egalitarian individualism. If such a slippery concept can be precisely defined, some truth may possibly be found in it." [12] But why only "some" truth? In what sense can we qualify attribution of egalitarian individualism to the Nilotic peoples?

The simple answer is that the Nilotic peoples vary significantly in their social structures and cultural patterns. At one end we have the Nuer, the Dinka, and to the south the Masai, with strong traditions of egalitarian individualism. At the other end we have the Alur and the Acholi, with more elaborate principles of stratification. But even in these latter societies the models of ranking were relatively simple as compared with those of some of their Bantu neighbors. There was a tendency among the Alur and the Acholi for political ranking to coincide with the ritual stratification.

> Thus, in Alur all those belonging to lineages descended from Chiefs are collectively called *rwodhi*, the term for the Chiefs themselves. . . . Alur commoners are collectively called *lwak*, which etymologically suggests the masses of subjects. In Acholi the same distinction is made between *kal* lineages, or those derived from and focussed upon the palace or homestead of the chief, [and] *lobong*, or subjects, a word that in other neighbouring Nilotic languages refers rather to serfs. [13]

Southall goes on to warn us against assuming that the "nobles" in such societies were a select minority. On the contrary, they could often be a majority in a particular community.

> This was always in the nature of the system, although it is true that colonial rule weakened or broke the bonds between serf or commoner clients and their noble patrons. . . . Nevertheless, given the principles of unilineal descent, cattle bride-wealth, exogamy and polygyny, noble lineages always on the average grew at a much larger rate than the commoner lineages, thus constantly diluting their nobility to the point of virtual extinction at the margin, preventing the development of a very hard line of distinction between all nobles and all commoners as such. [14]

The Luo of Kenya are even less hierarchical than this. Their degree of decentralization bears comparison with that characteristic of the eastern Nilotes. [15]

---

12. Aidan W. Southall, "Rank and Stratification among the Alur and Other Nilotic Peoples," in *Social Stratification in Africa*, ed. Arthur Tuden and Leonard Plotnicov (New York: Free Press, 1970), p. 36.

13. *Ibid.*, p. 38.

14. *Ibid.*

15. The Nilotic peoples are scattered throughout an area which encompasses northeastern Zaïre, northern Uganda, northern and western Kenya, southwestern Ethiopia, and southern Sudan. Analysts used to divide the area into the Nilotic and the Nilo-Hamitic segments. The appellation which has been gaining currency is that which emerged from Joseph H. Greenberg's linguistic classification. The Nilotes of old are now described as western Nilotes, and the Nilo-Hamitic groups are described as eastern Nilotes.

Egalitarian individualism as a cultural inheritance is mobilizable either in the direction of a private-enterprise system or in the direction of socialism. It depends upon whether it is the component of *individualism* or the factor of *egalitarianism* which gains ascendancy in unfolding political interaction.

A related distinction is, once again, that between culture and structure. Culture is that complex of values which seeks to control or motivate conscious social behavior; but structure in this context is mainly concerned with relationships of power and their organizational apparatus. Location can sometimes be an important structural variable. Structural elements go beyond the mere organization of the community within itself, encompassing power relationships with neighboring groups. Tribes included within the same national boundaries assume structural relationships to each other.

The Nilotes of Uganda were easy to mobilize into a mood of opposition to feudalism. Not only were they culturally more egalitarian than the neighboring Bantu kingdoms, but during the colonial period they had also been placed structurally in a position of relative deprivation as compared with the monarchical south.

But which direction should Uganda take after abolishing feudalism? The Nilotes might agree on the abolition of feudalism, but should feudalism be succeeded by a private-enterprise system or by a socialistic arrangement? Should the egalitarianism or the individualism in their cultural heritage be permitted supremacy? On the eve of independence important Nilotic leaders were already sure that some degree of socialism was needed, but they were far less certain that this should go to the extent of trying to suppress the spirit of individualism. Naphlin Akena Adoko, who later became one of the most powerful political figures in Uganda, captured the Nilotic dilemma in a speech he gave in Gulu on the eve of independence. He was addressing a meeting of leading residents of the town. Adoko said landownership in Lango and Acholi before the advent of Europeans had both socialistic and individualistic characteristics. Land was under the umbrella of the tribe or clans, but personal property was still permitted.

> It is my submission that what we need is a judicious mixture of individualism and socialism. We in Uganda have a degree of a mixed economy — what we need is a golden mean between socialism and individualism.

The meeting was held under the chairmanship of the secretary general of Acholi. It was so successful that its organizer, Okot p'Bitek, assessed that there was enough interest in such meetings to warrant one a week in Gulu.[16]

The factor which for a while came to tip the scales in favor of greater radicalism was the personality of Milton Obote and his own order of priorities, but this factor was combined with a national history which made it possible to utilize antifeudalism as an argument in favor of socialism. Much of Obote's Common

---

16. *Uganda Argus* (Kampala), May 16, 1962.

Man's Charter was oriented toward fighting the remnants of feudalism in the country. There was a persistent warning in the charter against the emergence of neofeudalism. There was an insistence that birth and heredity should forever cease to be determinants of status and privilege. But a capitalist need not favor feudalism. To some extent that was what the American Revolution was all about. It was at once a great initiation of a capitalistic civilization and a strong rebellion against British feudalistic tendencies. American political culture has included a persistent theme of opposition to a hereditary aristocracy. The idea of social mobility as an imperative is well within the complex of values of American civilization. That civilization is pre-eminently capitalistic, solidly derived from concepts of rugged individualism and private enterprise. But at the same time that civilization remains, at least in relation to its domestic preferences, opposed to feudalism and hereditary titles.

The asset which Obote had in his mission to move Uganda toward socialism ultimately lay in the availability of antifeudalism as a mobilizational resource. But did Obote stand a chance of success in persuading his supporters that socialism was the only legitimate alternative to feudalism? The answer to that question had begun to unfold before Obote was deposed in January, 1971. There seemed to be greater support for his socialistic policies among his own people in Lango than among some of the other northerners in the country. The Acholi are adjacent to the Langi, but indications at the time seemed to suggest that their enthusiasm for socialism was limited. Could the reason lie partly in the fact that the Acholi were less culturally egalitarian and less structurally underprivileged during the colonial period? The relevance of culture for ideological attitudes continued to be important, but it also remained difficult to measure with any degree of certainty.

Radicalism and the Kenya Nilotes

When President Kenyatta visited Luoland in October, 1969, to open the Soviet-financed hospital in Kisumu, he gave a speech which provoked a political reaction from the supporters of the opposition party, the Kenya People's Union. Mzee Kenyatta accused the people of Nyanza, the Luo, of some deficiencies in their commitment to nation-building. His taunts included the charge of "laziness." It was quite clear that the Luo had been commercially and even agriculturally less innovative and less dynamic than the Kikuyu. The president suggested that the relative slowness of economic development in that region was due in part to inadequate exertion by the local people.

The president's analysis of Nyanza behavior was exaggerated, but he was pointing to an important element in Luo social behavior and cultural orientation. The history of the Luo in Kenya did seem to indicate that their cultural genius in the modern period might lie more in proletarian organization and intellectual excellence and less in entrepreneurial vigor. While the Kikuyu soon displayed a readiness to move out of their tribal areas and establish businesses in Luoland and other regions, the Luo had an even longer history of mobility with longer distances traversed in search of opportunities. But the opportunities which the Luo sought were not in business and commerce. The Luo were great proletarians and great intellectuals without being great businessmen.

On the intellectual side, the Luo were soon attending the university in Nairobi in numbers disproportionate to their size. Tensions in university politics were sometimes created by the fact that the academic leaders seemed to be disproportionately drawn from Nyanza. Recruitment had not been distorted to produce such a result. The Luo tribe in the first few years of Kenya's independence simply produced more academics than any other single community in the country or, indeed, in East Africa as a whole.

On the proletarian side, the Luo of Kenya have been exceptionally mobile as a labor force, crossing boundaries and establishing their presence in important fields of employment outside their homes. Although the Luo, like the Kikuyu, are in some important respects basically a rural people, their role in Kenya's nationalism has been basically that of an urban class. The impact of the Luo on trade-unionism in Kenya and Uganda has been impressive. The mobility of the tribe across national frontiers has helped to give them a cosmopolitan. dimension rooted in relative urbanism. Tom Mboya, a Luo, emerged as a founding father of African trade-unionism in Kenya and a great fighter for fair wages in the towns.

The fact that the socialist party of Kenya, the Kenya People's Union, had its base in Luoland was due to a variety of factors, some of which might have had nothing to do with the cultural predispositions of the Luo as a people. Yet it seems almost certain that these cultural predispositions were not entirely irrelevant in sharpening the confrontation between the Kikuyu and the Luo. The Kikuyu conviction that the Luo were lazy and expected advantages disproportionate to their exertion was based on Kikuyu values in relation to agricultural innovation and entrepreneurial vigor. In these fields the Luo had not proved especially outstanding. Unlike the Kikuyu, they were neither great farmers nor great businessmen.

Yet the Luo have a history of mobility in search of better opportunities and have established their presence in university institutions as well as in trade-unionism. The conclusion to be drawn is that some of their cultural predispositions have oriented them toward these alternative fields of endeavor. The question which arises is whether the proletarian orientation of the Luo contributed toward their ideological radicalization under Oginga Odinga. It is not clear that the attitude of Luo intellectuals to radicalism in Kenya politics is prevalent as an ideological position or that this attitude is culturally determined. It remains to be seen if Luo intellectualist leanings will also turn out to be especially congenial to ideological radicalization in the years ahead.

Luo orientation toward urbanization was connected with their attitude to land. In the words of B. A. Ogot:

> This was concrete, matter of fact, and utilitarian. Such mystic categories as Earth cult, Goddess of fertility, or the mystic connection between the Mother soil and the man working it — so often attributed to the peasantry wherever they may be — were signally absent from their minds and civilisation. . . . The people had thus no great love for the land on which they lived, as long as there was enough of it for their cattle and their crops. A man would readily leave his father's grave and build a new home several miles away, if the land in the latter place was better, and enemies fewer.[17]

Ogot goes on to observe, however, that some important changes in Luo attitudes toward land had taken place. The Luo migration from the north had taken them to areas where rearing cattle was not quite as profitable, and where the agricultural economy had begun to foster some attachment to settlement. The acute shortage of land in western Kenya had accelerated this tendency and had given land a little more mystique in the Luo complex of values than it had had before.

But even after allowing for these changes, there is still a hard core of relative utilitarianism in Luo attitudes toward land and readiness to move elsewhere in pursuit of alternative opportunities. The Luo component in migrant labor across territorial boundaries in East Africa has been disproportionate to the number of Luo in the region. After independence the Kikuyu gained new mobility in the pursuit of commercial opportunities; but, for many years before independence, the Luo had sought to explore new economic areas as mobile proletarians. Trade-unionism, both in Kenya and in Uganda, was spearheaded in part by Luo initiative.

Innovators versus Revolutionaries

Is there a potential clash between political radicals and economic innovators? We have attempted to indicate some relationships between cultural factors and political dispositions to account for the distinctive political systems emerging in East Africa. The question which now arises is how these systems in turn affect economic and political performance in the countries concerned.

A major premise of this analysis is that while Tanzania has in its political revolutionary fervor moved toward centralized political systems, it has also moved *ipso facto* in the direction of reduced potential for economic innovation. Kenya, on the other hand, is likely to develop a high level of economic innovation,

---

17. B. A. Ogot, *A History of the Southern Luo* (Nairobi: East African Publishing House, 1967), Vol. I, *Migration and Settlement*, pp. 38–39.

partly because it has so far fallen short of a political system centralized enough to control the economy.

At this stage we need to follow Ralph Linton and distinguish between *basic inventions* and *improving inventions*. Linton defines a basic invention as one that involves the application of a new principle or a new combination of principles.

> It is basic in the sense that it opens up new potentialities for progress and is destined, in the normal course of events, to become the foundation of a whole series of other inventions. It involved the use of a new principle and became the starting point of a whole series of improving inventions, such as those which culminated in the laminated bow, crossbow, and so on. A more modern example of such a basic invention would be the vacuum tube, whose potentialities for use are only beginning to be understood.[18]

An improving invention is a modification of a pre-existing device, usually made with the intention of increasing its efficiency or rendering it available for some new use.

Linton argues that a basic invention seems to be valuable mainly as the starting point for a series of improving inventions. Many basic inventions appear on the scene without the capacity to be used efficiently or satisfactorily.

> Thus the first automobiles were little better than toys or scientific curiosities. They did not play their present important role in our culture until they had been refined and perfected by literally hundreds of improving inventions.[19]

Basic inventions are the nearest to primary scientific inventions as such and therefore can be made regardless of the centralization of a political system. In other words, they are seldom subject to variations in political culture and control.

But the range of improving inventions feasible in a society is something that is subject to changes and differences in the political and economic cultures of that society. Thus, although the Soviet Union has perhaps as good a potential for basic inventions as the United States, it has a significantly lower capacity for improving inventions. The United States is, for the time being, the most highly developed nation in the world, with a capacity for sophisticated utilization of technology, even in the most simple areas of domestic life. American gadgetry is slowly conquering the rest of the globe, and the idea that life is often made more comfortable by an imaginative use of gadgets and gimmicks is something which is gaining ground. Americans have gone the furthest in domesticating technology and making it help not simply the scientist in his laboratory and

---

18. Ralph Linton, *The Study of Man* (New York: Appleton Century Crofts, 1936), p. 316.

19. *Ibid.*, p. 318.

the factory worker in his plant but also the housewife in her kitchen. The vigorous propensity to improve gadgetry and perfect areas of utility has a direct relationship to domestic competition within the American system. In other words, improving inventions are more subject to localized competitive conditions than are basic inventions. The latter, by their association with primary science and primary technology, can derive their impetus and incentive from international competitive conditions rather than localized ones.

In a capitalistic system the localized pool of incentives is partly an interaction between the competition of the producers and the preferences of the consumers. Again, it is in the nature of such a system that improving inventions and secondary innovativeness are permitted to achieve a high level of vigor.

It is feasible for a centralized system to produce important political and economic innovations. It is arguable that Obote's Document No. 5, concerning four constituencies for each parliamentary candidate, would not have been conceivable as a proposition in 1964 or 1965, when Uganda was a neofederal polity. Obote produced such an innovative document in a situation where at least power, if not the polity, had been centralized. The centralization of power on its own can mean little more than the monopolization of power. It tells us very little about the extent to which the center has succeeded in penetrating the periphery. It tells us very little about the manipulative capability of the center in relation to what goes on in the rest of the society. The centralization of power merely means that when the chips are down it is the center and its preference that prevail. The centralization of the political system, or the polity, requires much more than that. It certainly must include significant capability for political penetration, as well as significant availability of political access.

By 1969 and 1970 Uganda had achieved centralization of power. Yet, in spite of this centralization, it is precisely in this period that some of the most important political innovations took place. Does this not nullify the argument about centralization and its lack of congeniality to inventiveness and innovation? In this case it does not, for the simple reason that Obote was the head of the state and the head of government. He was at the apex of power. Institutions of an original kind can be invented by the top man in a centralized system partly because he is the least subject to the centralization of power. He retains the freedom to innovate and experiment. He retains the freedom to be bold in his imagination. It would have been a more convincing argument against our proposition if a new electoral system had been born out of the imagination of the discontented Baganda, seeking ways of reconciling their lot with the new political situation.

It is not only in relation to the political system that a spirit of innovation is assessed. Here, too, we are thrown back to the complex of cultural norms and predispositions in a given society. It is in this regard that we have to evaluate the cultural traditions of individual African ethnic groups and the extent to which they are congenial to a spirit of innovation. A generalization can be attempted from the outset — namely, that settled, traditional communities have a lower potential for innovation than rapidly modernizing states. The pull of custom in a traditional community can be a form of centralization. Just as a centralized polity in a modern state can too often stifle areas of secondary innovation, so can the blanket of custom suffocate a spirit of secondary, or even primary, inventiveness. As Horace M. Kallen once pointed out, innovators are not necessarily rebels, and the temper of innovation is by no means the temper of revolt. Nevertheless, a situation which demands a good deal of conformity is one which minimizes responsiveness to innovation. There is, in the case of all innovation, an initial inclination toward resistance within the social organization. As Kallen put it:

> Innovators are forced into a combative position. For their novelties enter a social organization most of whose establishments are going concerns and enter as competitors and deprecators of one or another. . . . Since all innovations animate readjustments in the distribution and organization of social forces they automatically evoke the antagonism of those who are disturbed. If the antagonism is pervasive and deep, the innovation per force lapses. If, however, it satisfies a want or nullifies an annoyance, however illusorily, it gathers a following.[20]

This, of course, exaggerates the degree of conformity demanded in individual East African communities. In any case there are important variations within the communities themselves. As we have indicated, the Baganda and the Kikuyu are similar in many respects, being large heartland tribes, central in the territories in which they are situated and cast in significant national roles in the histories of Uganda and Kenya, respectively. Yet the pulls of conformity were greater among the Baganda than among the Kikuyu.

This brings us to another distinction to bear in mind in the case of innovation. Some innovations flourish in situations of large-scale organization, and others in situations of individual autonomy. Innovations concerning man's preparation for interplanetary travel are of the kind which need immense economic resources and large-scale organization of technocratic and scientific expertise. Innovations concerning special types of wrist watches and their capacity to resist this or that disturbing force of nature might well require a different kind of atmosphere, certainly one which puts a premium on the skills of the individual watchmaker.

This is also true of political institutions. Innovations concerning institutions to govern large-scale society take place more easily in situations of large-scale organization. But innovations in terms of coping with the natural elements and pursuing areas of social fellowship and amity, without highly organized institutions of coercion, flourish in different kinds of conditions.

We might again note that during the colonial period the Baganda responded very effectively to the colonial presence and became leaders in important new

---

20. *Encyclopedia of the Social Sciences*, 1937 ed., s.v. "Innovation."

sectors of the economy. But an important element in their success was the relative decentralization of power in Uganda and the autonomy enjoyed by Buganda as a region. The Baganda's capacity to take advantage of the new culture and its skills was greatly facilitated by the relatively privileged status they were granted almost from the outset. The Kikuyu, being decentralized when the British arrived, lacked the kind of institutions of large-scale organization which could impress that side of the British temperament which admired such organization. In addition, the Kikuyu had to face the nearness of a settler community. There could be no question of enjoying the type of autonomy and vigorous independence accorded the Baganda. The Kikuyu were already a threat to the settler community, even in their relative submissiveness. The settler community proceeded to devise ways of containing the apparent cultural vigor of the Kikuyu.

It might well be that, had the Kikuyu been permitted the same latitude of responsiveness to the new skills which came with colonialism, their range of innovativeness and development would have been greater. There are certainly many indications of semisuppressed enthusiasm and vigor. Some of the schools with which they experimented during the colonial period are an indication both of latent responsiveness to the Western impact and of inner innovation. In trade there were also indications of a community wanting to burst out and experiment with economic risk-taking and entrepreneurial adventure. The Kikuyu needed the release of independence to liberate these energies of change.[21]

Elite Initiative versus Mass Spontaneity

We are back to our distinction between structural and systemic transformations, for it is partly the heightened experimentation and innovativeness in Kenya which is releasing structural change without the aid of revolutionary planning. Along with all its disruption and social costs, Kenya's experience remains one of a revolution without revolutionaries at the helm. But are there no prospects of a total revolution in East Africa? Must a revolution be either structural or systemic? Can it not be both?

In fact, there is in East Africa an example of a revolution that has been both structural and systemic, however imperfect the model — namely, the revolution in Zanzibar. This introduces us to yet another important distinction concerning instigated revolutions. Revolutions can be instigated either from above or from below. When a revolutionary outburst is instigated from below, what we have is a highly militant assertion at the grass-roots level. In such cases the line separating spontaneity from instigation can be very thin indeed.

---

21. See Margaret Katzin, "The Role of the Small Entrepreneur," in *Economic Transition in Africa*, ed. Melville J. Herskovits and Mitchell Harwitz (London: Routledge & Kegan Paul, 1964), pp. 184–85.

East Africa's experience would seem to suggest that revolutions instigated from above are safer and more manageable than revolutions instigated from below. This may sound somewhat snobbish, but the evidence is compelling in the East African context. Grass-roots revolutions can be devastating, but revolutions led by an elite stand a better chance of realizing their objectives.

The two parts of Tanzania offer a perfect illustration of this proposition. Zanzibar experienced a grass-roots revolution, both structural and systemic, instigated from below. The result has not been a transformation of the political system as such but a devastation of the polity, a dislocation of the economy of the country, a general sense of insecurity in the population, a lack of sense of direction in national policies, and a rapid erosion of human values. The revolution on mainland Tanzania, on the other hand, is calmly led by an intellectual, Julius "Mwalimu" Nyerere. There is a purposefulness in it all, a sense of direction, a sense of balance, a sense of popular support, and an elegant sensibility to human considerations. The lesson which East Africans seem invited to draw from this experience is that if they must have revolutions, let the ultimate instigation and guidance come from the top rather than from the grass roots. Revolutions may be best carried out for the sake of the masses, but they are not necessarily best initiated by the masses.

Obote's Uganda was much more like mainland Tanzania than like Zanzibar. The Obote "revolution" might have been *for* the common man, but in the initial stages it was not *by* the common man. There can be no doubt that the Obote "revolution" was being instigated from the top. There was, to begin with, no revolutionary fervor in Uganda at the grass-roots level. The revolutionaries were drawn from the ranks of the elite. And why not? The paradox of successful revolution is that it is most creative when it is fundamentally elitist. That is what happened in Russia when it was decided that the proletariat as a whole could not be entrusted with the revolution; responsibility had to pass to a *vanguard* of the proletariat. V. I. Lenin, like Julius Nyerere and Milton Obote, was a member of the intelligentsia, not a common man drawn from the ranks. There developed among Russians a rapid awareness that the masses alone do not constitute the best revolutionaries. Lenin once quoted with approval Karl Kautsky's assertion that it is "absolutely untrue" to regard socialist consciousness as a direct result of the proletarian class struggle. Kautsky said:

> Modern socialist consciousness can arise only on the basis of profound scientific knowledge. . . . The vehicle of science is not the proletariat but the *bourgeois intelligentsia:* it was in the minds of individual members of this stratum that modern socialism originated; it was they who communicated it to the more intellectually developed proletarians who, in their turn, introduced it into the proletarian class struggle where conditions allowed that to be done.[22]

---

22. Quoted in Lenin, *Selected Works* (Moscow: Foreign Languages Press, 1960), Vol. I, *What Is to Be Done?* p. 156 (Kautsky's emphasis). See also Hannah Arendt, *On Revolution* (New York: Viking, 1963).

Lenin credited the working classes with a capacity for spontaneity but not with an automatic capacity for socialist consciousness. The birth of socialism was, according to Lenin, inseparable from the history of intellectualism.

> The theory of socialism . . . grew out of the philosophic, historical, and economic theories elaborated by educated representatives of the property classes, by intellectuals. By their social status, the founders of modern scientific socialism, Marx and Engels, themselves belonged to the bourgeois intelligentsia.[23]

This theory does not seek to keep the masses out of revolutionary creativity. All that is being asserted is that the masses must be responsive to guidance, leadership, and discipline from the top. In the Russian context the formula was that in order to get *action* the nation needed *unity*, in order to get unity the nation needed *discipline*, and in order to get discipline the nation needed *obedience*.

It was out of such assumptions that the doctrine of "democratic centralism" came into being in Russia after the Communist Revolution. The term implied what has been called "a combination between the principle of mass participation at the bottom and the concentration of leadership at the top."

None of the East African cases has yet approached the Soviet example, either in structural or in systemic transformation. Nor is even Nyerere's ideology as yet at the level of comprehensiveness and cohesion which has characterized Soviet communism. But East Africa has so far produced one country which is undergoing rapid structural change (Kenya); one country which briefly attempted systemic change but had yet to accomplish structural transformation (Uganda); one country which has carried out systemic change and has initiated important structural innovations, including *ujamaa* villages (mainland Tanzania); and, finally, an island which has undergone the agonies of both systemic and structural transformation, with a devastation that can be partly explained by the fact that this revolution was a revolution from below (Zanzibar).

In conclusion, we should bear in mind that a revolution brings to an end an old order and, at the same time, seeks to initiate a new order. Until the new order has been clarified and consolidated, the revolution is incomplete. This is particularly true of systemic revolutions, where we seek to know what new sociopolitical system has replaced the old. It is even more true when the systemic revolution is clearly instigated by a set of idealized objectives. We then seek to know whether those objectives have been fulfilled.

The three systemic revolutions in East Africa have been the one in Zanzibar, the one in mainland Tanzania, and the Obote attempt in Uganda. The case of Zanzibar is one of brutal termination of an old order. The style of life,

---

23. Lenin, *What Is to Be Done?* p. 149. For a useful analysis of the social origins of revolutionaries, see also Crane Brinton, *Anatomy of Revolution* (Englewood Cliffs, N.J.: Prentice-Hall, 1938).

the arbitrariness, and the sense of drift in Zanzibar are all indications of an inconclusive revolution. In the case of mainland Tanzania something approaching a new order is coming into being under Nyerere's leadership. In the case of Uganda we know that 1966 marked the end of neofederalism and monarchism. That might well be Obote's most enduring legacy to Uganda. Although an old order was ended, the country has yet to create a stable alternative order.

[13]

Political Culture and Economic Socialization

We have defined political culture as the values and mores that determine political behavior. Ideology is, of course, a central part of political culture; but here we ought to make a distinction. Explicit ideology is that which is enunciated and worked out, sometimes in elaborate formulas, to be a guide to action in a given society. Implicit, or immanent, ideology is that which may not have been adequately enunciated or given a formal framework of interconnection between its parts, but which nevertheless is the basis on which certain political choices are made and certain political responses or reactions are evoked. Political culture inevitably colors men's conceptions of their self-interests and of their ultimate ambitions. It also helps to shape the kinds of institutions which societies evolve.[1]

Economic socialization, on the other hand, signifies a process by which young people, and sometimes older people, are enabled to acquire the kinds of assumptions and values which then determine the nature of their behavior as economic beings. Such persons are gradually immersed in a universe of preconceptions and transmitted mores, and these influence the kinds of economic choices they might make in given situations in the course of their lives. Impulses to acquire or not to acquire, to consume or to conserve, have economic dimensions which are in part fostered by a process of economic socialization. It will be seen that this process presupposes a kind of economic culture comparable as a category to the phenomenon of political culture. Economic culture is the total complex of norms, desires, aversions, aspirations, and inhibitions which condition the society's economic behavior.

In each of the East African countries there are pre-existent economic traditions at play which have a great bearing on the nature of economic development and the pace of response to political exertions. In the preceding chapter we looked at some of them in relation to concepts of revolution. Let us now observe the broader background of the economic man in East Africa.

---

1. One kind of political culture is civic culture. See especially Gabriel Almond and Sidney Verba, *The Civic Culture* (Princeton: Princeton University Press, 1963). See also Lucian W. Pye and Sidney Verba, eds., *Political Culture and Political Development* (Princeton: Princeton University Press, 1965).

The Nonautonomy of Economics

Within the different economic traditions in East Africa, the economic role of the individual is almost always interrelated with the other roles that the individual has to play. This is a factor which, in different forms, has been observed by at least two generations of social scientists in East Africa. It has been pointed out that in societies regulated by reciprocity and status rather than by formal contract, the elements of the economy are embedded in noneconomic institutions, the economic process itself being instituted through kinship, marriage, age-groups, secret societies, totemic associations, and public solemnities. In such societies the term *economic life* would therefore have no obvious meaning.[2] Land or cattle or goods would pass at betrothal or marriage, marking a change of status. Gifts of food would move from one person to another according to the rules of the social context. There is no exact quantification, for "reciprocity demands adequacy of response, not mathematical quality."[3] R. Firth has made a similar observation in a different context:

> In a primitive society, there is no relationship which is of a purely economic character. . . . . Therein lies the strength of primitive society, in that it enlists the binding forces of one aspect of society to support those of another.[4]

Partly because of this difficulty in separating economic motivation from other aspects which condition human behavior, there were instances in East Africa when the behavior of Africans was regarded as being devoid of "economic sense." Cyril Ehrlich cites an early case in which a cattle-owner in Uganda refused 600 shillings for a beast but was prepared to exchange it quite happily for a bicycle worth 300 shillings, and another case in which Baganda peasants sold trees worth 100 shillings for 10 shillings. Lucy Mair has cited similar cases in Uganda, and Elizabeth Hoyt in Kenya. The idea of accepting a bicycle worth 300 shillings rather than 600 shillings in cash in exchange for a beast finds some kind of explanation in the following hypothesis of Lucy Mair's:

> When one compares the reason why cattle are desired with the reason why barkcloths are desired, it becomes clear that different commodities are valued from points of view so different that the values cannot be reduced to a single common denominator. . . . The possession of most goods is prized for its own sake, rather than for the sake of other goods which might be acquired by disposing of them.[5]

2. See Karl Polanyi, Conrad M. Arensberz, and Harry W. Pearson, eds., *Trade and Market in the Early Empire* (Glencoe, Ill.: Free Press, 1957).
3. Guy Hunter, *The New Societies of Tropical Africa* (London: Oxford University Press, 1962), pp. 80–81.
4. Quoted in *ibid*.
5. Lucy P. Mair, *An African People in the Twentieth Century* (London: Routledge,

If, then, things are valued by different criteria, it makes sense for a person who is exchanging a beast to accept a bicycle (which he specifically wants) and to reject 600 shillings in cash (to which he cannot assign an immediate function). Yet, if it does make sense to behave in this way, the sense involved is evidently not distinctively "economic."

This relative inseparability of economic motivation from other factors is relevant to an understanding of the interplay between ideology and the realities of economic behavior in East Africa. The behavior of ministers who accumulate wealth, the failure of an African businessman who goes bankrupt in a couple of years, the risks involved in preventing political leaders from participating in entrepreneurial activity in accordance with Tanzania's Arusha Declaration, the hazards in Kenya of trying to create an African entrepreneurial class and to disseminate the idea of shareholding in private enterprise — all of these are issues which are profoundly affected by the nonisolatability of economic motivation in the socioeconomic culture of East African peoples.

Prestige Motive versus Profit Motive

The foremost area of conflict between ideology and economic reality in East Africa is the attempt to forge an operational profit motive on the one hand and the attempt to tame or transform a pre-existent prestige motive on the other. Although groups like the Kikuyu in Kenya and the Baganda in Uganda have sometimes displayed striking entrepreneurial skills, their business performance is impressive only when compared with that of other tribes. There is room for further entrepreneurial stimulation. The prestige motive in East Africa arises in part out of the collectivistic sensitivities of individuals in traditional societies. The approval of the tribe, clan, or extended family is a powerful influence on behavior. The desire for prestige within the traditional unit is therefore often a stronger impulse than any individualistic profit motive of the Western type. The disapproval of the traditional unit of identity serves as a powerful deterrent for the individual.

This prestige motive in traditional society raises serious economic problems — among them, as has often been pointed out, the problem of getting people to save. Earnings are expended on entertainment and hospitality; on ostentatious weddings, expensive funerals, and initiation ceremonies. In addition, there is the all too familiar desire to fulfill obligations toward distant cousins and aunts. Many a struggling African businessman has at best a blunted profit motive — torn as he is between the desire to make money for himself and the desire to let his kith and kin benefit from what his enterprise yields.

1934). See also Elizabeth Hoyt, "Economic Sense and the African," *Africa*, XXII (1952). I am indebted to Hunter, *New Societies of Tropical Africa*, for bibliographical guidance as well as for some insights concerning these issues.

It can be seen at once that of the two types of motives the profit motive is clearly more isolable as an economic impulse than the prestige motive. The latter does have economic implications and often very important economic consequences, but it is clearly a more complex type of motivation than the profit motive. The prestige motive is socially more ethical than the profit motive. The profit motive can be too self-centered, sometimes too selfish. But the prestige motive seriously attaches value and importance to the opinions of one's peers.[6]

The term *prestige motive* is not intended to denote merely a quest for personal glamour. When an African has to support a wide range of kin or has to welcome reluctantly a group of unexpected guests, it is not glamour he is after. Sometimes his behavior is simply due to a fear of social disapproval. The canons of hospitality and of kinship obligations are maintained partly out of conviction and partly out of a wish to be respected, but ultimately out of a desire to maintain the sense of belonging to the social group and to avert the burden of its disapproval. Precisely because the prestige motive encompasses this web of complex impulses, it is a motive which defies any attempt to compartmentalize its elements and single out the source of economic animation.

One of the main components of economic policy in Kenya and Uganda has been the commitment to create an African commercial class. Much of the entrepreneurial activity of these countries has been in the hands of nonindigenous peoples. The shopkeepers, the chief clerks, the shareholders in businesses, and the major owners and managers of industries were quite often people of non-African extraction. In these sectors of commercial activity the Asians were particularly conspicuous, partly because they penetrated remote areas in search of business and opportunity. Some of the recent governmental schemes in Kenya and Uganda have been designed to capture some of these opportunities for Africans and to replace the preponderance of Asians in certain sectors as an entrepreneurial elite.

Loans have been given to potential African businessmen to encourage them to establish a viable foothold in private enterprise. Sometimes licensing procedures have been manipulated to ensure an African entry into areas previously dominated by others. Ministers of government and sometimes even the heads of state have reaffirmed a need for a more rapid Africanization of economic activity in Kenya and Uganda and have demanded more cooperation and sacrifice from the nonindigenous economic elite to enable the admission of Africans to their ranks.

The major stumbling block in the way of an adequate realization of governmental ambitions has been the prevalence of the prestige motive behind African behavior in the economy and the continued integration of the economic factor with the complex of African motivations. What is needed is a capacity to accept the proposition that business is business. In that tautology lies a universe of

---

6. See Ali A. Mazrui, "Is African Development Plannable?" in *On Heroes and Uhuru-Worship* (London: Longmans, 1967), pp. 137–38.

economic socialization and acceptance of certain postulates. That tautology seeks to assert the autonomy of the economic factor, to isolate the commitment to the success of business from other considerations that may distort its perspective. But many aspiring African businessmen have yet to be socialized into a complete acceptance of the tautology that business is business. They may sell something to a customer who is a kin of theirs at a loss to themselves; or they may succumb to family pressures for special concessions in business relations, often reducing the whole economic exercise into a noneconomic venture. The prestige motive is at work in the form of hypersensitivity to kinship obligations and special loyalties. Sometimes ministers in Uganda have complained that African businessmen leave their shops at the slightest social pretext. At important hours of business they leave to attend a funeral or an initiation ceremony and close up the business. Far too often, customers relying on African shopkeepers have had to divert their trade to the more persistently businesslike Asians.

It is true that the African businessman is sometimes reluctant to attend an initiation ceremony or funeral during business hours. What causes him, in the end, to attend is not so much his unwillingness to invoke the excuse of "the pressure of business" as the inability, or the presumed inability, of the rest of his kin to accept such an excuse as a legitimate one. Arguments that one could not attend an important family ceremony because it was held at a crucial business hour are interpreted to mean that the defaulter is prepared to sacrifice loyalty to his people for the sake of an extra penny earned at his shop. Such a charge is usually a very serious one for most members of African social groups.

The Quest for Social Deviance

This discussion brings us back to the phenomenon of marginality as a psychological factor with regard to potential entrepreneurial behavior. And the concept of marginality is linked in East Africa to a related concept which at times is almost interchangeable with marginality, but only in specific areas of experience. The related concept is that of *deviance* from social or cultural norms or from the prevalent ethnic identity of the area. Attention has been drawn repeatedly to the important role of marginal individuals in the economic activities of many of the underdeveloped countries of the world — the Chinese in various South Asian countries; the Lebanese in West Africa, Latin America, and elsewhere; and the Indians in East Africa. We can also mention the Jews in different European countries and later in the United States — a group whose relative cultural deviance resulted in major achievements in a few selected areas of endeavor. Robert E. Park, who originated the concept of social marginality and recognized its significance, has argued that marginal individuals, because of their very ambiguous position in society, have been impelled to make creative adjustments and attain special heights of social accomplishment as a route to fuller absorption. Genuine innovations in social behavior have thus been born out of the deviance of specific individuals and the marginality of specific groups.[7] There has therefore been an attempt in East Africa to evoke deviance from some members of indigenous groups. The Asians have been marginal because they have been more conspicuously distinct as a minority ethnic group, and they have therefore developed special protective features of nonconformity. Each African tribe is also, of course, ethnically somewhat different from all others. But the level of cultural variance among tribes has been obscured precisely by the presence of large and influential economic groups who are conspicuously more different — the Asians and the Europeans of East Africa's economies. How do you create social deviance among indigenous groups? How do you get them to rebel against the constraints of the prestige motive and the fear of social disapproval? How do you get them to defiantly affirm the tautological proposition that business is business? A world of economic socialization is required to achieve and induce this form of deviance.

Spreading the Entrepreneurial Gospel

In Uganda and even more militantly in Kenya the solution invoked has simply been a major propaganda campaign to interest Africans in the idea of holding shares in business industries. The Ministry of Commerce in Kenya has even undertaken at times the actual work of distributing shares in the private sector and attempting to get greater involvement of ordinary people in the business of calculating profit and loss in the commercial sector of life. Kenya's new immigration regulations and its greater commitment to the utilization of local people in secretarial and clerical positions is one part of this militant attempt to help the growth of an African managerial and bureaucratic class.

It has sometimes been argued that Kenya has chosen to leave the ranks of socialists and is instead engaged in the process of Africanizing capitalism at home. For our purposes there is perhaps no special need to quarrel about labels and to argue that what is happening in Kenya is or is not socialism. What has to be noted is that within the political culture of most African countries it is not always the egalitarian commitment that is deemed paramount. There is also the commitment to development. In other words, socialism in African countries is torn between its role as an ethic of distribution and its role as an ideology of development. If rapid development is the paramount goal, distributive equality might sometimes have to be sacrificed. If equality is the paramount goal, there is the danger of a significantly slow growth in the economic evolution of the nation.

---

7. See Bert F. Hoselitz, "Non-economic Factors in Economic Development," *American Economic Review*, XLVII, no. 2 (May, 1957), 38–41.

Where commitment is primarily to development, the need is sometimes felt for an African entrepreneurial and managerial class capable of efficiently undertaking tasks which in the past have been done more prevalently by non-Africans. To create this segment of African managers and African risk-takers, it becomes important to try to conquer the inhibitions of some traditional modes of motivation. One way of conquering them is a persistent exercise in economic proselytism. Kenya's attempt to distribute widely shares in private enterprise for purchase by ordinary Africans is precisely such a case of economic proselytism. The idea is to win converts in limited numbers and to promote among them a greater readiness to take risks of this kind. The converts would, after a period, presumably disseminate their new commitments to their descendants. Within a few African families the process of new forms of economic socialization would thus be started. The successful African businessman would literally produce his own successors as the new complex of values is transmitted to at least one member of his progeny.

Even more important as a method of widening the area of proselytism is the simple phenomenon of a demonstration effect. Increasing numbers of fairly successful and affluent Africans in commerce may help to demonstrate that economic risks are capable of yielding positive dividends. For the convert to the new economic creed in East Africa, paradise need not be in the hereafter; it may be realized concretely here and now, not long after conversion to the creed.

It may be that Kenya and Uganda are a little naïve in some of the methods they have used in this exercise of economic proselytism. But the deficiencies in managerial and entrepreneurial skills among local people are readily apparent. There is no doubt that some measures are needed to create greater self-reliance in this area of life. Kenya and Uganda have attempted to promote some degree of cultural deviance and thereby create effective successors to the Asian and European marginal men.

Of course, deviance would gradually become institutionalized. In the words of Hoselitz:

> Once a form of deviant behavior can find the shelter of an institution, it becomes routinized, it ceases to be deviant, and it tends to become an accepted mode of social action. But the institution in which it is "laid down" forms an advance post, so to speak, from which further deviance is possible. Thus the institutions which arose in Western Europe before the Industrial Revolution and in Japan before the Meiji restoration were already the end product of the process of social change; but they, in turn, made possible, by their very existence, further social and economic change.[8]

Self-reliance is an important component of the kind of ethos which produces

---

8. *Ibid.*, pp. 38–39.

effective entrepreneurs. The spirit of self-reliance very often needs to be inculcated or inadvertently promoted in a child at a very early age. This is a case of socialization in its most literal and natural form. But there are occasions when a society cannot create certain values in children without achieving some kind of transformation in the values of the parents. Socialization into the norms and prejudices of Christianity or Islam in ultimate generations of Christians or Muslims inevitably presupposes a moment of conversion in an earlier generation of grown-ups. A first step toward the creation of an "achievement-oriented ideology" must be either a conscious reform movement or an accidental adjustment in the values of the next generation, coming as an unintended effect of present-day socioeconomic tendencies. Both a conscious reform movement and an accidental transformation of values in children are perhaps well under way in important sectors of East African life and may interact and reinforce each other in the normal course of events.

Absent Fathers and Socialization

We might look first at the accidental transformation that is likely to result from what is happening outside the realm of policy. David C. McClelland has argued that the ethos of individual self-reliance in children can sometimes be accelerated in its growth by a historical development which keeps authoritarian fathers away from home at crucial periods of socialization. The kind of spirit which leads to effective entrepreneurial talent was what McClelland called "n-Achievement." His assumption was that children can develop a high n-Achievement in situations where fathers are not too domineering and not likely to interfere too much with the children's independence.

> One incidental consequence of prolonged wars may be an increase in n-Achievement, because the fathers are away too much to interfere with their sons' development of it. And in Turkey, [N.M.] Bradburn found that those boys tended to have higher n-Achievement who had left home early or whose fathers had died before they were eighteen.[9]

The phenomenon of a father's long absence from home while at war in distant lands is rare in modern Africa. There have been civil wars, pre-eminently in Congo and Nigeria, and these have sometimes involved extended absences from home for large numbers of fighters. But, in general, African countries have not entered into military commitments resulting in prolonged separations of members of families.

---

9. David C. McClelland, "The Achievement Motive in Economic Growth," in *Industrialization and Society*, ed. Bert F. Hoselitz and Wilbur E. Moore (The Hague: UNESCO and Mouton, 1963), p. 92. McClelland was citing N. M. Bradburn, "The Managerial Role in Turkey" (Ph.D. diss., Harvard University, 1960).

While there have been few cases of Africans leaving home on military expeditions, there have been many cases of husbands and fathers moving some distance from home in search of work and a livelihood. The phenomenon of labor migrating between the mines and the villages and the partial or seasonal depopulation of the countryside as young men seek work in towns and at industrial centers have created punctuated family life in Africa. The migrant laborer is at times in a predicament reminiscent of that of the sailor in the coastal towns of Europe in the days when some went out to sea on long, hazardous journeys. The wives and families waved them farewell as they set sail on their long voyages; they returned later, only to set sail again. These were the ancient maritime punctuations of family life for the many who were engaged in recurrent traveling in quest of work and livelihood on the high seas. The African equivalent is the movement of young people, husbands, and fathers in search of work in strange cities and hazardous mines.

If this phenomenon of the absence of fathers sometimes contributes to greater self-reliance in their children at a formative stage of socialization, migrant labor is part of the process by which Africa might in time create a class of self-reliant entrepreneurs. Since migration of workers has been going on for a while, it might be said that if an entrepreneurial class were to result from this migration, greater evidence of this development would be apparent. But this argument overlooks an important constraint. While the absence of fathers might contribute toward the growth of self-reliance in young people, much of village life is still so collective that not enough of this self-reliance is permitted to emerge. What is gained by the absence of fathers is lost by the intervention of other members of the extended family in controlling the young. Nevertheless, there is in the phenomenon of migration, when it eventually is coupled with the increasing atomization of family life in the villages, the potential for greater individualization and for more distinctively self-reliant forms of economic motivation.

McClelland has asserted that "the campaign to spread achievement-oriented ideology, if possible, could also incorporate an attack on the extreme authoritarianism in fathers that impedes or prevents the development of self-reliance in their sons." Migration of labor might itself contribute toward the dissolution of any lingering parental authoritarian control. Another way that McClelland suggests to dilute the father's impact is to promote the rights of women, both legally and socially. He asserts that one of the ways to undermine the dominance of the male is to strengthen the rights of the female. One of the ways of transmitting self-reliant norms to children is to release elements of self-reliance in mothers by accelerating their social emancipation.[10]

Much of McClelland's discussion on the importance of feminism assumes an oriental kind of subordination of the female to the male. This form of subordina-

---

10. McClelland, "Achievement Motive in Economic Growth," p. 93.

tion tends to suggest the exclusion of women from processes of economic activity and their assignment to more concentrated forms of domesticity. In other words, a woman in traditional society in the Orient and in the Islamic world outside Africa tends to be very much a domestic animal or a closely guarded and protected domestic possession. Liberation of the woman in these terms implies her greater involvement in processes of life outside the home and sometimes an actual involvement in the economy with a full-scale career.

This segregation and specialization in domestic work is by no means unknown in some African societies. But there are other African societies in which female subordination does *not* imply female withdrawal from the economic process. On the contrary, in such societies there is often a direct female involvement in the utilization of land and the augmentation of the productive forces. There are times when female work in a traditional economic system is, in fact, more important than the labor contributed by the male. In these cases what implies subordination is not withdrawal from the productive process but answerability and accountability to male direction.

The female involvement in work on the farm would have the potential of self-reliance if excessive accountability to male control were to be drastically reduced. Here, again, the phenomenon of labor migration might be gradually contributing toward greater emancipation of women in the villages and the promotion of their greater self-reliance. Women among the Kikuyu, for example, continue to work very hard on the farms. Self-reliance in the sense of self-exertion is certainly present. But with the increasing incidence of prolonged absences by the male members of the family, female self-reliance might achieve greater meaning through a reduction in masculine control.

The impact of women as agents of economic socialization would then be enhanced. What they transmit to their children when many male members of the extended family are away could contain greater potential for entrepreneurial independence than was possible when mothers were still essentially subservient and dependent. The dissolution of male authoritarianism over children growing up and the augmentation of female independence while men are away at work might combine to produce a climate hospitable to new forms of economic socialization in East Africa. Although many of these assumptions are oversimplified, what is being discussed here is the direction of certain tendencies as constraints on the entrepreneurial spirit are weakened. The full emergence of that spirit may take time. Indeed, weakening constraints on it, though a necessary condition for its emergence, is by no means the only condition. The women might be liberated, and the sons might be less dominated by their uncles and their fathers; and yet the specific ethos of self-reliance might remain unrealized because other components have yet to be added to complete the cluster of favorable preconditions.[11]

---

11. For some related issues, see J. W. Atkinson, "Motivational Determinants of Risk-taking Behavior," *Psychological Review*, LXIV (1957), 359–72; David C. McClel-

What might be added to these favorable preconditions? This is where the issue of deliberate policy, or conscious reform, becomes relevant. Conversion to new modes of economic behavior might require more than structural changes in communal life or long punctuations in family life. Once these accidental predispositions have been achieved, further progress might still require conscious exhortation and proselytism. There are occasions when the proselytism is not intended to transform economic behavior as such. It may indeed constitute a new religion and create new demands on social behavior, but its *economic* components might be less direct.

Calvinism and the Arusha Declaration

Max Weber's thesis on the Protestant Reformation affords pertinent insights into the nature of economic socialization. Weber argued that the transformation of values which the Reformation brought about had direct implications for the economic culture of the Western world. A moral justification of worldly activity emerged from the Reformation and gave to Lutheranism and, even more dramatically, to Calvinism a commitment to modes of economic behavior, the cumulative consequence of which was the rise of capitalism.[12]

This was a case of proselytism of a noneconomic, spiritual order affecting the economy and leading to a transformation of economic habits of thought and economic values. It is true that Weber sometimes came dangerously near to a theory of religious determinism in his thesis. But one does not have to accept his postulates in entirety in order to accept the relevance of religion for the transformation of economic culture.

Although there is a Calvinistic component in Tanzania's Arusha Declaration, there are important differences between the declaration and the doctrine of Calvinism. Historical Calvinism was antiostentation without being antiacquisition. But Tanzania's socialism seems to take it for granted that to be antiostentation one must also be antiacquisition, for the acquisitive instinct is what gives rise to social exhibitionism. This equation in Tanzania's socialism may well result in delaying the emergence of an effective entrepreneurial class.

Max Weber distinguished between capitalists and bureaucrats, yet many of the characteristics he attributed to bureaucrats were precisely those of an entrepreneurial kind. Since then, studies of the motivation of the bureaucratic and managerial class seem to indicate that the primary impulse is not the acquisition of money because of what it can buy.

---

land, *The Achieving Society* (Princeton, N.J.: Van Nostrand, 1961); N. M. Bradburn and D. E. Berliew, "Need for Achievement and English Economic Growth," *Economic Development and Cultural Change*, X, no. 1 (1961), 8–20; E. C. Rosen, "Race Ethnicity and Achievement Syndrome," *American Sociological Review*, XXIV (1959), 47–60.

12. See Max Weber, *The Protestant Ethic and the Spirit of Capitalism*, trans. Talcott Parsons (New York: Scribner's, 1958).

Had these entrepreneurs been above all interested in money, many more of them would have quit working as soon as they had made all the money they could possibly use. . . . These men were really motivated by a desire for achievement rather than by a desire for money as such. . . . [They] were interested in money without wanting it for its own sake, namely, [because] money served as a ready quantitative index of how well they were doing — e.g., of how much they had achieved by their efforts over the past year. The need to achieve can never be satisfied by money; but estimates of profitability in money terms can supply direct knowledge of how well one is doing one's job.[13]

Tanzania has experimented with an ethos which definitely has Calvinistic components. The demand for dedicated exertion, the suspicion of certain forms of consumption, the eulogization of the virtues of frugality and self-denial — all of these seem to be qualities which Tanzania's socialism has shared with that Calvinistic spirit which, in Weberian terms, contributed to the emergence of capitalism. But whereas Calvinism in its historical role was opposed to indulgent consumption but not to determined acquisition, Tanzania's socialism has manifested a disapproval of both. There has been a tendency to feel that the spirit of accumulation must inevitably lead to a spirit of luxurious indulgence.

The dangers of Tanzania's policies have included the possibility of slowing down the emergence of genuine entrepreneurship because of the lack of an adequate incentive to acquire. Entrepreneurs are not necessarily economic animals, committed to ostentatious living and antisocial exuberance. On the contrary, they may often be more interested in profit as an index of achievement than as a gateway to opulence. They may be both anticonsumption and antiacquisition on this scale. Tanzania's socialism may be retarding the emergence of a fully spirited managerial class.

It may be argued that this would not be regrettable, since Tanzania is committed to the prevention of class-formation in its society insofar as this is possible. But there is a risk which ought to be borne in mind. Karl Marx did not adequately differentiate between the motivation of those who own and the motivation of those who manage. Much of Marx's analysis presupposed that those who owned were the same as those who managed. The exploitation undertaken was a conscious exploitation of worker by capitalist in the face-to-face society of the factory. But the evolution of society in industrialized countries has tended to emphasize more than ever the complex relationship between skills of management and motivation of ownership. Shareholders very often have become distant from the day-to-day workings of a particular industry, exerting only the remotest control on the workers or the methods and policies of a given firm. The idea of "the managerial revolution" emphasizes the distinction between a class of

---

13. McClelland, "Achievement Motive in Economic Growth," p. 85. See also Jason L. Finkle and Richard W. Cable, eds., *Political Development and Social Change* (New York: Wiley, 1966), pp. 147–48.

managers on the one hand and a class of shareholders on the other. In nineteenth-century Europe, where the owners and the managers were the same, the level of exploitation was often direct and had a greedy immediacy. As European countries and the United States attained a complexity in economic relationships, it became possible to buy impersonal shares. The manager of a given firm became able to manifest a relatively rational spirit of organization and detachment in the process of committing himself to increasing the profit margin. Although the profits made were often not for his own pocket, they constituted an index of his achievement in the management of the industry. When managers regard the profit motive merely as an index of achievement, such a motive may often attain autonomy from mere considerations of greed. It may thereby help to tone down the excesses of exploitation which Tanzania regards as inherent in capitalism.

Yet, in January, 1967, the National Executive Committee of the Tanganyika African National Union (TANU), meeting at Arusha, enunciated resolutions for every officeholder in the governing party and every officeholder in the government. This significantly large class of potentially enterprising people, in a country short of individuals with this degree of sophistication, was declared to be divorced from any entrepreneurial activity in the private sector. No TANU or government leader was to hold shares in any company, nor were they to hold directorships in any privately owned enterprise. Investment in real estate was also taboo, for no TANU or government leader was to own houses which he rented to others. These were the resolutions which sought to insulate the potentially most enterprising group of Tanzanians from a potentially crucial economic activity.

It was possible that this exercise in insulation would, in fact, result in integrating ownership and management more closely than ever in Tanzania. The party and government leaders were potential shareholders who might conceivably have promoted by their examples greater participation in shareholding in the country. And certainly their exclusion from holding shares would tend to throw back some of those shares to businessmen with a more immediate involvement in the management of their firms. What was implicitly demanded by the Leadership Resolutions of the Arusha Declaration was functional specialization in the different sectors of Tanzanian leadership. In a sense, it was almost like saying that leaders in the political life of the nation ought to have no significant leadership role in the economic life of the nation. It amounted to insisting that professional businessmen should retain ownership as well as management and direction. The continuing merger of these roles might well aggravate more than ever the exploitative potential which Karl Marx discerned in the relationship between the worker on the one side and the managing owner on the other.

In other ways, too, the political culture that Tanzania is seeking to create and foster seems to inhibit certain aspects of economic resocialization which might otherwise help to accelerate the rate of economic growth. Tanzania is determined to create a particular kind of national self-reliance. What is not certain is whether the creation of collective self-reliance might not militate against the emergence of deviant individual self-reliance. It is the old problem of collectivism in relation to individual exertion. Is an egalitarian society which seeks to deny certain forms of reward for certain forms of achievement really antiparasitic? Or is it, on the contrary, a fertile breeding ground for those who would hide their indolence behind collective exertion and feed on what has been communally produced by others? After all, kinship obligations and the demands of intratribal solidarity and hospitality have been effective breeding grounds for parasitism. Yet these kinship bonds have been described by Nyerere as the ancestral origins of African socialism. The parasitic tendencies of newly urbanized Africans to live on the earnings of their relatives might rear their ugly heads when newly "mobilized" individuals are permitted to enjoy the full benefits of the fruit of collective effort.[14]

Further complicating the Tanzanian case are some elements in the political culture of indigenous groups. Especially in mainland Tanzania, the spirit of self-reliance has been up against one of the most attractive qualities of the peoples there — the gentleness which they have long manifested in the course of their political evolution. The phenomenon of Nyerere's control on the country has a good deal to do with this quiescent component in Tanzania's political culture. No other African leader can claim similar success in exerting such broad control over his country with relatively such little force. But we must remember that the effect of a leader is to be attributed not simply to his qualities but also to the characteristics of those who follow. Among the characteristics of some peoples of Tanzania must be included the readiness to accept intelligent leadership.

Is this quality likely to be a fertile ground for the emergence of self-reliance? Or is a spirit of individual self-reliance likely to be diluted by the sheer quiescent gentleness within the political habits of the peoples of Tanzania? At the moment these are fair questions to ask. Yet political culture, like other aspects of the cultural make-up of a society, can change. A new note of militancy might enter the political behavior of the peoples of Tanzania before long; but, at present, this is uncertain. What is certain is that gentleness is still part of political behavior in Tanzania. The policy of collective self-reliance gains ready acceptance mainly because it is promulgated by the leaders. It is the paradox

---

14. Garry Thomas has argued that collectivism as a mode of rural organization in Tanzania, as envisaged by Nyerere in 1967, might retard rural development without achieving any striking alternative ideal. "As for the industrious farmers on settlement schemes who rise above apparent restraints and earn many times the income of people enjoying the same opportunities, it is likely that those who drew up the Arusha Declaration would be more alarmed with the farmers who were content with a minimum income than with the entrepreneurial-type farmers. . . . If indeed the goal is economic classlessness, the quarrel then is more with the cash economy than with the farmer entrepreneurs involved" (Thomas, "Let Economic Strata Stay: Agricultural Capitalism and Rural Development in Tanzania," *East Africa Journal*, IV, no. 7 [November, 1967], 31).

of being self-reliant in response to directives. That quality of deviance which is so necessary for entrepreneurial innovation may find it harder than ever to find life and effectiveness in Tanzania.

Economic Man in Uganda and Kenya

Uganda and Kenya have taken several paths toward the economic resocialization of their peoples. On July 4, 1966, Uganda's National Assembly approved the National Trading Corporation Bill, setting up a new body to accelerate African participation in trade and commerce. This was the culmination of a number of different experiments and appeals by the Uganda government to achieve greater indigenous involvement in these sectors of the economy. A month before the bill was passed, the minister of commerce and industry told a meeting of the National Economic and Social Advisory Council that a situation had to be created in which Africans could be helped to become commercially effective. "They must learn commercial tricks and trade tricks, and be ready to burn their fingers." It was easy to open a shop, but perseverance was needed to keep it open.[15]

Concurrent with tendencies toward socialistic public enterprise, there definitely seems to be a groping by the Uganda government for methods by which Africans can, in the words of the minister, "learn commercial tricks and trade tricks, and be ready to burn their fingers." The National Trading Corporation was intended to facilitate this process of experimentation with African involvement in commercial activities.

In 1967 there was a slight feeling of unease among non-African businessmen in East Africa. Tanzania had nationalized certain industries. In Uganda and Kenya there seemed to be increasing militancy in the process of Africanizing commerce. The Uganda government decided that the non-African businessmen needed reassurance. Addressing the Uganda Chamber of Commerce at its annual meeting, the minister of commerce and industry urged the businessmen not to regard the National Trading Corporation as a threat:

> It is not this Government's intention to see that all non-African businessmen go out of business. Far from it, it is the intention to see that there is a proper balance between Africans and non-Africans in the distributive trade.

The minister asked the businessmen to cooperate in achieving greater racial integration in commerce. Private enterprise had a challenge to meet. The minister asked the businessmen to rally the best qualities of business in support of integra-

---

15. See the speeches by the minister of commerce and industry and the minister of planning and economic development, *Uganda Argus* (Kampala), July 3, 1966.

tion as they had in support of other issues. "I do look for an attitude of energy, vigour and of willingness to take reasonable risks," the minister asserted.[16]

The Uganda government has sometimes put faith in commercial education and training as part of the process of economic resocialization. While training in accountancy, bookkeeping, secretarial skills, and even personnel management does not constitute an induction into entrepreneurial behavior, such education is perhaps supportive of economic readjustment and psychological reorientation. In May, 1966, the minister of education announced that new steps to expand the range of commercial education in Uganda were being taken. Some of these steps affected the role of the Uganda College of Commerce, which was already in existence but whose scope was under review. Discussions between the government and Makerere University led to a scheme to introduce accountancy at degree level at Makerere, supported by legal studies with a special orientation toward business law.[17] The government then requested Makerere to set up a Department of Commerce by 1969. This has since come into being. Graduates in commerce are in great demand in government, in parastatal bodies, and in the remaining sectors of private enterprise.

To some extent the government has, in this effort, attempted to utilize the mystique of education as a way of giving an extra boost to the reputation of commercial activity. The craze for education in East Africa has always been striking, and initiatives toward its acquisition have been the order of the day. But the attraction of commercial activity has, for a long time, been uncertain. Can the mystique of education be utilized to create a mystique of commerce? And is commercial education the right approach to the transplantation of prestige? The skills which are being taught in commercial education continue, to some extent, to be purely supportive of rather than fundamental to the creation of an African commercial class. Nevertheless, the new faith in training for business and private enterprise is part of Uganda's groping for effective means of economic resocialization.

Meanwhile, in 1968 the government set up the special Mugenyi Committee on Africanisation of Commerce and Industry in Uganda. The commission submitted a report recommending rapid Africanization to be completed in five years. The government rejected the idea of setting up a deadline but accepted the idea of rapidity. The government issued a white paper on Africanization of commerce and industry, followed by legislation in 1969 to introduce scheduled areas of trade and to conrol immigrant competition with local enterprise.

Kenya's policy in this sphere of national life has been strikingly similar to Uganda's. To some extent Kenya's problem has been more severe. For one thing, there are more Asians in Kenya than in the rest of East Africa. For another, Africans had a longer history of successful participation in middleman

---

16. *Ibid.*, April 29, 1967.
17. See "More Training in Commerce" (editorial), *ibid.*, May 21, 1966.

economic activity in Uganda than they had in Kenya. Prosperous African farmers and merchants were known in Uganda well before independence. In Kenya, however, the growth of a prosperous African class was much more manifestly a postindependence phenomenon. Farming in Kenya had continued to be dominated in its cash-crop aspects by Europeans, and distributive trade was controlled overwhelmingly by Europeans and Asians. A resettlement scheme in the Kenya Highlands helped to give an increasing share of this sector of the national economy to Africans, but there was still a good deal to be done. Progress in the commercial sector was in many ways less spectacular than the resettlement schemes. There was an early commitment to the Africanization of commerce and to the creation of an effective African business class. Sessional Paper No. 10 on African Socialism, published in 1965, was in part an undertaking to Africanize the rudimentary capitalism which Kenya had created.

At first the methods used were mainly those of appealing to immigrant business-men to involve more and more Africans in commercial activities. However, many Asian businesses were essentially family businesses which did not lend themselves very easily to acquiring partners outside the family circle. Since the distribution of work and method of involvement had a strong personal element rooted in family relationship, it was not easy to find a place for a new African partner in the business. In addition, the creation of an African commercial class could seriously undermine the livelihood of some of the poorer shopkeepers in immigrant communities. The government's appeals were virtually inviting certain Asians to commit commercial suicide. Finally, Africans were seldom effectively competitive in commerce, even when given a little push. This brings us back to the need for economic resocialization in the creation of an effective African commercial class.

Francis Nduati Macharia is one African businessman who achieved sufficient eminence to become president of the Kenya National Chamber of Commerce and Industry, the country's main organization of businessmen. In an interview late in 1967 he implied that the African in Kenya had yet to acquire the discrimination and single-mindedness which would enable him to affirm the tautological proposition that business is business — and is not something else. In the words of Macharia: "Many Africans are completely confused. They don't know whether they want to do business or farming or something else — and there is a tendency to look on business as a hobby." [18]

Because the loose appeals to Asian businessmen were ineffective, and because many Africans who did become businessmen were unsuccessful, the Kenya government became increasingly militant in its policy of trying to push Africans into effective business behavior. One method was simply to reduce the opportunities open to non-Africans in the hope that the resultant gaps would be filled

18. Francis Nduati Macharia, "On the Carpet: Finance and Know-How Are Big Weaknesses," *Sunday Nation* (Nairobi), December 3, 1967.

by Africans who might otherwise have been too timid or too disorganized to compete with those who had previously responded to such opportunities. Out of this grew the idea of the Trade Licensing Act, designed to Africanize trade. The method was to license businesses in Kenya more systematically and to limit the duration of licenses to one year. Certain geographical areas of trade were to be reserved for citizens. If the minister was convinced that a certain business could be handled by a citizen, he would have the right to refuse a noncitizen a license for that business. Measures of this kind were in principle intended to be nonracial, and those immigrants who had become citizens of Kenya were not to be penalized. But ultimately the purpose was to achieve a greater Africanization of some openings in business which could be created only by a deliberate elimination of some Asians and Europeans from certain areas of commercial activity. This side of the Kenya government's policy was designed not to increase African competitiveness but to decrease the competition that the African had to face from others. Policy-makers hope that the security which these new African businessmen enjoy will gradually have a healthy demonstration effect on other aspiring Africans. Future generations of African merchants might be forced to manifest a more meaningful faith in risk-taking than this overprotected first generation is being called upon to do.

The Kenya government is also utilizing other methods of economic transformation. It has taken measures to increase the number of African traders without necessarily ousting their rivals. One experiment undertaken by the minister of commerce, Mwai Kibaki, in February, 1967, was to sell shares in a major Asian industry at cheap rates. The industry, the House of Manji, offered the shares to the ministry for this kind of distribution and intended to attract significant African participation in what had previously been a large family business. Although that particular experiment encountered difficulties, the Kenya government is still convinced that one can learn to invest only by investing. Africans must therefore be encouraged to take the risks of buying shares and must familiarize themselves with this exercise.

At times Kenya's policy has echoed the policy which was pursued in Sweden in the 1950s — that of trying to create "an ownership democracy." It has even echoed John Stuart Mill. In the opinion of Mill, political participation by individuals is the most effective and educative method of creating political consciousness. In the opinion of the Kenya government, economic participation by individuals serves the same purpose in the effort to create economic consciousness and sophistication.

The East African Economic Reformation

We have mentioned that economic behavior in Africa has very often been a struggle for supremacy between a prestige motive derived from ancestral values and a newly fostered profit motive sometimes associated with a spirit of entrepreneurship. East Africa is feeling the need for a certain transformation of values in the economic field to make possible a greater commitment to socioeconomic changes in the populace. Political culture is often intimately connected with problems of economic socialization. The erosion of certain inherited political-cultural traits might well be a prerequisite for the creation of new economic cultural dispositions.

We have seen that Tanzania's resocialization scheme not only borrows from Calvinistic doctrine the disapproval of ostentatious acquisition but even opposes determined, nonshowy acquisition. In its distaste for social classes, however, Tanzania is overlooking the economic necessity of a class of managers — those who may exercise their duties impersonally and without ownership. The Leadership Resolutions of the Arusha Declaration also ignore economic realities in their attempt to keep a large portion of the competent, educated population out of the economic sphere and, instead, to keep business entirely in the hands of professional businessmen.

We mentioned that in Kenya and Uganda the attempt to resocialize the population in the economic field has taken the form of trying to propagate an ethos of investment and shareholding in large sectors of the society. The governments of both of these countries seem committed to the creation of an African commercial class and have been experimenting with institutions and legislation calculated to Africanize some of the existing rudimentary capitalism. Kenya has been more consistent. Uganda is torn between state enterprise and the Africanization of private enterprise.

The danger in Kenya and Uganda is that specific forms of the prestige motive might survive the resocialization — and survive in a form not entirely beneficial to the body politic. The Kenya government and the Uganda government might succeed in creating a significant business class from the ranks of the indigenous people; but the quest for prestige, which comes from some aspects of traditional political culture, might take a more modern and more luxurious form. The prestige that survives the resocialization might be simply that which concerns itself with self-glamorization in the social context. The degree of consumption which would accompany this residual prestige motive might militate against certain directions of economic growth and, indeed, of political stability.[19]

---

19. Some of these aspects of new developments in Africa are discussed in Ali A. Mazrui, "The Monarchical Tendency in African Political Culture," *British Journal of Sociology*, XVIII, no. 3 (September, 1967), 231–50, reprinted in *idem, Violence and Thought: Essays on Social Tensions in Africa* (London: Longmans, 1969), pp. 206–30. For the Leadership Resolutions of Tanzania, see the Publicity Section, TANU, *The Arusha Declaration and TANU's Policy on Socialism and Self-Reliance* (Dar es Salaam, 1967), pp. 12–20. The implications of these resolutions for social stratification are also discussed in Ali A. Mazrui, "Political Superannuation and the Trans-Class Man" (Paper delivered at the Seventh World Congress of the International Political Science Association, Brussels, September, 1967). A classic on the "managerial revolution" in the modern world is, of course, James Burnham, *The Managerial Revolution*, (1941; reprint ed. with preface by Michael Young, London: Penguin, 1962).

That Calvinistic capacity to approve of acquisition while condemning ostentatious consumption may not be adequately met in Kenya. Tanzania's error is perhaps in throwing out the baby with the bathwater. The risk which Kenya is taking is in retaining not only the baby but also the dirty water. Uganda is trying to avoid both risks, but the ambivalence between socialism and Africanized capitalism has its own dangers.

Large areas of uncertainty must remain. The interplay between political culture and economic socialization is complex, and its consequences are not easily discernible. Where new economic values are derived from foreign traditions, the process of economic resocialization is basically a process of economic acculturation. But in East Africa the situation is not simply an interplay between indigenous traditional habits and imported Western norms. There is also the conscious attempt to determine directions of change which are at least semiautonomous of both Westernism and local traditionality. What East Africa is experiencing might well be its reformation in the economic field, complete with the tensions of institutional fluidity and the quest for new political bearings.

[14]

The National Service and
Economic Conscription

The concept of "economic conscription" can be used in analyzing some of the phenomena we are observing in East Africa. The definition of *conscription* as given in the *Concise Oxford Dictionary* is "compulsory enlistment for military or naval service." In East Africa the idea of a national service is partly economic in motivation, concerning issues of development more than those of defense. But the rhetoric of economic exertion in such cases often uses military imagery, and the concepts of discipline demanded within the national services and related programs are again conceived in neomilitaristic terms.

The image of being at war with poverty is at the root of the Tanzanian ethos of economic development. In his inaugural address in December, 1962, President Nyerere said:

> I know there are still a few people who think we are joking when they hear us using the word "war." Let me assure them that we are not. . . . Even if one were to take, for example, the Maji Maji Rebellion and the Slave Wars, one would find no parallel to the slaughter of our people which has stemmed from poverty, ignorance and disease. . . . In the same way the famine last year [1961], if it had caught us unprepared, could have killed many more of our people than ever died in battle during the Maji Maji Rebellion.[1]

This neomilitaristic conception of Tanzania's problems of development was an established part of Nyerere's ideology. It can be traced back to the day of independence and even farther. In terms of policy it resulted in two interrelated guiding principles — first, social discipline and, second, mobilization of human resources for difficult tasks in the countryside.

The issue of discipline was also behind the single-party structure and the refusal to adopt the liberal value of free interplay between antagonistic factions. To use Nyerere's words, "*This is our time of emergency*, and until our war against poverty, ignorance and disease has been won, we should not let our

---

1. Julius Nyerere, *Freedom and Unity — Uhuru na Umoja* (Dar es Salaam: Oxford University Press, 1966), pp. 176–87. The address was given on December 10, 1962.

unity be destroyed by somebody else's book of rules." [2] The definition of self-reliance in the Arusha Declaration starts with the subheading *"We are at war."*

My own concept of economic conscription is related to an older concept of social mobilization that can be found in the literature of the social sciences. Karl W. Deutsch of Harvard University has offered the following as a definition of social mobilization.

> Social mobilization can be defined . . . as the process in which major clusters of old social, economic and psychological commitments are eroded or broken and people become available for new patterns of socialization and behavior. . . . In this fashion, soldiers are mobilized *from* their homes and families and mobilized *into* the army in which they serve. Similarly, [Karl] Mannheim suggests an image of large numbers of people moving away *from* a life of social isolation, traditionalism and political apathy, and moving *into* a different life of broader and deeper involvement in the vast complexities of modern life, including potential and actual involvement in mass politics.[3]

Deutsch links the image of mobilization to Mannheim's concept of "fundamental democraticization," leading to increasing involvement in the modern process as villagers are uprooted from old ways. Political mobilization is sometimes the more explicit process of getting the masses more involved in the political process.

There are two important differences between this older concept of mobilization and my own concept of conscription as used in this figurative sense. First, mobilization implies large-scale involvement of the masses, whereas conscription can imply the involvement of a single individual or a very narrow class of people. Second, mobilization does not by definition, imply compulsion. Deutsch's notion of social mobilization refers to a process which is almost *ad hoc* and uncontrolled, as new values try to entice those who have been released from old values, and old patterns of life give way to newly formulated ones. There need be no governmental policy of mobilization in this social sense. Like Mannheim's "fundamental democraticization," this can be a process of social chance rather than the implementation of a political policy. Conscription, on the other hand, does imply compulsory enlistment for specific national or social goals. Although in our notion of economic conscription the goals may include defense, they are more often primarily developmental.

The Tanzanian Scheme

In Tanzania the National Service was voluntary to begin with and could therefore not be regarded as "conscriptive." It started, following the mutinies

---

2. Julius Nyerere, "One Party Government," *Transition*, I, no. 2 (December, 1961), 10. Emphasis original.

3. Karl W. Deutsch, "Social Mobilization and Political Development," *American Political Science Review*, LV, no. 3 (September, 1961), 493–94. Emphasis original.

of 1964, with an appeal from President Nyerere: "I call upon all members of the TANU Youth League, wherever they are, to . . . enrol themselves." Later on, as the National Service was institutionalized, the approach continued to be an appeal to young people to avail themselves of this training in discipline and national purpose. Among the disappointments in this initial approach was the fact that the best educated did not volunteer. The second vice-president, Rashidi Kawawa, told the National Assembly in October, 1966, that the government had been forced to make the service compulsory "in view of the very poor response from the educated group to join the service for the good of our nation." The vice-president also reported that less than twenty-five educated people had joined the National Youth Service voluntarily since May, 1965, when President Nyerere had made an appeal to the youth of Tanzania. "President Nyerere made the appeal realising that discipline and some sense of responsibility and leadership were virtues which could only be acquired through proper training," said Kawawa.[4] The proposals of 1966 made the National Service obligatory for sixth-form-leavers, those who had attended university, those who had graduated from professional institutions, and all persons who had obtained employment through the National Service. The move was indeed from exhortation to conscription.

There are important differences in militaristic imagery between the National Service as it has evolved in Tanzania and the National Service Proposals in Obote's Uganda. It is true that the Obote proposals also were made in terms of being to some extent "at war with poverty." Article 4 of the proposals states, "The National Service should not be based on training in arms of war, but in arms for the sustained development of the economy." And the very first article of the proposals utilizes the concept of mobilization: "The basic objective of the National Service will be to mobilise all able-bodied persons to develop a real sense of individual and collective responsibility to society, within the overall national goal of One country — One people." With regard to the concepts of development and defense, the Obote approach for Uganda was more clearly developmental and more remotely defensive than can be said of Tanzania's scheme. The training that the Tanzanian service provides clearly has both military and developmental purposes. The young people have even been informally referred to as "The Green Guards" by President Nyerere.

The arrangements in Tanzania include a commitment to serve for five months in a camp. Part of this period is spent in manual work, often cultivation of a local crop. Thus, maize would be cultivated in an Arusha camp and sisal in Tanga. Other forms of manual work include participation in community projects where these are in close proximity. The other part of this period is spent in military training — for example, learning the use of firearms and the discipline and drill of parades. Apart from the manual work and communal living, the experience in the camp includes lectures in political education. There

---

4. *Daily Nation* (Nairobi), October 4, 1966.

is less emphasis in the Tanzanian scheme than in the Uganda proposals on providing opportunities to young people to acquire technical skills.

For those who are graduates of university institutions the period in camp is followed by eighteen months in the substantive post for which the person is qualified. In such a role the individual is guaranteed the minimum wage of Dar es Salaam (200 shillings per month now, but 180 shillings at the time the National Service was inaugurated) plus 40 per cent of the remaining part of the normal salary for the job. This is the *posho*, or subsistence allowance, and is not subject to tax during those eighteen months. In addition, the graduate is entitled to a modest housing allowance and to two sets of uniforms. After the eighteen months the graduate returns to the camp for one concluding month of refresher training.

There has since been some attempt to channel students into the National Service after they have received their higher school certificates and before they have actually entered a university. A number of such students from Tanzania have started their academic careers at Makerere after going through the five months of camp experience.

The Obote National Service Scheme

One of the criticisms which might be leveled against Obote's proposals for national service in Uganda is that the proposals confused two different problems: the problem of how to provide a socializing experience for every able-bodied citizen and the problem of what to do with school-leavers — those students who leave school after obtaining a school certificate. The training camps and centers at regional, parliamentary constituency, and subcounty levels seemed designed to be centers of national education for the population as a whole. Article 10 of Obote's proposals emphasized that the training camps were to be primarily, even if not exclusively, for adults. The ideological inspiration behind the training camps for adults was partly *integrative*, partly *agrarian*, and partly *egalitarian*. Although President Obote's proposals had not been fully implemented when he was overthrown by the army in January, 1971, they constitute a distinctive scheme well worth analysis.

First, the ideological inspiration was *integrative* in that there was a clear emphasis on the need to afford Ugandans from different regions the opportunity to live together. One of the major goals of the National Service was the imperative of oneness — "the overall national goal of One Country — One People." The ambition of the service therefore included the aspiration "to eradicate factional feelings and loyalties, and to consolidate National unity through creative participation of the people in the task of national building" (Article 5 [c]). The camps as "miniature Ugandas" were to serve as institutionalized opportunities for ethnic intermingling. As Article 3 of the proposals put it:

The Service will further aim at the promotion of an intercourse amongst all the people of Uganda and provision of facilities for people of different backgrounds to participate in national and community projects, thereby affording to all participants in such projects opportunities to know more and more about Uganda and her people, and to develop new values and attitudes towards the Nation.

All these ideas fell within the general integrative purpose of the National Service, as did the projected courses on "national consciousness and promotion and advancement of culture" (Article 10).

Second, the ideological inspiration was *agrarian* in that there was a tendency to emphasize training in agricultural methods and to sensitize the trainees to the situation in a country which was primarily agricultural. The proposals urged that those called into the National Service in each of the training camps should not only come from all parts of Uganda but should also "participate in agricultural, animal husbandry and related activities irrespective of their professions or occupations" (Article 10). For those engaged in crop-production and mixed farming, arrangements were to be made to advance their knowledge in their occupations during their service in the camps. But the others, whether they were originally doctors, lawyers, engineers, or lecturers in moral philosophy, were all to be called upon to participate in agrarian activities. The choice of the sites for the camps therefore depended not only on such questions as whether there was an easily accessible source of water but also on whether there was good farming land in close proximity (Article 9).

All these considerations pertain to the task of ruralizing the perspectives of Ugandans from urban areas. But the proposals were well aware of the preponderance of rural Ugandans in the population. "Since the majority of citizens of Uganda live in rural areas where the standard of living is low and amenities are few, it will be the principle concern of the National Service to encourage and promote new patterns of rural life that are compatible with modern requirements and standards" (Article 4). The proposals envisaged the establishment of state farms for the production of carefully selected commodities (Article 30).

Third, the ideological inspiration was *egalitarian* in that the goal was not simply to bring Ugandans from different regions and from different tribes to live together but also to bring Ugandans from different social strata and different social classes to live together. The living conditions for all were to be at the same level. There was to be no hierarchy in the organization of the camp which would, for example, accord different "high table" eating privileges or different accommodations to different categories of residents. "Any person doing his National Service in any of these camps irrespective of his status in Uganda and irrespective of whether or not he is a lecturer, demonstrator or trainee, will be provided with the same accommodation and will be living, eating, working and playing together and subject to the same regulations and treatment" (Article 15).

The National Service Proposals provided for an entirely different kind of exercise in relation to school-leavers. In each of the rural parliamentary constituencies of Uganda, training centers were to be established for, firstly, primary-seven-leavers who had not gone on for further education in postprimary institutions and, secondly, unmarried youths between the ages of fourteen and twenty-one who did not fall in the first category but who had attended school and reached primary six or primary seven.

The ideological imperative of promoting national integration through greater national consciousness was regarded to be as valid for the young people as it was for the adults in the National Service. The cultivation of national consciousness in the young people and the promotion of African culture in their activities were both regarded as very important. But it was further proposed that these young people, who already knew how to read and write and who had a working knowledge of English, but who had had no opportunity to proceed further with their education, should be enabled to undergo a further course of advanced training on a broad basis in academic subjects, technical skills, art in various forms, some African languages (particularly Swahili, Luganda, and Lingala), as well as in games of various kinds and in leadership (Articles 17–19).

An agrarian element remained pertinent in this part of the National Service Proposals. As part of the training, each student who was accepted for a full course at the Constituency Training Centres "should own a plot of land and benefit from the proceeds of that plot, and further, . . . any such student who takes an interest in any technical subject, any other form of handwork, or any cultural activity should benefit financially from any such work or activity" (Article 21).

Primary-seven-leavers who undertook the four-year course in the Constituency Training Centres and who showed enough promise to benefit from further education were to be selected, subject to the number of places available in the postprimary boarding institutions, to spend at least two months in such institutions every year. It was recommended that at the end of each first term in the postprimary institutions, trainees in the Constituency Training Centres join the postprimary institutions for two months. In turn, it was recommended that students in such institutions join the Constituency Training Centres for the same period. It was suggested that this exchange take into account geographical areas of birth of the youths concerned. It was proposed that at the end of the full course, students who showed sufficient promise to gain by higher and further training be found places in appropriate institutions, and that the rest be settled, not necessarily on the basis of the constituency or district in which they were born, but on a Uganda-wide basis (Article 23).

With regard to youths between the ages of fourteen and twenty-one who did not fall within the first category of primary-seven-leavers, Obote's proposals urged that they be given an opportunity to undergo training and acquire skills at the Constituency Training Centres. But because of their age it was proposed that their courses be different from those of the primary-seven-leavers who joined the centers directly from school. The courses were to take two years, spread over four terms of six months each. When not undergoing a course of training, the youths were required to return to their homes and work under the supervision and guidance of the National Service for the same period.

The Obote proposals went on to say that although Constituency Training Centres would be run within the policy of the National Service, this would not mean that the young trainees who went to such centers would, after four or two years, have completed the requirements of a call-up for the National Service. After completing this course of training, they would be called up for twelve months of continuous service in any area or areas of Uganda.

It is this mixture of camps for adults and Constituency Training Centres for primary-seven-leavers and other young people between the ages of fourteen and twenty-one which exposed the Obote National Service Proposals to the charge of confusing two separate needs. One was the need to inculcate in adults a greater awareness of the nation in all its regional and ethnic diversity, a greater sensitivity to rural problems, and a greater acceptance of egalitarian values and the reduction of disparities between different strata of society. The other need was to afford additional opportunities for training to young people who had not had the opportunity to go further in their education. Why were these two very different national ambitions bracketed together?

In reality this was defensible if the different ambitions of the National Service were reduced to the central idea of *social toil.* If Obote's National Service Proposals were ultimately animated by what the proposals called ''a spirit of dedicated service to the Nation'' (Article 4), then a shared experience of exertion and toil by Ugandans from different regions, tribes, and strata was the most central of all the ambitions of this scheme. We are, in fact, back to the concept of economic conscription.

The Tanzania National Service scheme of 1966 definitely included the purpose of initiating the educated into the rigors of manual labor. Exertion in this case included the experience of working with one's hands and participating in nation-building activities involving physical labor. In the Obote scheme this aspect was not quite as explicit as it was in the arrangements in Tanzania. Yet the obligation imposed on all in the Uganda National Service to participate in agricultural activities seemed calculated to promote a readiness in people from different professions to engage in social toil and exertion.

Problems of Social Redundancy

The opposite of toil and exertion is, quite simply, idleness. There are, in fact, three forms of idleness to take into account: the idleness which comes with not being able to get a job, with suffering the deprivations of unemployment;

the idleness which comes with being privileged or rich, with being part of a leisure class; and the idleness which arises out of special cultural attitudes to "unnecessary exertion." Idleness brings the primary-seven-leavers into an orbit of shared relationship with privileged members of the Uganda elite; the school-leavers suffer the idleness of the unemployed, while the elite enjoy the idleness of the leisurely class.

Professor B. A. Ogot, head of the Department of History at the University of Nairobi, once suggested that the stability of a country depends on what its citizens do between 5:00 P.M. and midnight. He described this as his "pet and simple theory." Most people are busy earning a living during the day. But during the leisure hours a choice has to be made between social and antisocial activities, between legitimate enjoyment of leisure on the one hand and scheming and maneuvering in ways detrimental to the nation on the other.[5] Ogot was suggesting that instability in a country arises out of what happens during the leisure hours. When people are busy earning their livings, there might not be an opportunity for certain political ills to flourish. And when people are provided with ways of passing leisure hours sufficient to afford cultural and psychological fulfillment, the stability of the society need not be in danger.

Ogot was making a valid point, but he might also have missed an important factor. He was taking leisure hours too literally as those *following* working hours. This is not difficult to understand in view of the fact that his speech was intended to appeal for the provision of greater government financial support for cultural activities in after-work hours. But of more fundamental sociological relevance for the issue of stability is the precise relationship between work and leisure. What happens between 8:00 A.M. and 5:00 P.M. — and what happens when idleness begins at 8:00 A.M. and lasts all day?

Article 5 (f) of Uganda's National Service Proposals did mention the need "to reduce the incidence of under-employment and unemployment, particularly of school-leavers, and to bring the benefits of our Independence, particularly to the rural population and urban workers." The Constituency Training Centres seemed to be in part oriented toward fighting this special kind of idleness imposed upon underemployed or unemployed school-leavers.

The problem is still present in Uganda, as elsewhere. It arises partly out of the pyramidal structure of education in East Africa. A few of those who go through primary education are chosen to go on to secondary education; and they undergo the second phase of training so that a few of them may go on to university education. At each stage on the way there is a great risk. Those who have completed only primary education might see themselves as "dropouts" with no special skills to enable them to play an adequate role in day-to-day life. Those who finish secondary education are at times similarly frustrated because they can get no higher on the educational pyramid and are

---

5. See *ibid.*, November 10, 1969. See also the editorial on that subject in the same issue.

not adequately convinced that the skills they have acquired are of relevance at their own level of educational accomplishment. In his perceptive essay entitled "Education for Self-Reliance," Nyerere has analyzed the implications of the elite orientation which lies behind the present educational systems in East African countries.[6] This elite orientation in its pyramidal structure continues to emphasize the belief that social achievement is vertical, that a person is successful only if he can push further and further upward and not necessarily if he can accomplish a great deal at his own level of the pyramid.

Meanwhile, schools proliferate in response both to the demands for social rewards for individuals and to assumptions about education as a dynamo for economic development. But each stage on the way — primary, junior secondary, and secondary — tends to be regarded not as a self-contained unit of training but as an incomplete stage toward the higher level of education. Because of this, the phenomenon of "social redundancy" begins to afflict African societies.

Social redundancy arises partly because education creates expectations about social roles for individuals which sometimes are not realized. A young person who has completed primary seven might be reluctant to accept a career or a style of life which he regards as not befitting his level of education. Social redundancy arises when individuals are no longer sure that there are suitable openings for them in society. There may be roles available which the individuals could perform effectively; but, because of expectations about "appropriate jobs" for each category of "dropouts," the diploma-holders in African societies are often underutilized or even completely unemployed. Social redundancy in Africa arises substantially out of a presumed social incongruity between this man and that job rather than out of a genuine shortage of jobs to fill.[7]

The problem of social redundancy in relation to the educational pyramid also has a pyramidal mode of growth. First there is social redundancy at the level of primary-school-leavers, the base of the pyramid; then, social redundancy at the level of secondary-school-leavers, unable to get into universities and also unable to obtain "appropriate" positions; and in the next decade or so there will no doubt be, in one African country after another, social redundancy at the level of university graduates. Some of them might find it impossible to obtain a job that would not offend their sense of social congruity. The important jobs are being filled. The universities are producing more people than can be absorbed into the kinds of jobs which have so far been presumed to be the right ones for graduates.

There is little doubt that in much of Africa the university degree is at the

---

6. Julius Nyerere, *Ujamaa — Essays on Socialism* (Dar es Salaam: Oxford University Press, 1968), pp. 44–75.
7. Social redundancy in relation to creative restlessness is discussed in Ali A. Mazrui, "Africa on the Eve of Tomorrow: Some Social Political Trends" (Paper delivered at the Conference on Africa in the 1980s, organized by the Adlai Stevenson Institute of International Affairs, Chicago, April, 1969). A version of the paper has been published in the *Bulletin of the Atomic Scientists*, Vol. XXV, no. 9 (1969).

moment overinflated in value. There is room for considerable deflation before a rational level of evaluation is achieved. Social redundancy in this case might serve as a deflationary device to help in rationalizing academic prices. But this is a problem for the future.

There are occasions when redundancy arises out of the attitudes of the parents rather than the presumed arrogance of the school-leavers. President Obote, in a speech to the Uganda Education Association in 1969, drew attention to the fact that some parents who have made sacrifices to send their children to school are reluctant to see them back in the village working on the farm after they have completed their secondary education. It is almost regarded as a disgrace to the family when a young man who has been exposed to a period of education returns to the rural area and starts with the implements of cultivation all over again. A return to the village by the educated becomes a symbol of failure and is therefore regarded as something that compromises the reputation of those who labored hard and sacrificed much to put their children through school. Yet, there are often no suitable jobs for the educated. Picking up the hoe and starting cultivation is at times the only alternative to being sentenced to a period of idleness and redundancy.

Problems of Privilege and Leisure

The second form of idleness, that of the privileged group, is more explicitly fought in the ideology of Tanzania than in what has evolved in Uganda. The concept of hard work has assumed the status of a full ideology in Tanzania. In "*Ujamaa*: The Basis of African Socialism," Julius Nyerere claims that in traditional Africa everyone was a "worker," distinct not only from an "employer" but also from a "loiterer" or an "idler." [8] Whether this is a justifiable interpretation of life in traditional African societies is arguable. But there is little doubt that Tanzania tried from the beginning to utilize the concept of work as a slogan of national mobilization. This effort can be traced back to the neat motto *Uhuru na Kazi*, or "Freedom and Work." Self-help schemes were devised in 1963, when expectations about aid had not fully materialized. The concept of self-help gradually evolved into the concept of self-reliance, both of which implied major exertions in the service of society.

In Tanzania's ideology there has been a profound disapproval of parasitism. If we go back to Nyerere's formulation of his socialism, we find the following arguments:

> Those of us who talk about the African way of life and, quite rightly, take pride in maintaining a tradition of hospitality which is so great a part of it, might do well to remember the Swahili saying "*Mgeni siku mbili; siku ya tatu mpe jembe*'

8. See Nyerere, *Freedom and Unity — Uhuru na Umoja*, pp. 162–71.

— or in English "Treat your guest as a guest for two days; on the third day give him a hoe."[9]

When the new proposals for the National Service were launched in 1966, there was a feeling that some of the educated had become parasitic. The National Service had been initiated after the army mutinies in 1964, but in the original scheme the well educated did not have to participate. Nyerere began to feel that this was anomalous. The National Service in Tanzania seemed to be catering only to the idleness of those whose ambitions had been frustrated (the unemployed) and not to the leisurely idleness of those whom society had enabled to get further in their education. The unemployed school-leavers had received little from society; but the graduates of University College, Dar es Salaam, had been maintained as undergraduates at a cost to the government of 24,000 shillings each per year. Soon after Nyerere expelled over 300 university students on October 22, 1966, following their defiant protest against the National Service, he gave a speech in which he further clarified the ultimate ambitions of the service, including the ambition to inculcate a sense of humility in the fortunate ones who had gotten far in their education, as well as to afford them the experience of working with their hands. The idleness which was being tackled in this case was the idleness of the fortunate. The danger which was being averted was the danger of producing an elite of leisure rather than an elite of labor.[10]

Toil and Cultural Behavior

The third form of idleness arises neither from social redundancy nor from habits of aristocratic leisure but from primordial cultural attitudes toward work. Is urgent insistence on work indigenous to Africa?

In an article published in 1953 on industrial efficiency and the urban African in Southern Rhodesia, Boris Gussman observed that the African traditionally worked extremely hard in his day-to-day tribal life when the occasion demanded. But life was so organized that prolonged work was rarely necessary. Needs were few, and people did not hoard goods or attempt to build up a surplus of wealth beyond their immediate needs. There was little competition, no money, and few emergencies apart from war. One year followed another with little variation in the program of life. Everyone knew the work he or she had to perform. The closely knit tribal system of reciprocity ensured that cooperation would be rewarded by social well-being rather than by material rewards for

9. *Ibid*., p. 165.
10. See Ali A. Mazrui, "Education and Elite Formation in East Africa" (Paper delivered at the Annual Conference of the Uganda Educational Association, Kampala, October 19, 1969).

services. Work was "the thing to do" for one's *Jamaa*, and it was often buttressed by ritual. "While work, and extremely hard work at certain times, was generally accepted with equanimity, it was rarely, if ever, undertaken for its own sake."[11]

More recently, William H. Friedland has also contradicted Nyerere in the latter's assertion that the urgency of work was part of traditional Africa. In analyzing some of the trends in African socialistic thought, Friedland observed that most African societies had subsistence economies and had not seen work as an ethic. He argued that the traditional view in Africa was probably closer to that of the Greeks, who looked upon work as an evil necessary for survival but not as a social obligation. Friedland added that the Judaeo-Christian ethic in the West did not look upon work with high regard until recent times. He cited Genesis as symbolic of the Judaeo-Christian conception. Adam and Eve lived in elegant idleness in the Garden of Eden, where work was unnecessary, as long as they were in a state of obedient harmony with God. When they ate of the tree of knowledge, God drove them out of the garden and ordered man thenceforth to labor. "In the sweat of thy face shalt thou eat bread." As Friedland put it, this was hardly a view which saw work as a blessing. The Almighty seemed to regard work as a punishment. It appeared as if the Almighty was sentencing Adam and Eve to the experience of earning their living for a change instead of living in idle splendor in the garden.[12]

Friedland and other scholars have drawn attention to the energies which have been devoted to community development in former British territories and to "human investment" in former French territories. These policies have been interpreted as yet additional attempts to create "an institutional apparatus pressuring people to work." Work in this case is seen in communal terms for specific projects such as the building of schools, the construction of roads, and other forms of individual contribution of labor to projects of social utility.

> On the whole, however, while there has been a great deal of community development and "human investment" the population generally has not yet developed the systematic work habits necessary for rapid economic growth.[13]

On balance the evidence seems to suggest that communal work in many African traditional societies was quite institutionalized and sometimes ritualized. The incentives to work were often in the following order: first, the search for the individual's basic needs and those of his immediate family; second, the individual's contribution to the welfare of neighbors and kinsmen, if this

---

11. Boris Gussman, "Industrial Efficiency and the Urban African: A Study of Conditions in Southern Rhodesia," *Africa*, XXIII (1953), reprinted in *Africa — Social Problems of Change and Conflict*, ed. Pierre van den Berghe (San Francisco: Chandler, 1965), pp. 396–97.

12. William H. Friedland, "Basic Social Trends," in *African Socialism*, ed. *idem* and Carl G. Rosberg, Jr. (Stanford: Stanford University Press, 1964), pp. 17–18.

13. *Ibid.*, pp. 18–19.

was customarily expected; and, third, the individual's interest in accumulating things for himself and aspiring to self-improvement as distinct from self-maintenance.

The ordering of priorities is quite significant. It is not correct to assume that the traditional African subordinated his basic needs to those of his community. His basic needs came first, those of his community and kinsmen came second, and the need for personal improvement came third. The incentives for hard work varied accordingly. Working hard for personal maintenance made good sense; working hard to meet one's normal obligations to one's kinsmen also made sense; but working hard for some undefined target of self-improvement was in many cases less clearly apprehended. The phenomenon of "target workers" in Africa — those who come to the cities to satisfy only certain needs and then go back home — and the phenomenon of workers working fewer hours as soon as they are paid more for the hours they do work have been interpreted by various economic anthropologists as indications of the low priority that self-improvement, regarded as an indefinite process of upward mobility, has in traditional African values.

The Tanzanian National Service is apparently in favor of maintaining this traditional order of priorities. It is in favor of a work ethic which makes it more important to serve prescribed communal needs than to serve an indefinite goal of individual self-improvement. Many of the camps afford opportunities only for cultivation, but there is a general interest in road-construction and assistance in building *Ujamaa* villages where camps are in suitable proximity. The passion against *kupe*, or parasites, is an ideological component of Tanzania's national ethic and influences the choice of jobs required under the National Service and related schemes.

The Obote National Service Proposals for Uganda seemed to be more individually oriented and less communal in emphasis in some respects than the Tanzanian scheme has been. The very first goal mentioned for the Uganda National Service was: "To produce economic returns for individual citizens and in turn to create wealth for the country, using, in the main, the efforts of the people" (Article 5). This was an attempt to marry individualism to a sense of communal responsibility. The fuller objective as given in the Obote proposals combined these two responsibilities. "The basic objective of the National Service will be to mobilise all able-bodied persons to develop a real sense of individual and collective responsibility to society, within the overall national goal of One country — One people" (Article 1). The proposals clearly recognized individual ambition as a major factor in human motivation. In the Constituency Training Centres there was also something approaching an attempt to socialize the young people into *individual* self-reliance. There was virtually an acceptance of the profit motive as one of the facts of life in economic development. This was in contrast to the Tanzanian scheme, which seemed afraid that modernization might reverse the traditional order of work incentives and make people more eager to pursue their own ambitions than to fulfill communal obligations. Tanzania was anxious to avert a scale of values which would put the individual's basic needs first, his self-improvement second, and communal obligations only third.

Obote's government, on the other hand, seemed disturbed that there was not enough commitment to individual enterprise in the economic culture of some local societies. The program of trying to create an African entrepreneurial class and of Africanizing commercial activity in the country had to be accompanied by a vigorous promotion of individual exertion and economic ambition among those who sought to try their luck in business. Nowhere in East Africa is individual improvement as a personal incentive for hard work and for better commercial organization as yet sufficiently developed among Africans. Hence, Obote's National Service scheme was interested in improving individual exertion as an ambition, as well as in improving the capacity of the people for serving their nation. This is illustrated in the following goals:

> To provide facilities and opportunities for those who participate in the National Service to acquire new skills and new attitudes which will enable them to make a greater contribution to their well-being and to society as a whole than would have been possible without the National Service [Article 5].

This line of reasoning sometimes sounds like Adam Smith's invisible hand, guiding the efforts of individuals who are seeking their own self-interests toward the promotion of the welfare of society as a whole. Although Obote's proposals did at times sound like this, there was in fact much greater balance between individualism and social commitment in them than is found in Adam Smith on the one hand and in the socialistic ethic of Tanzania on the other.

The National Service and National Security

There is a clearer link with the military in the history of the Tanzanian National Service than is discernible in the Obote proposals. Following the mutiny of the armed forces in Tanzania, President Nyerere was deeply shaken and turned to the youth of the country for a solution to the problem. The main thing in Tanzania was to build an army loyal enough to resist the temptation of challenging civilian authority. A previous army had, at least indirectly, failed that test. For a couple of days the world wondered what had happened to Julius Nyerere. When the president finally re-emerged, invited British toops to disband the mutineers, and addressed the nation on where to move next, he was impelled to say:

> I call on all members of the TANU Youth League, wherever they are, to go to the local TANU office and enrol themselves. From this group we shall try to build a nucleus of a new army for the Republic of Tanganyika.[14]

---

14. *Sunday News* (Dar es Salaam), January 26, 1964.

The National Service was in part a preparatory experience for young people prior to entering the armed forces. The notion of a people's army drawn in this way, having links with the political party, emerged substantially out of the deeply disturbing experience of the mutinies of 1964. The Tanzanian National Service proposals of 1966 were, it is true, concerned more with nation-building than with preparation for military engagement. But the component of military training has remained in the scheme, even as it was revised and reformulated in 1966.

There are convincing arguments as to why there should be a military component in the Tanzanian scheme and why there should be none in any scheme in Uganda. Tanzania's main dangers in military affairs have been, first, the threat of mutinous elements among the troops and, second, that of hostile contiguity with Portuguese Africa and the racist regimes of southern Africa. As an answer to the mutinous tendencies of professional soldiers, Nyerere decided to promote the nucleus of a people's army. He seemed to regard military training for ordinary citizens as a safeguard against a professional military challenge from regular troops. Tanzania's contiguity with colonialists and hostile neighbors also resulted at least in selective training for people in areas bordering hostile neighbors. In April, 1967, the second vice-president, Rashidi Kawawa, announced that all able-bodied men in Tanzanian villages bordering Mozambique were being "trained in the art of defending themselves." The immediate cause of equipping some villagers with arms seems to have been a series of incidents on the border involving military action by the Portuguese.[15] We might therefore say that from the point of view of balancing the power of professional soldiers and reducing the temptation to mutiny on the one hand, and from the point of view of being ready to deal with hostile neighbors on the other, there is a case for including military training in the Tanzanian National Service.

The situation in Uganda was different. The Obote proposals asserted that "the National Service should not be based on training in arms of war, but in arms for the sustained development of the economy, the raising of the standard of living, and the inculcation of national unity, integrity and a spirit of dedicated service to the Nation" (Article 4). In the philosophy of Obote's proposals there was, then, even more emphasis on the National Service as an exercise in national construction rather than as an exercise in military preparation.

In one sense Uganda might be considered not very different from Tanzania; both countries had experienced border conflicts and had been threatened by mutinous soldiers in the ranks. The army mutinies of early 1964 and the American-bought planes which disturbed the tranquility along the border with Congo-Kinshasa (now Zaïre) in 1965 indicated a degree of vulnerability to military hazards in Uganda comparable to that in Tanzania. But Uganda, with or without Obote, has an additional problem. It has internal ethnic cleavages which are

---

15. See "Tanzania Villagers Armed," *East African Standard* (Nairobi), April 19, 1967.

deeper than anything that Tanzania has experienced so far. Several parts of Uganda have been declared disturbed areas or have been placed, for basically domestic reasons, under a state of emergency, explicit or implicit. Actual confrontations between the central government's military forces and rebellious groups in different parts of the country have been known. In this kind of situation it does not make sense to maximize training in the use of arms or to disseminate such training widely throughout the population. Because Uganda faces the third danger of internal ethnic cleavages, with precedents ranging from the Rwenzururu uprising to the Buganda defiance, the country cannot really afford a National Service which makes a virtue of disseminating military skills or military sophistication throughout the population.

Some argued at the time that the lack of a military component in the Obote proposals exposed the country unnecessarily in its relations with other states. It left a large section of the population unready to meet the challenge of potential external aggression. But, in reality, internal disturbance is also a major factor to bear in mind. Tanzania is justified in its distrust of establishing a specialized professional army with a monopoly of military skills. But Obote, in contrast, was justified in insisting on such a professional army with precisely such a monopoly of military skills. The greater national integration that Tanzania had achieved, and its more extensive cultural homogeneity, supported its choice of policy; the special problems of Uganda justified an alternative approach.

In Tanzania the idea of popular readiness to defend the country against external aggression has been recurrent in political rhetoric for some time. The first vice-president of Tanzania, Sheikh Abeid Karume, was most enthusiastic in his vision of a militarized Tanzania. He had been known to forecast that by the year 1975 Tanzania would have an army of 2,000,000, and that "every able-bodied Tanzanian [would] be able to use a gun in defence of his motherland." Karume emphasized that it was through fighting and not through constitutional means that the people of Zanzibar and Pemba redeemed their rights and humanity. "It is through the barrel of the gun that those rights will be upheld."[16]

Although Karume carried the notion of a militarized democracy to an extreme, the idea has not been absent in Nyerere's rhetoric. On the eve of the first anniversary of the Arusha Declaration, Nyerere told thousands of young people at a mass rally that there were two weapons with which they could uphold the revolution — the first was the plow and the second was the gun. "The nation should have the spirit to develop its economy and the power to defend its independence."[17]

The Tanzanian National Service was conceived as a school to bridge these two ambitions of development and defense. At first, against the background of the mutinies, the values of discipline and obedience were strongly emphasized.

---

16. *Uganda Argus* (Kampala), February 7, 1968.
17. *Ibid.*, February 6, 1968.

Speaking at a passing-out parade of four companies of National Service youths who were about to join the Tanzania People's Defence Forces in May, 1965, Rashidi Kawawa stressed that the National Service was designed for hard work and obedience. "You must keep the discipline you have got from the National Service and not leave it in the camp. . . . Tomorrow you are going to join the army, but don't think that you will already be soldiers. You will always have to educate yourselves."[18]

In Uganda, on the other hand, domestic law and order continued to be a more immediate worry than external aggression. Arming civilian trainees might have increased rather than diminished the risks to internal law and order. But there was an alternative whereby the National Service could contribute to domestic tranquility that was to include in it a component of training for police duties. In April, 1969, the minister of state for the National Service in Obote's government, J. O. Anyoti, announced in the National Assembly that the National Service Bill had a provision for police work. His ministry would contribute effectively to the maintenance of law and order and the control of crime in general. In September, 1968, President Obote had held a meeting with senior police officers to discuss the proposals for including a provision for police work in the National Service Bill. The suggestion had been welcomed by the police. In elaborating the proposals, it had been indicated that recruitment in the villages of able-bodied men for the National Service would bear in mind their being trained in keeping law and order. The training would be sufficient to enable them to operate according to the basic rules of security work. The recruits would be given specific duties, and in some of the border regions they would get special training to deal with the peculiar nature of the situation existing there.[19]

In spite of these measures for handling border infiltrations and for dealing with militant refugees, it remains true that the basic thrust of Obote's National Service was, from the point of view of security, toward police work for domestic law and order rather than toward military preparedness for defense against external aggression or the creation of a people's army to reduce the danger of a challenge from a professional army. The Obote proposals stated that those young people who would be called up to do part of their national service in the subcounty camps "will also be trained in security work, particularly police work at the village level, concerning maintenance of law and order. Persons trained in this police work will be liable for call-up for police duties in their areas" (Article 27).

This may be the nearest that the Obote proposals came to approaching a literal sense of conscription. But on the whole the impulse behind the Uganda National Service was developmental in both an economic and a political

---

18. *Standard* (Dar es Salaam), May 1, 1965.
19. See *Uganda Argus*, April 3, 1969.

sense — integrative, agrarian, and egalitarian. The National Service was directed in part against all three kinds of idleness in the evolving social system of the country — the idleness of social redundancy and unemployment, the idleness of leisure, and the idleness of a culturally inhibited commitment to personal self-improvement. The Tanzanian experiment was less concerned with the last kind of idleness, since to cure it might be to release the ferocious demon of rugged and ambitious individualism. Behind both the Obote and Nyerere experiments was the search for effective ways of "mobilizing" resources and personnel for the long, drawn-out battle against economic underdevelopment and political fragility.

[15]

Cultural Engineering and
Socialized Technology

So far we have used the term *engineering* in a figurative sense, implying an analogy between nation-building and, for example, the construction of a bridge. The term *social technology* is also often used figuratively, denoting the technical and sociological know-how which is needed by the "social engineer." In this chapter we shall examine technology in its literal sense — the techniques of industrial and mechanical sciences, both basic and advanced. These techniques affect social structures and cultural patterns, and it is to this interplay of industrial and mechanical techniques on the one hand and social variables on the other that we shall now turn.

We shall first take a broad sweep of the subject and examine some of the major points which have emerged from the literature about the relationship between technological innovation and sociocultural change. We shall then focus the analysis more directly on Africa's experience and discuss not only the fact of technological change but also the speed of that change and its implications for the structure of values in African societies. Particular attention will be paid to President Nyerere's view of technological gradualism and what this implies for an ideology of socialistic transformation. The views of Kwame Nkrumah on the place of applied science within socialism will provide a foil to Nyerere's position. Finally, we shall consider the role of the plow in the development of a rural economy.

Material Challenge and Cultural Response

William F. Ogburn once distinguished between material culture and adaptive culture. By material culture he meant elements like factories, houses, machines, raw materials, manufactured products, foodstuffs, and the like. Material culture contains certain techniques for handling the elements involved in it. How a factory floor is organized, how a tool is handled, and what architectural style is used in building a house are all techniques *immediate* to material culture. But Ogburn pointed out the effects of material culture on a wider area of cultural behavior. Laws, political institutions, philosophical outlooks, systems of belief, and customs at large have an area of interaction with material conditions.

> One important function of government, for instance, is the adjustment of the population to the material conditions of life, although there are other governmental functions. [William Graham] Sumner has called many of these processes of adjustment "mores." The cultural adjustments to material conditions, however, include a larger body of processes than the mores; certainly they include the folkways and social institutions. These ways of adjustment may be called . . . "the adaptive culture." The adaptive culture is therefore that portion of the non-material which is adjusted or adapted to the material conditions.[1]

Ogburn pointed out that some parts of the nonmaterial culture are immediately adaptive, such as rules governing the handling of technical appliances, whereas other parts of the nonmaterial culture are only indirectly or partially adaptive, religion being one example. Family life and its organization are also part of the nonmaterial culture. The family makes some adjustments in response to material conditions, while other aspects of family life remain constant. Therefore, according to Ogburn the family is a part of the nonmaterial culture which is only selectively adaptive.

> When the material conditions change, changes are occasioned in the adaptive culture. But these changes in the adaptive culture do not synchronize exactly with the change in the material culture. There is a lag which may last for varying lengths of time, sometimes, indeed, for many years.[2]

So far Ogburn is quite persuasive. He becomes less so in his hypothesis that changes in the material culture precede changes in the adaptive culture. At first sight, he might appear to be right by definition. After all, the word *adaptive* implies that it is this sector of social life that is responsive, while material conditions pose the challenge. Yet the choice of the adjective *adaptive* in a manner which distinguishes it from material conditions begs the whole question. Material culture, in the sense of how houses are built or how factory life is organized or what kinds of tools are used, can "adapt" to nonmaterial institutions in the same way that material culture can condition nonmaterial culture.

Ogburn's position is certainly not a crude form of economic determinism; but it is a variation of historical materialism. His concept of a "cultural lag" between material changes and cultural adjustments echoes the concept of a moving equilibrium, which is implicit in certain schools of historical materialism. The main issue to be noted, however, is that Ogburn's concept of what is material is wider than the mere concept of what is economic. Another point to be noted is that Ogburn is eager to emphasize that his assertion regarding the primacy of the material culture is "not in the form of a universal dictum."

---

1. William Fielding Ogburn, *Social Change* (New York: Viking, 1922), pp. 202–3.
2. *Ibid.*, p. 203.

Conceivably, forms of adaptation might be worked out prior to a change in the material situation, and adaptation might be applied practically at the same time as the change in the material conditions. But such a situation presumes a very high degree of planning, prediction and control. . . . It is not implied that changes may not occur in non-material culture while the material culture remains the same. Art or education, for instance, may undergo many changes with a constant material culture. . . . Adjustment is therefore a relative term, and perhaps only in a few cases would there be a situation which might be called perfect adjustment or perfect lack of adjustment. . . . [However,] the collection of data, it is thought, will show that at the present time there are a very large number of cases where the material conditions change and the changes in the adaptive culture follow later.[3]

Even if we do reject Ogburn's assumption about the primacy of material phenomena, at least we have to concede the reality of reciprocal influence between cultural arrangements and the material conditions of life. Industrialization has profoundly changed certain aspects of the life style of the Japanese; but the organization of the factory, the relationship of discipline and deference to productivity, and the hours of work and rates of pay and their influence on the rate of industrialization illustrate the reverse impact of a hierarchical political culture upon the organization of productive forces.

We have discussed the manipulation of cultural factors in the direction of predetermined national goals and policies. We have analyzed throughout this book different aspects of this phenomenon of cultural engineering. But, as we have noted, the term *engineering* has so far been used figuratively. The question which now arises is whether there is a place for technology in the literal sense as an agent for cultural engineering. Alvin M. Weinberg posed the problem in this way: "Can technology replace social engineering?" Social problems are, after all, more complex than technological ones.

A social problem exists because many people behave, individually, in a socially unacceptable way. To solve a social problem one must induce social change — one must persuade many people to behave differently than they have behaved in the past. One must persuade many people to have fewer babies, or to drive more carefully, or to refrain from disliking Negroes. By contrast, resolution of a technological problem involves many fewer individual decisions. Once President Roosevelt decided to go after atomic energy, it was by comparison a relatively simple task to mobilise the Manhattan Project.[4]

Weinberg discusses the immense problems of trying to change motivational patterns, trying to modify habits deeply embedded in tradition. He cites the

---

3. *Ibid.*, pp. 211–12.
4. Alvin M. Weinberg, "Can Technology Replace Social Engineering?" *Bulletin of the Atomic Scientists*, XXII (December, 1966), 5.

example of rice-eaters in India preferring starvation to a diet of wheat imported from the United States. He contrasts the difficulties of the social engineer with the relative simplicity open to the technological engineer. The rocket, the reactor, and the desalination appliance might be expensive to develop; but their feasibility is more immediate, and their success is easy to achieve once the scientific principles that underlie them are mastered.

Weinberg then moves on to the critical issue. In view of this simplicity of technological engineering in contrast to the complexity which meets the social engineer, to what extent can social problems be circumvented by reducing them to technological problems?

> Can we identify quick Technological Fixes for profound and almost infinitely complicated social problems, "Fixes" that are within the grasp of modern technology, and which would either eliminate the original social problem without requiring a change in the individual's social attitudes, or would so alter the problem as to make its resolution more feasible? . . . To what extent can technological remedies be found for social problems without first having to remove the causes of the problem? It is in this sense that I ask: "Can technology replace social engineering?" [5]

One example Weinberg gives is ideologically controversial. He argues that the Marxian view of poverty has been overtaken by technology. In the Marxian view, economic problems are regarded as being primarily an outcome of maldistribution of goods. In Marx's later theory of value, the question of poverty is reduced to the issue of profit. Marx envisaged the abolition of poverty in terms of the elimination of profit in economic relations. Marx was, therefore, primarily a social engineer — trying to convince or coerce many people to forgo their short-term profits in the belief that this renunciation would result in the long-term welfare of the society as a whole.

But technology has greatly enhanced the productive capacity of technologically advanced societies. Distribution of goods is still uneven and might be regarded as unfair by Marxian standards, but advances in the technology of energy, of mass production, and of automation have indeed resulted in the affluent society.

> Technology has provided a "Fix" — greatly expanded production of goods — which enables our capitalist society to achieve many of the aims of the Marxist social engineer without going through the social revolution Marx viewed as inevitable. Technology has converted the seemingly intractable social problem of widespread poverty into a relatively tractable one.[6]

---

5. *Ibid.* See also Hasu H. Patel, "Technology and Culture: Some Problems and Prospects for Africa," in *Proceedings of the International Seminar on Africa in World Affairs: The Next Thirty Years*, Makerere University, Kampala, December, 1969.

6. Weinberg, "Can Technology Replace Social Engineering?" p. 5.

Marx's prediction that the poor of the capitalist world would get poorer while the rich would get richer was partially nullified by something that he himself had witnessed — the coming of the sophisticated technological era. The rich of the capitalist world did get richer, but the poor did not get poorer. The latter prediction was negated by the expanding activity afforded by technological breakthroughs.

A more modest illustration concerns the issue of safety on the roads. How can traffic deaths be reduced? How can people be taught to drive more carefully? Weinberg cites Ralph Nader's observation that a safer car, and its development and promotion by the car industry in the United States, is a quicker and probably a surer way to reduce traffic deaths than is a campaign to teach people to drive more carefully.

This area of experience might be called "socialized technology." The word *technology* is used here in a literal sense, implying a scientific, technical body of knowledge which uses principles of physics and natural forces to meet specified practical needs. Technology is normally, in any case, utilized for some social purposes. But our concept of *socialized* technology examines the functions of technology not only in terms of their primary purposes but also in terms of their wider social repercussions. New breakthroughs in the utilization of energy may result in expanded productivity. Thus, increased productivity might be seen as falling within the primary purposes of the innovation. But if the diffusion of the new modes of production also results in rising levels of affluence in the society, in better-fed children, for example, these latter repercussions would fall within the secondary, and wider, social significance of the innovations.

When technology is deliberately utilized with the secondary as well as the primary purposes in mind, it has indeed become socialized. When a society does embark on utilizing technology in this way, any innovation in productive techniques is assessed not merely in terms of balance of profit and efficiency of output but also in terms of impact on the quality of life of all those engaged in that enterprise. Technology, then, becomes an agency for social reform as well as an instrument for material innovation. To return to the terms we used previously, socialized technology purposefully manipulates material conditions in order to effect changes in the "adaptive culture."

Montesquieu, the French philosopher, attributed important conditioning power to climatic factors. Climate was, in his view, part of the explanation for political behavior and even for certain types of political institutions. A more modest claim might be that fluctuations in the weather affect political behavior. Samuel Huntington has suggested that race rioting in the United States can be correlated with hot, humid weather. The social engineer would seek to cope with race rioting by improving race relations and eliminating the causes of discontent. But a "technological fix" for the same problem would entail installing air conditioning and free electricity in the black ghetto to reduce the riot potential of humid heat.

[251]

Technological Gradualism

What is sometimes at stake in planning for technological change is not so much a question of deciding to introduce a certain technological innovation in order to affect certain patterns of social behavior as a question of deciding the *speed* of technological change. Of the three East African countries, Tanzania has been most conscious of the relevance of speed in the interaction of technology and social principles. Nyerere's Tanzania has been attempting a combination of ideological revolution and technological gradualism. In ideology the commitment is to the creation and maintenance of a revolutionary egalitarian ethic, seeking to create social accord and economic development without creating social and economic inequalities. Combined with this revolutionary egalitarian quest is a belief in technological pragmatism, a reluctance to undergo rapid technological change in spite of the commitment to rapid social transformation. To some extent, it is almost as if Nyerere were aware that the relationship between technology and egalitarianism is a tense one. The most egalitarian African societies have been the least technologically advanced.

Class differentiation is due not only to income but also to life style. Life styles in the less technologically advanced African societies are relatively even. The principle of distribution of goods was developed partly because the existing technology allowed neither for diversity of production nor for effective ways of preservation and exchange of products. There was a limited amount of grain that a chief could eat; what he had accumulated beyond his own consumption capacity became subject to general distribution. The situation echoed some of the postulates of John Locke's theory of the origins of society. According to Locke, the earth was given to mankind in common to share, but each individual had a right to invest his labor in production and thereby derive a title to what he produced. But each man was entitled only to that which he could meaningfully make use of without waste. Accumulation beyond the limits of individual consumption and utilization was wasteful and therefore illegitimate. This, of course, presupposed a society that had neither elaborated an efficient system of preserving the fruit of the earth nor created an effective system of exchange by barter or monetary circulation.

Whatever the reasons in the case of Africa's experience, the simpler societies managed, by the very rudimentary nature of their technology, to maintain a system of distributive equity and limited power differentials. In the words of Max Gluckman:

> The tribal economy was simple and undifferentiated: even in a good year the available technology did not allow a man to produce much beyond his own needs. There was little trade and luxury, so even a conqueror could not make himself more comfortable than he had been before. One cannot build a palace with grass

and mud, and if the only foods are grains, milk and meat, one cannot live much above the standard of ordinary men.[7]

The social complexities which came with technological efficiency gradually sharpened differences in life styles and increased gaps in power. In such African societies, technology had the effect of disrupting the egalitarian inclinations of traditional modes of organization.

In Tanzania, Nyerere's ambition has been to move from the egalitarian principles of some of these traditional African societies to modern socialism, without passing through the inequalities of capitalistic industrialization. Nyerere's concept of *Ujamaa*, implying the transformation of the bonds of kinship into a kind of socialistic solidarity, seeks precisely to emphasize this transition from primordial egalitarianism and fellowship to modern socialism. Nyerere has recurrently emphasized that Africa does not need to be taught socialism, for the principles of hospitality and social obligation are rooted in African organization.

In reality, the egalitarianism which Nyerere has mentioned was more effectively demonstrated in technologically simple African societies, and so technology has become a major factor to be borne in mind in deciding whether Tanzania can move from tribal collectivism to modern socialism without undergoing the pangs of social inequities. The trouble is that very modest technological innovation can have profound consequences for social stratification. If social stratification includes the factors of prestige and life style as well as income, even modest innovations coming into African societies can have unintended social repercussions.

Leonard W. Doob once referred to the complex repercussions following the introduction of the bicycle in a developing society. Here the issue of primary functions and secondary functions becomes relevant. At the level of the primary functions of a bicycle, its introduction entails the need to learn "a new set of motor skills" if the users are to keep their balance and pedal forward. These skills are predictable. But, in addition, there is the secondary level of the bicycle's functions.

> Other consequences of learning to cycle . . . may have little or at least no definite, predictable relation to the machine itself — the status of those who buy and ride it, the kind and amount of impediments (other than people) transported by cycle, the effects on social relations resulting from the greater freedom to move about, or, in general, the personality traits of the cyclists that are modified or acquired.[8]

There are other aspects of technological change. Goods arising out of

---

7. Max Gluckman, "The Rise of a Zulu Empire," *Scientific American*, CCII, no. 4 (1960), 166.

8. Leonard W. Doob, "Psychological Aspects of Planned Developmental Change," in *Perspectives in Developmental Change*, ed. Art Gallagher, Jr. (Lexington: University of Kentucky Press, 1968), pp. 41–42.

technological advancement profoundly affect consumption patterns in African societies. Expectations of style of life and levels of luxury had to be transformed when certain items appeared on the market and seemed to be not entirely beyond acquisition. The phenomenon of migration to the cities, the contraction of subsistence agriculture, the growth of wage-labor, and change in the life style of rural areas were all inevitably brought about in certain African countries by the impact of technology on individual ambition and consumption patterns. Philip Gulliver observed that wage-labor has become a means of acquiring nontraditional commodities such as radios, Western clothing, and bus tickets, as well as more traditional commodities such as cattle, tools, and bridewealth.[9]

With independence, consumption patterns have expanded in some sectors of society. The Mercedes Benz, for example, has become a symbol of modernity, at once mechanized and luxurious. Political leaders have attacked utilization of the Mercedes Benz more often than they have defended it. But Tom Mboya once defended the Mercedes in Kenya as a symbolic device for raising the ambitions of people. A country without symbolic goals for the exertions of its citizens was, in Mboya's view, "a colourless society." In a country which permits social mobility and enables people to rise and acquire things they did not have before, new levels of luxury are themselves incentives for citizens to plan for their futures and struggle for achievement. In order to make people apply themselves more, it is necessary to convince them that it will make a difference in their lives. New levels of exertion demand a demonstration that things are, in Mboya's words, "going to happen." The Mercedes Benz as a piece of technological opulence becomes for the ambitious citizen a symbol of "new worlds to conquer." Mboya said:

> If I can afford it there is no reason why I shouldn't buy one. We don't all have to go on bicycles to show that we are committed to our people. In fact our people need to have some ambition as a driving force in their efforts to self improvement. . . . You can't really think you're going to try and create a colourless society in this country. . . . It has been tried before in Russia and it was decided that no one should earn more than three hundred roubles regardless of his job, his station in life and so on. This is the kind of attitude or approach which is really negative because it can lead people to assuming that things are not going to happen.[10]

But technology does not simply influence consumption; it also influences production. Nyerere in Tanzania has attempted to curb both the trend toward domestic technological opulence and the tendency toward premature commitment to rapid industrialization. The Leadership Resolutions of the Arusha Declaration,

---

9. Philip H. Gulliver, "Incentives in Labor Migration," *Human Organization*, XIX, no. 3 (Fall, 1960), 159–61.

10. Tom Mboya, "This So-called Elite," interview by Viviene Barton, *Sunday Nation* (Nairobi), April 27, 1969.

and the entire ethos of an austere life style for Tanzania's leaders, have attempted to handle the issue of social ostentation arising out of new levels of domestic consumption. The austerity has not gone to the extent of frowning on the use of refrigerators in houses, though it has resisted the idea of having national television. Tanzania is the only country in East Africa without television. As for the task of resisting the rapid application of sophisticated technology, this has been more an attitude of mind than a formal policy. But it has been an attitude of mind that is very conscious, influenced in part precisely by the desire to prevent a very rapid leap from the egalitarian simplicity of traditional Tanzania to a destabilizing mechanization of the countryside.

On August 5, 1967, Nyerere spoke at a teach-in on the Arusha Declaration organized by the branch of the TANU Youth League at University College, Dar es Salaam. To this teach-in Nyerere said:

> Our future lies in the development of our agriculture and in the development of our rural areas. But because we are seeking to grow from our own roots and to preserve that which is valuable in our traditional past, we have also to stop thinking in terms of massive agricultural mechanisation and the proletarianisation of our rural population. We have, instead, to think in terms of development through the improvement of the tools we now use, and through the growth of cooperative systems of production. Instead of aiming at large farms using tractors and other modern equipment and employing agricultural labourers, we should be aiming at having ox ploughs all over the country. The jembe [hoe] will have to be eliminated by the ox plough before the latter can be eliminated by the tractor. We cannot hope to eliminate the jembe by the tractor.[11]

On Science and Self-Reliance

In linking socialism to technological gradualism, Julius Nyerere was following a path somewhat different from that taken by the other great figure in the stream of socialistic ideas in Africa, Kwame Nkrumah. To Nkrumah, both socialism and science were processes of modernization, and they needed to go together. Nkrumah did not interpret the concept of "scientific socialism" merely in the Marxist sense of principles of socialism arrived at through a scientific method of analysis; he interpreted "scientific socialism" as an ideology which believed not only in the pursuit of social justice but also in the quest for scientific progress. Socialism to Nkrumah was both an ethic of distribution and an ideology of development. In its capacity as an ideology of development, socialism had to put a premium on science and technological advancement as principles of social reform. In the ceremony at which he laid the foundation stone of Ghana's

---

11. Julius Nyerere, "The Purpose Is Man," in *Freedom and Socialism* (London: Oxford University Press, 1968), p. 320.

atomic reactor center in Kwabenya, near Accra, Nkrumah said that neither Ghana nor Africa could afford to lag behind other nations in the nuclear age. Development was, in part, a utilization of power.

> We have therefore been compelled to enter the field of atomic energy because this already promises to yield the greatest economic source of power since the beginning of man. . . . We must ourselves take part in the pursuit of scientific and technological research as a means of providing the basis for our socialist society. Socialism without science is void.[12]

New nations are attracted to socialism sometimes because they presume that since it is a rationalistic ideology, it must also have a scientific outlook. Radical reformers in Africa, like those in China before them, sometimes see in the scientific spirit the fuel of historical mobility and social dynamism. David E. Apter once said:

> In so far as Marxism is a philosophy of science, it is also a philosophy of social engineering and can therefore be thrust into the heart of the ancient high culture of a country such as China to destroy the past in the name of the future — a process which is also going on in Africa. This is one of the reasons why socialism is so prevalent as a political ideology among political leaders.[13]

But Apter touched upon an important distinction in bringing us back to the dichotomy between the laboratory and the workshop. Although there are times when political leaders are not fully sensitized to the difference between pure science and applied science and might be inclined to revere both forms, it is in reality the applied phenomenon which, in sober moments, commands special respect.

> Faced with the immense problems of building new societies and preventing chaos, it is the political leaders of new nations who come closest to the scientific culture, since as social engineers they possess an optimism similar to that of the scientists. . . . In new countries, immediate service to the community is the sole object of science. . . . As a result, it is not those who represent the scientific culture who find a place in the new nations, but rather the men whom [C.P.] Snow regards as falling away from that tradition in its philosophical sense, i.e., the engineers and the technicians. These practical men set the goals in most new nations, along with the social engineers — the politicians.[14]

Apter was exaggerating the interaction of engineers and politicians in new nations,

---

12. *Ghana Today*, VIII, no. 21 (December 16, 1964), 1.
13. David E. Apter, "New Nations and the Scientific Revolution," *Bulletin of the Atomic Scientists*, XVII, no. 2 (February, 1961), 61.
14. *Ibid.*, pp. 62–63.

but he was certainly right in his assumption that applied science has a special mystique to social and cultural engineers. In Nkrumah's vision of social transformation, which Apter studied in depth and at close quarters, Apter did find ample evidence for this interpretation.

What must not be overlooked is the alternative school, represented by Julius Nyerere. In Nyerere's view, the introduction of technology is most compatible with socialism when that technology is subject to the principle of planning. And planning, in turn, has to be assessed by criteria which include the principle of self-implementation. Thus, technology has to be introduced into a developing society piecemeal, taking into account the capacity of the society to absorb it and putting a premium on the ideas of self-implementation and self-management.

It is because of this frame of reasoning that Tanzania's socialism since 1967, and to some extent before that, has placed a high value on the ethic of self-reliance. The Arusha Declaration was a declaration of *Ujamaa na Kujitegemea* ("Socialism and Self-Reliance"). A number of principles have been derived from the union of these concepts. The National Service scheme of 1966 was beginning to emphasize the idea of exertion. And, even before that, the schemes of self-help in 1963 augured well for the ethic of maximum utilization of local resources by local energies.

The interpretation of development within the Arusha Declaration began to put more emphasis on the availability of labor in Tanzania and less on the importation of capital. The Arusha Declaration asserted that those who saw development in terms of the importation of foreign investment and foreign aid mistook the subsidiary for the fundamental. Foreign investment and foreign aid could help development, but development in Tanzania did not rely on money. Money was what came after development had taken place. The ultimate power of the people of Tanzania in relation to the task of development was their readiness to work hard and use the means at their disposal.

> We will continue to use money; and each year we will use more money for the various development projects than we used the previous year, but this will be one of the signs of our development. What we are saying, however, is that from now on we shall know what is the foundation and what is the fruit of development. Between *money* and *people* it is obvious that the people and their *hard work* are the foundation of development, and money is one of the fruits of that hard work.[15]

But, in the scientific age, when is an African country self-reliant? Nkrumah's answer was that self-reliance consisted in a speedy entry into the nuclear age. The nuclear reactor that he inaugurated was an extravagance which Ghana could

---

15. Nyerere, "The Arusha Declaration: Socialism and Self-Reliance," in *Freedom and Socialism*, pp. 246–47. Emphasis original.

not really afford. Part of the extravagance lay in the fact that Ghana was not yet capable of self-managing or self-implementing projects based on the availability of the reactor.

In the case of Nyerere, on the other hand, it is not enough to call technology "applied science." There is still the question, Who does the application? If Tanzania's capacity for technology is still rudimentary, that should be taken into account in planning the phases and steps for introducing technology. In the words of the Arusha Declaration:

> Because of our emphasis on money, we have made another big mistake. We have put too much emphasis on industries. . . . The mistake we are making is to think that development begins with industries. It is a mistake because we do not have the means to establish many modern industries in our country. We do not have either the necessary finances or the technical know-how. It is not enough to say that we shall borrow the finances and technicians from other countries to come and start the industries. . . . Even if we could get the necessary assistance, dependence on it could interfere with our policy on socialism.[16]

In August, 1967, when Nyerere was elaborating on the meaning of the Arusha Declaration at the teach-in in Dar es Salaam, he formulated his theory of technological gradualism more clearly.

> Instead of thinking about providing each farmer with his own lorry, we should consider the usefulness of oxen-drawn carts, which could be made within the country and which are appropriate both to our roads and to the loads which each farmer is likely to have. Instead of the aerial spraying of crops with insecticide, we should use hand-operated pumps, and so on. In other words, we have to think in terms of what is available, or can be made available, at comparatively small costs, and which can be operated by the people. By moving into the future along this path, we can avoid massive social disruption and human suffering.[17]

The Plow and the Green Revolution

It is in the same context that we should place Nyerere's vision of a move from a culture of the hoe to a culture of the plow in rural Tanzania. Indeed, one of the main reasons why large areas of Africa were left behind even in elementary agricultural technology was that the plow bypassed those areas.[18] To revert to Ogburn's distinction, Nyerere's recommendation that the hoe be replaced by the ox-plow might cause a change in material culture; but, historically,

---

16. *Ibid.*, pp. 241–42.
17. Nyerere, "The Purpose Is Man," p. 320.
18. See Jack Goody, *Technology, Tradition and the State in Africa* (London: Oxford University Press, 1971), p. 25.

such replacements have also brought about changes with wide consequences for the "adaptive" culture. At the more immediate level flow the consequences of higher productivity. The area of land an individual can cultivate increases significantly. Surplus food for exchange may promote specialist crafts. Accumulation of the proceeds of productivity, combined with the availability of newer luxury goods, may cause an emphasis on differences in life style and sharpen the cultural class divergence between urban and rural areas. Moreover, the cultivation of bigger tracts of land increases the importance of the principle of individual possession, reduces the possibility of moving from plot to plot, raises the value of arable land, and initiates the end of shifting agriculture.

Other areas of the adaptive culture might also be reformed by replacing the hoe with the plow. Among these is the status of women and their role in the economic life of society. In many parts of Africa women have had a critical role in the economy, and they have certainly been important agents of cultivation on the farm. The economic power of women has not always resulted in their having a high social status, though it has sometimes done so. But experience elsewhere in the world suggests that the hoe culture tends to give a big and sometimes weary role to women in farming, whereas the plow culture reinstates the supremacy of men in the economy.

William McNeill traces a progression from hunting and gathering to hoe agriculture and then to plow agriculture. In hunting societies and pastoral societies, men tended to rank higher than women. Killing wild animals or controlling large domestic animals was regarded as primarily a man's job. With the coming of the hoe and settled agriculture, masculine primacy in the economy was no longer automatic. On the contrary, many hoe societies developed a central economic role for women, which sometimes evolved into an elaborate matrilineal organization. With the coming of the plow, pulled by an animal, men in the history of Europe and Asia became, once again, the principal providers of food. Nor was it only the immediate economic culture that was affected. Masculine primacy was resurrected in the family and in society at large. Patrilinealism began to reassert itself among plowing peoples in the Middle East. Over a period of time, religion also responded to these changes. The emergence of male deities and male priests, characterizing the new spiritual organizations of Egypt and the Fertile Crescent, may also have been connected with the new masculine role in agriculture.[19]

Many centuries later, when an African president in Tanzania sounded a clarion call to replace the hoe with the ox-plow, he was in fact urging a change which elsewhere had had a variety of repercussions. In East Africa, the stabilization of the ox-plow as the central aspect of agriculture might affect the sexual division of labor in the economy. This, in turn, might also affect other areas of adaptive

---

19. See William H. McNeill, *The Rise of the West: A History of the Human Community* (Chicago: University of Chicago Press, 1963), pp. 24–26.

culture. The phenomenon of labor migration in Africa, with men going to the towns and to the mines while women tend the farms, could be significantly modified, if not arrested. The re-emergence of masculine primacy on the farm might discourage men from drifting to the cities and the mines and keep them busy in the rural areas tending the oxen and sharpening the plow-blades.

Men have drifted from the countryside partly because the women could cope with the scale of agriculture practiced there and partly because the output of that agriculture was not enough to meet the new levels of consumption generated by improvements elsewhere. The effective introduction of the plow could undermine both these reasons for labor migration. It could make it more difficult for the women to cope with the new technology and with the larger areas of land under cultivation. It could also result in significantly increased productivity, which would make farming economically more rewarding than wage-labor in the towns.

Until now, animals have been used in East African societies for milk, meat, and bridewealth. They have not been used as "horsepower" or "oxpower." But, again, the history of Europe and Asia offers illuminating precedents:

> Perhaps a growing shortage of cultivable land compelled or encouraged technical innovation and improvement. . . . The problem this presented to peoples accustomed to slash-and-burn agriculture was solved by two basic inventions. One was fallowing, the other the traction plough. The two were closely connected. Only the most back-breaking labour could maintain a substantial area of fallow in good tilth without the use of animal power. But once someone had hit upon the idea of hitching a modified spade behind one or more animals and exploiting the beast's strength to break the ground, it became relatively easy for an ordinary family to cultivate more land than was needed to feed its members.[20]

In East Africa, the persistence of labor migration has been partly due to the persistence of subsistence agriculture. By helping to push agriculture beyond the limits of mere subsistence, the ox-plow, if introduced widely in East African societies, could stabilize the rural population precisely by making agriculture more productive. In some areas an important precondition for such a technological breakthrough might be more effective control of the tsetse fly. Oxen and horses must be able to survive before they can become agricultural power. In other areas more subtle cultural changes might need to be brought about before animals highly prized for other purposes could be used for tilling and plowing the land. The range of customs likely to be affected by the introduction of the plow in East Africa may vary from bridewealth to labor migration and from diet to sexual division of labor.

The full acceptance of the plow might also initiate social and economic change among such obstinately pastoral peoples as the Masai in Kenya and Tanzania

---

20. *Ibid.*, p. 24.

and the Karamojong in Uganda. The culture of these peoples has been predicated on the utilization of cattle. But that utilization, as we have intimated, has tended to limit itself to milk, meat, and the use of cattle for exchange relations. The question which arises is whether the use of animals for cultivation might be for the pastoralists less of a leap than the adoption of the hoe. Certainly, the adoption of the hoe has tended in some of these groups to have all the connotations of female labor and has therefore fallen short of full masculine dignity. But cultivating the land with animal power, with the man still semicontrolling an ox but with a more immediate job in hand, might be just the intermediate stage necessary to help the defiant pastoralists of East Africa move on to mixed agriculture. Here, again, the precedent set in the history of Europe and Asia provides pertinent insights:

> The use of animal power also established a much more integral relation between stockbreeding and agriculture. Mixed farming, uniting animal husbandry with crop cultivation, was to become a distinguishing characteristic of agriculture in western Eurasia. It made possible a higher standard of living or of leisure than was attainable by peoples relying mainly or entirely upon the strength of merely human muscles.[21]

Jack Goody attributes the slow arrival of the plow in Africa partly to the absence of that other basic technological innovation, the wheel. The wheel did indeed cross the Sahara, both in the west, as two-wheeled chariots engraved on Saharan boulders indicate, and in the east, namely, in Ethiopia and in the Sudan. But in much of the rest of precolonial Africa the wheel was absent; and this affected, among other things, the pattern of agricultural organization and delayed the evolution of the more sophisticated plows.[22]

A start has been made. Even in Karamoja the ox-plow has made a modest appearance. But, whatever the reasons for the delay in the arrival of the plow in East African societies, its increased promotion could transform the lives of the Karamojong and the Masai. A new green revolution could come to East Africa. Such a transformation might be a measure of the substantial developmental power of a modest technological innovation in relation to cultural change at large.

---

21. *Ibid.*, p. 26.
22. Jack Goody, *Technology, Tradition and the State in Africa*, pp. 25–26. See also Thomas R. de Gregori, *Technology and the Economic Development of the Tropical African Frontier* (Cleveland: Press of Case Western Reserve University, 1969), esp. chap. 4, "The Technological History of Sub-Saharan Africa," pp. 83–182.

[16]

Cultural Engineering and Militarized Technology

Technology in East Africa has made a difference not merely in the economic sphere but in the military sphere as well. Changes of profound political and psychological significance have arisen out of the modernization of military skills and the emergence of armed forces as actors on the national scene. From the point of view of political sociology, the most important consequences of the emergence of the modern army in Africa are reducible to two areas of impact. The first area concerns the consolidation of statehood, and the second concerns the diversification of the class structures.

It is a hypothesis of this chapter that the emergence of the modern army in African countries is a critical variable toward the centralization of power in the polity and therefore an important stage toward the emergence of state structures of authority. A second hypothesis is that the emergence of the modern army in African countries has broken the correlation between political power and Western education, interrupting the trend toward the dictatorship of the educated class in modern African history. The *Lumpenproletariat* is a mass of disorganized workers and ghetto-dwellers in the developed world; but the *Lumpenmilitäriat* is that class of semiorganized and semiliterate soldiers which has begun to claim a share of power and influence in what would otherwise have become a heavily privileged meritocracy of the educated.

The third hypothesis of this chapter is that the history of modernization in independent Africa might well be a gradual transition from the political supremacy of those who hold the means of destruction, as might be the trend in the first two or three decades of independence, to the future political supremacy of those who control the means of production. The initial phases of technological development in a relatively backward society, to the extent that they are applied to both military and civilian areas of life, tend to widen the gap of power between the unarmed citizenry on the one side and those who control the new means of war on the other. It is only after the society has become more technologically complex, and factories and laboratories have generated their own power-holders, that the means of production become critical enough to the survival of national systems to provide a countervailing balance to the power exercised by the military.

Those who control the means of production — workers, managers, and owners — are most powerful in relation to soldiers in situations of technological complexity. They are weakest in relation to soldiers in situations of rudimentary technology, symbolized both by the new cotton mill in the midst of rural backwardness and by the machine gun in a society which still experiences cattle raids with spears.

Technology and Centralization of Violence

In the first hypothesis, that the emergence of the modern army is a step toward the consolidation of statehood in African countries, the concept of statehood is derived partly from the implication of Max Weber's definition. Weber asserted that the state could not be defined sociologically in terms of its ends. Maintenance of law and order, preservation of society, promotion of the well-being of the community, and control or suppression of deviant behavior may all be central to the purposes of the state. Yet Weber's point was that there is scarcely any task performed by the state which some political association has not taken in hand, and that there is no task which has always been exclusive and peculiar to those associations which are designated as political ones. To Weber, the modern state could be defined sociologically only in terms of the specific means peculiar to it, namely, the use of physical force.

Weber quoted Trotsky's belief that "every state is founded on force." Weber conceded that force is not the normal or the only means of the state, but he regarded it as a means specific to the state.

> Today the relation between the state and violence is an especially intimate one. In the past, the most varied institutions — beginning with the sib — had known the use of physical force as quite normal. Today, however, we have to say that a state is a human community that "successfully" claims the monopoly of the *legitimate use of physical force* within a given territory. Specifically, at the present time, the right to use physical force is ascribed to other institutions or to individuals only to the extent to which the state permits it. The state is considered the sole source of the "right" to use violence.[1]

Uganda was the first East African country to experience a military coup. Yet it can hardly be stated that the use of physical force in Uganda has been concentrated in the hands of the institutions of the state. On the contrary, one of the staggering aspects of life in Uganda is the phenomenon of decentralized violence. The country has one of the highest per capita rates of homicide in the world. Nor is the violence perpetrated only by deviants and antisocial crimi-

---

1. Max Weber, "Politics as a Vocation" (Speech delivered at Munich University, 1918), in *From Max Weber: Essays in Sociology*, ed. H. H. Gerth and C. Wright Mills (1946; reprint ed., London: Routledge & Kegan Paul, 1957), p. 78.

nals. On the contrary, there is the recurrent phenomenon of thieves or suspected thieves being beaten to death by indignant villagers. In other words, villagers take the law into their own hands, judge the suspects they have captured, and inflict the often fatal punishment. This form of physical coercion is therefore by no means monopolized by the state or the institutions of the central government. Local communities in different parts of Uganda have assumed the right to initiate violence as retribution against thieves and other antisocial elements.[2]

When the army took over in Uganda, on January 25, 1971, *kondoism*, or robbery with violence, was already common. Obote's government, in desperation, had even made robbery with violence a capital offense — to the consternation of those who feared that this would not reduce the violence but increase the number of murders committed in eliminating witnesses to robberies. Following the coup, in the wake of instability and uncertainty about the survival of legitimate authority, *kondoism* occurred even more frequently. There was also suspicion that some members of Obote's Intelligence Department, stripped of power and disgraced, used the firearms they had acquired from the previous regime for new purposes. It was suspected that old informers were becoming *kondos*, taking up gangsterism and armed thuggery.

What is even more significant from the point of view of this analysis is the way in which the military regime sought to claim a monopoly of the legitimate use of physical force. On the night of March 18, 1971, the government issued two decrees. The first gave the armed forces the power to search houses and other buildings, vehicles, and aircraft, and to take possession of vehicles, stolen property, and dangerous weapons. The campaign was designed, in the words of the attorney general, to "stamp out the scourge of *kondoism*." The second decree gave members of the armed forces and prison officers the power to arrest persons for offenses against public order, against other persons, relating to property.

> In simple terms the offences listed are the sort of offences committed by *kondos*. For example, armed robbery and armed attacks on defenceless members of the community. Members of the armed forces and prison officers are given power to search houses and other buildings and motor cars and aircraft if they have reason to believe that a person who is to be arrested is in any of those places or anything stolen may be found in such places. They may also take possession of vehicles, stolen property and dangerous weapons. . . . The Decree will remain in force for twelve months. It is hoped that before that time has expired *kondoism* will have been banished from Uganda.[3]

---

2. These issues are discussed more fully in Ali A. Mazrui, "Civic Violence and Political Violence in Uganda and the United States" (Paper delivered at the World Congress of the International Sociological Association, Varna, Bulgaria, September, 1970). See also Colin Leys, "Violence in Africa," *Transition*, V, no. 21 (1965), 17–20.

3. Statement by the attorney general, *Uganda Argus* (Kampala), March 19, 1971.

Even before these decrees, soldiers were being used to patrol certain streets of Kampala, following repeated burglaries. There was also a vigorous attempt to prevent armed political victimization of supporters of the former Obote regime by other civilians.

In general, what the new military regime was doing in trying to centralize power and monopolize violence was what was to be expected of any central government in such a situation. The relevance of military technology to this phenomenon arises out of the gap which modern weaponry creates between the army and armed civilians in African conditions. In parts of East Africa military skills are still assessed in terms of prowess in handling spears and in using the bow and arrow. The centralization of power and the consolidation of authority in Uganda would have been even more difficult if the armed forces had not been equipped both with relatively modern weapons and with relatively rapid technological mobility.

Even the use of the metal spear was a significant variable in emerging kingdoms in Africa. A culture using metal was at least closer to statehood than was a combat culture based on the bow and arrow. In the words of Jack Goody:

> The bow and arrow is essentially a democratic weapon; every man knows how to construct one; the materials are readily available, the techniques uncomplicated, the missiles easy to replace (though more difficult with the introduction of iron that affected even hunting people like the Hadza of Tanzania and the Bushmen of the Kalahari). . . . With the technologies of the bow and stone-tipped arrow any kind of centralization is almost impossible. But with the introduction of metals, kingdoms are on the cards.[4]

In the case of the original kingdoms, the uneven distribution of raw materials involved systems of exchange and often long-distance trade, which therefore necessitated systems of control and security. Centralization was also encouraged by the relatively complicated process of manufacturing metal weapons.

> In some areas of West Africa we find special kin-guilds of blacksmiths who hand down their traditions among their members; and in centralised groups such as Mossi the members of the guilds often have a special relationship with royalty, who are often their major patrons. But elsewhere (among the acephalous LoDagaa, for example), smiths are not restricted. Even here, however, such individuals have a special role to play in the maintenance of peace, perhaps to counter-balance their role as manufacturers of arms.[5]

With the coming of the rifle in colonial Africa and the tank in independent Africa, military elitism became even more pronounced. The old days of military

---

4. Jack Goody, *Technology, Tradition and the State in Africa* (London: Oxford University Press, 1971), pp. 43–46.
5. *Ibid.*, p. 46.

democracy, when everyone passed through the warrior stage and the weapons were the simple ones capable of being manufactured by the warrior himself, were replaced by the era of professional military specialists, with weapons requiring a high level of technological skill to manufacture and some specialized training to use. The Uganda Army might not have a monopoly of armed force; it has even lost a monopoly of certain types of firearms, partly because of theft from the armories. But in the totality of concentrated technological power of destruction, the army in an African country like Uganda is in a position to assert special rights of primacy.

There is a built-in inclination on the part of a national army to engage in active prevention of separatism. Although there have been civil wars in Africa which have included the defection of important sectors of the armed forces to support regional or ethnic separatism, even those civil wars illustrate the compelling urge at the center of power to prevent a successful bid to secede. In the absence of external warfare and preparation for distant military adventures, national armed forces in Africa very often find a special sense of mission in seeking to keep the inherited territories intact. And, given the fact that Africa was in an age of postspear combat, the capacity of national armies to maintain national integrity has been much enhanced by modest improvements in weaponry and military carriers.

Slight differences in technological capability between different segments of the armed forces can be decisive in affecting the fortunes of a coup. For example, the coup in Uganda was a victory of the mechanized battalion in control of armored vehicles against the numerically more preponderant soldiers from Acholi and Lango in possession of less mobile weaponry. A relatively small segment of the armed forces in Uganda succeeded in outwitting the rest of the army and in ejecting Milton Obote after eight years in power, simply because that small segment had acquired technological superiority by pre-empting the control of armored vehicles.

But in Uganda, too, the political intervention of the armed forces has consequently generated separatist tendencies in areas that are not firmly under control. Nevertheless, the propensity of the central army to maintain territorial integrity remains as effectively illustrated in Uganda's experience as elsewhere. And the technological superiority enjoyed by the forces of the central army retains a critical relevance in the slow evolution of structures that seek to monopolize violence and centralize power.

On Soldiers and Social Stratification

According to the second hypothesis of this chapter, the emergence of the modern army in African countries has interrupted the trend toward rule by the well educated. Precisely because military technology puts such a substantial power differential on the side of the soldiers, the phenomenon has a profound relevance for the diversification of the class structure in independent Africa. As Africa approached independence, there was considerable evidence that it was evolving a power elite based on education. In some African societies an oligarchy based on birth and ascription was developing, as was the case in some traditional societies. In other societies oligarchical systems based on wealth differentials were developing, with the rich exercising power because they were rich. There seemed to be emerging in Africa a class assuming critical influence and prestige because it had acquired the skills of modern education.

The elite started in part as a bureaucratic elite. Major positions in the civil service were rapidly Africanized, and the criteria for such Africanization placed a premium on modern Western education. But the emergence of an educated bureaucratic elite was accompanied by the emergence of a slightly less educated political elite. The triumph of anticolonial movements had thrust leaders into the forefront of affairs, leaders who would not have attained such pre-eminence had they not had at least some basic exposure to modern schools. Indeed, many of the modern successful leaders, and certainly a high proportion of the politicians, were drawn from the schools where they had previously served as teachers. The modern educational system had served the cause of politics by contributing some of its pioneer African teachers to the political profession. The most prominent of these pioneers in East Africa is President Julius Nyerere of Tanzania. We have noted that he is still called Mwalimu, signifying "teacher" or "mentor."

We have seen that the need for educational credentials in order to participate in national politics in a country like Uganda was partly derived from the issue of language. Where political power was acquired through communication and interaction with a wide variety of groups, a lingua franca was necessary. And the lingua franca which gradually attained the status of a national language in Uganda was English. A person without the command of English could become a party official in a local constituency, but he could not become a member of Parliament. Moreover, in Uganda the English language normally was not acquired in the streets and the markets but through exposure to formal education. In brief, those African countries which did not have an indigenous language widely understood in different ethnic communities were developing a system based on the primacy of the educated class.

It was in this kind of situation that Milton Obote, as president of Uganda, began to lament the inequalities which were evolving in the country and aspired to raise the mystique of the common man. He was all too aware of the inevitable functions of the English language in some areas of national life. But he was also aware of its propensity to confer certain privileges on those who had acquired an adequate command of it. Obote noted that in the colonial period English had been the language of the central administration in Uganda. Many Ugandans had learned English in order to serve in the administration in the days of imperial supremacy.

There was one section of the population in Uganda, interethnic in composition, which was not using English as the primary qualification for professional ascent. This section was the armed forces. It was in the armed forces that Swahili played virtually its only official role in independent Uganda. The commanding heights of the military profession, unlike any other major profession in Uganda, did not require any special fluency in English. Skills of weaponry, courage, efficient military behavior, loyalty, and discipline counted for more than a command of the metropolitan language. The man who came to command the armed forces of Uganda rose to the rank of major and received the title of commander of the armed forces with little formal education behind him and limited eloquence in English. If Obote was looking for a model of social mobility that did not require a command of the metropolitan language, he had it right there, in the barracks of his armed forces.

Yet, for a while, the implications of this situation escaped President Obote's attention, in spite of his commitment to the mystique of the common man. Obote was aware that education and Western culture continued to widen the gaps between certain sectors of Uganda's population. In the Common Man's Charter he elaborated upon Benjamin Disraeli's concept of the "two nations." Disraeli had been concerned about the trend toward polarization in British society; Britain was divided into two essentially antagonistic "nations within the nation" — the poor and the rich. Obote's Common Man's Charter took the Disraeli analysis a stage further and related it to the situation in Uganda. The worry in Uganda was not simply about a division between the rich and the poor but also about a cultural division between those who had been exposed to Western culture and those who had retained traditional ways. Both forms of fragmentation needed to be arrested.

> We cannot afford to build two nations within the territorial boundaries of Uganda: one rich, educated, African in appearance but mentally foreign, and the other, which constitutes the majority of the population, poor and illiterate. . . . We are convinced that from the standpoint of our history, not only our educational system inherited from pre-Independence days, but also the attitudes to modern commerce and industry and the position of a person in authority, in or outside Government, are creating a gap between the well-to-do on the one hand and the mass of the people on the other. As the years go by, this gap will become wider and wider. The Move to the Left Strategy of this Charter aims at bridging the gap and arresting this development [Articles 21, 22].

In some societies some families were rich to begin with; through their wealth they became politically powerful, and through their power as well as their wealth they were able to provide their children with the best education available. But in Africa the trend of causation was reversed. It was through education, at least at certain levels, that some figures managed to enter Parliament and organize political parties; and it was as a result of capturing political power that they made themselves rich. Instead of political power emerging out of the support of wealth, in this case wealth came at the end of the career afforded by political power.

One reason why John F. Kennedy succeeded in being elected president of the United States was that he had wealth in his family behind him. Someone from a poverty-stricken Irish Catholic family would not have stood a chance of rising to that level of pre-eminence, even someone with a Harvard education. Milton Obote, on the other hand, or Kwame Nkrumah before him, started by having at least a modest exposure to Western education before capturing national power. And it was, at best, only after capturing national power that they were able to consolidate their economic positions. In fact, Obote seemed to have done far less in consolidating his economic position than some of his colleagues in the cabinet. But the main point to be grasped here is the reversal of the chain of causation. In Africa's first decade of independence, economic achievement has been the fruit of political power rather than the seed from which political power has sprung.

Obote fell short of controlling his colleagues in their propensity for economic consumption. His Communication from the Chair, in April, 1970, did attempt to curb the special privileges of the civil service. But the civil service was even better educated than the majority of politicians. And the civil servants' morale could not be reassured if they were forced to make sacrifices while ministers and other politicians continued to reap the rewards of their political positions.

A song of the common man in Uganda continued to be sung in spite of these paradoxes and ironies. And then, on January 25, 1971, a modestly educated Lugbara voice haltingly read out to the nation eighteen reasons why the army had taken power. From a linguistic point of view, the voice which came across Radio Uganda was indeed the authentic voice of the common man — probably coming from a peasant family in West Nile, with limited exposure to Westernism and formal education, and retaining his deep roots in the indigenous soil.

Not long afterward a more educated voice, that of Chief Inspector of Police Oryema, announced that power had been taken over by the armed forces, that the police had concurred, and that the man in charge was going to be Maj. Gen. Idi Amin Dada. Again, from a linguistic point of view and in relation to standards of education, General Amin sounded much more like a common man than Obote ever did. And, from a cultural point of view, he was more authentically African than the people whom the Common Man's Charter dismissed as "educated, African in appearance but mentally foreign."

In a sense which was at once glorious and tragic, Obote's song in honor of the common man had at last come to haunt him: a Lugbara voice on Radio Uganda enumerating eighteen charges against the prophet of the common man, and a new president for Uganda emerging from the womb of the countryside far from the capital, equipped with less than a complete primary education and, to some extent, self-educated. The *Lumpenmilitäriat* had staged its revolution.

From Rebellious Soldiers to Revolutionary Strikers

This brings us to the third hypothesis in our discussion of military power and political efficacy, that control of the means of destruction is more decisive than control of the means of production in technologically underdeveloped countries. Marx assumed that the common man, or, to use his term, the proletarian, would derive his revolutionary power from his position within the processes of production. In Marx's view, technology would be on the side of the workers in industrialized societies, though indirectly. The capitalists would have a vested interest in improving the methods of production in order to enhance their own levels of profit. The factories and workshops, "the material forces of production," would therefore be undergoing improvement all the time. But in the very process of improving their technological efficiency the capitalists would be digging their own graves.

> The bourgeoisie cannot exist without constantly revolutionizing the instruments of production, and thereby the relations of production, and with them the whole relations of society. . . . The bourgeoisie, during its rule of scarce one hundred years, has created more massive and more colossal productive forces than have all preceding generations together. Subjection of nature's forces to man, machinery, application of chemistry to industry and agriculture, steam navigation, railways, electric telegraphs, clearing of whole continents for cultivation, canalization of rivers, whole populations conjured out of the ground — what earlier century had even a presentiment that such productive forces slumbered in the lap of social labor? [6]

Technological change outstrips changes in relations between classes and between individuals engaged in the processes of production. What Marx and Engels described as "the epidemic of overproduction" begins to create revolutionary conditions. The revolutionary forces are, in fact, the productive forces, which have become too vast and too extended to serve merely the interests of bourgeois property. The stage is set for an economic civil war.

> The weapons with which the bourgeoisie felled feudalism to the ground are now turned against the bourgeoisie itself. But not only had the bourgeoisie forged the weapons that bring death to itself; it has also called into existence the men who are to wield those weapons — the modern working class — the proletarians. [7]

---

6. Karl Marx and Friedrich Engels, *The Manifesto of the Communist Party*, in *Marx and Engels: Basic Writings on Politics and Philosophy*, ed. Lewis Feuer (New York: Doubleday, Anchor Books, 1959), pp. 10–12.

7. *Ibid.*, p. 13.

In this Marxian picture of the emergence of the supremacy of the common man there is the insistence that ultimate power lies in controlling the forces of production. The forces are initially controlled through ownership, since the law gives the means of production to the bourgeoisie as their property. But gradually the means of production fall under the *de facto* control of socialized labor. The principle of legal ownership is then challenged, and a domestic economic war seeks to resolve the imbalance between technological progress and the lethargy of antiquated social relations.

At the turn of the century Georges Sorel proposed the *general strike* as the appropriate weapon of the proletarian revolution. Sorel's theory of purposeful violence through industrial action was worked out, consciously analogous to theories of more conventional warfare. To Sorel the road to revolution was not through the control of the army; for the army was there to protect the state, and the state to exploit the masses. As a syndicalist, he saw salvation through, first, a technological revolution strong enough to make capitalism vulnerable and, second, industrial action to bring a technological civilization to a halt.

Sorel ridiculed military writers who discussed the new methods of war that had been necessitated by the employment of troops "infinitely more numerous than those of Napoleon, equipped with arms much more deadly than those of his time" — and yet who did not imagine that wars could be decided in any way other than that of the Napoleonic battle. Nevertheless, said Sorel, those writers did make a point when they looked at every battle and every skirmish as preparation for a more decisive international confrontation.

> The revolutionary Syndicates argue about Socialist action exactly in the same manner as military workers argue about war; they restrict the whole of Socialism to the general strike; they look upon every combination as one that should culminate in this catastrophe; they see in each strike a reduced facsimile, an essay, a preparation for the great final upheaval.[8]

But Sorel, like Marx before him, was all too keenly aware that technological advancement had to occur before industrial action could become a true revolutionary weapon. Until that happens it is not the control of the means of production that can be used to transform the balance of power in a particular society; it is the control of the means of destruction. It is therefore fitting that the gradual ideological legitimation of the skills of *war*, as against the skills of *work*, came to be undertaken by Marxists from less-developed societies. The collection of schools of guerrilla warfare and radical organization for military purposes derives its inspiration precisely from the ambition to manipulate the skills of war rather than the skills of industry against those who hold and wield

---

8. Georges Sorel, *Reflections on Violence*, trans. T. E. Hulme, introduction by Edward A. Shils (New York: Collier, 1967), pp. 114, 119–20.

the power. Such ideological positions in relatively underdeveloped countries range from the position taken by Mao Tse-tung, that power comes from the barrel of the gun, to the vision of Ernesto "Che" Guevara concerning the guerrilla genesis of the Cuban Revolution.

In East Africa the nearest thing to a people's revolution has been the Zanzibar Revolution. Again, control of the forces of destruction was a critical variable in the situation. The importance of technological advantage on a modest scale was grotesquely illustrated on that Isle of Cloves. John Okello, who spearheaded the revolution, had an army of his own. Yet, by Okello's account, his army did not come into possession of a single "modern weapon" until the attack on the government was initiated. The group skillfully approached the principal armory at Ziwani in Zanzibar. Okello claims that until he personally seized the rifle from the sentry guarding the armory, his soldiers were equipped only with bows and arrows, spears, and *pangas*. Control of the armory made all the difference in this confrontation with the age-old sultanate. The attackers were armed with primitive weapons; the government had a modern armory in readiness. The technological imbalance had to be reversed or at least reduced before the attack could stand a chance.

The strategy for tilting the balance depended on *surprise*. After the little group had overcome the guards at the armory, they proceeded, in a swift, surprise move, to distribute arms and ammunition to the revolutionaries. "Thus, when dawn broke on Sunday morning (January 12, 1964), and reporters on the scene caught their first glimpse of the revolutionaries, they saw a fairly well equipped soldiery." [9]

Okello was later eased out of the power structure of the Zanzibar Revolution and suffered indignity and detention in all three countries of East Africa. But the legacy of the barrel of the gun as the ultimate source of revolution was not forgotten in Zanzibar. Sheikh Abeid Karume, the leader of the Afro-Shirazi party and the first vice-president of the union between Zanzibar and Tanganyika, continued to reaffirm this. Sheikh Karume emphasized that it was through a violent confrontation that the people of Zanzibar and Pemba won back their rights as human beings. "It is through the barrel of the gun that those rights will be upheld." [10]

The Zanzibar Revolution had a demonstration effect on the mainland, culminating in the armed mutinies of 1964. The revolution was the first challenge of this kind from people who, in other circumstances, were not regarded as elite.

Then, on January 25, 1971, an army coup on the East African mainland took place. The successful combatants were, in comparison with the civilians they had overthrown, only modestly educated and indubitably non-Westernized.

---

9. Michael F. Lofchie, "Was Okello's Revolution a Conspiracy?" *Transition*, VII, no. 33 (October–November, 1967), 37. See also John Okello, *Revolution in Zanzibar* (Nairobi: East African Publishing House, 1967), pp. 30–34.

10. *Uganda Argus*, Fébruary 7, 1968.

As we have indicated, they were, in relation to the movement of meritocracy in colonial and postcolonial Africa, people drawn from the semiliterate countryside rather than from the polished, sophisticated, Westernized elite. The barrel of the gun had once again asserted supremacy in a situation of technological underdevelopment.

Triumph of the Powers of Destruction

We began with a hypothesis that control of the means of destruction — the guns and the armored cars — is more decisive in a situation of technological underdevelopment than is control of the means of production. Marx has been at once vindicated and contradicted by Africa's experience. He has been vindicated in his assumption that the means of production becomes relevant as a weapon for revolutionary efficacy when industrial sophistication has been achieved as a result of continuing investment in technical improvement. He has been contradicted by the emergent primacy of the military factor as a basis of power, overshadowing the economic domain in this regard.

It is, of course, arguable that both industrial action and military action are means of destruction. The former, bringing technological civilization to a standstill, is destructive of the ultimate purposes of productive capacity. The latter, using gunpowder or nuclear power, is physically destructive of life and property. Both modes of revolutionary action are, in their ultimate animation, countercreative.

Yet this equation overlooks the important distinction between withholding productivity on the one hand and unleashing destructiveness on the other. Industrial action and manipulation of economic power as a form of political sabotage is basically a case of withholding productivity, or jamming the processes of economic creativeness. But destroying a factory with cannonfire, throwing a grenade into a restaurant, or bringing a post office and a radio station under army control are different utilizations of power. They do entail a display of destructive power rather than a display of productive power being withheld at enormous costs.

Georges Sorel's ideas provide the link between these two forms of countercreativeness. By looking upon the general strike as a mode of purposeful proletarian violence, Sorel was indeed seeking to obliterate the distinction between revolutionary efficacy based on the control of the means of production and revolutionary assertion springing from the powers of destructiveness. But even his attempt to obliterate this distinction must always presuppose a high degree of industrial sophistication.

> The Marxian theory of revolution supposes that capitalism, while it is still in full swing, will be struck to the heart, when — having attained complete industrial efficiency — it has finally achieved its historical mission, and whilst the economic

system is still a progressive one. . . . . It is very important always to lay stress on the high degree of prosperity which industry must possess in order that the realisation of Socialism may be possible. . . . The dependence of the revolution on the constant and rapid progress of industry must be demonstrated in a striking manner.[11]

In a country like Uganda, the peasantry could not be expected to seize power. The urban workers proved to be no less vulnerable to the power of the state. They were increasingly bullied into discipline by the Obote regime, their Labour College for industrial training was abolished with ease, and they were compelled to enter into a consolidated trade-union movement by a mere pronouncement from the Ministry of Labour. Neither the proletariat nor the peasantry in Uganda could use their economic roles to force their wishes on the rest of the population or on the government. After all, subsistence agriculture in the countryside is not the kind of labor that can be wielded against the power structure. And the utilization of industrial countervailing power, so characteristic of the rise of collective bargaining in industrialized Western countries, was distant from the political realities of Uganda. The common man had to resort to the barrel of the gun to challenge the ultimate heights of power in a technologically backward country.

---

11. Sorel, *Reflections on Violence*, pp. 92, 137.

[Conclusion]

Toward a Theory of
Nation-Building

We have discussed different dimensions of cultural engineering and social policy in East Africa and have drawn from experiences elsewhere on the African continent for further theoretical illumination. What remains is the task of focusing more narrowly on the central and fundamental processes of nation-building in East Africa.

Nation-building involves five major processes. These are: first, the achievement of some degree of *cultural and normative fusion*; second, the promotion of *economic interpenetration* among different strata and sectors of society; third, the process of *social integration*; fourth, the building of institutions for effective *conflict-resolution*; and, fifth, the psychological accumulation of a *shared national experience*.

The process of *cultural and normative fusion* ultimately involves the acquisition of shared values and modes of expression and a shared life style and view of one's place in the universe. Of special importance for this process is cultural interaction among the different subgroups of society. The paramount medium for cultural interaction is, quite simply, *language*, both oral and written. We have paid special attention to the role of language and the written word in historical consciousness, literary communication, political penetration, and political recruitment.

The promotion of *economic interpenetration* and exchange relationships between subgroups is, in part, a commitment to the idea of economic interdependence. In other words, the economic dimension of nation-building is the process by which the different subgroups within a country develop a conscious vested interest in the national economy.

The process of *social integration* is that process by which the gaps between the elite and the masses, the town and the countryside, the privileged and the underprivileged, are gradually narrowed.

The routinization of *conflict-resolution* involves building institutions and consolidating procedures at different levels of society to enable leaders to emerge and to permit clashes of interest, divergences in values and opinions, and disputes over rights and duties to be resolved with minimal social disruption.

The psychological accumulation of a *shared national experience* is that process of acquiring a consciousness of having undergone some important experiences in the past *together*. When this fifth dimension interacts with the first process of cultural and normative fusion in African conditions, tribal subidentities gradually merge into a new national identity.

Cultural Fusion and Enlarged Empathy

One of the most fundamental political problems confronting African countries generally is the crisis of national integration. It arises because different clusters of citizens do not accept each other as compatriots. The sense of a shared nationality has yet to be forged. It can therefore be seen that a process of cultural fusion — leading to an enlarged empathy, a shared language, or a shared life style — is a contribution toward the integrative process. We have discussed the study of history as a process of socialization. The commitment to indigenize what is foreign, idealize what is indigenous, nationalize what is sectional, and emphasize what is African is central to the process of cultural fusion in African conditions. We have also discussed the role of creative literature in bridging the gap between metropolitan and local modes of artistic expression and in defining an area of shared aesthetic experience in spite of the ethnic diversity which characterizes African national populations.

In this task of cultural fusion the problem of a national language cannot be overemphasized. As we have indicated, in Tanzania Swahili is a shared language and in some respects a shared culture. The government's policies on language include a commitment to develop Swahili for use in more and more areas of common endeavor. The appointment of committees to compile a fuller legal vocabulary in Swahili, the promotion of literary competitions in Swahili, the encouragement to write textbooks in Swahili, and President Nyerere's work in translating Shakespeare into Swahili are all part of a determined attempt to make the language useful in a greater area of national life and to make national life more systematically interpenetrated by that shared language.

In Kenya the aftereffects of British cultural policy during the colonial period have been different. When Kenya became independent, there was a large number of languages recognized in both the educational policies and the policies of the Department of Information and Broadcasting. But independence meant a reduction of this plurality. The number of languages used on the radio was drastically reduced; except for a few hours of special service, programs were broadcast exclusively in English or Swahili. And the country has moved increasingly in the direction of promoting Swahili. The ruling party, the Kenya African National Union, has already declared itself in favor of the systematic promotion of Swahili as a national language. President Kenyatta has also appeared as a strong champion of Swahili for that purpose. We must remind ourselves that only a small number of Kenyans speak Swahili as their first language, but that an increasingly large number have acquired it as a means of communicating with members of other tribes. The English language is still important in Kenya, both as a medium of instruction at the higher levels of education and as the lingua franca of the elite. But the ultimate base for Swahili lies in its role as a lingua franca of the masses. The promotion of a shared language, with the ultimate ambition of cultural homogenization, is part of the process of national integration.

At one time it was likely that Uganda would also become a domain of Swahili. In the late 1920s the British colonial authorities put forward a strong case for the adoption of Swahili as a medium of education and administration in Uganda. The arguments put forward at that time have since been echoed in some of the current debates in the country about the utility of Swahili. The British administration in Uganda believed that there was a case for establishing close cultural ties between the new areas of knowledge that the British were introducing and the traditional background of the people. There was also the view that if Uganda came to use an African language other than Swahili as its lingua franca, it would simply be isolating itself. The most sensible thing for Uganda to do, the British colonial authorities argued in 1927, was to vigorously pursue policies calculated to spread Swahili widely and deepen its roots in the life of the nation.

Resistance to Swahili came from the Baganda, the biggest tribal community of Uganda. The Baganda had a complex system of government and a highly developed cultural heritage. They were also in a strong position to spread their language and culture to other groups in the country and thus strengthen their own credentials for leadership. The introduction of Swahili as a lingua franca would threaten their cultural credentials for national leadership. Therefore, they resisted this linguistic intrusion. The British authorities, after attempting to promote Swahili in the educational system, abandoned the endeavor and acquiesced in the Ganda bid to foster their own cultural hegemony in the country.

In 1966 there was a confrontation between the independent central government of Uganda and the regional government of Buganda. The central government won, and the king of Buganda fled to England, where he lived in exile until his death in November, 1969. At that time of the confrontation, the only official role that Swahili had in Uganda was its role as the language of command in the armed forces. One consequence of this was that Swahili had its strongest enthusiasts among the soldiers. In any case, the political decline of the Baganda had, by itself, improved the prospects of Swahili in the country. Ugandans from the Nilotic and Sudanic areas of the north much preferred Swahili to Luganda as a transtribal language among the grass roots. In April, 1970, the Language Association of Uganda passed a resolution urging the government to take steps to promote Swahili as a potential national language. The resolution was hotly debated in the press, but the very idea of passing such a resolution in support of Swahili would have been almost inconceivable a few years earlier.

In October, 1970, at the inauguration of Makerere University, President Obote promised to introduce Swahili into Uganda schools. Obote was overthrown before he could implement that policy. But the military regime did something that Obote had long wanted to do but had never done. The soldiers introduced Swahili as one of the languages of the domestic services of Radio Uganda.

All three countries of East Africa are seeking ways of increasing cultural intercourse among different linguistic groups. The quest for a national language capable of being spread among the masses and of being identified as native to Africa is part of the restless search for greater cultural fusion.

The Economics of Nationhood

The second dimension of nation-building is the process of economic interpenetration among different sectors and groups. The different tribal communities in an African country could, conceivably, simply coexist Although the boundaries of the country had put them together on the map, there would be little contact between some tribes and others. A more advanced stage of integration exists when the tribes have some contact with each other. The process of economic interaction and exchange would increase this contact and maximize situations of bargaining and compromise.

Tanzania has, as we have indicated earlier, idealized the concept of self-reliance. Perhaps national self-reliance deserves to be so idealized, provided the idea does not drift into one of autarky and isolation. But, from the point of view of the integrative process, there is little worse than tribal self-reliance. When each tribe is called upon to depend only on itself for its needs, the society is not allowing itself the opportunity to foster *tribal interdependence*, which is achieved when groups from one community find that they have to exchange with groups from another. The market becomes a mechanism for ethnic interpenetration. Goods flow from one community to another in exchange for other goods or for services. The nation moves from a collection of coexisting groups to a collection of interacting groups.

But economic interaction can be dangerous to the nation. Karl Marx was right to assume that the production and exchange of goods would have the potential for generating conflict, but he was wrong to assume that this conflict would be a class conflict. In African conditions ethnic divisions are often deeper and more fundamental than class divisions. Even where economic interaction does take place, the tensions which are created are only partly economic — quite often, only secondarily economic.

Exchange and economic interaction as a pathway toward nation-building suffered a serious setback in Nigeria's experience. The Ibo as a community were impressive entrepreneurs, and their activities in this sphere enabled them to penetrate other regions and communities as tradesmen. The economic mobility of the Ibo and their ability to establish enterprises outside their regions, to make business contacts, and to facilitate movements of goods or money, either as capital or as subsidies to their relatives, from one region to another, were conducive to a greater degree of interpenetration within Nigeria. They were, in other words, contributing to national integration. Yet tragic massacres of the Ibo in Northern Nigeria in May and September, 1966, were in part attributable precisely to their entrepreneurial endeavors and their economic mobility. They had moved north to fill important sectors of regional life, both public and private. They had provided significant services and had helped to enrich and diversify the regional economic system. But, partly because of these activities, and partly because of their distinctness as an ethnic group external to the region, the Ibo generated the kind of tension which later erupted on such a tragic scale. Of course, the brutal nature of the first Nigerian coup, in January, 1966, especially the Ibo predominance in its execution, was a major ignitive factor behind the riots and massacres that took place later, as the Hausa rose to avenge themselves on the Ibo. Nevertheless, part of the price of economic interaction and exchange as fostered by the Ibo in Nigeria had been the intensification of certain areas of interethnic conflict.

A question which inevitably is raised is whether a centralized economy or a market economy with free enterprise is a better mechanism for fostering ethnic interdependence. In East Africa, Tanzania under Nyerere and Uganda under Obote opted for a substantial measure of state ownership and state direction of the economy. Tanzania began in 1967 with the Arusha Declaration, the nationalization of banks and other key enterprises, and substantial government control of the rest of the economy. Then, on May 1, 1970, Obote announced far-reaching socialistic measures designed in part to give the state a 60 per cent share of all major industries in the country. When the policy was to be implemented, Obote's government began to modify it; and the military regime which followed him even started to reverse it.

For much of 1970, Kenya was the odd one out in this scheme of things. The word *socialism*, once used as frequently in the rhetoric of Kenya as in that of, say, Obote's Uganda — perhaps even more so at one time — has since been getting rusty. Under Kenyatta's government, the country is embarked on the path of promoting private enterprise. There is a clear commitment in Kenya to create an indigenous entrepreneurial culture. At the time of independence, much of the exchange trade was in the hands of Indians and Europeans. Government plans have aggressively initiated measures designed to decrease the economic control of Indians and Europeans in the nation and to raise the level of participation of indigenous Africans in commercial activity. Institutions have been set up to help African businessmen establish themselves. Legislation has been passed to reserve certain areas for African businessmen and exclude from those areas the competition of immigrants, especially those who have not taken out Kenya citizenship. The Immigration Regulations in Kenya, and those in Uganda as well, are designed to indigenize much of the exchange sector of the economy and other categories of personnel in national life.

The Trade Licensing Acts in both Kenya and Uganda have been designed to increase private initiative of Africans and to protect them from excessive challenge from longer-established immigrant business enterprises. But, in the case of Uganda, the Trade Licensing Act of early 1969, which became operational at the beginning of 1970, was for a while overtaken by the socialistic measures announced by President Obote on May Day, 1970. The post-Obote policies of Uganda are, in part, a return to the presocialistic days.

From the point of view of national integration, state ownership seems to be a less effective way of promoting ethnic interdependence than a free-enterprise economy would be. State ownership may reduce the challenge of creating new classes in East Africa. But it may also reduce the degree to which different tribes learn the arts of bargaining with each other and the skills of economic exchange. The market as an institution in East Africa is, in any case, much less developed than it is in West Africa. And the tradition of economic initiative among East African tribes is, on the whole, of briefer historical duration than that of, say, the Yoruba in West Africa. The establishment of state control in East Africa before an adequately vigorous economic culture has been created and before the tradition of rational economic initiative has fully matured might slow down that aspect of nation-building which relies on maximizing ethnic interdependence and economic interaction.

It is arguable that state ownership would strengthen governments. Should it have such an effect, it would be contributing toward the consolidation of political legitimacy, even if it would slow down the process of political integration. But such an assumption is perhaps a little hasty. Does state ownership in situations of fragile central institutions enhance or strain political legitimacy? We are not yet in a position to be sure. But it is at least arguable that the assumption of major responsibilities by the state might prematurely promote a tendency to hold the state responsible when things go wrong. As the state takes over more and more of the economy, it is indeed assuming responsibility for these ventures. But responsibility in this sense implies accountability; and accountability implies the acceptance of blame when things go wrong. The pace of development in such countries is bound to be slow, and setbacks are bound to be recurrent; occasions for articulated recrimination or silent grievance are bound to arise from year to year. Setbacks which might otherwise have been blamed on businessmen or blind market forces or immigrant communities are increasingly attributable to failings in state policies. The real danger posed by state socialism in a society with fragile institutions is not the danger of making the government too strong but the risk of making the government more conspicuously ineffectual. Yet the very effort to make the economy work could, if it were to include a significant amount of genuine participation by indigenous workers and peasants, foster the kind of economic interaction necessary for nation-building.

Pluralism and Social Integration

The third process of nation-building is social integration. Let us recall the distinction made earlier, in Chapter 7, between national integration and social integration. For our purposes in this conclusion we may say that national integration has both a special sense and a general sense. In its special sense, employed in Chapter 7, national integration is the merger of subnationalities into a wider national entity. It is the combination of the first process of cultural and normative fusion and the fifth process of accumulating collective experiences on the broad national scale. The merger of tribe with tribe on the slow road to modern nationhood is the meaning of national integration in this narrow, specialized sense. But national integration as a broader and more general concept encompasses all five processes of nation-building. When a collection of social subgroups is undergoing cultural and normative fusion, economic interpenetration, social integration, institutionalization of their methods of resolving conflicts, and the accumulation of country-wide collective experiences, that collection of subgroups is becoming nationally integrated in the more general sense.

Social integration is the process by which the gaps between the elite and the masses, the rural and the urban classes, the privileged and the underprivileged, are gradually reduced or leveled off. We have emphasized that social integration is not necessarily a process by which the difference in income between the richest man and the poorest man in the country is minimized. The requirements of social integration are satisfied if there are, between the richest and the poorest, many people with intermediate incomes.

In transitional societies an important mitigating factor for the problem of social integration is the phenomenon of the transclass man. We have attempted to show how social distance between the elite and the masses in Africa can be narrower than is sometimes assumed, simply because many members of the elite belong, in effect, to more than one social class.

The role of metropolitan forms of education in the process of social stratification is critical in East Africa's experience; and the English language is an important agent of social differentiation as well as of cultural integration. By providing a means of transtribal communication between educated elites drawn from different ethnic groups, English does serve the cause of normative interaction and shared acculturation. But, by opening up certain privileges to those who command it in such countries as Kenya and Uganda, the English language is one factor behind a widening gulf between the masses and the elites.

What should be remembered is that both social integration and national integration in the narrow sense are, in essence, processes of *depluralizing* society. Although pluralism never completely disappears, a society ceases to be a plural society when the stage of full national integration is reached. Put another way, there is pluralism in every society, but not every society is a plural one. Whether or not a society is a plural one depends on the nature and depth of the pluralism. After all, one might also say that there is some *nationhood* in every independent

African country, but not every independent African country is a nation. Again, whether or not a country is a nation depends upon the nature and depth of that sense of nationhood.

When Harold Laski rebelled against the notion of "Man *versus* the State," he suggested a view of society which thought of political life in terms of relations between groups rather than relations between the government and the individual. The theory that Laski was putting forward was one of pluralism.

If a plural society is not simply a society with pluralism, what distinguishes plural societies from others? The extreme case of a plural society is a society of total identities — of self-contained cultural systems or exclusive racial groups. This is perhaps the kind of plural society which, as J. Clyde Mitchell suggests, comes nearest to being "a contradiction in terms." Relationships between the groups are at either the level of bare coexistence or that of minimal contact. This is perhaps the "pure type" of plural society.[1]

As the integrative process gets under way, the total identities are increasingly partialized. By the time coalescence is reached, the society has been substantially depluralized in this special sense. The society might retain a highly structured, class pluralism, as has been the case in England. Yet England has ceased to be a plural society and is, on the contrary, almost a "pure type" of integrated nation. Complete coalescence with the Scots and the Welsh has not been fully achieved, though it is well advanced. The relationship of the English and the Northern Irish is perhaps still basically a compromise relationship, but one with substantial areas of coalescence. The preponderant English, however, have achieved cohesion. The process of national integration among the English has virtually come to an end.

Yet, as long as certain forms of pluralism persist, there is room for further depluralization. England has virtually completed national integration in the narrow sense, but there is considerable room for social integration. There is room especially for increased erosion of class distinctions.

While national integration in this narrow sense is finite, social integration is not. Perhaps the ultimate error of Marxism is to assume that if all classes were abolished, there would be an end to social integration. Having made that assumption, Marxism logically then assumes that there would be an end to the need for the state as well — that it would "wither away" on attainment of classlessness. Perfect social integration would indeed make the state redundant. Yet, because social integration is an infinite process, the state continues to be necessary for the purpose of giving it direction.

Nevertheless, in its formulation of the role of conflict in social change and in its conception of perfect coalescence, however unrealizable, Marxism still affords useful insights into the nature of the integrative process. As an ideology,

---

1. "If [such societies] are 'plural,' can they be societies?" See J. Clyde Mitchell, *Tribalism and the Plural Society* (London: Oxford University Press, 1960), p. 25.

Marxism often creates conflict; but as a methodology, it helps us to understand conflict. After all, the integrative process is, in the ultimate analysis, the story of conflict and its role in socializing man.[2]

Conflict-Resolution and Political Legitimacy

The fourth process of nation-building involves the creation of institutions for effective conflict-resolution. The most fundamental of human institutions have often grown in response to the need to contain conflicts of interest, divergences in values, and disputes over rights and duties.

The cumulative experience of conflict-resolution is indispensable to national integration. Conflict may have a propensity to dissolve social relationships, but the *resolution* of conflict is an essential mechanism of integration. The experience of jointly looking for a way out of a crisis, of seeing mutual hostility subside to a level of mutual tolerance, of being intensely conscious of each other's position and yet sensing the need to bridge the gulf — these are experiences which, over a period of time, should help two groups of people move forward into a relationship of greater integration. It cannot be repeated too often that conflict-resolution, even if it is not a sufficient condition for national integration, is certainly a necessary one.

As for what makes conflict-resolution possible, it is sometimes the cumulative power of precedent, of having overcome crises before. The experience of previous clashes sharpens the capacity to discover areas of mutual compatibility on subsequent occasions of tension. Another factor which makes conflict-resolution possible is awareness of reciprocal dependence.

Not only does the routinization of conflict-resolution require stable institutions for such purposes at the center of national life; it also needs a diversity of secondary institutions at the lower levels of national life. The routinization of conflict-resolution is, in fact, a process of institution-building and consolidation of procedures. But conflicts and disputes should not all involve the state. Mechanisms for resolving private disputes, or for assuring an acceptable outcome of a private bargain, need to grow on all the different levels. We have paid special attention to political recruitment and electoral experimentation, partly because they involve the shared mechanisms of leadership and tension-management at both national and local levels.

Authority at the center of national life can continue to grope for resilience. The problem of political obligation is, in a sense, the old problem of why

---

2. These points are discussed more fully in Ali A. Mazrui, "Pluralism and National Integration," in *Pluralism in Africa*, ed. Leo Kuper and M. G. Smith (Berkeley: University of California Press, 1969), pp. 333–50. The same chapter appears in Mazrui, *Violence and Thought: Essays on Social Tensions in Africa* (London: Longmans, 1969), pp. 102–21.

and when one obeys, or ought to obey, the government. Where legitimacy is secure, the citizens do not question the government's right to govern, though they may question the wisdom of this or that governmental action. When it is not secure, challenges to authority may allow little differentiation of dissent, insubordination, rebellion, and outright treason. In addition, there is in African conditions the distinctive problem of civilian-military relations, which is often, though not always, an aspect of the crisis of political legitimacy. This crisis has as its base the struggle to ensure that every opposition remains a loyal opposition. It is a quest for a situation in which one can challenge the government's decisions without challenging the government's right to execute them.

In the final analysis there is the ultimate problem of *consensus*. There is a distinction between primary consensus and secondary consensus. Primary consensus is what makes us accept a certain degree of force from the government, even if we complain about that force, without feeling that the government lacks the right to govern. Agreement behind institutions is the essence of primary consensus. Secondary consensus, on the other hand, is consensus on this or that policy, or agreement behind a leader. In this case what is accepted is the substance of a particular policy (for example, a new tax on cigarettes or a greater emphasis on secondary education) or the leadership of a particular individual. The institution which that individual occupies, or through which those policies are arrived at, might remain very fragile, subject to sudden change or collapse, and might be bereft of the sanctity of widespread and deep acceptance. In short, then, consensus on methods, procedures, and the sanctity of institutions is primary consensus, while consensus on policies and leaders is secondary consensus.

None of the three East African countries has as yet arrived at a situation of secure primary consensus. Tanzania has a highly developed level of secondary consensus behind President Nyerere and, for the time being, behind his policies of socialism and self-reliance. Tanzania, in other words, has secondary consensus at both the level of policy and that of leadership.

Kenya has substantial secondary consensus at the level of leadership. There is acceptance of Mzee Kenyatta as the guardian of the nation, and there is, on the whole, acceptance of his lieutenants because they are his lieutenants. But secondary consensus behind policies in Kenya is more fragile. This is partly because there is greater haziness about concrete national directions in Kenya than there in Tanzania and partly because Kenya's mechanisms of socialization and propaganda in support of policies are less organized than are those in Tanzania. In addition, factors of tribal nepotism in the course of the implementation of policies help to aggravate secondary dissension over the policies themselves.

In regard to this problem of consensus, the situation in Uganda is even a little worse than that in Kenya, let alone that in Tanzania. In Uganda there has not been quite as much agreement behind either the national leadership or the policies as there has been in the other two countries. Under Obote, Uganda considered having a one-party state. It is clear that the reasons for Obote's choice of the one-party state were radically different from the reasons that led Tanzania to adopt the same system.

In mainland Tanzania the case for a one-party system was based on the observation that the country was solidly united. The Tanganyika African National Union argued that the laws of the country should reflect the realities of the country — and one reality was that Tanganyikans, or mainland Tanzanians, had massively voted for single-party dominance. In announcing the intention in 1963 to form a one-party system *de jure*, President Nyerere defended the decision partly on the grounds that without a one-party system Tanganyika would not enjoy real political contests in its elections. TANU was so overwhelmingly supported that opposing candidates stood no chance. Only a one-party system in which candidates belonging to the same party could compete for election would restore the principle of choice to the Tanganyika electorate — so he argued.

Obote's path toward the one-party system sprang from exactly opposite considerations. There was a conviction that the previous multiparty system had been basically divisive and prone to violent eruptions. Obote saw Uganda as needing a one-party system, not because, as in the case of Tanzania, the country was solidly united, but because the country was dangerously divided.

If we further compare the two countries, not only with each other but with a more developed and more stable entity, other points of theoretical interest emerge. The people of mainland Tanzania are united in support of a particular political party and particular political leadership. The people of Great Britain, on the other hand, are united in support of a particular set of institutions and a particular system of government. Tanzania under Nyerere has had more secondary consensus than is normally possible in Britain. No head of government in Britain can hope to have the overwhelming support that Nyerere enjoys in mainland Tanzania, and no sets of policies in the United Kingdom are likely to enjoy as much popular backing as seems to lie behind some of Nyerere's policies on socialism and self-reliance. There is no doubt that in terms of mobilizing support for a particular personality in politics or a particular set of policies, Tanzania is more mobilizable in peacetime than is the United Kingdom. But there is no doubt that the United Kingdom enjoys far greater primary consensus than has as yet been achieved in Tanzania. The system of government under which the United Kingdom is ruled does not pose the question of whether it will survive the present head of government. Institutions in Tanzania, devised substantially under Nyerere's inspiration, may outlive him as a major feature of the country, but that is by no means certain. For the time being, the institutions derive their authority from Nyerere's standing; Nyerere does not derive his authority from the sanctity of the institutions.

In Britain, prime ministers come and go, but the system of government — though always changing in a number of subtle ways — continues to demonstrate its stable resilience as it has for a substantial period of history. In some respects, however, Tanzania is better off than the United Kingdom. Where institutions have already acquired primary consensus to back them, they are difficult to change. This is all right as long as the institutions are desirable in themselves and serve the nation well; but many of the British institutions were born in a period when men were not engaged in rational and purposeful nation-building. The institutions were not products of reflection, calculation, and rational choice, but were the outcome of historical accidents.

What is distinctive about the last few decades of world history is the greater self-confidence shown by societies in their readiness to experiment with new social institutions. Even among the Tories in the United Kingdom, there is now greater preparedness than ever to try things out and to attempt to control factors of production and social change. Nationalization of an industry is no longer taboo — as the nationalization of Rolls Royce by a Tory government in February, 1971, illustrated.

A country like Tanzania, with wide secondary consensus but as yet uncertain primary consensus, is, in a sense, cast in a situation in which social choice is possible. The secondary agreement behind the leadership and the policies can be used as a basis for experimenting with carefully selected institutions and gradually creating primary agreement behind those institutions. The people started off united behind TANU and Nyerere but relatively indifferent toward the actual system of government and social organization. In other words, TANU and Nyerere had a wide area of latitude as to the direction in which they could take the nation.

Because Tanzanians were united on Independence Day behind TANU and Nyerere, it made sense for TANU to set up a commission to explore how one-party unity could be reconciled with democratic values. It was a purposeful engagement in social engineering; but it was social engineering of the most central kind — the decision to erect a structure of government and administration as an act of conscious political choice. Having set up a one-party state *de jure*, the nation could then set about slowly acquiring primary consensus behind the new system should this be feasible.

Uganda is in a different situation. It did not emerge into independence with the sanctity of primary consensus, like that in the United Kingdom, or with the blessing of secondary consensus, like that in Tanzania. Under Obote, Uganda gradually drifted into a system of greater coercion. There are occasions when coercion is thought of as a functional alternative to consensus. Zaïre is less united than Uganda; therefore, Zaïre needs more coercion in its system than does Uganda. Tanzania is more united than Uganda; therefore, Tanzania needs less coercion for minimal system-maintenance than does Uganda. In this sense coercion and unity, or consensus, are functional alternatives as bases for governmental action.

Integration and Collective Emotions

In the long and slow process of national integration, it is not enough that people achieve a degree of cultural fusion; it is not enough that they interact economically; it is not enough that they integrate socially; it is not enough that they socially evolve a multiplicity of institutions for resolving conflict. There is a fifth process required to pull these other four together and focus them toward the center, namely, the collective cumulation of a shared national experience.

The spread of the Swahili language, though it does introduce significant cultural interaction in the country, does not ensure that one part of the country knows much about another part, or that there is a conscious identification of those who speak Swahili in the northern tip of Tanzania with those who speak it in the southern tip. Economic exchange, though going on all over the country, usually involves relationships between subunits of the nation — a shopkeeper and his customers, a firm and another firm, a parastatal body and its clientele. Through social integration gaps between the elite and the masses are minimized. The routinization of conflict-resolution can be resolution between subunits of the nation, or between the central government and one particular subunit at a given moment. None of these experiences really need involve, in any fundamental sense, the population as a whole. These experiences may have repercussions all over the country; but in general the processes of cultural fusion, economic interaction, social integration, and routinization of conflict-resolution may be basically processes of integrating subunits but not necessarily of *nationalizing* them all in a shared moment of particular experience.

In order to give these four other processes a central focus and to promote in the population mutual identification as nationals of the same country, some additional area of experience is needed; and this additional centralizing process is what might be called a collective cumulation of shared moments of national experience.

In *Representative Government*, John Stuart Mill defined a nationality in the following terms:

> A portion of mankind may be said to constitute a Nationality if they are united among themselves by common sympathies which do not exist between them and any others — which make them co-operate with each other more willingly than with other people, desire to be under the same government, and desire that they should be governed by themselves or a portion of themselves exclusively. This feeling of nationality may have been generated by various causes . . . but the strongest of all is identity of political antecedents; the possession of national history and consequent community of recollections; collective pride and humiliation, pleasure and regret, connected with the same incidents in the past.[3]

---

3. John Stuart Mill, *Representative Government* (1861; reprint ed., New York: Dutton; London: Dent, Everyman's Library, 1962), pp. 359–60.

Mill is emphasizing the importance for nationhood of the kind of shared experiences which lead to shared prejudices and shared emotional dispositions. When a group of people begins to feel proud about the same things or humiliated by the same things, pleased or saddened collectively by the same incidents, that group of people is acquiring the capacity for collective selfhood. The process of nation-building at the psychological level therefore entails the cumulative acquisition of common emotional dispositions and common potential responses to the same stimuli. To be capable of being angry about the same incident is to share an area of fellow feeling. The shared resentment of colonialism in African countries often constituted the beginnings of national consciousness. Where elections are permitted to take place in independent Africa, the general participation in campaigning and the widespread disputes over policies and personalities are a form of political interaction on a national scale. To that extent general elections, no matter how painful and even violent, are part of the cumulative acquisition of collective memories by an African people. It is not enough that Africans rewrite their history. It is not enough that they permit the study of history to socialize them. It is sometimes also necessary for them to make history, or at least experience it, together.

Social engineering in the new African states has sometimes taken the form of purposeful collectivization of emotions in a bid to make the populace share a moment of empathy. The collectivization of anger, for example, sometimes results in the nationalization of protest. A capacity for what Mill calls "collective pride and humiliation" is a particularly important feature of a sense of shared nationhood. It is precisely because of this that anger as an emotion is so central to the growth of nationhood. After all, offended pride gives rise to anger. Collective humiliation is a deeper stage of offended pride. This, in turn, generates anger, either overtly or in a subdued, silent form. Connected with the cumulative acquisition of a capacity for collective pride and collective humiliation, shared moments of collective anger become part of the process of national integration.

President Obote was particularly aware of the importance of promoting shared emotional dispositions and collective responses to the same stimuli. Faced with a country deeply divided ethnically, Obote tended at times to turn precisely to the devices of collectivizing moments of anger and nationalizing protest. On Saturday, February 13, 1965, some Congolese planes bombed the villages of Goli and Payida in the West Nile District of Uganda. Obote was angry that this should have happened; but, more importantly, he saw the moment as one that afforded the opportunity for arousing collective patriotic anger among Ugandans. He perceived that being angry with the Congolese for violating Uganda's borders in such a violent way was not adequate. The planes which had crossed the border were American-made, deliberately sold or given to Tshombe's regime in Congo by the United States. There was a possibility of directing the collective anger of Ugandans against the United States, as well as against Tshombe's regime. A diplomatic confrontation between Uganda and the United

States had the air of a David and Goliath confrontation. Aroused in proud anger, the weak were confronting the mighty in a posture of defiant protest. Obote said to his countrymen:

> We blame the government of the United States. . . . We have been attacked without provocation on our part. I cannot say whether we are going to retaliate. . . . We must all be prepared to throw sand, and sacks of sand, in the eyes of the mighty.[4]

Even then the question arose as to why Obote was dramatizing the bombing incident instead of minimizing it. One reason might have been the obvious one — the desire to take a justifiably indignant stand at having had the frontiers of one's country violently violated. But it also seemed likely that Obote perceived the political functions of collectivized wounded pride. An important problem confronting every African government is how to transform the old, race-conscious nationalism of the anticolonial struggle into a new, state-conscious patriotism of postcolonial days. How could the anti-imperialist protests of transformation be converted into cumulative dispositions of shared national identity?

In the case of the bombing incident in Uganda in 1965, there was something very "sovereign" about having to defend one's borders against hostile planes. That must have been one reason why Obote, when he spoke on television on the night following the bombing incident, felt impelled to remind his countrymen that on October 2, 1962, the country had become *independent*. To be attacked by enemy planes from across the border could almost be a status symbol for a new state. Inevitably, the diplomatic protests that followed had the ring of newly acquired sovereignty.

If an African leader was dedicated to creating a state-conscious patriotism in his people, he had to utilize a variety of factors — from flags to air space — as symbols of sovereignty. This is what made the "destruction" of a village in the West Nile District of Uganda something that could be used in constructing a moment of national cohesion; for Ugandans in a moment of joint outrage were Ugandans united.

The government therefore arranged for popular participation in national anger. A national demonstration was scheduled for Tuesday afternoon, February 16, 1965. There were ministerial appeals to employers to release their workers for the great march to the American embassy and for the rally to follow. At least metaphorically, Ugandans were up in arms — or so the great march was supposed to demonstrate. Even the wounded soldier in a West Nile village was elevated to a symbolic state hero. As Obote put it: "Our one officer has already spilled blood for all of us. It will be our duty to redeem that blood."[5]

---

4. *Uganda Argus* (Kampala), February 15, 1965.
5. *Ibid.*

The Uganda government could have protested directly to the Congolese government or to the government of the United States. But this would have been
a government-to-government form of protest. Instead, what Obote was out to
do was to collectivize anger and to popularize protest as a way of nationalizing
that anger. There were a number of miscalculations in the arrangements that
were made, and not everything went according to plan. But a demonstration
did take place. The American embassy was momentarily besieged, and the
American flag was burned. Diplomatic protest at the government-to-government
level was one thing; but Obote was out to promote protest at the grass-roots
level and, in so doing, to add one more thin layer of experience to that slow,
cumulative acquisition of a sense of shared pride and shared humiliation among
Ugandans.

The history of Uganda under Obote included other moments of attempted
nationalization of political indignation. The growth of national identity is inseparable from the process by which prejudices become to some extent homogenized
and emotional dispositions become collectivized in the population. Sometimes
fear as a source of protest is also relevant to this process. The fear of an
enemy, the anger arising out of wounded pride, and the ambition to create
the foundations of nationhood have often interacted on those occasions of shared
responses in new states.[6]

Toward a National Memory

These, then, are the five dimensions of nation-building illustrated in East
Africa's experience. The quest for a national language, like the quest for a
shared literary and historical consciousness, is in part a quest for a shared
cultural heritage. Part of the process by which a collection of individuals or
subgroups becomes a people occurs when they succeed in forging a common
universe of perspectives and a capacity for mutual communication. Cultural
and normative fusion does not presuppose identity of values or uniformity of
thought and cultural behavior. It simply presupposes a high degree of mutual
influence in cultural perspectives among groups and individuals, tending toward
a shared language of cultural discourse.

Economic interpenetration of groups and sectors of society promotes a shared
interest in the economic fortunes of the country. In East Africa, where there
has been a history of expatriate dominance, the issue is also connected with
the policies of indigenizing the economy. At their most extreme, the approaches
have amounted to a choice between African socialism and black capitalism.

Class-formation is one aspect of social change that has been influenced by

---

6. For further elaboration of Uganda's experience in this regard, see Ali A. Mazrui,
"Leadership in Africa: Obote of Uganda," *International Journal*, XXV, no. 3 (Summer,
1970), 538–64.

economic interaction. Tanzania is seeking to achieve social integration through social equality, an approach based on the example of integrated traditional societies. Kenya, on the other hand, has been pursuing social integration through social differentiation and functional diversification among the African populace. Uganda is caught between the two approaches. Meanwhile, the policies of progressive depluralization continue, with language policies as well as economic policies central to the whole process.

Whether encouraged or frustrated, class-formation generates areas of conflict. There are other forms of conflict as well in East Africa, ranging from ethnic tensions to ideological disputes. Nation-building must therefore include the construction of institutions — electoral, judicial, and others — for the resolution of these multiple conflicts. The experience of institutional experimentation and the constant search for ways of containing conflict are perhaps the most explicitly political of all the dimensions of nation-building. The crisis of political authority and legitimacy is a crisis of institutional fluidity, a crisis concerning the government's ability to solve some of the critical disputes of politics. In this respect nation-building becomes a search for a viable system of tension-management.

Finally, we have discussed the unifying impact of collective experiences on a people. Colonialism was, in many African countries, such an experience, and the struggle against colonialism was another. The very fact of having been ruled by the same colonial power for half a century or more was an important factor behind the relative unity and similarity of Uganda, Kenya, and Tanzania as contrasted with Congo, which was ruled by a different imperial country. After independence, such phenomena as party politics, electioneering, national service, induced collective indignation, and special central crises have focused attention on each country as a unit of selfhood. Cultural engineering as a quest for purposeful change becomes a shared moment in the stream of conscious history. These are the experiences which cumulatively evolve into a shared national memory. And a national memory is the historical dimension of nationhood, giving this particular form of collective history its roots in time.

Index

Abbas, Ferhat, 29
Abdulaziz, M. H., 48
Acculturation, 39, 41. *See also* English
language; Indigenization; National
integration; Resocialization; Social
integration
Achebe, Chinua, 36, 43, 44, 91
Achole (people), 33, 117, 122, 123, 174,
178, 197, 198, 199
Adoko, Akena, 70–71, 142, 179, 198;
and documentary radicalism, 70–71
Aesthetic dualism, 39, 40, 45, 47, 48, 49.
See also Indigenization; Resocial-
ization
African history. *See* History
African literature. *See* Literature
Ajayi, J. F. A., 17–18
Akan (language), 120
Algeria, 29
Allen, John, 48
Alur (people), 197
Amin, Major General Idi, 162, 175, 176;
coup by, 161, 179, 270; detribalization
of military, 179, 180; supporter of
Swahili, 91; wives of, 142
Anyoti, J. O., 245
Arabic, 5; and Quran, 73
Arabs, 29, 95–96
Army, British, 170; use of in Kenya,
163–65, 179; use of in Tanganyika,
163, 165, 169–71, 179; use of in
Uganda, 161–63, 175, 179
Arts, traditional, and modern education,
45, 46, 47. *See also* Indigenization;
National integration; Resocialization;
Social integration
Arusha Declaration (Nyerere), 71, 211,
227, 244, 258; Calvinist qualities of,

219–23; and conspicuous consumption,
254–55; as documentary radicalism,
67, 69; and economic development,
230, 258; and entrepreneurship,
221–23; and National Service, 257
Ashanti (people), 118, 119
Asians: as entrepreneurs, 106, 107, 212,
213, 225; marginality of, 213–14
Ateso (language), 101, 104
Autobiography, in East Africa, 26–30,
46. *See also* Mau Mau
Automobiles, as symbols of affluence,
155–56
Azikiwe, Nnamdi, 54, 90, 112

Baganda (people), 15, 18, 118, 124;
and civil service, 174–77; compared
with Jews, 194; compared with
Kikuyu, 193–95, 204–5; compared
with Samurai, 194; and constitutional
rights, 117; and English language, 99;
as entrepreneurs, 211; military tradition
of, 173–74; opposition to Swahili,
89–90, 98, 279; remilitarization of, 179
Baldwin, James, 51–52
Banda, Hastings, 187
Bantu (people), 196; in administration
and politics, 174, 176. *See also*
Baganda; Swahili
Banyoro (people), 71
Barnett, Donald L., 28–29, 189
Biafra, 20, 48, 115, 143–44. *See also*
Ibo; Nigeria
Blundell, Sir Michael, 105
Blyden, Edward, 49
British army. *See* Army, British
Buganda (kingdom), 30, 195; decline of
influence of, 98, 124; defeat of,

[295]

Resocialization: as prerequisite for viable
literary culture, 41–43; of schoolchildren, 50; through taking new arts
to the people, 45–46
Revolution:
instigated, 205; in Tanzania, 185, 206;
in Uganda, 185, 206
spontaneous, in Europe in 1848, 185
structural: in England during Industrial
Revolution, 184; in Japan after Meiji
Restoration, 183–84; in Kenya,
184–85, 205
systemic: in China, 185, 188–89;
in Cuba, 185; in Egypt, 185; in
Russia, 185, 206–7; in Tanzania,
207–8; in Uganda, attempted by
Obote, 207–8; in Zanzibar, 207–8
Robert, Shaaban, 88
Roman Catholic church, 154; and
polygamy, 144
Rubadiri, David, 36, 187

Sectional elements of culture, nationaliza-
tion of, 17–19, 101
Self-criticism, 81; in literature, 36–37
Senegal, 91
Senghor, Leopold, 91; as French-
language writer, 47; and negritude, 27,
36 n, 76–77, 79, 91; as political
thinker, 80
Sessional Paper No. 10 (Kenya), as
documentary radicalism, 69
Shakespeare, William, 24; translated into
Swahili, 36, 45, 47, 48, 51–52, 68, 92
Shikoku, Milton, 147, 157
Slogans, political, 78–79, 80
Social integration, 97, 277, 283–85,
289; and English language, 98, 107–8,
283; in Kenya, 106–7, 293; in
Tanzania, 106, 293; in Uganda, 107,
293. See also English language;
Indigenization; National integration;
Resocialization
Social stratification, 148–49
Socialism, 80; "African socialism," 80,
93, 155, 256; socialistic revolution,
186
Soyinka, Wole, 36, 91
Suffering, and postindependence revolu-
tionary commitment: in Kenya,
186–88; in Malawi, 187; in Tanganyika, 186, 188; in Uganda, 187;
in Zambia, 187

Swahili, 5; criticized as child of Arab
imperialism, 95–96; expressing
African socialism, 93; first used for
translating, 92; in Kenya, 88, 89;
as literate language, 48, 72; modernization of in Tanzania, 47, 48; radio
broadcasts in, 100, 280; in Tanzania,
87, 100; as transtribal language, 89,
94; in Uganda, 98, 269, 279–80

Tanganyika, 111; opposition to English
language, 96; and Swahili, 105. See
also Tanzania
Tank Hill party, 63
Tanner, Ralph, 48, 82
TANU (Tanzanian African National
Union), 94, 111, 171, 221, 231,
255, 287, 288
Tanzania, 36, 40, 47, 84, 111, 154;
and African socialism, 93; and Swahili,
87, 88, 94, 95–96, 105. See also
Tanganyika
Technology: importance to the military,
263, 266–67, 271, 273; social applica-
tion of, 249–51; use of tools and animal
power, 26–61
Temu, Peter, 92, 93
Theatre, Makerere traveling project,
45–46, 50
Trade-unionism, 200–201, 275
Transition, 35, 47, 50, 58, 91, 108, 177
Translation: creating understanding, 46;
enriching African languages, 92; in
literature, 35–36; taking new arts to
the people, 47, 91, 92; vindicating
African languages as literary media,
47–48
Transnationalism, 34–35; as identification with other literatures, 35
Trevor-Roper, Hugh, 7–8, 11, 14, 15, 24
Tribalism, 30; and confidence in govern-
ment, 132–37; and nationalism, 30,
154–55; and party system, 120–25;
and polygamy, 142, 143. See also
Detribalization
Tutuola, Amos, 25, 50

Uganda, 15, 17, 18, 20, 40, 45, 46,
47, 58, 63, 84, 111; and documentary
radicalism, 69–71; military coup in,
161, 179, 270, 273–75; and Move
to the Left, 69–71, 269; parliamentary
institutions in, 117–18; and Swahili,

ATE DUE